Springer Textbooks in Law

Springer Textbooks in Law compiles high-quality educational content aimed at undergraduate and graduate students in all areas of law. All self-contained volumes are authored by accomplished academics and suitable for use in class as well as individual study. Many of them include chapter abstracts, definitions of technical terms, cases and self-assessment exercises, as well as recommended reading sections. This series is an invaluable resource for students and lecturers alike and spans the full range of topics in international and European law, including fundamentals of law and comparative law. Special attention is paid to current and emerging topics such as IT law, intellectual property, human rights as well as dispute resolution, mediation, arbitration – and many more.

Urs Saxer

The Law of Global and European Organizations

Institutionalized Cooperation in Disruptive Times

Springer

Urs Saxer
University of Zurich (UZH)
Zürich, Switzerland

ISSN 2509-999X ISSN 2510-0009 (electronic)
Springer Textbooks in Law
ISBN 978-3-032-00066-8 ISBN 978-3-032-00067-5 (eBook)
https://doi.org/10.1007/978-3-032-00067-5

This Springer imprint is published by the registered company Springer Nature Switzerland AG
The registered company address is: Gewerbestrasse 11, 6330 Cham, Switzerland

Preface

We live in disruptive times. In a world that has become multipolar, common international norms steering conduct of states and other international actors seem to be on the decline. Unilateralism appears to increasingly prevail over multilateralism: Instead of relying on agreed solutions to common problems and conflicts, some states adopt measures dictated by national self-interest at the expenses of other states, others pursue a strategy of regional dominance to further their interests, and others use unilaterally military force to reach a favorable outcome in a conflict. However, all this does not change the fact that in a world that has become smaller, interdependencies are so dominant that striving for power and dominance or the use of military force does not represent valid alternatives to institutionalized multilateralism. Even in disruptive times, international organizations are a factor of order. No state can it make alone.

This book deals with the law of international organizations as a special area of international law. International organizations embody the institutionalized system of states. The activities of these international organizations have a major impact not only on international politics, but also on our daily lives. When one state attacks another state militarily, as Russia did in 2022 against Ukraine, this affects organizations such as the UN, the OSCE, NATO, and the EU. When the American president deliberately imposes tariffs on individual states, it must be examined whether this is compatible with WTO obligations. When it comes to daily life, then we fly from one country to another thanks to the International Civil Aviation Organization. Foreign products and services are available thanks to the WTO agreements. We can settle financial obligations in foreign currencies because currencies are generally convertible thanks to the IMF. During the corona pandemic, international coordination through the WHO played an important role. Our human rights are monitored by numerous regional and international human rights bodies, notably by the UN Human Rights Committee. And the UN and regional organizations mediate in conflicts and tensions – often successfully, sometimes not. These are just a few examples. They show: international organizations matter. Of course, they cannot work miracles. They are sometimes slow and inefficient. Nevertheless, they are often fundamentally pivotal for the international system and for people. Without them, life and politics would be (even) more difficult. They are necessary, which is why they were established by states—across ideological, political, and cultural boundaries and controversies. It is no exaggeration to say that these organizations, along with states, embody *the structural and institutional foundations of the international system* and make it capable of acting. They also reflect the system's dynamics, especially in the advancement of international law, which occurs primarily in and through these organizations.

International organizations are also the law-based *institutionalized framework of international politics*. The interconnection between international law and the law of international organizations is evident. Evident are also the very close links between international organizations and international politics. This book cannot and will not ignore these political aspects because to deny this would result in an anemic undertaking, far away from the realities of international institutionalized relations. The focus of this book is therefore clear: the legal foundations create the normative framework for political action, hopefully in the common interest of states and of mankind, and that is what the book is about: the *institutionalized normative framework of international politics on the global and regional level.*

In the international system, there are different types of organizations, institutions, networks, and regimes that are sustained by different actors: intergovernmental organizations, nongovernmental organizations (NGOs), informal regimes such as the G7 and G20, or global public policy networks between states, and multinational companies for specific purposes. Given its focus on international law, this book concentrates on traditional state-based international organizations such as the UN or the WTO, as well as the EU as a supranational organization; it further addresses NGOs as an organizational form of civil society at the international level. Other international institutions are not considered. Their academic appreciation and analysis belong rather to the academic domain of International Relations.

The author has been teaching the law of international organizations for decades at various universities, but especially at his home university, the University of Zurich. Experience has shown that the treatment of different organizations in the sense of a mere juxtaposition is unsatisfactory, because then the common bracket in the sense of the shared, general legal dogmatic and theoretical aspects is too little recognizable. On the other hand, the purely abstract discussion of the legal issues associated with international organizations does not do justice to the very practical impact these organizations have and is not sufficiently illustrative.

For these reasons, this book begins with a general part of the law of international organizations, which also highlights the latter's close links with general international law. Subsequently, various international organizations are discussed in more detail. The choice is at least partly obvious: the UN is the central global organization of the state system, and the UN Charter is part of the constitutional structures of the international system. There is no way around it. Numerous problems of the law of international organizations can be discussed using its example. The EU is the prototype of a supranational organization as the next higher level of intergovernmental cooperation, which is based on a partial integration of state functions. The

WTO, as the most important international economic organization, is primarily an institution that monitors and, if necessary, enforces states' compliance with the central trade agreements GATT, GATS, and TRIPS. It has numerous mechanisms for implementing and developing the multilateral conventions that govern it. These include, above all, a very efficient dispute settlement mechanism which, however, currently is unfortunately blocked as the US refuses to participate in filling vacancies in the Appellate Body. The Bretton Woods institutions have special features, which make them interesting not only because of their obvious global economic importance but also from a legal point of view. These certainly include not only their structure and functioning, which is modeled on private-sector enterprises, especially in the area of decision-making, but also their concrete activities, which are very close to the financial economy.

As to regional organizations, the European ones are in the foreground. In that sense, this textbook is somewhat Eurocentric. There are indeed many organizations in other parts of the world that are also of importance and interest. Their discussion must, however, be reserved for a later or separate edition; for to include them in the present textbook would either make the book too voluminous or the discussion of the individual regional organizations would have to be superficial.

The OSCE is an organization based solely on soft law. At the same time, it is an organization under Chapter VIII of the UN Charter. The Council of Europe is a very traditional organization, but it has specific features related to the organs and as a consequence of the close connection with the European Court of Human Rights. Finally, NATO has special features with regard to decision-making, the organs, and cooperation with third states. All of these organizations, then, have their distinctive features, and together all of them provide a multifaceted picture of the impact of international organizations in the international system.

Given the variety and importance of the global and regional organizations covered in this book, it cannot be more than an overview. However, it is the author's hope that the book will help to better understand international organizations as important actors, to better frame international policy issues and problems institutionally, and ultimately to gain a deeper understanding of the institutional basis of the international system – even in disruptive times.

Zürich, Switzerland Urs Saxer

Acknowledgments

Over the years, many have contributed directly or indirectly to this book. I am particularly indebted to students who assisted me with research, compiling materials, and contributing to first drafts of chapters on the basis of my lecture notes and PowerPoint presentations. These students include:

Victoria Törner (General Part); He Jiawei (United Nations); Claire Ann Smith (Regional Organizations and European Union); Dr. Dominic Staiger (World Trade Organization, Institutions of Bretton Woods, Non-Governmental Organizations); Steven Rüttimann (United Nations and World Trade Organization); Ulrike Heinrich (Regional Organizations, European Union, and the Institutions of Bretton Woods).

Special thanks to Dominic Staiger, Ulrike Heinrich, and Steven Rüttimann also for assisting me as a group in many respects. It was a very rewarding teamwork and an exceptionally pleasant cooperation. Also, Ya Lan Chang helped with research and editing, Giordana Campagna PhD reviewed an early draft of the entire book and gave important material input. Moritz Senn MLaw did the prefinal editing, and Leo Tibergien, PhD candidate, made with his many very helpful remarks the book much more readable to students. Justin Kuhn, a law student at the University of Zurich, did the final editing. Finally, Olga Lieder, Dipl.-Jur., did an excellent job when compiling the index. I would like to express my sincere thanks to all of them.

Errors and omissions are, of course, the author's sole responsibility.

Contents

List of Abbreviations

App.	Application
Art.	Articles
AU	African Union
ASEAN	Association of Southeast Asian Nations
cf.	confer
COE	Council of Europe
COMECON	Council for Mutual Economic Assistance
CSCE	Conference for Security and Cooperation in Europe
EAEC	European Atomic Energy Community
ECF	Extended Credit Facility
ECSC	European Coal and Steel Community
ECOSOC	Economic and Social Council
ECOWAS	Economic Community of West African States
EDC	European Defence Community
EEC	European Economic Community
ed.	editor
edn.	edition
eds.	editors
EEC	European Economic Community
EFF	Extended Fund Facilities
EFTA	European Free Trade Organization
EJIL	European Journal of International Law
EPAC	European Partners Against Corruption
EPC	European Political Community
EURTAOM	European Atomic Energy Community
EU	European Union
e.g.	exempli/for example
FAO	Food and Agriculture Organization
FCL	Flexible Credit Lines
FRG	Federal Republic of Germany
GATT	General Agreement on Tariffs and Trade

GEF	Global Environmental Facility
HIPC	Initiative for Heavily Indebted Poor Countries
ibid.	ibidem/in the same place
IBRD	International Bank for Reconstruction and Development
ICAO	International Civil Aviation Organization
ICC	International Criminal Court
ICCPR	International Covenant on Civil and Political Rights
ICISS	International Commission on Intervention and State Sovereignty
ICJ	International Court of Justice
ICSID	International Centre for Settlement of Investment Disputes
ICTR	International Criminal Tribunal for Rwanda
ICTY	International Criminal Tribunal of Former Yugoslavia
IDA	International Development Association
id.	Idem/the same person
IFC	International Finance Corporation
ILO	International Labour Organization
IMO	International Maritime Organization
ITU	International Telecommunication Union
IAEA	International Atomic Energy Agency
i.e.	id est/that is
LAFTA	Latin American Free Trade Union
LAS	League of Arabic States
LGDJ	Librairie Générale de Droit et de Jurisprudence
LoI	Letter of Intent
LoF	League of Nations
MDR	Multilateral Debt Relief
MERCOSUR	Mercado Común del Sur
MIGA	Multilateral Investment Guarantee Organization
MoU	Memorandum of Understanding
NAFTA	North American Free Trade Agreement
NATO	North Atlantic Treaty Organization
NGO	Non-governmental organization
no.	number
OAS	Organization of American States
OAU	Organization for African Unity
OEEC	European Economic Co-operation
OSCE	Organization for Security and Co-operation in Europe
OTIF	Organization for International Carriage by Rail
para.	Paragraph
paras.	Paragraphs
PfP	Partnership for Peace
p.	page
pp.	pages
PRGT	Poverty Reduction and Growth Trust

Pt.	Part
RCF	Rapid Credit Facility
RFI	Rapid Financing Instruments
RoE	Rules of Engagement
SBA	Stand-By Arrangements
SC	United Nations Security Council
SCF	Standby Credit Facility
SG	United Nations Secretary General
s.	and the following page
ss.	and the following pages
UN	United Nations
UN DESA	United Nations Department of Economic and Social Affairs
UN GA	United Nations General Assembly
UNCF	UN Children's Fund
UNDCP	UN International Drug Control Program
UNDP	United Nations Development Program
UNEP	United Nations Environmental Program
UNESCO	United Nations Educational, Scientific and Cultural Organization
UNHRC	United Nations High Commissioner for Human Rights
UNIDO	United Nations Industrial Development Organization
UNPF	UN Population Fund
UNWTO	United Nations World Tourism Organization
UPU	Universal Postal Union
VCLT	Vienna Convention on the Law of Treaties
vol.	volume
WEU	Western European Union
WEP	World Food Program
WHO	World Health Organization
WIPO	World Intellectual Property Organization
WMO	World Meteorological Organization
WTO	World Trade Organization
WWI	First World War
WWII	Second World War

Chapter 1
International Organizations: Principles and General Rules

1.1 Why International Organizations Matter

Over the last century, international organizations have become central actors in the international system. Today, they are the most important form of long-term institutional co-operation between states on various subject matters. They exist because many of the *world's problems are global or regional in nature*. Hence, these problems can only be solved through close co-operation between states in the framework of common international institutions devoted to dealing with these issues. Of course, certain issues can be regulated by bilateral or multilateral treaties, however such a static, limited approach often does not suffice. This is because the most significant contemporary problems tend to be long term and dynamic in nature and require institutionalized resolution mechanisms. Due to the ever-closer web of interdependencies in the global system it is insufficient for general abstract norms alone to regulate these interdependencies and steer them towards common purposes. The sharp increase in number of international organizations since the Second World War (WWII) is clear evidence for an *obvious necessity of international co-operation between states within an institutional framework.*

International organizations deal with a vast scope of subject matters. A central task is the preservation of *international peace and security*, which is also one of the central goals of the international legal order. The significance of this goal has given rise to international norms prohibiting the use of force. However, even though these norms are pivotal to the international system, their mere existence does not secure general compliance in a structurally decentralized international order composed of sovereign states. There is a need for an overarching framework monitoring compliance and imposing sanctions against perpetrators. This task is being taken seriously primarily by the United Nations (UN) and other global organizations as well as regional organizations like the Organization for Security and Co-operation in Europe

---

Special thanks to Victoria Törner for her important contribution to the elaboration of this chapter.

U. Saxer, *The Law of Global and European Organizations*, Springer Textbooks in Law, https://doi.org/10.1007/978-3-032-00067-5_1

(OSCE) or African Union (AU). Hence, *monitoring states' compliance with international norms* is one of the main reasons why international organizations exist.

In the traditional decentralized international order, if states find themselves victims of a public international law violation, they can have recourse to traditional public international law measures to secure compliance with international norm. Such measures include retorsion, countermeasures and reprisals. These self-help measures can be unilaterally taken by the victim states, which means that they themselves carry out the task of law enforcement to force the perpetrator to comply. In contrast, within the framework of international organizations, states become *"institutionally relieved"*, as institutionalized and therefore multilateral collective measures can be taken to enforce legal norms instead of states acting unilaterally to protect their interests. An important form of such collective measures is, e.g., the UN Security Council's powers under Chapter VII of the UN Charter in the event of a breach of international peace and security.

International organizations deal, however, with more than just international security and the maintenance of peace. An important area that falls under their authority is the *economy*, including the economic development of less developed parts of the world. The European Union (EU), the European Free Trade Organization (EFTA), the Economic Community of West African States (ECOWAS) or MERCOSUR came into being as a form of regional economic cooperation.[1] Globally, the World Trade Organization (WTO) is the most important economic organization. The Bretton Woods Institutions, as financial organizations, also regulate the global economy and have adopted development-oriented policies over time. In addition, there are many further regional organizations and institutions devoted to the economy and development.[2]

Other important areas that organizations focus on are the *protection of human rights* and the *strengthening of the rule of law*. The Council of Europe (CoE) is arguably the most effective regional organization in this regard. Other organizations that share these purposes include the OSCE, the Organization of American States (OAS), and the African Union (AU, former Organization for African Unity OAU). On the international level, the UN is also tasked with the protection and promotion of human rights. This is reflected in the adoption of many landmark international

[1] Although the EU has two distinct purposes when it was conceived. One of the prevention of war through ensuring limited access to coal and steel and the second of creating an economic community in which trade flows freely.

[2] One example of a regional organization focused on economic development is the Economic Community of West African States. Its purpose is to 'foster interstate economic and political cooperation', available at <https://www.ecowas.int/about-ecowas/history/> (accessed 8 March 2025). Another example is the Asian Development Bank. Consisting of 49 members in the Asia-Pacific and 19 in the rest of the world, it aims to 'promote social and economic development' by 'providing loans, technical assistance, grants, and equity investments' to members and partners, available at <https://www.adb.org/who-we-are/about> (accessed 8 March 2025). Similarly, the Islamic Development Bank promotes social and economic development in its member states and 'Muslim communities worldwide', available at <https://www.isdb.org/who-we-are> (accessed 8 March 2025).

human rights treaties, in particular the International Covenant on Civil and Political Rights and the International Covenant on Economic, Social and Cultural Rights, both adopted by the UN General Assembly in 1966. In addition, the UN's commitment to human rights has led to the establishment of UN bodies such as the Human Rights Council and the Human Rights Committee.

International organizations also extend their reach into more *technical areas*. In fact, the first few international organizations, e.g. the Universal Postal Union established in 1874, were technical organizations. Today's international technical organizations deal with a variety of issues such as transborder traffic, postal services or communication. The International Telecommunication Union (ITU) regulates news transmission via TV and radio, but also the technical aspects of internet communication, and the Intelsat, regulates the worldwide commercial news transmission via satellites. Other such international organizations include the Intergovernmental Organization for International Carriage by Rail (OTIF); the International Maritime Organization (IMO), the International Civil Aviation Organization (ICAO) and the World Tourism Organization (UNWTO). There is evidently a large number of organizations operating in various specific technical fields. Many of these organizations aim to set uniform standards, i.e. to generate legal, technical and economic harmonization in their fields. There are also organizations devoted to *cultural issues*, most notably the United Nations Educational, Scientific and Cultural Organization (UNESCO), or to health like the World Health Organization (WHO). International organizations' scope of involvement has significantly expanded over time, covering almost all areas of state activity and most aspects of human life.

One can distinguish international organizations between those with a *general political aim* and those with a more *technical and functional purpose*. International organizations with a general political approach have a vast, almost limitless, ambit of competence. Even though their primary concern is often the settlement of disputes, the maintenance of peace, and the advancement of human rights (e.g. UN, OAS, AU), they also have other concerns. These include the economy, development, ecology, and standard setting in many other policy areas. International organizations dedicated to technical and functional issues usually have a more rigid and limited set of goals and activities and are often less politicized than those with general political goals. This has a lot to do with interdependencies: It is in the interest of all the states including those in conflict with each other that, e.g., the rules of international communication, transportation and civil aviation are observed, and their compliance be monitored by international institutions also in times of high political tensions.

For all these reasons, international organizations play a crucial role in shaping the development of the world and of international law. Although international organizations are primarily dependent on their member states, it is necessary for their organs to have some autonomy from their members to perform properly. The will of the international organization should therefore constitute *more than just the lowest common denominator* of the wills of the member states. It is also vital that these organs possess the ability to supervise co-operation between the member states and ensure that the norms of the organizations are observed and enforced by them.

All this has also a crucial impact on general international law and its development. International law is very often drafted by organs of international organizations, not by states. These organs contribute to established legal practice by interpreting these international norms. There are, therefore, many reasons why international organizations matter.

1.2 History

International organizations are a *special, institutionalized form of co-operation between states*. It is the notion of institutionalization that distinguishes them from co-operation, e.g., based on bilateral and multilateral treaties. Institutionalization in this context is thus the creation of *international state-autonomous structures* arising from the co-operation between states, forming organs of international organizations. Unlike bilateral and multilateral treaties, these organizations are autonomous entities, i.e. separate from the states that created them and usually have their own legal personality. Historical developments evidence a steady trend towards more institutionalized cooperation between states.

1.2.1 International Cooperation Before the 1815 Congress of Vienna

1.2.1.1 Precursors; Early Alliances

In the historical development, institutionalized constructions that enable stable and permanent state co-operation has always existed. One early arrangement that somewhat resembles the international organizations of today is the co-operation between the ancient Greek cities to protect the sanctuary of Delphi.[3] This co-operation had its own army and even acted as an arbitrator to resolve political disputes among Greek cities. The old Greek city-states were, however, not comparable to modern states; further, at that time, there was no international legal order comparable to what developed later in Europe and the world during the centuries after the Peace of Westphalia.

Throughout history, states occasionally entered into alliances. These alliances, established for common purposes such as defense or common economic benefits, can be regarded as precursors of today's regional organizations. One example is the confederation of Etruscan states, located in modern-day Tuscany and part of Umbria, created during the Antiques before the establishment of the Roman Empire Another

[3]For an in-depth discussion of co-operation in ancient Greek cities, see Butler (2009), especially Chapter II: Greek Cities.

example is the Hanseatic League, which started off as an interest group for German merchants abroad, but which then transformed into a confederation of these merchants and their cities. The old Swiss confederation can also be regarded as a precursor of an international organization.[4]

1.2.1.2 After the Peace of Westphalia; European Peace Conferences

A landmark achievement for international relations was the signing of the Peace of Westphalia in 1648. This event is widely hailed as laying the foundation for the modern nation-state 'characterized by principles such as sovereignty and the balance of power'.[5] The peace treaties negotiated in Westphalia ended the Eighty Years' War between the Spanish and the Dutch Crowns, and the Thirty Years' War. With this peace treaty, the tradition of diplomatic state conferences in Europe started, which often took place after wars and regulated their outcomes. These conferences are often regarded as the political precursors of international organizations. For instance, Mangone wrote that, even though the Congress of Westphalia had little resemblance to twentieth century peace conferences, its significance lay in its successful *negotiation* of multilateral peace treaties.[6] The conferences generally sought to establish how peace treaties should regulate the aftermath of wars. Accordingly, their objectives were security issues in Europe and the settlement of territorial issues during a time when territory was often equated with power.

1.2.2 The Nineteenth Century

1.2.2.1 Holy Alliance and Concert of Europe

It has been said that the nineteenth century is the 'era of *preparation for* international organization'[7] due to significant developments in international cooperation. The Congress of Vienna 1815 is considered the beginning of international cooperation that laid the groundwork for today's international organizations.[8] The Congress aimed to draw up a long-term peace plan for Europe after the Napoleonic wars which had disrupted balance of power in Europe and violated various international principles. Two achievements emerged from the Congress: The Holy Alliance and the Concert of Europe, both of which embodied the *soft institutionalization of international and/or European relations.*

---

[4] For an overview of these alliances, see Mangone (1954), 19 s.

[5] Reinalda (2009), p. 17; For a contrary view, see Osiander (2001), p. 251.

[6] See Mangone (1954), p. 22.

[7] Amerasinghe (2005), p. 5.

[8] For an in-depth discussion of the Congress of Vienna, see Reinalda (2009), 17 ss.

The Holy Alliance,[9] established on the initiative of Tsar Alexander I of Russia, was formed to institutionalize the relations between the main Christian European powers; namely, Russia, Austria and Prussia. The Alliance sought to permanently influence the political conditions in the European states and the ideological underpinnings of Europe by promoting and defending Christianity and the monarchic political order.

The Concert of Europe can be understood as a board of directors comprising important states of Europe. Remarkably, it was able to influence Europe's political direction in the nineteenth century. The main European powers such as Prussia, Russia, Britain and France decided on important European issues together by employing 'a new method of diplomacy—diplomacy by congress or conference'.[10] The Concert of Europe was essentially based on a *coordination of national policies without common institutions*, as it was made possible by the European powers coming together to solve international crises and maintain peace. In this sense, it lacked the structural features of an international organization as we understand the term today. Nonetheless, there is a similarity between the UN Security Council's actions regarding international peace and security, and the Concert of Europe in the nineteenth century: the Concert of Europe was a common Directorate consisting of state representatives who decided on the status of contested territories, settled conflicts and debated political issues of common concern.

1.2.2.2 River Commissions

The Final Act of the Congress of Vienna of 1815 also established the Central Commission for Navigation on the Rhine, a technical commission which, like a national administration, was responsible for administering the navigation of the Rhine River. It had the power to make formal decisions directed towards ship owners and ship crews. The legal basis of the Commission has changed multiple times, but it still exists today. In 1856 the Danube Commission was created, which administered navigation on the Danube. The Commission was endowed with far-reaching powers over the Danube states and was able to act through its own organs. It adopted ordinances and had the right to collect fees and to impose fines on individuals. These Commissions can be considered as precursors to supranational organizations because they had their own law-making powers and could directly enforce its laws against individuals.

[9]For a discussion of the history of the Holy Alliance's treaty, see Knapton (1941), 132 ss.
[10]Elrod (1976), p. 162.

1.2.2.3 International Administrative Unions

The second half of the nineteenth century witnessed the establishment of so-called *international administrative unions* to regulate technical transborder activities of common concern and to coordinate the national administrations in these areas. The first was the International Telegraphic Union, later renamed International Telecommunication Union (ITU) founded 1865; it was followed by the Universal Postal Union (UPU) founded in Bern (Switzerland) in 1874. The administrative unions of the nineteenth century had common features: (1) they were based on an international treaty between the member states; (2) their competences and jurisdiction were limited to administrative tasks designated to the administrative union; (3) for the purpose of these tasks, secretaries were instituted as organs of the unions. The secretaries could act in the name of the union and express the will of the union, though the Secretariat had no influence on the formation of the union's collective will. This was usually formed at conferences that gathered all the member states. However, since state sovereignty was pivotal in the nineteenth century, all the unions' important decisions based on unanimity. The will of the union was thus merely a reflection of collective individual wills of all the member states. The task for the Secretariat was mostly confined to enforcing the resolutions decided by the states and supervising the member states' implementation of the resolutions. Importantly, the Secretariat was politically impartial in performing its task. Moreover, it acted as a forum for information exchange between the member states.

The basic structure of administrative unions, i.e. a conference of member states unanimously forming the unions' wills, and the creation of independent organs, has continued to influence the structure of today's international organizations.

1.2.3 The Interwar Period: Collective Security and the League of Nations (LoN)

The end of the First World War (WWI) marked an important change in the development of international organizations. After the devastation inflicted by WWI in Europe, the main powers realized that national decisions to go to wars could no longer be tolerated as a normal consequence of state sovereignty, and that measures would have to be taken to enable states to settle their disputes peacefully. Hence, the signing of the Treaty of Versailles in 1919 created the League of Nations as the *first institution devoted to collective security* as a new common response by states to international security issues. It established a political and legal framework that sought to deter states from engaging in military conflicts by threatening collective sanctions against aggressors and by offering states political and legal procedures to settle conflicts. Thus, the *concept of collective security was born*. Article 11 of the Covenant of the League of Nations stipulated the following rule:

Article 11. Any war or threat of war, whether immediately affecting any of the Members of the League or not, is hereby declared a matter of concern to the whole League, and the League shall take any action that may be deemed wise and effectual to safeguard the peace of nations.

By deeming war or threat of war against a member state as an attack against all member states, collective security served to deter potential aggressors.

The League had a purpose and the structure comparable to today's international organizations, as it sought to promote not only peace, but general co-operation between states with a focus on economic, cultural and social matters. Such interaction was achieved partly by the organs of the League itself, and partly through special organizations with their own legal personalities but which were closely linked to the League. The League of Nations' structure was more complex than that of the nineteenth century organizations. It comprised of the following organs: the Council, the Assembly and the Secretariat. In the Assembly, all states were represented. The Council had a limited number of member states, some permanent and some elected. The Council acted as the executive organ of the League, usually requiring a unanimous vote for its decisions, which were usually non-binding. The combination of permanent and elected members resembles the Concert of Europe and corresponds to the composition of the UN Security Council. Further, the Permanent Court of International Justice was created by the League, but it was institutionally independent from the League.

The League of Nations was the *first international organization with a genuine political purpose*, i.e. peace and security. However, it never achieved universal membership; only sixty-three countries were member states throughout its history. Most member states were European countries, with a minority of states from South America (e.g. Bolivia and Colombia) and Asia (e.g. Japan, China and Thailand). Notoriously, the United States of America never became a member despite that President Woodrow Wilson 'publicly supported the general principle of reforming the international system', a support which 'lent credibility to the various unofficial schemes for a League of Nations'.[11] The League was further weakened when Adolf Hitler came into power in 1933. Angered by the League's refusal to grant Germany military parity, Germany withdrew from the League 9 months after Hitler's ascension to power. In 1939, the Soviet Union was expelled after attacking Finland in 1939. Furthermore, the League struggled with its decision-making mechanism that often-required unanimity, which hindered it, e.g., from effectively imposing sanctions.

Despite shortcomings, the League of Nations was a considerable step forward from the nineteenth century administrative unions in terms of the extent to which international relations were institutionalized. This was true as well for special-purpose organizations established at that time, such as the International Labour Organization (ILO) , also created by the Treaty of Versailles in 1919 and which

[11] Armstrong (1982), p. 2; For a detailed account of Wilson's role, see 6 ss.

still exists today. The ILO did not only regulate interstate co-operation but had a main role in setting norms. Moreover, it had and still has a tripartite structure for the International Labour Conference, the organization's plenary organ: national delegations to the Conference consist of one worker's representative, one employer's representative and two government representatives, thereby changing the traditional approach of only governmental representation in international organizations.

The perception of international organizations was considerably enhanced as a result of the creation of the League of Nations and its special organizations. In contrast, regional organizations did not play a role during this time.

1.2.4 The Post-WWII Period

1.2.4.1 Establishment of the United Nations (UN)

The end of WWII and the creation of the UN mark the beginning of the heyday of international organizations. Contrary to the League of Nations, the UN is a *truly universal organization* by having almost all existing states as members: Indeed, out of approximately 200 countries in the world, 193 are members of the UN. This demonstrates that the UN has had exponentially more success than the League of Nations in becoming a universal organization, at least on the face of it.[12]

The UN was created with the flaws of the League of Nations in mind. It has a more elaborate system of collective security than the League of Nations, which makes the UN more efficient and better able to maintain international peace and security. This is due primarily to the powers of its executive organ, the Security Council. The Security Council is composed of fifteen member states with five permanent members. These are the main victorious powers of the Second World War, i.e. the United States, the Soviet Union (present-day Russia), United Kingdom, France and China. The five permanent members have the power to veto UN Security Council resolutions. This is sometimes an impediment to the proper functioning of the Council as the main organ responsible for peace and security. This is why the veto is often criticized but at no avail: it is and remains a political reality. The General Assembly, consisting of all UN members, meets regularly, and unlike the Security Council, all members have equal voting power. In contrast to the League of Nations, the resolutions of the Security Council and the General Assembly do not require unanimity, and the Council's resolutions are often legally binding. The other main organs of the UN are the Secretariat, presided over by the Secretary-General; the Economic and Social Council (ECOSOC); the Trusteeship Council (inactive since 1994); and the International Court of Justice (ICJ).

[12]The UN, as an organization of states, is vulnerable to realpolitik machinations and power play. This will be discussed in more detail in the chapter on the UN.

Additionally, the UN has various special agencies which are partly a continuation of the League of Nations' auxiliary organizations set up under the auspices of its Covenant. The entire UN system consists of the UN as the main organization and its special organizations, programs, funds and agencies. Examples include the Food and Agriculture Organization (FAO), the UNESCO, ICAO, the Bretton Woods Institutions consisting of the International Monetary Fund and the World Bank Group, the WHO, the World Meteorological Organization (WMO) etc. These various and diverse special agencies demonstrate the complexity of the UN and its significance to our daily lives.

The creation of the UN heralded also a new era of international law which no longer merely regulates interstate relations but purports to coordinate national policies within the framework of international institutions. One can also speak of a new dimension of international law being created, i.e. the *law of an organized international community*. The law created by the UN guides states in their organization of peace and security; increasingly, the UN's influence has extended to the states' domestic affairs.[13] Specifically, a so-called *international constitutional order arose around the UN Charter serving as its constitution.*[14] The UN Charter has thus come to play an important role in the international system. In this sense, the creation of the UN marked a very important turning point in the development of international law.

1.2.4.2 The Establishment of Regional Organizations

The UN is thoroughly imbued with the idea of collective security, as are some of the regional organizations which emerged progressively after the creation of the UN. Regional organizations were mainly established after WWII. Examples include the creation of the League of Arab States (LAS), later renamed as Arab League, already in 1945, the Organization of American States (OAS) in 1948, and the Organization for African Unity (OAU), later renamed as African Union, in 1963. In Europe, the Western European Union (WEU) was founded as a defense union shortly after WWII. Further, in 1949 the North Atlantic Treaty Organization

[13]For instance, the UK Parliament enacted the United Nations Act 1946 to allow the UK to implement UN Security Council Chapter VII resolutions. In this regard, the UK enforced Resolution 1373, adopted on 28 Sep 2001 and aimed at preventing the financing of terrorism and terrorist acts, by enacting domestic legislation to freeze assets with links to terrorism. There has also been debates amongst US scholars on whether UN Security Council resolutions create domestic legal rights. Cf. Brand (1976), 298 ss.

[14]Bardo Fassbender argues that the UN Charter has a 'double constitutional character': it is the constitution of the UN, and also 'the constitution of the international community': Fassbender (2009), p. 1 (emphasis removed). Jan Klabbers, however, was unconvinced by Fassbender's argument and called it 'wishful thinking, often asserted rather than carefully argued…and too circular to be plausible'. One reason for this criticism is that Fassbender is unsuccessful in bridging the gap between domestic constitutional law, which regulates public authority, and international law, a 'largely horizontal legal order, made up of sovereign states': Klabbers (2009), 667 ss.

(NATO) was established, comprising at the time ten European States, Canada and the US.

Regional organizations became increasingly important with the partial paralysis of the UN Security Council during the Cold War. This paralysis was caused by the veto power used by the two competing superpowers, the US and the USSR, who also represented the larger world conflict between western style democratic states based on market economy and communist states. This conflict had a significant impact on the UN Security Council's operations. For example, in 1950, the USSR boycotted the UN Security Council in 1950 to protest the UN's refusal to recognize the People's Republic of China as the official representative of China as UN member instead of the Republic of China (Taiwan).[15] At other times, the Cold War had led to stalemates in other international crises, such as the Suez Canal Crisis in 1956. The Security Council was prevented from acting in the crisis due to vetoes by Britain and France. In the end, the General Assembly had, based on its subsidiary powers with respect of the maintenance of peace and security, to step in to resolve the conflict between Israel and Egypt by calling for a ceasefire.

Contrary to the UN Security Council's ineffectiveness during the Cold War, regional organizations were and are less likely to be affected by geopolitical and ideological conflicts because they are comprised of *states who share similar regional interests*, which tend to lead to close cooperation between the states and even integration. This is especially so within the areas of security and the economy. For example, African Union (AU; former OAU) has as its goal the settlement of disputes between African states and economic development in the region. In 1967 the Association of Southeast Asian Nations (ASEAN) was founded; its original members were Indonesia, Malaysia, the Philippines, Singapore and Thailand. Now, ASEAN has been expanded to include Vietnam, Myanmar, Laos, Brunei and Cambodia. In South America, the Latin American Free Trade Union (LAFTA) was in operation between 1960 and 1980. In 1992, the North American Free Trade Agreement (NAFTA) was established between the United States, Canada and Mexico. Argentina, Brazil, Paraguay, Uruguay and Venezuela (currently suspended) are members of Mercado Común del Sur (MERCOSUR), a customs union focused on promotion of free trade that was founded in 1995. The East African Community, seeking to promote free trade in the area, existed between 1967 and 1977. The Economic Community of West African States (ECOWAS) was founded in 1975. This organization has expanded its activities from mere economic co-operation to an approach that also includes the preservation of peace, including Peace-Keeping Operations (PKO) in internal conflicts.

[15] As a result of the USSR boycott of the Security Council, the US was able to intervene, based on an authorization of the Security Council, in Korea, already then divided into a communist-controlled North and US-controlled South. When the North invaded the South, the US brought the Korean situation to the UN Security Council as it knew that it would not have to face a Soviet veto. The Security Council passed Resolution S/RES/83 (1950) of 27 Jun 1950, allowing the United States and its allies to repel the communist invaders.

1.2.4.3 The Process of European Integration: The EU and Supranationalism

The process of European integration started with the establishment of the Council of Europe (CoE) in 1949. Winston Churchill had already advocated for a united Europe in 1946 in a speech delivered in Zurich (Switzerland). "If Europe were once united in the sharing of its common inheritance," Churchill said, "there would be no limit to the happiness, prosperity and glory which its 300 million or 400 million people would enjoy."[16] Churchill had thus envisioned an economic and political union to which member states would relinquish some of their sovereign powers; in other words, *supranationalism*. As the first European organization responsible for all European concerns except security-related matters, the CoE was designed as a traditional international organization at the time because the concept of supranationalism was not yet a concrete issue. Hence, the CoE is an intergovernmental organization based on the principle of sovereignty and mere co-operation between the member states. It has a general purpose, albeit excluding regional peace and defense matters, with a particular focus on the protection of human rights and the advancement of the rule of law.

A different approach was adopted in 1951 when the Paris Treaty established the European Coal and Steel Community (ECSC), the first precursor to the European Community (EC) and the European Union (EU). The aim of the ECSC was to merge the French and German coal and steel industries, which played a key role in WWII, under the umbrella of a common institution with an administration vested with genuine, independent powers. The ESCS was inspired by the so-called Schuman Plan, conceptualized by Robert Schuman, the French Minister of Foreign Affairs at the time. Schuman envisaged that mere interstate co-operation was not sufficient to rebuild the countries and prevent wars in Europe, and so inspired the creation of ECSC together with Jean Monnet, a French Entrepreneur and high official of the French government who became the first president of the ECSC's High Authority (later renamed Commission). The ECSC was to be regulated and administered by the High Authority as a supranational organ, which then led to a new species of international organizations, i.e. supranational organizations. The ECSC's structure was unique as compared to traditional international organizations. It had the following organs: The Commission, made up of independent members with powers to enact regulations and render decisions; the Council, made up of government representatives; the Assembly, made up of representatives of the national parliaments; and an independent court. This marked the beginning of *supranationalism as a new political and legal concept* and posed a new challenge to national sovereignty.[17]

The EU, in its current form, has a similar structure, but its organs' tasks have changed and expanded. Its main organs include the Commission, the Council, the

[16]The complete text of the speech is available at <https://winstonchurchill.org/resources/speeches/1946-1963-elder-statesman/united-states-of-europe/> (accessed 8 March 2025).

[17]This will be explained infra Sect. 4.2.

Parliament and the European Court of Justice. The EU has gone through different stages in its development before it became the organization that it is today. In 1957, in addition to the ECSC, the European Economic Community (EEC) and the European Atomic Energy Community (EURATOM) were founded by the Treaty of Rome. In 1967, these three existing communities were merged into the European Community (EC). In 1992, the EU was established by the Maastricht Treaty and consisted of three pillars: the European Community, the Common Foreign and Security Policy, and Justice and Home Affairs. The EU at that time did not have international legal personality, but only the EC. This changed in 2009, when the Lisbon Treaty amended the Maastricht Treaty by merging the three pillars under the EU as one legal entity. From an international point of view, the Lisbon Treaty also united the organization on foreign affairs matters by establishing the European External Action Service, headed by the High Representative of the Union for Foreign Affairs and Security Policy. One of the tasks of the High Representative is to ensure consistency in the EU's external actions and policies.

The process of European integration has made important contributions to the theory and practice of international organizations. It is based on the concept that states are integrated into a unified structure which places increasing limits, and even replaces, to a certain extent, state sovereignty.[18] This involves *transferring some sovereign powers to a supranational institution,* which demonstrates that EU states are willing to relinquish some powers for the benefit of integration. In contrast, the UN were and are still based on *sovereign co-operation between member states*, and no transfers of power to the organization takes place, despite the UN Security Council's competences to decide on coercive measures.

The process of European integration is based on the *idea of functional economic integration*. This means that the organization's powers transferred by the states for the sake of integration will increase and alter according to growing and changing economic and political needs. Integration is therefore an on-going process which has witnessed an expansion of the organs' powers, a deepening of the integration of the member states, more autonomous institutions and organs, as well as an enhanced international role.

[18] For a criticism of this practice, see Coughlan (2004), 33 ss. Coughlan contends that respect for state sovereignty is a 'fundamental democratic principle and the cornerstone of international law', and the concept of shared sovereignty on which the EU is premised is 'propaganda [cover] for having one's laws and policies decided by European Union bodies one does not elect', 39–40; For a more charitable take on the EU and national sovereignty, see Bellamy (2017), 188 ss. Bellamy characterizes the EU as 'a republican association of sovereign states that is designed to overcome the possibility for their mutual domination while providing a mechanism for their securing certain global goods and avoiding various global bads', 189.

1.2.4.4 Other European Organizations

The EEC in 1957 was an exclusive community comprising only the six Western European founding states (France, Germany, Italy, Belgium, Netherlands and Luxembourg.) This led to the establishment of a competing free trade union in 1960, the European Free Trade Association (EFTA), composed at that time of seven non-EEC European countries. Its structure was and is much more in line with traditional international organizations. It only has one representative organ, the Council, which is responsible for enforcing agreements reached by its members; these agreements can only be reached by unanimity. In addition, the EFTA has a secretariat in Geneva, and a court in Luxembourg.

The longing for *integration as a consequence of increasing regional interdependencies* was not only confined to Western Europe; similar efforts during the Cold War were made in Eastern Europe. The states under Soviet influence formed the Council for Mutual Economic Assistance (COMECON) in 1949. COMECON was the Soviet response to Western Europe's Organization for European Economic Co-operation (OEEC). The OEEC was responsible for administering the Marshall Plan, an economic recovery program initiated by the United States to help rebuild Europe after WWII.[19] In 1955, the Warsaw Treaty of Friendship, Cooperation, and Mutual Assistance (commonly known as the Warsaw Pact) was established as a military alliance of communist countries[20] and in response to NATO.

The OSCE is another example of a regional European organization. It started as a permanent conference, the Conference for Security and Co-operation in Europe (CSCE) and served as a discussion forum for Western and Eastern European states, with the participation of the United States and Canada. The CSCE was not an organization from a legal point of view, but rather a *permanent negotiation process*. One of its main achievements was to bring human rights to the forefront of European relations. Part VII of its Helsinki Final Act 1975, a soft law document adopted at the end and as a result of the first negotiation round, is dedicated to respect for human rights. In particular, it states:

> *The participating States will respect human rights and fundamental freedoms, including the freedom of thought, conscience, religion or belief, for all without distinction as to race, sex, language or religion.*

Of particular significance, too, is its provision on national minorities, given Europe's WWII persecution of certain national minorities:

---

[19] For more information on the Marshall Plan, see <https://www.marshallfoundation.org/marshall/the-marshall-plan/history-marshall-plan/> (Accessed 8 March 2025).

[20] These countries were the Soviet Union, East Germany, Poland, Hungary, Czechoslovakia, Romania, Bulgaria and Albania.

The participating States on whose territory national minorities exist will respect the right of persons belonging to such minorities to equality before the law, will afford them the full opportunity for the actual enjoyment of human rights and fundamental freedoms and will, in this manner, protect their legitimate interests in this sphere.

In 1994, the CSCE was transformed into the OSCE, thus becoming a international organization, properly understood, with a complex, sophisticated structure.

1.2.4.5 Global Economic Organizations

At the global level, the conclusion of the General Agreement on Tariffs and Trade (GATT) as well as the establishment of the Bretton Woods Institutions formed an important step in the development of international organizations. One of the main reasons to establish these institutions was to prevent a worldwide economic decline as it happened in the interwar period with the Great Depression of the 1930s which also gave rise to political extremism, and which was largely responsible for the "Machtergreifung" of Hitler in 1933. The lack of any international intergovernmental institution at that time devoted to trade and the economy at large was co-responsible for the economic depression because there was no institutionalized cooperation between states, and the unilateral measures of states to protect their own economy made things even worse. Thus, the global regulation of trade was an important issue on the political agenda after WWII to lay the foundation for a prospering international economy. There was a widespread impetus to establish an international organization dealing with foreign trade and international competition and to establish global rules for trade to be monitored by an appropriate international institution.

a) GATT
Hence, on 24 March 1948, the Havana Charter was signed with the intention to create the International Trade Organization (ITO). Apart from trade, the ITO was designed to regulate the protection of foreign investment and to establish antitrust regulations. However, the Havana Charter was opposed by the US Congress. Without the participation of the US, by far the most important economic power, the creation of the ITO made no sense; as a result, the ITO was never established. Only the GATT, a treaty aimed to reduce trade barriers, and which was part of the ITO, survived. It became operational in 1947 based on a provisional protocol regulating its early application before the ITO's coming into existence which, however, for the reasons explained never occurred. The GATT then continued to remain in force based on said provision protocol until the World Trade Organization (WTO) was established to succeed the GATT in 1994. Despite a weak legal basis, the GATT had a remarkable impact on international trade as it played a leading role in regulating and promoting it.[21]

[21] For a history of the GATT and its impact on international trade policy, see Kock (1969).

The basic idea behind GATT is the "Most Favoured Nation" (MFN) clause between the GATT members. It states that trade concessions between two member states are automatically applicable to all member states. Other goals and achievements of the GATT were broad reductions of discriminatory quantitative restrictions on imports and exports, and the reduction and abolition of tariffs in many economic sectors. These policies helped to develop international trade at a rapid pace. Remarkably, the GATT was not an intergovernmental international organization with its own legal personality, but merely a multilateral treaty. Although only treaty-based, it managed to build up rudimentary organizational structures throughout the years until the WTO was finally established. In 1960, a permanent council was set up as a plenary body with decision-making powers between the formal meetings of the contracting parties. The GATT also had a Secretariat based in Geneva headed by a Secretary General. The Secretariat conducted arbitrations to settle disputes between the contracting parties that could not be resolved by consultation, which is a form of dispute resolution introduced in the GATT. It took place between two parties to a dispute with a view to resolving it without resorting to litigation. These practices have come to form the basis of the WTO's dispute settlement procedures.

b) Institutions of Bretton Woods: IMF and World Bank

After WWII important international financial organizations were established. The International Monetary Fund (IMF) and the World Bank are the two core Bretton Woods institutions. Their creation goes back to 1944 at the UN Monetary and Financial Conference in Bretton Woods in New Hampshire, USA. The purpose of the Conference was to establish a new monetary policy order post-WWII. The IMF was founded with the purpose of achieving equal growth and development of international trade, stabilizing international exchange rates, assisting a multilateral system of payments and eliminating foreign exchange (FOREX) restrictions. The IMF also helps states with balance of payment problems, as well as offers loans to countries in need. To achieve this financial stability, a system of fixed exchange rates between the currencies was initially put in place. However, in the early 1970s, the system broke down when the US unilaterally left it; since then, currencies are allowed to float.

The World Bank consists of the International Bank for Reconstruction and Development (IBRD) and the International Development Association (IDA). These organizations became operational on 27 December 1945. Other Bretton Woods institutions were established later as part of the World Bank Group: the International Finance Corporation (IFC); the International Centre for Settlement of Disputes (ICSID); and the Multilateral Investment Guarantee Agency (MIGA). The World Bank's initial purpose was to rebuild and support member states' economic development through capital investments after WWII. Over the years, however, the World Bank's functions have changed. Today, the Bank mostly grants loans to economically weak or developing countries and offers them technical assistance on a very broad range of issues, such as improving skills, development training for migrant workers, improving irrigation service delivery e.g. in Peruvian Sierra, and helping e.g. India meet its solar energy targets.[22] Generally, these loans are mainly invested in infrastructure projects. The same is true for the IFC and the IDA. Hence, the World Bank is essentially an international institution that provides financial assistance to developing countries to reduce poverty. In line with this aim, the World Bank promotes private foreign investments by offering guarantees for loans or sharing of loans to the investors.

1.2.4.6 Conclusion

After WWII, international organizations became increasingly important. This trend reflected the *growing interdependencies and interconnectivity of an increasingly constitutionalized international system* and the *need to cooperate in an institutionalized framework to steer and regulate these interdependencies*. Therefore, states on the regional and global level established common institutions and became members of these organizations because they considered them necessary for their own advancement. This was particularly true for decolonized, newly independent states. For these new states, membership in international organizations, especially the UN and its specialized agencies, was regarded as the culmination of their journey to statehood and independence.

The UN's partial inability to cope with important global problems due to the rivalry between the two superpowers, the Soviet Union and US, during the Cold War contributed to the creation of regional organizations with a political purpose. Integration efforts in the areas of regional security and economy demonstrated important and mostly successful regional self-organization efforts. The most advanced attempt was the process of European integration within a supranational institutional framework.

1.2.5 Post 1989

1.2.5.1 End of the Cold War and an Expanded Role for the UN

1989 marked the end of the Cold War, and thus of the antagonisms between the Western democracies and the Eastern socialist states. This had an important structural impact on the global political system, as well as the role of global and regional organizations. Since 1989, many global and regional organizations have expanded their activities and strengthened their competences. At the same time, the number of member states in organizations increased, particularly in Europe.

---

[22] See <https://www.worldbank.org/en/who-we-are/ibrd> (accessed 8 March 2025).

a) Gulf Conflict 1990/1991

A good example illustrating these developments is the UN: Since 1989, i.e. after the end of the East-West conflict that had paralyzed the UN, the organization was finally able to pursue its goals set by the founding members, i.e. ensuring international peace and security. The Kuwait crisis in 1990/1991, which saw Iraq invade and annex Kuwait, marked the turning point. After decades of Security Council ineffectiveness due to US and Soviet vetoes, the UN, for the first time, was able to manage a conflict efficiently by ousting Iraqi troops from Kuwait under a US-led military operation. This operation of US troops and its allied states was approved by UN Security Council Resolution 678[23] adopted under Chapter VII UN Charter which authorizes military action e.g. when the prohibition on the use of force in Article 2(4) has been breached. Article 2(4) states:

All Members shall refrain in their international relations from the threat or use of force against the territorial integrity or political independence of any state, or in any other manner inconsistent with the Purposes of the United Nations.

Article 39, under Chapter VII, provides that:

The Security Council shall determine the existence of any threat to the peace, breach of the peace, or act of aggression and shall make recommendations, or decide what measures shall be taken in accordance with Articles 41 and 42, to maintain or restore international peace and security.

Article 42 allows the UN Security Council to authorize force. It states:

Should the Security Council consider that measures provided for in Article 41 would be inadequate or have proved to be inadequate, it may take such action by air, sea, or land forces as may be necessary to maintain or restore international peace and security. Such action may include demonstrations, blockade, and other operations by air, sea, or land forces of Members of the United Nations.

Hence, Iraq's invasion of Kuwait was a blatant breach of Article 2(4). After determining, in UN Security Council Resolution 660,[24] that the invasion was a breach of international peace and security, the UN Security Council authorized member states to use 'all necessary means' to, inter alia, restore international peace and security. The case thus saw the UN Security Council taking coercive measures against Iraq and became a precedent for many subsequent UN Security Council resolutions under Chapter VII in many conflicts.

[23] S/RES/678 (1990).

[24] S/RES/660 (1990).

b) UN Involvement in Internal Conflicts

During the past three decades, the UN Security Council has involved itself primarily in internal conflicts threatening international peace and security. The following conflicts were particularly salient: Yugoslavia in the 1990s and the UN's action in Somalia, Cambodia, Haiti, Rwanda, Libya and other states. Since 1989, the number of peacekeeping missions has grown immensely. The Security Council has also employed instruments such as stationing peacekeeping forces in conflict zones to prevent violence, and authorizing troops to use force. This kind of involvement was unthinkable during the Cold War because it was thought that the UN had no authority to intervene in internal matters of the member states, which shows that state sovereignty also played a role in hindering the UN Security Council in achieving its purpose.

The 1990s brought a dramatic change to this approach. The UN Security Council's practice suggested that the notion of domestic affairs being a matter of national sovereignty was very much relativized, and that these matters were usually susceptible to the Security Council's collective action. This indicates a change in the balance of power between international organizations and member states: the national sovereignty of the member states has been shrinking due to the increasing regulatory powers of international organizations which themselves reflect dramatically increasing global and regional interdependencies. Activities traditionally regarded as falling under the domestic domain are also on the Security Council's work desk, such as human rights, system of government and rule of law.[25]

c) Setbacks

However, the UN has not only experienced relative successes lately; it has had serious setbacks due, e.g. to unauthorized unilateral military interventions. One important example is NATO's intervention in Kosovo 1999[26] which helped establishing an independent Kosovar state against the will of Serbia. Other examples include the US-led invasion of Afghanistan in 2001 which ousted the Taliban from power, and of Iraq in 2003 which brought to an end the rule of the longtime dictator Saddam Hussein.[27] An extreme challenge of the authority of the UN at large and of the Security Council in particular was Russia's attack on Ukraine on March 24th, 2022, which took place during a meeting of the Security Council on the conflict between Russia and Ukraine. Hereinafter, Russia vetoed all the Council's decision on the conflict.

---

[25] For the tension between state sovereignty and human rights, see e.g. Walling (2013). For a collection of scholarly perspectives on the UN's impact on state sovereignty, see Paolini et al. (1998).

[26] For some critical perspectives on these military interventions, see Krisch (1999), 59 ss.; Henkin (1999), 824 ss.; Wheeler (2000), 144 ss.

[27] For an analysis of how the Iraq War has impacted international law and the world order more generally, see McGoldrick (2004). For scholarly critical perspectives, see e.g. Falk (2007); Santhanam et al. (2003); and Yoo (2003), 563 ss.

Nonetheless, the UN remains an indispensable international organization. As such, it has many expectations to fulfill, but it does not always have the requisite resources to meet them. Consequently, it has to be selective of the measures it adopts. The structure of the UN, in particular the Security Council, also suggests that its policies are sometimes influenced by the self-interests of some of the permanent members of the Security Council, which in turn might undermine the organization's legitimacy. The UN Security Council has recently increasingly found itself incapable of acting due to vetoes, e.g. from Russia and China in the Syrian conflict before the end of the Assad regime[28] and above all in Russia's military aggression against Ukraine.

1.2.5.2 European Integration Efforts

The process of European integration is paradigmatic for a trend towards closer institutionalized cooperation among states of a region after the end of the Cold War. Already in 1986, the Single European Act (SEA), the first major revision of the 1957 Treaty of Rome, set the tone for institutional developments and reforms within the then-EC. The SEA's goal was to create a "Single Market" in the Community by 1992. To achieve this, it provided for a more collaborative legislative process, later known as the cooperation procedure, which strengthened the role of the European Parliament and gave it real powers in the process of legislation. At the same time, the SEA introduced more majority voting in the Council of Ministers. Moreover, the SEA codified the European Council and the European Political Co-operation, later the Common Foreign and Security Policy, for the first time, and contained provisions for closer co-operation on economic and monetary policy and justice.

After having achieved the single market, the Maastricht Treaty led to the creation of the EU in 1992. The next stage of the process was the creation of the European Monetary Union (EMU) and the treaty framework for the common currency, the Euro. In 1994, the European Economic Area (EEA) was formed, comprising EU and EFTA countries, but excluding Switzerland (on its own accord). The EEA allows the non-EU states Iceland, Norway and Liechtenstein to participate in the internal market on the same conditions as the EU member states.

An important transformation occurred in Eastern Europe after the breakdown of the socialist regimes in 1989/1990. The COMECON and the Warsaw Pact were dissolved. Since then, almost all of the Eastern European states have applied for membership in the EU; many of them became members in 2004 and 2007. Most of them are also NATO members. All former Eastern Bloc states, except Belarus, also became members of the CoE. The EU, the CoE and the OSCE all played an

---

[28] The conflict in Syria has been raging since 2011 between the Ba'athist Syrian Arab Republic, led by President Bashar al-Assad and his allies, and various opposing forces. The opposing forces, in turn, oppose each other. The UN Security Council has met many times to pass resolutions to address the conflict, but the proposed resolutions have been vetoed by Russia and China. For more information, see Gifkins (2012), 377 ss.

important role in transforming the former Eastern European communist states into states governed by the principles of democracy, rule of law and a free market economy. The integration of these states into regional organizations was regarded by the states themselves as key to their transformation. The transformation of both the organizations and Europe itself illustrates how instrumental the organizations were in bringing about change.

The reconfiguration of politics since 1989 has had a profound effect in the EU regarding its expansion and thus, the extent of integration of its member states. However, in recent years, particularly during the Eurozone crisis that began in 2008, the EU's supranationalism has been exposed and subject to critical scrutiny. The Eurozone's flaws, revealed by the crisis, as well as the refugee crisis that began in 2015 have caused states to be cautious of transferring powers to the central EU authority and taking for granted the benefits of integration. This scepticism culminated in the Brexit vote of the UK in 2016, but also in the rise of integration-sceptic, nationalist parties in many European countries.[29] By contrast, at the beginning of Russia's war against Ukraine, the EU appeared very united and strengthened. Over time, however, more and more divergent views emerged in the individual member states.

1.2.5.3 Regional Integration Efforts Outside Europe

Other examples of regional integration include the African Union (AU; successor to the Organization of African Unity), Mercosur, ECOWAS and the Asian-Pacific Economic Cooperation (APEC). The AU comprises all African states as members. The organization's aims include to promote of political and socio-economic integration on the continent and of African interests internationally; peace and security in Africa; and the promotion of democratic institutions, good governance and human rights. The AU and some of the other regional organizations have all taken steps towards further integration and even supranationalism.

1.2.5.4 Establishment of the WTO

In the 1990s, also WTO as a new, powerful institution was established and officially started as an international organization in 1995. Uniting the basic agreements GATT, GATS and TRIPS under a common institutional framework, the WTO covers not only goods but also services (GATS) and intellectual property (TRIPS), thus liberalizing many areas of international trade. It moreover contains a permanent dispute settlement mechanism. The transformation of the GATT into the WTO showed that,

[29] For a discussion of Euroscepticism in France in response to Europe's successive crises since 2008, see Ivaldi (2018), 278 ss.; For a similar discussion, but with a focus on Italy and the Netherlands, see Pirro and van Kessel (2018), 327 ss.

particularly in the world of economy, the ever-increasing economic interdependencies force states to co-operate, both for their own interests and a major part of the international community.

1.2.5.5 Russia's War Against the Ukraine; China's Geopolitical Ambitions; The BRICS States

Russia's war against Ukraine in 2022 and China's geopolitical ambitions pose a major challenge to the international order and the architecture of that order, as these countries, together with other states, particularly the BRICS states,[30] intend to establish a multipolar international system with several power centers.

The Russian aggression against Ukraine has severely damaged some organizations, such as the OSCE, which, before the war, with Russia's consent, was heavily involved in the conflict in Ukraine and sought to mediate, or the UN Security Council, which was completely disavowed by its permanent member Russia when it started the military invasion of the Ukraine. On the other hand, the very decisive reactions of, for example, the EU and the Council of Europe, but also the General Assembly of the UN, and the sudden sharp increase in the importance of NATO, show that in the face of Russian aggression, countries are strongly considering institutionalized cooperation in joint organizations to meet the challenges posted by the Russia's military aggression.

China is a member of all relevant international organizations and a key promoter of the in population world's largest regional organization, the Shanghai Cooperation Organization (SCO), founded in 2001 and headquartered in Beijing.[31] China's rise has led to a political and economic rivalry with the US that is having a major impact on geopolitics. China's foreign policy is characterized by an increasing self-confidence and, to some extent, hegemonic aspirations which are inter alia reflected in territorial disputes with neighboring states, and military threats against Taiwan.

BRICS is an informal organization comprising the emerging states Brazil, Russia, India, China, South Africa, Iran, Egypt, Ethiopia, and the United Arab Emirates.[32] Originally designed as a gathering of emerging states with common economic interest,[33] it has increasingly become an institution with geopolitical ambitions.[34] These states are driving economic and political South-South cooperation to alter the international system on the basis of the increasingly influential non-Western part of

---

[30] For more details as to BRICS see infra Sect. 1.3.1.3.

[31] Members states of the Shanghai Cooperation Organization are China, Kazakhstan, Kirgizstan, Russia, Tadzhikistan, Uzbekistan, India, Pakistan and Iran.

[32] For more information see https://en.wikipedia.org/wiki/BRICS (accessed 8 March 2025).

[33] The BRICS states have established the BRICS Development Bank, also labelled New Development Bank, a multilateral development bank with a purpose and activities comparable to the World Bank; see https://www.ndb.int/ (accessed 8 March 2025).

[34] The BRICS states represent more than 40% of the World population and more than 20% of the world's GDP; see Bono (2023) 464 ss., 466 et seq.

the World. So, also the BRICS states strive for multipolarity in international relations. It is to be seen what the impact on international organizations will be.

1.2.5.6 Conclusion

International organizations used to be strongly dependent on their member states, and originally often only embodied the lowest common denominator of the will of the member states. In contrast, *member states today are increasingly dependent on international organizations*. The need for international co-operation in the face of global and regional interdependencies, which in turn calls for institutionalized co-operation, significantly impairs the power of states to act unilaterally and in isolation. States' domestic measures are no longer able to address alone new international problems, as e.g. the Covid-19 pandemic showed. Hence, states are compelled to accept international organizations as the most competent institutions in certain areas and to cooperate in this institutionalized framework. This has allowed international organizations to become authoritative actors in the international system, which can be seen as one of the most significant developments since the beginning of the twenty-first century.

1.3 Types of International Organizations

1.3.1 Definitions and Distinctions

1.3.1.1 Definition

There is no clear definition of the term 'international organization' in international law. There is, however, a quasi-official definition of the term in the 2011 ILC Articles on the Responsibility of International Organizations.[35] Legal doctrine as well as practice usually refer to this definition in Article 2 (a). This definition, which is functionally linked to the subject of the ILC codification, i.e. the responsibility of IOs, is very generic and maybe undercomplex as it does not, despite its very general nature, grasp the enormous variety of international institutions. Nonetheless, the ILC definition has authority and is certainly useful as a starting point for analysis. Article 2(a) states:

> *"International organization" means an organization established by a treaty or other instrument governed by international law and possessing its own*

---

[35] Available at <https://legal.un.org/ilc/texts/instruments/english/draft_Articles/9_11_2011.pdf> (accessed 8 March 2025).

international legal personality. International organizations may include as members, in addition to States, other entities.

This conforms with legal doctrine and practice which has developed criteria to distinguish international organizations from other international institutions. Accordingly, the features of an international organization as an institution of international law are, quite in line with the ILC definition, as follows:

1. A multilateral treaty or similar international legal instrument as the legal basis, which reflects a will to establish a permanent institution for a common purpose. An international legal instrument could, for example, be a resolution of an international organization.[36]
2. Membership by states or international organizations.
3. An autonomous will distinct from the will of its members, autonomous decision-making procedures and an international legal personality (i.e. subject of international law).
4. Organs capable of forming the will of the international organization and vested with powers to represent it.

The most authoritative characteristics include a *multilateral treaty as the legal basis, states or international organizations as members, international legal personality and permanent independent organs*. Sometimes other characteristics are also referred to, such as, e.g., sovereign equality of members or a partial transfer of sovereign power from the states to the organization. The latter is more characteristic of a supranational organization as a special category of international institutions. In addition, looking at today's organizations, equality between member states is not always relevant. Sometimes states have different degrees of power in an international organization. An example of this is the EU's weighted voting according to the countries' population, or, for the Breton Woods institutions, according to the members' financial contribution.

1.3.1.2 Basic Criteria

a) Based on a Treaty or Another International Legal Instrument

International organizations are usually based on a treaty. However, there are exceptions. An international organization not based on a multilateral treaty is the OSCE, which originated as an institutionalized multilateral conference. Although the CSCE increasingly took on an organizational structure and became the OSCE in 1995, this

[36] An example of this is the International Criminal Tribunal of Former Yugoslavia (ICTY), which is based on a resolution by the UN Security Council under Chapter VII.

is not based on a treaty. In fact, the OSCE's legal basis is soft law, i.e. legally non-binding interstate agreements.[37]

Other legal instruments may include *resolutions of an international organizations*. Examples of international institutions based on resolutions include the war crimes tribunals for Yugoslavia and Rwanda, established by the UN Security Council.[38] Theses tribunals are international institutions and have international legal personality, but they are not inter*governmental* organizations because they do not have member states.

b) States as Members

Membership of international organizations usually consists of states. However, current practice shows that international organizations can also be members of other international organizations. A good example is the EU's membership in the WTO. Membership may occasionally also be conferred on non-sovereign territories. India, for example, became a member of the UN when it was still under British colonial rule. Furthermore, the Byelorussian Soviet Socialist Republic (now Belarus) and the Ukrainian Soviet Socialist Republic (now Ukraine) were also full members of the UN despite being constituent republics of the Soviet Union. Taiwan is member of some international organizations despite that the People's Republic of China (PRC) considers Taiwan as part of the PRC, and Taiwan itself never declared its independence from China. These were and are, however, exceptions due to particular political circumstances.

c) International Legal Personality

International organizations have their own international legal personality. The existence and extent of the legal personality are determined by its founding members and are expressed or implied in the founding treaty. The founding treaty should thus state whether the organization has the capacity to enter into treaties or entertain other legal and/or political relations with other international subjects. Absent explicit regulations in the treaty, these powers have to be inferred from the treaty provisions, based on the established methodology of organization treaty interpretation. However, sometimes multilateral treaties with a particular organizational structure, e.g. just a

[37] Given this, it might seem that the OSCE's status as an international organization can be questioned. However, the practice by states and other international organizations, in particular the UN, has shown that the OSCE, despite its lacking international treaty, is in fact recognized as an international organization with its own legal personality. The OSCE further has the status of a regional arrangement under Chapter VIII of the UN Charter. In this light, it can be said that although the OSCE is not based on a multilateral treaty, it still has the status as an international organization because of its international recognition.

[38] International Tribunal for the Prosecution of Persons Responsible for Serious Violations of International Humanitarian Law Committed in the Territory of the Former Yugoslavia since 1991 (ICTY), S/RES/827 (1993), and International Tribunal for the Prosecution of Persons Responsible for Genocide and Other Serious Violations of International Humanitarian Law Committed in the Territory of Rwanda and Rwandan Citizens Responsible for Genocide and Other Such Violations Committed in the Territory of Neighbouring States, between 1 Jan 1994 and 31 Dec 1994 (ICTR), S/RES/55 (1994).

Secretariat without any plenary organ, do not explicitly state whether there is an intention to confer international legal personality to this structure. An example is the GATT before the establishment of the WTO. The GATT did not express the intention of establishing a legal personality but developed in that direction through practice. However, it remained a mere treaty. The same is true for some international human rights instruments with bodies monitoring compliance.

The scope of an organization's international legal capacity is determined on a *functional basis*, i.e. the organization must be entitled to take actions that are covered by its functions and its purposes as set out in the founding documents.[39]

d) Own Organs

Finally, an international organization must have its own organs. This is a necessary consequence of the permanent institutionalization of co-operation between member states to pursue a common purpose, hence distinguishing an international organization from traditional international treaties. The organs are permanent and work continuously towards accomplishing and maintaining the aims of the organization. Thus, international organizations have at least one organ to uphold and express the will and intention of the organization. Without such an organ, there is no international organization.

1.3.1.3 International Institutions Without an International Legal Basis; Regimes

There are international institutions established by states which have neither a legal basis in international law nor international legal personality but are nonetheless institutions. An example is the Commonwealth of Nations, a political association of former Colonies of the British Crown which has a secretariat, and which is partly based in the Statute of Westminster 1931, an act of the UK Parliament setting the basis for the relationship between the Commonwealth realms and the Crown, and the London Declaration of 1949. Another example is the G20, an intergovernmental forum of 19 countries and the European Union (EU) established in 1999 without any legal basis and without legal personality. It is most probably the most influential international political institution apart from the UN, dealing foremost with the world economy and international financial stability, but increasingly with many other issues such as climate change and sustainable development. Very often issues to be decided by international organizations, above all by the institutions of Bretton Woods, are pre-discussed and pre-decided in the framework of the annual G20 summits. Another international institution without legal basis is the BRICS group of states.[40] Since 2009 the BRICS group has been holding annual summits. There is also a rotating pro tempore president. In spite of this, BRICS does not have formal

[39] *Reparation for Injuries Suffered in the Service of the U.N.*, Advisory Opinion, ICJ Rep. 174 (1994).

[40] See Bono (2023), 464 ss.

structures. However, the BRICS states have established the New Development Bank and, based on an international treaty,[41] the Contingent Reserve Arrangement (CRA) which should protect states in liquidity problems against international pressures.

The G20 and the BRICS group are examples of international regimes. This term was developed by international relations scholars. Stephen Krasner, e.g., defines regimes as "institutions possessing norms, decision rules, and procedures which facilitate a convergence of expectations in a given area of international relations".[42] The concept of regimes is thus much broader than that of an international organization. It encompasses arrangements between several, including non-state actors that consist of principles, norms, rules, and procedures, i.e. a norm system that regulate specific international issues and problems.

1.3.1.4 NGOs; Special Cases

Traditional international organizations, sometimes also labeled intergovernmental organizations (IGO), are distinct from Non-Governmental Organizations (NGO). NGOs are not created by states based in an international treaty. They are organizations under national jurisdiction with private (often civil society) instutions and private individuals as members. They are established by private initiative, are based on voluntary association, are governed by the law of the state in which they are incorporated, have only private legal capacity, and are not subjects of international law. However, NGOs, like international organizations, have an institutional structure and concern themselves with transnational activities.

Some key features of NGOs are:

(a) Public purpose independent of state interests
(b) Established on private initiatives
(c) A minimal institutional structure
(d) Headquarters
(e) Transnational activities
(f) Governed by national law

Other features include the requirements that the NGO is non-religious, non-military and not engaged in illegal activities. NGOs can be both national and international NGOs. There are about 40,000 international NGOs today and even more national ones. Some famous NGOs include Amnesty International, Greenpeace and the International Olympic Committee.

---

[41] Cf. the Treaty for the Establishment of a BRICS Contingent Reserve Arrangement, signed in Fortaleza in Jul 2014; http://www.brics.utoronto.ca/docs/140715-treaty.html (accessed 8 March 2025).

[42] See Krasner (1983), p. 2.

The International Committee Red Cross (ICRC)[43] is a special international institution. It has a very international humanitarian purpose but is not based on a multilateral treaty. It is a Swiss association based on Swiss national law. In accordance with its statutes, the members of the ICRC are all Swiss citizens. Therefore, the ICRC is an NGO, however with some features typical of an international organization[44] It enjoys partial international legal personality as a result of the 1949 Geneva Conventions which endow the ICRC with some international rights and duties.[45]

1.3.2 Types and Classifications

There is no generally accepted classification of international organizations, but different types can be identified. There are the distinctions between traditional intergovernmental organizations and supranational organizations; between regional and universal organizations; and between organizations with a general purpose and those with a special purpose.

1.3.2.1 Supranational Organizations

a) Main Feature: Transfer of Powers from the Member States to the Organization[46]

Although the term "supranational organization" is most used to describe the EU, there are other organizations that possess features of supranationalism.

There are important structural differences between traditional international organizations and supranational organizations, in particular regarding the organization's powers, the decision-making and, generally, the relations to the member states. The term "supranational organization" is used as a general label to describe international organizations that have a *higher degree of integration between member states* compared to traditional international organizations which primarily coordinate national policies in certain policy fields. This higher degree of integration stems from a *transfer by the member states of some of their sovereign powers to the supranational organization*.

This is the main feature of supranationalism: matters previously under national competence come under the supranational organization's purview. Supranational

[43] See <www.icrc.org> (accessed 8 March 2025).

[44] For more information on the ICRC's legal status, see Debuf (2016), 319 ss.

[45] As to the details see infra, Sect. 6.2.2.2.

[46] For a more detailed analysis of supranationalism see infra Sect. 4.2.

organizations are thus international organizations which are granted powers formerly reserved to the member states. This has important structural consequences: Organs within the supranational organization are established to independently administer and exercise the powers so transferred.

b) Characteristics

The most important elements of supranational organizations which distinguish them from traditional organizations are thus *the consequences of the transfer of powers* from the states to the organization. These features include:

(a) The capacity of the organization to *enact laws binding the member states* which are directly applicable in the member states, thus establishing rights and obligations of the inhabitants as well as of private legal entities such as companies. This is the necessary consequence of the general responsibility of the organization for certain policy areas which were originally member state prerogatives. This responsibility includes the duty to develop and implement policies by enacting the necessary domestic legal rules.

(b) A special structure of the organization with *state-like features* based on a separation of powers, comprising of law-making bodies, an executive organ and a court.

(c) Decision-making is usually based on the *(often qualified) majority principle*. Adhering to the unanimity principle would certainly preserve the member states' sovereignty but would be impracticable given that the member states have transferred some of their sovereign rights and that decisions are required in the policy areas for which the organization has responsibility.

(d) *Direct applicability and immediate effect* of, at the minimum, a part of the organization's legal rules (the so-called secondary law) in member states without specific national implementation measures. This is also the necessary consequence of the organization's overall responsibility to regulate certain specific issues.

(e) The capacity of *individuals and companies to invoke the law* of the supranational organization against member states and against the organizations' organs.

(f) A *court system with compulsory jurisdiction* that ensures a uniform application of the organization's laws by its organs and member states, and to preserve minimum rule of law standards for private individuals and companies directly affected by the organization's laws.

The term supranationalism is primarily used to describe the EU. Nonetheless, other international organs and organizations occasionally act in a manner that resembles supranationalism. One pertinent example is the UN Security Council's enactment of coercive measures under Chapter VII of the UN Charter, in particular when these measures are directed at individuals. An example of such measures are resolutions that call for the freezing of assets of individuals, such as Resolution 1333[47] which froze the financial assets of Osama bin Laden.

The overall point is that the stronger the necessity to integrate on an international or regional plane, the stronger the supranational aspiration of an organization. The need to integrate is usually influenced by the extent to which the problems to be tackled are transnational and cross-border, with either an international or regional dimension and how strong the interdependencies are. As more and as stronger states are interdependent in policy areas, as more there is a need to establish common rules by common institutions. Against the background of a general trend towards ever increasing interdependencies, also supranationalism has the potential to become a general trend.

1.3.2.2 Universal and Regional Organizations

The territorial reach of membership of an international organization is usually the basis to distinguish between universal organizations and regional organizations. The term "regionalism" is mostly defined in relation to geographic territory. Examples include the CoE, AU and the OAS. For other international organizations, e.g. the NATO, it is not the regional nexus that is the main cause for its co-operation, but rather the common political and military interests. The same can be said about the OSCE, which is Europe-centered but has American and Asian members.

1.3.2.3 General Political and Special Purpose

The distinction between organizations with a general political purpose and organizations with a special, technical and functional purpose has already been mentioned:[48] organizations with a general purpose are usually concerned with the preservation of peace and security over and above other concerns, but they also have other broad purposes including the protection of human rights, the advancement of the economy, the promotion of the rule of law etc. Such organizations include the League of Nations, the UN, the OSCE and the AU. International organizations with special purposes, in contrast, have more specific goals. This is the case for all the specialized Agencies of the UN, such as the WHO, the UNESCO or the FAO. Goals may include the removal of barriers to trade, the integration of the economy or the co-ordination of health policy. Also these organizations are involved in politics: there are often overlaps between functions with political and technical aspects.

---

[47] S/RES/1333 (2000).

[48] See Sect. 1.1.

1.4 Establishment and Dissolution of International Organizations

International organizations are based on legal documents that set out and regulate an organization's purpose, structure and activities. The organization's legal basis also forms the basis of the organization's international legal personality. Once its organs have been elected, the organization is able to act.

1.4.1 Treaty-Based Organizations

As mentioned,[49] the most common legal foundation of an international organization is a multilateral treaty concluded between states and/or other international legal subjects under international law. An international organization is born when the founding treaty enters into force. This treaty must express the intention to create an international organization, i.e. an organization with its own legal personality and organs to perform its tasks. In so doing, the founding treaty, which can also be referred to as the *international organization's constitution*, usually regulates the organization's purpose and functions, its basic structure and organs, decision-making, including law-making, membership, the rights and obligations of the member states and the organization, and the relations between the organization and its member states, the relations between the organization and its member states.

The Vienna Convention on the Law of Treaties (VCLT) is applicable to the founding treaty. Article 5 states:

> *...the present Convention applies to any treaty which is the constituent instrument of an international organization and to any treaty adopted within an international organization without prejudice to any relevant rules of the organization.*

As the founding treaty is a multilateral treaty between states, it often stipulates the number of ratifications required before the organization is formally established. Absent such provision, the founding treaty enters into force if and when all the founding member states have ratified the treaty.

In public international law, the principle of freedom of contract, in particular the form of the contract, also applies to treaties. Accordingly, an organization can be established by an informal agreement between the founding members, though this is

[49] Section 1.2.1.1.

very exceptional. An example of it in practice was the establishment of the Nordic Council in 1952.[50]

Many constituent instruments *do not allow reservations by member states.* However, if the treaty is silent on this issue, Articles 19–23 VCLT apply. Article 20(3) VCLT states that a reservation requires the acceptance of the competent organ of the organization, which is the organ that decides on membership.

1.4.2 Organizations Based on Decisions by International Bodies

The organs of international organizations may also create other organizations and institutions with their own legal personality. The legal basis is then not a treaty but a resolution of an international organization. Well-known examples are the criminal courts established by the UN Security Council under Chapter VII of the UN Charter, the most prominent being the ICTY. Another example is the Global Environmental Facility (GEF),[51] an institution with 182 members, created as a pilot program by the World Bank. In 1992, during the Rio Summit, the GEF moved out of the World Bank. In 1994, it became an independent institution when its constituent instrument was adopted after it was accepted by representatives of the States participating in the GEF and by the three implementing Agencies of the GEF, i.e. the United Nations Development Programme, the United Nations Environment Programme, and the World Bank.[52]

1.4.3 Legal Personality and the Ability to Act

The legal personality of an international organization is determined by its constitutional document and is therefore contingent upon the founding treaty's entering into force. Some organizations require ratification by a certain number of states for this to occur. The international organization acquires its international legal personality as soon as its founding instrument has been ratified by the requisite number of states. Only when the organs have been properly set up, either elected or nominated, does the international organization gain its ability to act.

[50] Later, cooperation between the Nordic countries was formalized in the Treaty of Co-operation between Denmark, Finland, Iceland, Norway and Sweden (the Helsinki Treaty). This Treaty was signed on 23 Mar 1962 and entered into force on 1 Jul 1962.

[51] <https://www.thegef.org/> (accessed 8 March 2025).

[52] See the Instrument for the Establishment of the Restructured Global Environment Facility, 7 Jul 1994, available at <https://www.thegef.org/documents/instrument-establishment-restructured-gef> (accessed 8 March 2025). This is a very hybrid, rather unique way to establish an international institution.

1.4.4 Establishment of an Interim Project Organization

Since there is usually a considerable amount of time between the establishment of the organization and the commencement of its activities, there is sometimes as an attachment to the founding treaties a protocol containing a time frame for the progressive realization of activities. Occasionally, the organization commences its activities even before the treaty has been ratified by the requisite number of states. In practice, states might have simultaneously agreed to establish an interim project organization when they signed the treaty. This interim project organization seeks to prepare the organization for the commencement of its activities. As soon as the founding treaty comes into force, the permanent organs then take over.

1.4.5 Headquarters Agreement with the Host State

The domicile of an international organization's headquarters is decided on at the time of its founding, when the newly founded international organization enters into a so-called headquarters agreement with the host state. Due to its neutrality and humanitarian tradition, Switzerland has entered into many such agreements and hosts various organizations in Geneva.[53] Headquarters agreements are an expression of the international legal subjectivity of international organizations, i.e. their capacity to enter into international treaties. Headquarters agreements usually contain provisions on the privileges and immunities of the organization, their tax exemptions, the recognition of the international organizations' functionaries as diplomats, relief from regulations on currencies, etc. A significant part of how these are regulated in headquarters agreements is determined by customary law, as stated in the relevant provisions of the Vienna Convention on Diplomatic Relations of 1961 as well as in the Vienna Convention on Consular Relations of 1963[54] which do, however, not directly apply to international organizations and their relations to states.

---

[53] Examples include the UN, the WHO, UNICEF, the UN High Commissioner for Refugees and the World Trade Organization.

[54] In addition, the provisions of the VCLT between States and International Organizations or between International Organizations of 1986, which is not in force yet, may apply as far as they constitute customary international law.

1.5 Dissolution of an International Organization

1.5.1 Lack of Rules in Constituent Instruments

International organizations are usually founded on a permanent basis as e.g. the UN or the EU. Their founding treaties are valid for an undefined period of time. The circumstances that incentivize states to co-operate in an international organization to solve issues of common concern are usually of the nature that a dissolution or temporary nature of an organization would undermine the states' efforts and run counter the very core reasons why international organizations are established. Nonetheless, international organizations can be established for a limited period, though this is very exceptional. The ECSC, for instance, was established for 50 years.

Generally, instances of a dissolution of international organizations are rare. Examples of a complete dissolution are the West European Union (WEU), COMECON and the WAPA. The League of Nations, too, was completely dissolved, however some of its functions were transferred to the UN. In theory, there are different reasons why and how an international organization is dissolved. Conceivable is (1) the replacement of an IO by another; (2) the absorption of an IO by another; and (3) the merger of IOs to establish a new IO. Special cases not implying the dissolution of an organizations are the separation of an organ to become an independent IO, and the transfer of specific functions. Contrary to the dissolution of an organization implying its liquidation, these examples are necessarily connected with a transfer of activities and/or assets to another organization. In practice, this almost never occurs, and if it does it is handled on an ad-hoc-basis. This is the main reason why there are no generally accepted rules of customary international law regulating dissolution that would apply.

The statutes of most international organizations do not contain a provision regulating the organization's dissolution. States prefer to regulate the dissolution and liquidation of an organization on an ad-hoc basis because this rarely happens, is very dependent on the concrete circumstances, and conflicts with the reason why an organization was established. Exceptions to this rule are the World Bank (Article VI (5) World Bank Agreement) and the IMF (Schedule K, IMF Agreement) since their dissolution would result in a liquidation of its financial assets. Therefore, their constitutions also regulate the dissolution of the organizations and the financial consequences thereof. The liquidation of these organizations is modeled after the liquidation of private companies.[55]

In the absence of legal rules in an organization's constitution regulating dissolution, how then is an organization legally dissolved? As to the legal basis, one has to look into customary international law and the VCLT. Both sources of law are, however, not conclusive.

---

[55] For details see infra, Sect. 1.6.4.

1.5.2 Dissolution by Contrarius Actus

International organizations without any specific dissolution rules can dissolve themselves by a so-called *contrarius actus*, i.e. a formal treaty dissolving the international organization. The legal basis would then be the VCLT. This would then formally be an amendment to the treaty establishing the organization and would be regulated by the original treaty's rules referring to amendments and thus also requires the ratification by the members, though they usually do not require all the members' consent.

One could argue, however, that dissolving an organization is the most extreme decision an organization may make and should therefore be supported by all of the organization's members. That said, unanimity may be unnecessary and inconsequential if a vast majority of the members wants to put an end to the existence of the organization with only a small minority of member states dissenting. There is no conclusive legal doctrine and practice as to this issue.

1.5.3 Dissolution by a Resolution of the Plenary Organ

An informal but pragmatic way to dissolve an organization is the adoption of a resolution to dissolve by the plenary organ. The League of Nations, for example, was dissolved by a decision of the organization's plenary organ, i.e. an Assembly resolution in 1946. This precedent shows that international organizations can be dissolved by a decision of the highest representative body. Even if dissolution is not unanimous, problems will only occur if a member is actively opposing it. The dissolution will still take place in case of mere acquiescence of some members. Generally, from a factual point of view an organization's viability depends on the support by its members. If the vast majority of the members desires to put an end to the organization's existence, the remaining opposing states will have to accept the decisions of the majority.

1.5.4 Liquidation

Upon a formal decision to dissolve, the organization faces liquidation. What happens to the treaties concluded by the organization and its assets or financial commitments? From a practical point of view, it is necessary to distinguish a complete liquidation of the organization from a partial or even entire transfer of the organization's activities to an existing or a new organization.

International law is unclear on these issues because there is little practice or precedents to follow, except for the provisions of the World Bank and the IMF. Practice is not conclusive and has so far been conducted rather pragmatically. The

UN for instance rejected the notion of being the formal successor of the League of Nations, although it took over a series of the League's technical functions. The UN was already established when the League of Nations dissolved, and the functions were accepted by the UN through General Assembly resolutions.[56] Additionally, the UN acquired the assets of the League of Nations under a treaty between the two organizations.[57] So, in practice, these issues are—as already mentioned—regulated ad-hoc. Absent such regulations, one may apply the general rules on state succession in treaties[58] and in non-treaty matters[59] *per analogiam.* These rules are, however, partly contested, often not supported by a clear international practice and do not always fit the specific situation of the dissolution of an organization.

1.6 Legal Status of International Organizations

1.6.1 Applicable Law

International organizations are subjects of international law. Therefore, International law is the legal system that governs international organizations and regulates their international legal rights and duties. As they are, contrary to states, just partial subjects of international law,[60] the question arises as to which international norms bind international organizations, and to what extent. International law recognizes three central sources of law: treaty-made law, customary international law and general principles of law.[61] It is generally recognized that international organizations are bound by all three sources. However, they usually have not to observe treaties concluded between states which have an impact on the areas of activity under the international organization's purview as they are not parties to these treaties. Likewise, they are normally not bound by decisions and resolutions of other international organizations. However, this does not preclude them from observing these legal sources on their own initiative without being obliged to do so or if these norms have become customary international law.

To give examples of these issues: Although all member states of the EU are also parties to the European Convention on Human Rights (ECHR), the EU itself is not a party to the Convention. Initially, the ECHR was only open to states, but an

[56] A/RES/24 (1946).

[57] A/RES/79, Annex 1 (1946).

[58] Cf. the ILC Vienna Convention on Succession of States in respect of Treaties of 1978.

[59] Cf. the ILC Vienna Convention on Succession of States in respect of State Property, Archives and Debts of 1983.

[60] For the explanation of the idea of a partial subject see infra, Sect. 1.5.4.

[61] In addition to these three sources of law, Art. 38 of the ICJ Statute lists an additional source: "judicial decisions and the teachings of the most highly qualified publicists of various nations". This, however, is only to be a "subsidiary means" to determine rules of international law.

amendment to the 14th Protocol allows the EU to also become party to the ECHR. When the Lisbon Treaty entered into force 1st December 2009, the EU became legally obliged to accede to the ECHR according to this treaty's provisions. However, the EU did not become a party, because the European Court of Justice (ECJ), on 18 December 2014, issued a negative legal opinion on the European Union's accession to the ECHR. The ECJ opined that accession would give an external body the power to review the application of EU law,[62] thus bringing the accession to a halt. Consequently, the EU is not formally bound by the ECHR. However, since the organs of the EU make decisions which directly affect individuals, the current situation is not satisfactory. In practice, the organs of the EU regard the ECHR as a part of the general legal norms in the European legal system. The EU is thereby indirectly bound by the ECHR.

The situation is similar with the UN. It is unclear whether UN peacekeeping operations, i.e. the Blue Helmets, ought to be bound by the 1949 Geneva Conventions and the 1977 Additional Protocols. The UN as an organization has never joined these treaties on humanitarian law, which are only open for ratification by states. Nevertheless, one can argue that the organization is bound by those rules through customary law. In practice, it is often stipulated in so-called Rules of Engagement (RoE) concluded between the UN and the host state and regulating the activities of UN-sponsored peacekeeping forces[63] that the troops should observe the Geneva Conventions and the Additional Protocols. Despite this, these agreements are not directly binding on the UN.[64]

In principle, international organizations cannot be bound by treaties between other international organizations or between states because of the *res inter alios acta* principle.[65] International organizations can thus only be bound by principles of customary law, or by their own unilateral adoption of certain legal norms concluded or decided by and applicable to other parties. Likewise, multilateral treaties signed by all member states do not bind international organizations. A good example is the ECHR to which all EU member states acceded, but which is not directly applicable to the organs and acts of the EU.

There is no clear answer to the question of how far international organizations can be bound by decisions made by other organizations. The following illustrates this. Article 103 of the UN Charter provides:

---

[62] ECJ, Opinion 2/13 of 18 Dec 2014 (ECLI:EU:C:2014:2454).

[63] "The use of force of any kind by a member of a peacekeeping contingent is defined by the rules of engagement (ROE). The ROE are tailored to the specific mandate of the mission and the situation on the ground.", United Nations Department of Peacekeeping Operations (2003), p. 140.

[64] The Secretary-General's 1999 Bulletin on *Observance by United Nations forces of international humanitarian law* states that IHL is applicable "to United Nations forces when in situations of armed conflict they are actively engaged therein as combatants, to the extent and for the duration of their engagement.".

[65] Legal basis of the principle is Art. 34, General Rule Regarding Third States, of the VCLT: "A treaty does not create either obligations or rights for a third State without its consent".

In the event of a conflict between the obligations of the Members of the United Nations under the present Charter and their obligations under any other international agreement, their obligations under the present Charter shall prevail.

Effectively, the UN, and particularly the Security Council's binding resolutions, enjoy primacy over the decisions and resolutions of other international organizations. International organizations are thus bound indirectly by binding resolutions, e.g. sanctions decisions, by the UN Security Council. This is an indirect consequence of the member states' Article 103 obligations. In theory, other organizations do not have any direct obligations to observe the resolutions of UN organs because they are not members of the UN. In practice, however, they must observe these obligations, too, because their member states are also UN member states. In addition, many UN Security Council resolutions set out obligations of international as well as of regional organizations, such as measures combatting terrorism. These obligations prevail over other obligations. Furthermore, regional organizations must observe the Security Council's binding resolutions in certain conflicts, e.g. when the resolutions call for the use of force or humanitarian aid. The UN's primacy stems from the universality of the UN, as well as the UN Charter being akin to a constitution of the state-based international system.[66]

As to the extent to which international organizations are bound by international law at large, their nature as partial subjects of international law sets limits. There are, e.g., international legal norms which are, by their nature, only addressed to states, such as rules relating to territory, citizenship or the internal political system. In addition, there are functional limitations stemming from an organization's purpose. An international organization's ability to have international rights and duties is limited by the organization's purpose; what clearly goes beyond this purpose may not be attributed to the organization.

1.6.2 Subjects of International Law; International Legal Personality

1.6.2.1 According to the Treaty Establishing the Organization

Intergovernmental international organizations are subjects of international law and thus possess international legal personality. International legal personality implies that they are independent holders of international rights and duties. These features are prerequisites for the international organizations to carry out their activities and achieve their goals. However, contrary to the unlimited international legal

[66] For a critical discussion of the legal relationship between the UN and the EU, see White (2006), p. 57.

personality of states, the organizations' international personality is partial and functionally limited to their purposes.

The precise legal nature of international institutions depends on the common will of the states that concluded the treaty, i.e. do they want to establish an international organization with its own legal personality and to what extent, or a treaty-based cooperation of states with some common structures but without legal subjectivity as is common with certain human rights treaty regimes? Very often (although not always), international legal personality is explicitly conferred on an organization in the treaty establishing the organization. Absent such an explicit provision, member states of international organizations implicitly recognize an international organization as an international legal subject through the ratification of its founding treaty if it is the will of the drafters to confer international legal personality to the organization. Ultimately, it depends on the proper construction of a treaty establishing an international organization whether it has international legal personality or not. In practice, this is generally not controversial because the states ratifying the treaty establishing the institutions usually know whether they confer international legal personality to the institution or not. In addition, the conclusion of a headquarter agreement with the host state and/or an agreement regulating the privileges and immunities of the organization and its officials is a conclusive presumption as to the international legal personality of an organization.

1.6.2.2 In Relation to Third Parties: Recognition

What about states that are not members of the organization and other international legal subjects? Do they have to accept the organization's international legal personality, or does this depend on recognition by third party states and other subjects of international law such as other organizations? To what extent does international legal personality depend on recognition? From a strictly positivist point of view, the legal personality has its basis in the founding treaty and is therefore only valid in relation to the member states, not in relation to third states. This is because the founding treaty is a *res inter alios acta* for third parties and therefore, the *pacta tertiis rule* applies: according to this legal principle, a contract cannot bind and adversely affect the rights of non-parties to an agreement. This means that there needs to be some kind of explicit or implicit recognition by third party states for an organization's international legal personality to affect third parties.

That said, the UN is an exception to this rule. In the *Reparations Case*, the ICJ, in its advisory opinion, stated that the UN is an "international legal person"[67] and enjoys the status of an international legal subject in relation to any third-party states. The ICJ stated that

---

[67] *Reparation for Injuries Suffered in the Service of the U.N.*, Advisory Opinion, ICJ Rep. 174 (1994). 179.

> *fifty states, representing the vast majority of the members of the international community, had the power, in conformity with international law, to bring into being an entity possessing objective international legal personality, and not merely personality recognized by them alone, together with capacity to bring international claims.*[68]

This is because of the universal nature of the UN and its unique international role. In practice, the international legal personality of other organizations is usually a matter of convenience and comity and is broadly accepted by non-member states and other international organizations.

1.6.2.3 Recognition by National Authorities and in Domestic Law

Another issue is whether the legal personality of international organizations is also recognized by states' domestic law and institutions, in particular national courts. The status of international organizations under domestic law is sometimes regulated in the treaties establishing international organizations: Member states often must recognize these organizations as subjects of private law in their own legal order. Where such provisions are absent in the founding statutes, the member states nonetheless generally recognize the international organizations' domestic legal personality. International organizations do, however, at times have difficulties when it comes to non-member states recognizing their legal personalities. In such cases the domestic courts of third-party states often refer to conflict of laws rules, which are usually applied to foreign corporations. The result is basically the same, namely the acceptance of the legal personality in the domestic legal order of duly established international organizations.

1.6.3 Functional Limitation of the International Legal Personality

States, as subjects of international law, virtually possess all conceivable international rights and duties.[69] This is different with international organizations; their international legal personality is *functionally limited to those rights and duties connected to the nature of international institutions*, i.e. to their goals and tasks. Thus, an international organization lacks, e.g., sovereignty: it has no territory protected by the UN Charter's guarantee of territorial integrity and political independence against foreign interventions or the use of military force, etc.[70] Therefore, international

---

[68] Ibid, 185.

[69] With the exception, of course of those rights and duties which are conferred to individuals such as human rights.

[70] Art. 2(4) UNCh prohibits the use of force against the "territorial integrity or political independence of any state".

organizations are considered partial subjects of international law. The functional limitation is relevant to, for example, international legal capacity as well as to the ability to act. The latter concerns, e.g., the organization's treaty-making power, its liability, privileges and immunities. Limiting the organization's capacity in this way thus has an impact on its international legal capacity, i.e. on its standing.

The decisive factor for determining the scope of the legal capacity of an international organization is the *intention of the founding states, i.e. the goals and purposes stipulated in the statute* of the international organization. This does not necessarily mean that international organizations merely have the rights and obligations expressed in the statute. In practice, the legal capacity expressed in the founding treaties is broadly interpreted. The main rules of interpretation are the doctrines of *effet utile*, *implied powers* and *inherent powers*.[71] These rules of interpretation essentially provide the international organizations with the powers and rights necessary to fulfill their purposes. These doctrines originate in the teleological method of interpretation, i.e. interpreting the legal capacities in light of the goals of the international organization.[72] Although the legal capacities of international organizations are broadly defined as a result, there is nevertheless a *functional limitation to international organizations' legal personality*.

1.6.4 International Legal Capacity

International legal capacity is vested in the international legal personality. It encompasses two concepts: the legal capacity itself, and the capacity to act.

International legal capacity means that an organization is *qualified to have international rights and duties*. An organization obtains the international legal capacity based on international legal personality when the treaty establishing the organization formally enters into force after the requisite number of ratifications by states has been reached, thereby creating a new international legal subject. International legal capacity encompasses the (functionally limited) rights and duties an organization can legally have based on general international law as well as based on its own law, including those rights and duties that are not expressed in the founding statutes such as implied powers.

An organization is able to act and thus to perform duties, and to enjoy rights *if and when the international organization's organs are elected or appointed* and are put in place so as to represent the organization internally in the relations with other organs of the organization and externally in the relations with other subjects of international law.

---

[71] See infra, Sects. 1.9.2 and 1.11.3.

[72] See supra, Sect. 1.11.2.

Some aspects of the international legal capacity of an international organization are particularly important: the capacity to contract (enter into legal relations); the international liability of an organization; and its privileges and immunities.

1.6.5 Capacity to Contract: Treaty-Making Power

The power to make treaties is an important power of international organizations. Even if this power is not explicitly recognized in an organization's constitution, it is nevertheless an *implied power flowing from the organization's legal personality*. International organizations conclude treaties with states, with other international organizations and with NGOs. The extensive use of treaties in practice has led to the development of a specific treaty law for international organizations. The *Vienna Convention on the Law of Treaties between States and International Organizations or between International Organizations of 1986* is largely identical to the VLCT of 1969, which only regulates interstate treaties. However, it is not yet formally in force.[73]

The most important treaties include the headquarters treaties, treaties concerning status and privileges, treaties that co-ordinate activities with other international organizations as well as treaties concerning the international organization's concrete activities (e.g. loan agreements by the World Bank, trade and association agreements with the EU etc.). Certain agreements are explicitly provided for in the statutes of international organizations, e.g. headquarter agreements or treaties regulating privileges and immunities. International organizations may, of course, conclude other treaties, i.e. treaties not explicitly mentioned in the statutes. The capacity to conclude treaties is functionally defined in light of the aims and purposes of the organization. If the subject-matter of the treaty does not fall into the overall competence of the international organization, it constitutes an *ultra vires* act. Except of this, there are no genuine limitations to the international organizations' treaty-making power. It is, if not explicitly regulated in an IO's constitution, an implied power. In addition, the 1986 VCLT IO contains rules regarding international organizations' treaty-making power. Article 27(2) of the 1986 VCLT IO states that *"an international organization party to a treaty may not invoke the rules of the organization as justification for its failure to perform the treaty"*. Article 46 of the VLCT IO 1986 further provides that an international organization cannot rely on its internal law to determine that an organ which has concluded an international treaty does not have the power to do so. There is only one exception to this rule, namely if the violation was manifest and concerned an organization's rule of fundamental importance. From the perspective of general international law, the treaty-making power of international organizations

[73] Art. 85 provides that the Convention will enter into force "on the thirtieth day following the date of deposit of the thirty-fifth instrument of ratification or accession by States or by Namibia, represented by the United Nations Council for Namibia".

consequently goes further than what has been granted by an organization's internal law.

In principle, the agreements concluded by an international organization bind the organization only and not its member states. A special case are the so-called mixed agreements between the EU and non-member states: They concern issues of both EU and member state competence and therefore must be adopted by both the EU and all the member states.[74] The EU can also have mixed agreements with other organizations.

1.6.6 Responsibility

1.6.6.1 Responsibility for Breaches of International Obligations

From an organization's international legal personality results, *inter alia*, its responsibility for its international unlawful conduct. As it is termed in Article 3 of the ILC Draft Articles on the Responsibility of International Organizations[75] under the heading "Responsibility of an international organization for its internationally wrongful acts": *"Every internationally wrongful act of an international organization entails the international responsibility of that organization."* Like other subjects of international law, international organizations are liable for infringements of international legal norms. In contrast, there is no general responsibility for lawful but harmful acts of an IO, e.g. in the framework of an UN peace enforcement that causes damages or casualties.

An international organization's actions are usually attributable to the organization and not its members. A member state is therefore not liable for an international organization's actions unless, on rare occasions, the international organization's statute provides for it[76] or in case of an illegal act committed jointly by an IO and a state.[77]

Treaties establishing international organizations do not usually contain any provisions regarding the organization's international responsibility, though the EU is a

[74]The EU has either exclusive competence or competence which is shared with EU countries. In case of shared competences, the agreement is concluded both by the EU and by EU countries. It is therefore a mixed agreement to which EU countries must give their consent. Art. 4 TFEU regulates which competences are shared.

[75]Draft Articles on the Responsibility of International Organizations for Internationally Wrongful Acts, adopted by the International Law Commission, at its 63rd session, at Geneva, Switzerland, from 26 Apr to 3 Jun and 4 Jul to 12 Aug 2011 in accordance with A/RES/65/26 (2010).

[76]A problem with secondary liability concerns the circumstances under which this secondary liability can be attributed to a member state. The ILC has determined that a strict secondary liability is out of the question, since it would jeopardize the separation of legal personalities between the international organization and its member states.

[77]Art. 14 of the ILC Draft Articles on Responsibility of International Organizations.

notable exception.[78] Generally, international responsibility of international organizations is governed by the same principles as those applying to state responsibility. Article 4 of the ILC Draft Articles on Responsibility of International Organizations states that responsibility is triggered when two elements of an internationally wrongful act by international organizations are made out. First, the *act needs to be attributable to the organization under international law,* and second, it needs to result in a *breach of an international obligation of the organization*. The act is attributed to the international organization by linking it to the conduct of an organ or agent of the international organization in performance of his/her duties. The sources of the obligation may stem from either general international law applicable to the organization or an international treaty signed by the organization.

It is undisputed that international organizations can also be *victims of violations of international law*, and may make claims against other international legal subjects, even if this type of action is not expressly provided for by the statutes. This is certainly an implied, most probably also an inherent power of the organization. This power was confirmed the ICJ in its 1949 Advisory Opinion on Reparation for Injuries Suffered in the Service of the United Nations.[79]

1.6.6.2 Responsibility for Infringements of Other Legal Norms

An international organization's conduct may not only infringe international legal norms, but also its own legal order or a state's domestic law. Where violations of the organization's own legal order occur, they often refer to alleged violations of the rights and interests of the organization's staff members by organs of the organizations. In many organizations special tribunals decide such controversies. Otherwise, such liability is often settled based on political considerations or in equity, if at all, because usually no legal remedies are available, and the organization's immunity is a shield against any actions brought before national courts.

The situation is similar as to legal transactions with international organizations as parties: When carrying out commercial activities or transactions, an international organization may incur tortious or contractual liability. In instances such as controversies over lease agreements concluded between an organization and a private tenant, domestic law will be applied, and a controversy can be tried in domestic courts or adjudicated by alternative dispute resolution mechanisms provided for by the organization.[80] However, an important impediment to the jurisdiction of state courts or to alternative dispute resolution are the *organization's immunities* which usually require an organization's consent to either court proceedings or dispute settlement. The organization's immunities thus sometimes complicate the

[78] See Art. 340 TFEU.

[79] Advisory Opinion of April 11, 1949 ICJ Reports 1949 174.

[80] As the name suggests, these mechanisms are an alternative to the state court system and usually involve third parties such as arbitrators or mediators.

enforcement of either the court's ruling or the outcome of the dispute settlement despite the organization's undisputed liability.[81]

The EU as a supranational organization is a special case because of its far-reaching powers. As a consequence, EU law provides also for extensive non-contractual liabilities to individuals or companies because of its powers to regulate or decide on matters with direct effect on them. The Court of Justice of the European Union (CJEU) has the power to decide on the EU's liability. Actions may be brought by individuals or member states who claim to have suffered damage and request compensation of such damage.

1.6.7 Privileges and Immunities

1.6.7.1 The Reasons for Privileges and Immunities

As a result of their special legal status as subjects of international law, international organizations benefit like states and their representatives from certain privileges and immunities which allow them to carry out their activities as freely and independently as possible from states. Privileges and immunities are granted *to secure an independent functioning of international organizations*. Therefore, the organization as well as its functionaries should not be subordinated to the law of any member state. Privileges and immunities protect the organization and its staff against undue pressure from member states, such as any kind of proceedings (civil, criminal or administrative) or enforcement measures. These privileges and immunities are therefore functional prerequisites of, and ensure, the organizations' proper performance.

The statutes of international organizations frequently, but not always, provide the explicit legal basis for these privileges. One example is Article 105 of the UN Charter, which establishes that the UN *"shall enjoy in the territory of each of its Members privileges and immunities as are necessary for the fulfillment of its purposes"*. In most cases, the constituent instruments are complemented by more detailed provisions set out, for example, in an appendix to the founding treaty, or in a separate agreement. In addition, the headquarters agreement concluded with the state hosting the organization may also contain such provisions. These privileges and immunities legally bind only the member states of the organizations. The UN, however, is an exception because, as the ICJ established in the *Reparations* case, the UN enjoys "objective legal personality".[82] Therefore, the UN's immunity and privileges are to be recognized by all states.

---

[81] For an analysis of international organizations' immunity, especially involving employment disputes, see Reinisch (2008), 285 ss.

[82] *Reparation for Injuries Suffered in the Service of the U.N.*, Advisory Opinion, ICJ Rep. 174 (1994), 179.

The regulation of immunity issues in the various international agreements are very similar and reflect general principles that have developed over the time. They are influenced to a very large extent by the regulations on state immunity.

1.6.7.2 Exemption from Domestic Jurisdiction

The most important privilege of international organizations is that *member states do not have jurisdiction over an organization;* therefore, the organization is immune from coercive measures by member states. This immunity does not mean that domestic law does not apply; it merely means that, procedurally, the law will not be enforceable against the international organization's will. International organizations can, however, waive these privileges and immunities in certain cases, e.g. in claims regarding purchase contracts or payment of rents. Some agreements contain clauses that waive the immunities of an international organization in specified circumstances. As is the case for states, in such instances, the international organizations' acts will be distinguished between acts *jure gestionis*, that is, commercial transactions performed by and contracts concluded by an organization's organs, and acts *jure imperii*, i.e. official acts of an organization as part of its activities. An organization will usually not wave it immunity for acts jure imperii.

Immunities are procedural barriers and are therefore disadvantageous for potential claimants against international organizations as whether claimants can sue in a certain state depends on an organization's acceptance of a state's jurisdiction.[83] In practice, organizations often seek settlements. Organizations that do not accept the jurisdiction of national courts sometimes establish their own arbitration bodies and procedures to settle disputes where domestic jurisdiction would normally apply, e.g. on issues of liability. The IMF, for instance, has an Office of the Ombudsperson for informal settlements of employment-related disputes.[84]

1.6.7.3 Inviolability of Assets, Premises, Archives and Communication

A further consequence of an international organization' immunity from member states' laws usually is, according to the agreement regulating immunity, that its assets, archives and premises enjoy the status of inviolability. Coercive measures by states against these facilities are accordingly not permitted, and so national authorities are not allowed to enter the premises of an international organization without its consent, not even to carry out an arrest or to serve a writ.

[83] For an in-depth study on how national courts deal with international organizations in cases before them, see Reinisch (2009); cf. Reinisch and Weber (2004), 59 ss.

[84] For an overview of the employment-related internal dispute settlement mechanisms of some international organizations, see Javits (2013), 223 ss.; cf. International Administrative Law Centre of Excellence (2016).

The premises of an international organization are, like foreign embassies, part of the territory of the host state and therefore the state's laws are in principle applicable. However, it is outside the host state's scope of enforcement. The headquarters agreement usually provides that the international organizations are responsible for regulating conduct on their own premises and enforcing it through their own organs.

The transmission of news by post, telegram, telephone, courier, e-mails or other digital means of communication etc. may neither be restrained by censorship or other restrictive measures by the host state or any member state. Both, representatives of member states as well as observers or persons officially invited by an organization must have secure access to and from the headquarters of an international organization. The organization's financial transactions may also not be subject to foreign exchange protection regulations.

1.6.7.4 Exemption from Taxes and Other Fiscal Burdens

International organizations do not pay any taxes and are exempted from custom duties and other fees. They are granted these tax exemptions to prevent the host state from benefiting from the membership fees paid and other financial contributions made by the member states, to protect the organization's assets and to secure that these assets serve to execute the organization's purpose.

1.6.7.5 Privileges and Immunities of Officials of International Organizations

Not only do the organizations themselves enjoy immunity, but the organizations' officials generally enjoy immunity for their official acts too. However, there is a difference between the immunity granted to ordinary officials and that granted to the international organization's top representatives. Average officials enjoy immunity only for their official acts, not private ones. In contrast, the top representatives normally enjoy the same privileges and immunities as diplomats, i.e. full immunity.

An example is an organization's Secretary-General, who is the chief administrative as well as executive officer, and enjoys full immunity. According to the Convention on Privileges and Immunities of the United Nations,[85] it is up to the UN Secretary-General to decide which categories of UN officials may receive the *laissez-passer* which gives them the full range of privileges and immunities.[86] All officials enjoy the privilege of exemption from taxation on their salaries and other

---

[85] 1 UN Treaty Series: Treaties and International Agreements registered or filed and recorded with the Secretariat of the United Nations, 14 Dec 1946, 15.

[86] See the Convention on the Privileges and Immunities of the United Nations, 13 Feb 1946, 1 U.N.T.S. 15, art. VII, § 26.

emoluments that they receive from the international organization.[87] This privilege also includes the prohibition to sequester the salaries of officials. Moreover, the officials and their families or dependents are immune from immigration or alien restrictions.[88]

The privileges and immunities of officials are functional in nature and are granted to them in the interest of the organization, and not for the officials' personal benefit. This means that the organization may waive these privileges and immunities when they are not in the interest of the organization. Hence, the privileges and immunities do not mean, e.g., that the officials can disregard the national legislation of their host states. However, since they work for international organizations, the host state cannot apply the principle of *persona non grata*. i.e. formally expel an organization's official as an undesirable person, even in case of serious crimes committed by an official. However, the host state may request the organization to waive its official's immunities or to terminate the official's engagement.

The privileges and immunities can also be invoked against any member state, including the home state of the officials, because they derive from a special international status of the organization in the interest of the organization. Thus, the home state may not assert jurisdiction based on nationality over its own citizen acting as an official of an organization.

Other persons protected by international law are those working for organs with special purposes, e.g. experts or members of armed forces in the service of international organizations. The legal status of the members of armed forces is usually regulated by agreements between an organization and/or the states sending the troops on one side and the state hosting them on the other side (so-called Rules of Engagement). These privileges and immunities may also be invoked against the person's home state.

1.6.7.6 Privileges and Immunities of State Representatives to International Organizations

States' representatives present at international organizations, e.g. attending official meetings, enjoy the privileges and immunities that are customary for foreign diplomats, in analogy to the Vienna Convention on Diplomatic Relations of 1961. As mentioned above, these representatives ought to have free access to the premises of the international organization. Privileges and immunities are further granted to member states' permanent representatives accredited to the international organization. These privileges are similar to those that are accorded to diplomats and consular staff. What distinguishes them is their emphasis on the functional basis of the privileges and immunities.

[87] Ibid., art. V, § 18(b).

[88] Ibid., art. V, § 18(c) and (d).

The 1975 Vienna Convention on the Representation of States in their Relations with International Organizations of a Universal Character attempts to standardize the applicable rules. However, this convention has never been ratified by the most prominent host states such as the US, Switzerland and Austria. Moreover, the UN has its own conventions, such as the 1946 General Convention on the Privileges and Immunities and the 1947 Specialized Agencies Convention.

The state representatives to an international organization are not accredited to the host states, but to the international organizations. Contrary to the requirement of the so-called *agrément* by the host state under Article 4 of the 1961 Vienna Convention on Diplomatic Relations, a formal agreement between the representative's state and the host state is not required, though in practice there is usually some sort of agreement between the sending state, the host state and the organization. A practical consequence is that the host state cannot declare a representative as a *persona non grata*, i.e. an undesirable person forced to leave the host state, which it could do regarding diplomats accredited to the host state. The host state must further accept representatives accredited to an international organization from states that it has not diplomatically recognized. The headquarter agreements concluded with the host state thus often specify that privileges and immunities need to be granted irrespective of the relationship between the sending state and the host state. The possibility of withdrawing accreditation remains with the organizations, who are obliged to do so under certain circumstances.

Moreover, international organizations need to secure privileges and immunities for non-government affiliated representatives, e.g. persons invited as observers. This is important for e.g. representatives of the ILO, not all of whom are government representatives.

1.7 Membership and Participation

1.7.1 Forms of Participation

Membership is the most typical and comprehensive way to participate in international organizations. Other forms of participation, which entail limited rights and duties, include the status of association, and participation as observer. The CoE is an example of an organization that regulates all these modes of participation.[89]

Membership in an organization consists of basic rights and duties such as the right to vote and participate in the organization's decision-making, and as duties the obligation to observe the organization's rules and pay the annual financial contribution. Members can either be founding members, i.e. original members, or members admitted subsequently. There are generally no differences in the legal status of original and subsequently admitted members.

[89] For details see infra, Sect. 3.4.2.

The term "association" denotes an attenuated form of cooperation with and participation by non-member states. There is no legal definition of association since its substance often varies from organization to organization. The concrete legal effects are regulated either in the organization's constitution, in its secondary law and/or by agreements between the international organization and the associated state(s) or international organization(s).[90] The EU, e.g. has concluded association agreements with, inter alia, developing countries which do, however, not convey any participation rights in the Union's organs.[91] Another example is the NATO program "Partnership for Peace". The program is open to European states and aims at creating mutual trust based on cooperation in security and military matters.[92]

Besides the association status of a non-member state, some organizations also offer the option of an observer status. Observers are present during discussions and may in some organizations participate in deliberation but have no right to vote.

. The admission of non-member states as observers is generally up to the organs of the international organization to decide. Switzerland, for instance, used to enjoy observer status at the UN until it became a full member in 2002. In some organizations, national liberation movements enjoy observer status. The Palestinian Liberation Organization (PLO) is an observer at the UN and represents the Palestinian people. The Holy See, the United States, Canada, Japan and Mexico have all acquired observer status at the CoE.

1.7.2 Accession

The conditions for becoming a member of an international organization depend on organization's statutes and may differ from organization to organization. Generally, membership is open to states and sometimes to other international organizations, but, e.g., not to the federated states within member states.[93] Non-sovereign territories may in particular instances become members of international or regional organizations.[94]

---

[90] Depending on an organization's concrete rules, international organizations may also qualify for an associated membership.

[91] These were concluded pursuant to Article 217 of the Treaty on the Functioning of the European Union (TFEU) which provides: "The Union may conclude with one or more third countries or international organizations agreements establishing an association involving reciprocal rights and obligations, common action and special procedure." A list of such agreements is available at <https://ec.europa.eu/trade/policy/countries-and-regions/negotiations-and-agreements/index_en.htm> (accessed 8 March 2025).

[92] For more details infra, Sect. 3.5.3.3.

[93] However, Belarus and Ukraine were, based on a political compromise with the Soviet Union, full members of the UN already before becoming independent from the Soviet Union.

[94] Greenland, e.g., is member of the Nordic Council.

Membership in international organizations is particularly important for newly created states. From a legal and political perspective, admission to the UN is practically equivalent to global recognition as a new state. It signals general acceptance that the process of creating the state is legitimate and has come to an end. A consequence of admission is that the territory of the new state is protected from external aggression, based on the prohibition of the use of force in Article 2(4) UN Charter. Hence, newly independent states usually apply for memberships of international and regional organizations immediately after the declaration of independence.

This is not the case with Kosovo, who unilaterally declared independence from Serbia on 17 February 2008, but still not is a UN member. This is primarily due to the precarious basis on which independence was declared. Although Kosovo's declaration of independence was illegal pursuant to Article 8 of the Serbian Constitution, which provides that the "territory of the Republic of Serbia is inseparable and indivisible", the ICJ has stated in an Advisory Opinion that the declaration of independence "did not violate any applicable rule of international law".[95] Nonetheless, only half of the states worldwide currently recognize Kosovo's independence, which can be partly attributed to Serbia's diplomatic campaign to suppress recognition of Kosovo's independence. This has consequences for Kosovo's prospective application for UN membership, which requires both the UN Security Council's approval and a two-third majority vote by the General Assembly. Russia as an ally of Serbia is against a UN membership of Kosovo. Therefore, the prospects of Kosovo's application for UN membership are uncertain.[96]

The statutes of some organizations provide that all states fulfilling the conditions for membership may become members. These are called *open organizations*. Other organizations limit their membership according to some specific criteria, e.g. geography. Article 49 TEU states that any European state that respects the values of the EU may apply for membership, thus limiting applicants by geography. However, geographical criteria can be broadly interpreted. For instance, the CoE regards Israel as a European state. In the OAS, the organization's statutes provide that any American state can become a member.[97] Organizations that do not admit members after their establishment are "closed" organizations, though such organizations are rare in practice.

Membership is not an entitlement; a non-member state does not have any enforceable rights to claim membership even in open international organizations, Admission as a member in an international organization depends on the *state's adherence to admission procedures and its fulfillment of the admission conditions*. In most organizations, the admission of new members must be approved by a (often

[95] *Accordance with International Law of the Unilateral Declaration of Independence in Respect of Kosovo*, Advisory Opinion, ICJ Rep. 452 (2010).

[96] For an analysis of the arguments in favour of Kosovo's membership in the UN, see Islami and Istrefi (2018), 331 ss.; For more details of Kosovo's quest for statehood, see Visoka (2018).

[97] Cuba's membership, however, has been suspended since 1962.

qualified) majority of the member states. In some organizations these criteria go even further. For admission to the EU, Article 49 TEU requires that all current member states conclude an agreement with the new member states, which is to be ratified in each member state. Prior to this, the Commission, the Council and the Parliament, as part of the admission procedure, have to agree with the admission of the candidate state. For admission to the UN, as stated earlier, a recommendation of the UN Security Council and an approval by two-thirds of the UN General Assembly is required. However, as has been discussed, members of the Security Council sometimes vote based on their own realpolitik interests. As such, the admission procedure is a *political process* and admission itself a *political decision of an organization*.

Some admission criteria are subjective, which leaves the international organization with a lot of discretion. An example is the criteria set out in Article 4(1) of the UN Charter. To become a member of the UN, a state needs to be "peace-loving" as well as able and willing to carry out the obligations under the UN Charter. These criteria inevitably leave space for political interpretation and have in earlier times been applied in an abusive manner in practice. In the UN Security Council, shortly after the establishment of the UN, the Soviet Union only consented to the admission of several Western states on the condition that some Communist states would be admitted, which the Western states in reality were reluctant to accept because of their poor respect for human rights and other international duties. The ICJ, solicited by the UN General Assembly, stated in an Advisory Opinion that

> *every application for admission should be examined and voted on separately and on its own merits; otherwise, it would be impossible to determine whether a particular applicant fulfils the necessary conditions.*[98]

Furthermore, international organizations can set reasonable conditions for membership. The ILO, for instance, requires applicant states to ratify certain conventions that are central to the ILO. Similarly, the OSCE requires its applicants to fulfill conditions relating to the protection of human rights and minorities as well as the observance of the rule of law. Admission to the CoE is de facto dependent on the ratification of the European Convention on Human Rights.

1.7.3 Rights, Duties and Suspension of Members

1.7.3.1 Rights and Duties

Membership of an international organization is a legal status entailing rights and duties. These can be found in the constituent instruments of the organization. The principle of equality of states governs the relationship between the members as well as between the members and the organization. Therefore, there is usually no legal

[98] *Conditions of Admission of a State to Membership in the United Nations (Art. 4 of the Charter)*, ICJ Rep. 57 (1948), 65.

difference between an original member and an admitted member. The UN Security Council, however, departs from the principle of equality between states because the five victorious WWII powers have permanent seats and veto power.

The rights of member states include voting rights and representation in an organization's organs. There are also rights that are specific to some organizations such as the right of financial assistance under the IMF Agreement. The duties mainly include observing the laws of the international organization and cooperating in enforcing the international organization's decisions. This includes implementing the organization's laws and decisions domestically. Member states also have to pay membership fees and bear other financial obligations.

1.7.3.2 Suspension of Membership Rights

The statutes of many international organizations usually contain provisions for the complete or partial suspension of membership rights as a sanction against a state violating its duties according to the organization's statute. Article 5 of the UN Charter is an example of such a provision. It states that a

> *Member of the United Nations against which preventive or enforcement action has been taken by the Security Council may be suspended from the exercise of the rights and privileges of membership by the General Assembly upon the recommendation of the Security Council.*

However, in practice, this Article is sparsely and inconsistently applied. In fact, a formal suspension under this article has not yet occurred.

An article that has been applied is Article 19 of the UN Charter, which states that a member state's voting powers are *ipso jure* suspended if it has failed to pay its fees for 2 consecutive years.[99] This Article has been invoked when a member state is in arrears in the payment of its membership fees. The UN General Assembly can freely revoke the suspension when it is satisfied that a member state has paid the arrears. Another practice, one particularly prevalent at the IMF and the World Bank, is the suspension of benefits if a state fails to fulfill membership duties. Generally, sanctions may vary according to an IO and may range from the mere interruption of particular benefits to the suspension of voting rights to the suspension of all the rights and privileges of membership.

It is controversial whether absent specific regulations, suspension is a justified and legal countermeasure in case of violations of membership duties. However, if the constitution of an international organization provides for the possibility of expulsion of a member state, which is almost always the case, the suspension of membership rights should also be permissible as a less far-reaching measure. In

[99] Cf. Art. 13(4) of the ILO Constitution which provides for voting rights to be suspended if a member is in arrears of its payment, and the arrears equals or exceeds two years' worth of payments.

some instances, organizations have taken measures resembling suspension, but which are not formal suspension. For instance, the treatment of the Socialist Federal Republic of Yugoslavia by UN organs after its dissolution in 1992 contained elements of both suspension and expulsion, as it was unclear which newly formed state would actually take on the international rights and duties of the Federal Republic. Therefore, the credentials of Serb diplomats were not accepted in the UN system.[100]

Also, in other instances, instead of suspending states, the UN has refrained from accepting the credentials of the diplomats representing a country against which it has invoked coercive measures. This was the case with South Africa under the white minority regime: Because of its policy of Apartheid, which denied basic human rights to the black majority, South African diplomats were excluded from the UN General Assembly. Thus, there is a form of quasi-suspension of membership, which means non-recognition or de-recognition, i.e. revoking recognition of representatives of member states.

A state usually retains its membership even under circumstances of domestic turbulence or upheavals. A change of government, a revolution or other radical changes does normally not affect the state's membership in international organizations as long as its statehood remains intact.[101] Even failed states continue to be members of international organizations despite lacking a government. However, in more recent times, certain regional organizations have tended to suspend a state's membership if it has undergone a non-democratic, violent change of government.[102]

1.7.4 Termination of Membership: Expulsion and Withdrawal

Membership can either be terminated by withdrawal or expulsion from an international organization.

1.7.4.1 Withdrawal

A state's withdrawal from an international organization is a termination of membership, legally based on a unilateral formal declaration by that state. In light of the general need of international co-operation, states usually strive to join international

[100]For more information on this, see e.g. Jovanovic (1997), 1719 ss.; and Blum (2007), 800 ss.

[101]For the explanations regarding issues of state succession as to membership in international organizations see infra, Sect. 1.7.6.

[102]For instance, the South American trading bloc Mercosur suspended Venezuela's membership in 2017 after the President imprisoned opposition activists, delayed elections and threatened to revamp the Constitution.

organizations rather than leave them. Nonetheless, many organizations have provisions regulating the right to leave the organization subject to certain conditions (e.g. a certain notice period or settling financial duties before the state's exit). The most important instances of withdrawal are Brexit, i.e. the UK leaving the EU, and Russia's withdrawal from the Council of Europe on March 15, 2022 as an attempt to prevent a vote on its expulsion.

Some organizations, such as the UN, do not have explicit exit rules. The question arises as to whether the lack of a provision for withdrawal means that such a possibility does not exist. Although Article 56 VCLT states that *"if there is no provision as to withdrawal, such withdrawal is only possible if it is established that the parties intended to admit it or if this right may be implied by the nature of the treaty"*, there are no clear general rules on this question, and practice by states and international organizations is inconclusive. It has partly become the prevailing view that, because of the principle of state sovereignty, states ought to be able to withdraw from an international organization even absent provisions regulating it.[103] The opposite view is that, pursuant to the principle of *pacta sunt servanda* that underpins international law, states are in principle not allowed to unilaterally exit an international organization's founding treaty. Consequently, if a state wants to exit an organization without a withdrawal clause, it needs the consent of the rest of the member states[104] or the organ deciding on membership. Generally, though, practice is governed by a degree of pragmatism. For instance, even if the UN Charter does not contain a right to withdraw, the general view is that there is a inherent right to do so, as was the case, e.g., when Indonesia temporarily withdrew from the UN on 9 January 1965 and then unilaterally resumed membership in the autumn of 1966.

Withdrawal from EU membership is more complicated because of the EU's supranational nature. Before the adoption of the TEU, a member state's unilateral withdrawal, from a legal point of view, would most probably have violated the treaties establishing the EC. That said, it can be assumed that the other member states would generally not have opposed the withdrawal of an unwilling member state to ensure that the integration process proceeds as smoothly as possible.[105] This is precisely the reason why a right to withdraw can be assumed in many organizations, even if it is not explicitly provided for. Letting members exit if they wish so serves the pragmatic purpose of ensuring the continued smooth operation of the organization. Allowing voluntary exits is thus a better solution than compelling the member state to behave badly to get itself expelled. Withdrawal from the EU is now explicitly regulated by Article 50 TEU.[106] The provision is a compromise between respect for a state's sovereign decision and the necessity of regulating, in an agreement, the

[103] See e.g. Singh (1958), p. 27.

[104] For a range of views on exiting international organizations, see Brölmann et al. (2018), 243 ss.

[105] Presumably, the withdrawing from the EU is as complicated as joining it, as Brexit shows.

[106] For analysis of a withdrawal by a member state from the EU on the EU, see Closa (2017). For an account of the origins of Art. 50, see Huysmans (2019), p. 155.

consequences of withdrawal as well as the future relationship between the Union and the former member state.[107]

When a member state withdraws from an international organization, it loses all related rights and duties. In some situations, certain rights or duties are retained, e.g. if some rights and duties have become customary international law. Also duties not based on the law of the international organization, but are contained in certain treaties, are retained. These treaties might incidentally be institutionally connected to the international organization (e.g. Article 58(3) ECHR).

1.7.4.2 Expulsion

Like suspension of membership rights, expulsion is a *coercive measure applied when a member state persistently violates its duties* and no longer conforms to an organization's basic norms. The prevailing opinion most probably is that expulsion not rooted in the international organization's constitution is prohibited; hence, expulsion must be explicitly regulated in the treaty establishing the organization. The opposite view qualifies an expulsion without explicit basis in an organization's constitution as a legitimate countermeasure in case of persistent, grave violation of membership duties and as an implied power of the organization.

An example of an explicit norm regulation expulsion is Article 6 of the UN Charter which states that *"a Member of the United Nations which has persistently violated the Principles contained in the present Charter may be expelled from the Organization by the General Assembly upon the recommendation of the Security Council."* Other international organizations have similar provisions. To date, Article 6 UN Charter has never been used, though for a long time there were serious discussions as to whether Apartheid South Africa and Israel should be formally expelled from the UN.[108] However, it is politically questionable whether such a sanction is useful. Expulsion of a member state means that the organization loses control of and over the state.[109] Expulsion also means that state's rights and duties cease to exist, though an international organization can have provisions ensuring a survival or continuance of certain duties. In this regard, pursuant to Article 58(2) of the ECHR, the European Court of Human Rights (ECtHR) retains its power to hear cases against a member state which deal with events before that state has been expelled from the CoE.

Expulsions happen rarely. The most recent instance is Russia's expulsion from the Council of Europe. On February 25, 2022, one day after Russia's attack on the

[107] As to the details in connection with the Brexit see infra, Sect. 4.4.21. and 4.4.2.2.

[108] As to the UN practice see infra, Sect. 2.7.3.

[109] This was the main reason why Russia and Turkey were not expelled from the Council of Europe despite flagrant and widespread human rights violations in these countries. Expulsion would have deprived victims of human rights violations to lodge appeals at the European Court of Human Rights.

Ukraine, Russia's membership in the Council of Europe got suspended. On 15 March 2022, Russia formally announced its withdrawal from the organization; its membership was due to terminate on 31 December 2022. However, on 16 March 2022 the Committee of Ministers voted to expel Russia from the council with immediate effect.[110] This decision did not have a direct legal basis in the statute of the Council of Europe. Six months after its exclusion from the Council of Europe, the Russian Federation ceased to be party to the European Convention on Human Rights, i.e. on September 2022. However, the European Court of Human Rights remained competent to deal with applications against Russia concerning actions or omissions occurring up until that date.

1.7.5 Sanctions/Coercive Measures Against Non-complying Members

Expulsion is one type of sanctions against a noncomplying member. International organizations' constitutional instruments often empower both the organization and its member states to impose other sanctions against states violating their obligations as members. The international organizations' statutes set out the procedures to follow when resorting to countermeasures such as sanctions. As these measures are collective measures, they are considerably more efficient than retorsions or reprisals that states might adopt unilaterally as self-help measures. Apart from violations of obligations *erga omnes*, self-help measures are only available for states adversely affected in their rights by another state's conduct. This is not necessarily the case if a state violates duties as a member of an IO. Therefore, collective measures by the organization which encompass all the member states are much more efficient enforcement tools.

If the statutes are silent on actions to be taken against states violating their membership obligations, the *general international rules of breach of contract apply. The 1969 VCLT is relevant here.* According to a general rule of international law, a treaty violation by one party does not frustrate the treaty for all parties. The multilateral treaties continue to be in force between the parties—including the state in breach.[111] Hence, a state cannot absolve itself of its obligations under multilateral treaties by breaching the treaties' provisions. That said, the organization and the other member states if affected are entitled to take countermeasures designed to frustrate the violating member state's membership benefits.

International law distinguishes between retorsions and reprisals. A retorsion is an unfriendly and harmful act often used as a soft method of retaliation against another state's harmful activities without infringing international law norms. Examples include economic and travel restrictions if there are no treaties regulating these

---

[110]CM/Res (2022) 2.

[111]See Art. 60 (2) VCLT.

issues, or the severance of diplomatic relations.[112] Reprisals, on the other hand, are acts which infringe norms of international law and are therefore illegal in principle. However, they are legitimate and considered to be exceptionally legal if they are adopted by one state in retaliation against a previous illegal act by another state.[113] Military sanctions, however, are not allowed, except if authorized by the UN Security Council.

Before international organizations or their member states adopt sanctions, they should appeal to their judicial authorities (if they have access to them), especially if international organizations have their own courts. However, this only applies to a small number of international organizations. In the EU, for instance, states can be brought to court if they have violated EU law.

Important is the distinction between military and non-military sanctions. While the latter can be adopted by all international organizations, *only the UN Security Council may adopt or authorize military sanctions*. There is a range of non-military sanctions available for international organizations and member states, which are:

(a) Mobilization of public opinion against the violating state(s);
(b) Suspension of all or some membership rights pursuant, e.g., to Article 19 of the UN Charter;[114]
(c) Authorization of measures against the violating states through the plenary or executive organ. Examples include the removal of membership benefits, economic or other sanctions;
(d) Cessation of payments to the member state;
(e) Expulsion of the violating state.

Non-military sanctions by the UN Security Council are important. Under Chapter VII of the Charter, the Security Council has the power to adopt both economic and other non-military sanctions against states that have violated the UN Charter.[115] Sanctions decisions are binding on all member states, and ought to be prioritized over any other obligation member states may have in relation to the violating state.[116]

Military sanctions are only permitted when authorized by the UN Security Council in response to a breach or a serious threat to international peace by a state.[117] The UN Security Council has authorized the use of force by individual states, groups of states, regional organizations or military alliances against violating

[112] For more information on retorsions, see Giegerich (2020).

[113] For more information on reprisals and retaliation, see Darcy (2015), p. 879.

[114] The Art. reads: "A Member of the United Nations which is in arrears in the payment of its financial contributions to the Organization shall have no vote in the General Assembly if the amount of its arrears equals or exceeds the amount of the contributions due from it for the preceding two full years. The General Assembly may, nevertheless, permit such a member to vote if it is satisfied that the failure to pay is due to conditions beyond the control of the Member".

[115] Art. 41 UNCh.

[116] Art. 103 UNCh; as to the details see infra, Sect. 2.11.2.2.

[117] Chapter VII UNCh, in particular Art. 42; as to the details see infra, Sect. 2.9.3.

states. Hence, regional organizations or regional military alliances are required to seek the UN Security Council's prior authorization to use force.[118]

The effects of sanctions by international organizations against states vary in practice. However, the practice of international organizations shows that the option of imposing sanctions as collective measures against violating states is an indispensable tool to enforce member obligations against a state infringing them.

1.7.6 State Succession of Membership

1.7.6.1 General Rules

Issues of state succession are generally complex, in particular relating to membership in international organizations. They usually arise in instances of profound structural changes in a country. The application of succession rules requires a prior analysis as to the identity and continuity of the state undergoing a structural change. The provisions of the 1978 Vienna Convention on Succession of States in Respect of Treaties can be applied analogously,[119] given that international organizations are usually treaty-based. The convention provides as a general, partly disputed rule for continuity of the treaties in force for the predecessor state also for a successor state. As membership in international organizations is concerned, however, there is, contrary to the convention's general rules, usually *no automatic continuity of the state's membership status by the new state* established on the territory of the old one. The main reason is that the decision on the membership status is political, and that organizations, therefore, reserve the right to assess whether a new state fulfills all the requirements for membership as established in the organization's constitution and practice. Therefore, the IOs rules as to how membership is obtained prevail over the rules of treaty succession.

1.7.6.2 Issues of Identity and Continuity of States

Problems with membership status may occur if the identity of a state changes. These problems arose, e.g. with the partition of India in 1947 which created two independent states, India and Pakistan. According to the legal considerations of the Sixth (Legal) Committee of the UN General Assembly on the legal problem raised by the admission of Pakistan as a UN member,[120] the general rule is that border adjustments or constitutional changes have no impact on the status of a member state because they do not constitute a change in identity. A state only *loses its membership when it*

[118] See infra, Sect. 3.2.2.

[119] However, this convention is only open for ratification by states.

[120] A/C.6/162.

ceases to exist as a subject under international law. Moreover, every newly created state, either on the territory of a UN member state (as is the case with Pakistan) or on the territory of a third state, must apply for UN membership.

This principle is executed in almost all international organizations. Usually, *new states must apply for membership* to allow the organization to assess whether the new state is fit for membership and willing to fulfill the membership obligations. Therefore, issues of identity and continuity of statehood are significant because they decide on the continuity of membership. In conformity with the main international rules on state identity and continuity, practice shows that incidents such as separation, dissolution or merger of states imply new identities and thus discontinuity. The consequence thereof that new states have to apply for membership. On the other hand, occurrences such as a change in territory, government, name or constitution usually do not affect a state's identity and therefore have no bearing on membership status.

1.7.6.3 Moving Frontier Rule

The moving frontier rule applies to the change of territory as codified in Article 15 of the Vienna Convention on Succession of States in Respect to Treaties of 1978. According to this rule, the effect of changes in state borders is that the treaty is automatically applicable within the new borders. This made, e.g. the EEC treaty applicable in East Germany after its reunification with Western Germany.

1.7.6.4 Practice of International Organizations: Special Cases

International organizations usually apply the aforementioned rules. However, in practice, particularly for the UN, state succession issues are sometimes resolved either pragmatically or politically. For instance, when the member states Egypt and Syria established the United Arab Republic (U.A.R.) as a new common state, this new state took over the previous membership of both states without a separate formal admission procedure. When the U.A.R. separated only 3 years later, the previous states' membership was reinstated. In contrast, as just explained, when Pakistan separated from India and Bangladesh seceded from Pakistan, the new states had to apply for membership.

The dissolution of the Soviet Union was a special case. The question arose whether Russia would, by way of state succession, automatically continue the membership of the former Soviet Union, or whether Russia would have to apply for membership. The answer had significant consequences given that the Soviet Union was a permanent member of the UN Security Council and possessed veto power. The Soviet Union was dissolved by a treaty between twelve of the originally fifteen Soviet Republics. In light of this, it could have been argued that the Soviet Union ceased to exist as a subject of international law. However, Russia was willing to continue the membership of the Soviet Union, and all the other UN member states agreed. In the absence of objections, Russia was able to take over the seat of the Soviet Union without any further decisions. All that occurred was a change of nameplates. Therefore, this was not as a case of state succession but as a case of continuity of statehood. In substance, however, this was a legal fiction influenced by political considerations.[121]

In contrast, the dissolution of the Socialist Federal Republic of Yugoslavia (SFRY) in 1991/1992 had the opposite outcome.[122] This was, once again, influenced by political considerations. The republics of Slovenia, Croatia, Bosnia and Herzegovina, and Macedonia, which were constituent members of the Yugoslav federation, left Yugoslavia successively. The remaining former Yugoslav republics, i.e. Serbia and Montenegro, adopted a new constitution and renamed themselves the Federal Republic of Yugoslavia (FRY). Like Russia, the Federal Republic of Yugoslavia announced that it continued the identity of the former SFRY and so its UN membership. However, the UN Security Council and the UN General Assembly took a different view and required the FRY to apply for membership. Due to the ongoing war in the former SFRY in 1992, and in particular the military involvement of the FRY in Bosnia Herzegovina, its application for membership at that time (1992) had no chance of success. Hence, the FRY obtained its membership only in 2000. Thus, interestingly, the SFRY's UN membership continued to exist as legal fiction between 1992 and 2000 even after its dissolution. Montenegro obtained its own membership after its separation from Serbia in 2006.

1.8 Structure, Organs, and Decision-Making

1.8.1 Issues

With every new international organization, a new independent legal community is established with its own legal order which legally constitutes the organization. This is also reflected in the organizations' structures, regarding the organs, decision-making processes, means and instruments.

There is a considerable variety as to the structures and organs of international organizations. Historical and political conditions at the time of establishment have an important impact, though it is the organization's specific goals that have the biggest influence. An organization focusing on maintaining international peace and security, for example, usually has quite different decision-making procedures, structures and instruments than an organization dealing primarily with technical issues, such as the International Telecommunication Union (ITU).

Despite this, most international organizations have *some structural issues and elements in common*. First, the structure is usually, because membership is limited to

[121] For an analysis of the relevant legal issues, see Blum (1992b), 354 ss.

[122] See e.g. Blum (1992a), 830 ss.; Wood (1997), 231 ss.; and Vitucci (2006), 105 ss.

states, state-dependent; member states represented by their governments are the main actors, and this is why intergovernmental organization is another term describing the nature of traditional IOs. Direct democratic representation of the people or of the peoples of member states does unusually not exist in international organizations. Insofar *there is no democracy in international organizations*.

Generally, an international organization needs to be able to form a will that can be represented externally. Therefore, organs forming that will have to exist as well as organs representing the organization in international relations. Therefore, all organizations have a main organ in which all the member states are represented, i.e. *a plenary organ*.

Also important are rules regulating the *structural relation between the members and the organization*. Generally, every international organization needs to maintain a balance between each member state's tendency to preserve its sovereign rights and the common goals of the states as members of an organization. Although the member states established the international organization to cooperate with each other, they still have their own will and their own rights, which they strive to protect as far as possible, also for reasons of domestic politics. This inevitably leads to difficulties in balancing the different interests, i.e. those of the international organization itself and the member states' particular interests. There is thus a potential conflict of interests. This conflict is also present in federal state systems, though they have different structures compared to international organizations. The structure also has an impact on how well the organization is able to create its own will rather than the lowest common denominator of the wills of the member states.

1.8.2 Statutory Organs

1.8.2.1 Introduction

The nineteenth century administrative unions had very rudimentary structures. During the sovereignty-oriented nineteenth century, a dominant concern of member states was to restrict the organizations' independent power as much as possible. Therefore, the organizations were intended to handle mere administrative tasks. The will of the organizations was manifested in an assembly, in which all the member states were represented with equal rights, and important decisions needed unanimity among members. The will of those organizations was consequently not more than the *lowest common denominator of the wills of all members*. The secretariats, which most administrative unions had, merely implemented the decisions made by the member states.

In the twenty-first century, such a structure is no longer viable for international organizations which must cope with many global challenges of common concern to the states as a consequence of increasing interdependencies and globalization. Already in the second half of the twentieth century, the organizational structure of international organizations has become more complicated because the areas of activity have also become more complex and comprehensive. Thus, the organizations' structure has to reflect these complexities. Today, an organization's usual internal structure comprises a plenary organ, an administrative organ and an executive organ. Almost all organizations further have special organs depending on their purpose and area of activity, and some organizations have a judicial organ or some other dispute settlement mechanism as well.

The structure of an IO is based on the idea of organs having different functions but supplementing each other and cooperating in pursuing the organization's goals. The relations are partly hierarchical: the *plenary organ is formally the highest organ*, but the executive organ usually has the concrete political power. In each organization there is a need to establish and *preserve an internal balance of the powers of the several organs and to avoid power conflicts.*

1.8.2.2 Plenary Organs

All international organizations have a plenary organ where all member states are represented. The plenary organs have different names, e.g. the General Assembly at the UN, the Committee of Ministers at CoE, and the Council at the EU. The purpose of the plenary organ is to give effect to the principle of sovereign equality of member states, which makes it essential that all member states take part, as a basic membership right, in the decision-making process of the organization. It is an organization's most representative and therefore usually *highest organ*. It sets standards as to the organization's policies, elects the office holder of other organs, establishes the organization's internal rules and makes generally the most important decisions as to the functioning of the IO.

In the plenary organ, the members are represented, usually by their governments, and usually have an equal say. A special case is the ILO which has a tripartite structure, i.e. consisting of government, employer and worker representatives. At the annual International Labour Conference, the organization's plenary organ, each member state sends four representatives: two government delegates, one employer delegate and one worker/employee delegate.

The advantage of plenary organs is that all states can participate and thus exercise a certain degree of influence over the organization. This also gives rise to a disadvantage in universal organizations where the vast number of member states leads to inefficiencies. This has had the consequence of many organizations *creating subsidiary organs under the plenary organs* that deal with specific subject-matters and facilitate the decision-making of the plenary organs by, e.g., drafting resolutions and submitting the drafts to the plenary organ. The UN General Assembly, for example, has six permanent main committees covering different activities, which prepare the decisions for the UN General Assembly.

1.8.2.3 Non-plenary Organs

International organizations also have non-plenary organs in which only some member states participate. Sometimes these members represent groups of states, such as in the IMF. They are created for efficiency reasons and as organ able to steer and direct the IO as well as the member states. The members usually represent their states (e.g. UN SC), but not always (see, e.g. the European Commission).[123] Sometimes they have decision-making authority (e.g. UN SC), sometimes they rather prepare and implement of decisions of the plenary organ.

The most famous non-plenary organ is the UN Security Council, which comprises 15 members from different parts of the world. Five of them are permanent members, the other 10 members are elected every 2 years. The UN's Economic and Social Council (ECOSOC) consists of 54 rotating members. Another example of a non-plenary organ is the Executive Board of the IMF.

Non-plenary organs like the Executive Board of the IMF are often created to boost efficiencies by giving an organ executive power that are easier to exercise on a regular basis. This is contrary to plenary organs which usually have only one annual session. Plenary organs like the UN General Assembly are usually not able to adequately steer the organization, its administration and its member states because of the infrequency of their meetings. Executive organs are much fitter to do this; they meet regularly and often establish special steering committees for that purpose.

1.8.2.4 Secretary-General; Administration

The international organization's administration is usually domiciled in its headquarters. The administration carries out the concrete work of the organization. It is headed and directed by a Secretary-General[124] such as the UN Secretary-General. Due to the expansion of most organizations' activities as a result of growing global and regional interdependencies, the significance of the administrations and the Secretary-Generals has substantially increased over the past decades.

The position of the Secretary-General is pivotal. As head of the administration, he or she represents the organization internally and externally and enters into treaties on the international organization's behalf. Secretary-Generals are often the organization's public face and play a political role. Besides heading the organization at the top of the hierarchy, they are concerned with administrative tasks for other organs, e.g. preparing for and taking minutes of meetings, the administration of budgets, the gathering of information as well as coordinating the various organs' activities. In addition, they often have political tasks which can be exercised through their right to raise important issues to the relevant organs. For example, Article 99 UN Charter states that the "*Secretary-General may bring to the attention of the Security Council*

---

[123] See infra, Sect. 4.7.5.2 as to the role of the European Commission.

[124] Some organizations use other labels such a Managing Director (IMF).

any matter which in his opinion may threaten the maintenance of international peace and security." The vast importance of Secretary-Generals is acknowledged, e.g., at the UN where the Secretary-General also plays an important role as peacemaker. In this regard, the Secretary-General carries out a range of activities, including good offices, mediation and dialogue processes in many conflicts. Usually, Secretary-Generals enjoy a degree of independence which elevates their status within the organization. As a result, they often have a role as one of the main organs of international organizations. Accordingly, Article 7(1) UN Charter, for example, recognizes the Secretariat as a main organ of the UN.

Even though the administration is obviously not the main decision-making organ, it plays a pivotal role. It is primarily responsible for the implementation of the other organs' resolutions and the practical work of the organization. Its workforce is composed of civil servants who are employed and accountable to the international organization only, and not to their home countries and who are elected also based on considerations of equitable geographic representations. The administration and the civil servants pursue their activities in a neutral way and work permanently for the organization while the other organs are composed of state representatives and sometimes only convene as little as once a year. In between these meetings, the Secretary-General, together with his or her administration, often must take over tasks that the plenary organ would normally be responsible for. Moreover, the administration knows the organization and its tasks best and has the most expertise compared to other organs. Its officers therefore can influence the development of the organization. The administration is also responsible for the organization's public relations and can thus impact the organization's public image as well. The administration further has the important task of monitoring the member states and publishing their observations of the states' implementation of the organization's policies. Administrations consequently exercise a sort of supervisory power over the member states.

The European Commission is an especially powerful administrative body because it exercises, as a supranational organ, both legislative and executive powers. The Commission is not only entrusted with the power of enforcing community rights but also exercises law-making powers by participating in the creation of secondary community law together with the Parliament and the Council.[125] This goes far beyond the powers of a Secretary-General of a traditional international organization.

1.8.2.5 Parliaments and Quasi-Parliamentary Organs

In some international organizations, especially in Europe, parliamentary organs have been created in response to a democratic deficit, because usually only government representatives participate in an organization's internal decision-making in its plenary organ. This deficit has increased due to amplified interdependencies, which

[125] For more details see infra, Sect. 4.7.5.2.

have caused national competences to become more internationalized and coordinated within international organizations. The consequence is that national parliaments lose control over ever more competences and/or have no other choice than to implement what has been pre-decided on an international level. For Switzerland, e.g., the decrease in national competences restricts the scope of application of direct democratic decision-making. (Quasi-) parliamentary organs have been thus created for this reason: to correct, at least to a certain extent, the democracy deficit. There are two ways to compensate for this increasing loss of powers of national parliaments.

The first is to ensure that *national parliaments are also represented on the international level* in a (quasi-)parliamentary organ of international organizations. A classic example is the Parliamentary Assembly of the CoE composed of representatives of the member states' parliaments. Another example is the parliamentary assembly of the OSCE. These organs have advisory functions only, and usually no lawmaking powers.

The second way to make up for the deficit is to have *a parliament as an organ of an international organization that is directly elected by the people.*[126] This is the case with the EU's Parliament whose members have been directly elected by the citizens of the member states since 1979. Over time, in particular after the Lisbon Treaty, the European Parliament has assumed additional responsibilities. It monitors the Commission and the Council and has an important role in law-making. This is the result of the so-called co-decision procedure and the ordinary legislative procedure in concert with the Council. The Parliament also approves the budget.[127]

Although quasi-parliamentary organs mainly exercise an advisory function, they sometimes also control other organs and even hold decision-making power, especially with regard to internal matter of the organization. However, they by far do not have the same standing in the international organization as national parliaments do in their countries, because they cannot legislate like a national parliament, and hence are arguably only an incomplete substitute for the growing democracy deficit. This deficit, in turn, is the result of a *steady increase in international policies and standards set by international organizations* which member states then must enforce domestically without these policies and standards first having gone through the domestic democratic process.

1.8.2.6 Expert Organs

Most international organizations have established expert organs; the personal expertise of those elected as members of these organs plays an important role. A good example is the *UN International Law Commission (ILC)*. The ILC initiates studies and produces draft codifications of various topics of international law as part of its

[126] For scholarly views on the EU's democratic deficit, cf. Müller (2016), 83 ss.; Beetz and Rossi (2017), 22 ss.; Zweifel (2002), 812 ss.; Kratochvíl and Sychra, (2019), 169 ss.

[127] See e.g. infra, Sect. 4.7.2.2.

task to contribute to the progressive development of international law. The codifications drafted by the ILC as the result of intense debates within the ILC are then presented to and usually adopted by the UN General Assembly and recommended by the Assembly to the member states for ratification. The ILC has initiated most of the important codifications of international law, most notably the VCLT.[128]

Another important expert organ of the UN is the *Human Rights Committee*.[129] The Committee monitors the implementation of the International Covenant on Civil and Political Rights (ICCPR) by, inter alia, reviewing state parties' reports on their implementation of the ICCPR, by issuing General Comments on how ICCPR rights should be interpreted,[130] and, as a quasi-judicial organ, decides on complaints of human rights violations lodged by individuals.

1.8.2.7 Judicial Organs

a) General Remarks

Judicial organs, i.e. courts, have increasingly gained importance. Even though they are not always formal courts, and the labels sometimes differ, some judicial organs are functionally equivalent to courts as they are tasked to decide on controversies arising from international law and/or on the law of a particular organization. The Human Rights Committee, for instance, is formally not a court but as expert organ it hears and decides human rights cases in a judicial manner. The most important international court is the International Court of Justice (ICJ), which is a main organ of the UN (Articles 7, 92–96 UN Charter). Some international courts, such as the ICJ, are organs of an international organization, while others are international institution with their own legal personality. Examples include the ICTY and the International Criminal Court.

b) Examples

The ECtHR is established by the European Convention on Human Rights (ECHR). The Court is institutionally linked to the CoE: the Parliamentary Assembly elects the judges for the Court. The ECtHR's human rights appeals process has been frequently utilized and, consequently, has increasingly become the victim of its own success.[131]

---

[128] As to the role of the ILC in international law-making see infra, Sect. 2.8.2.4, label (d).

[129] Note that the Human Rights Committee is not to be confused with the Human Rights Council, which is a political body made up of states to promote human rights around the world. The Human Rights Committee, in contrast, is an expert body.

[130] See e.g. General Comment No. 36 on Art. 6—the Right to Life (30 Oct 2018).

[131] As one commentator puts it, this is due to a combination of factors, including the ECtHR's "positive public reputation, its expansive interpretations of the Convention, a distrust of domestic judiciaries in some countries, and entrenched human rights problems in others", thus leading to a "docket crisis of massive proportions" of "tens of thousands of new individual applications annually": Helfer (2008), p. 126; cf. Greer (2008), 680 ss.

The Court of Justice of the European Union (CJEU consists of two courts. The first is the Court of Justice, informally known as European Court of Justice (ECJ)) which is the judicial organ of the EU and hears applications from national courts for preliminary rulings, annulment and appeals. The second court is the General Court, which hears applications for annulment from individuals, companies and, less commonly, national governments (focusing on competition law, state aid, trade, agriculture and trademarks).

The ICTY is a good example of how international organizations can extend their powers. It was created by UN Security Council Resolution 827 for the

> *sole purpose of prosecuting persons responsible for serious violations of international humanitarian law committed in the territory of the former Yugoslavia between 1 January 1991 and a date to be determined by the Security Council upon the restoration of peace.*[132]

The ICTY is an international institution in its own right, possessing its own legal personality and its own founding statute. It was created in 1992 whilst the conflict in the former Yugoslavia was still on-going, which shows that international organizations sometimes respond quickly to serious humanitarian situations. Similarly, the International Criminal Tribunal for Rwanda was established in 1994 by UN Security Council Resolution 955 to prosecute crimes committed in the Rwanda genocide.[133] This suggests that there is a growing awareness of the importance of holding perpetrators of international crimes to account, though the international criminal courts and tribunals have been plagued by problems of legitimacy.[134]

Further, there is a tendency to establish appellate bodies to monitor the jurisprudence of lower international courts. The most important example is the WTO's Dispute Settlement mechanism which provides for a special appellate body.

c) The Courts' Roles and Functions

The genuine function of courts is *to decide on controversies*. Some international courts like the ICJ have in addition the *power to give advisory opinions*. These opinions may also concern the legality of resolutions of international organizations.

The controversies that international courts adjudicate include those (a) between states, (b) between states and international organizations, (c) between organs of an international organization, (d) between individuals or corporations and a state, and (e) between individuals or corporations and an international organization.

The first category describes the traditional function of international courts. The most notable of such courts are the ICJ, the WTO's dispute settlement mechanism,

---

[132] S/Res/827 (1993), para 2.

[133] Furthermore, the International Criminal Court (ICC) was created in 2002 pursuant to the 1998 Rome Statute. It investigates and tries individuals charged with the gravest crimes of concern to the international community, i.e. genocide, war crimes, crimes against humanity and the crime of aggression. For a history of the ICC, see Çakmak (2017); cf. McGoldrick et al. (2004).

[134] See e.g. Cassese (2012), 491 ss. (focusing on the legitimacy of the ICTY and the Special Tribunal for Lebanon); Boas et al. (2012); de Hoon (2017), 591 ss.; and Roach (2013), 619 ss. For an analysis of the relationship between the ICC and the UN Security Council, and a defence of the ICC, see Lentner (2019).

and, but only exceptionally, the ECtHR, which deals mainly with complaints by individuals against states.

The second category refers to disputes between organizations and their member states, which are settled by the judicial organs of the organization. The ECJ is a good example of this; it adjudicates disputes between member states and the organs of the EU. The applicable law is usually the law of the international organization, including both primary and secondary legislation. In contrast, within the framework of the UN, disputes between the UN and its member states cannot be settled at the ICJ. The UN cannot be the claimant nor be defendant in cases before the ICJ because only states have legal standing. Therefore, the ICJ has no power to act as the UN's judicial organ. However, the UN Security Council, the UN General Assembly and other organs may ask the ICJ to give advisory opinions. Such advisory opinions may concern the relation between the UN and its member states or between the UN Security Council and the UN General Assembly or other organs. The advisory opinions are not legally binding but are nonetheless of substantial authority as the opinions of the ICJ as World Court.

Only very few courts have the power to decide on controversies between organs of an international organization. The most prominent example is again the ECJ, which has the capacity to adjudicate disputes between the organs of the EU. As to the fourth category, i.e. controversies between individuals or corporations and a state to be decided by a court linked with an international organization, again the ECJ is a good example. It decides cases between individuals or corporations and a member state on the conformity of the member state's acts with the law of the EU. Moreover, in the realm of the protection of human rights, individuals can bring claims against member states for human rights violations. The most prominent example of this is the legal protection within the framework of the ECHR, enforced by the ECtHR. A similar but less developed system of legal protection is the UN ICCPR, enforced by the UN Human Rights Committee as mentioned earlier. Such systems have also been developed in other regions of the world, e.g. by OAS in America.

The fifth category, i.e. controversies between individuals or corporations and an international organization, refers foremost to the relations between an international organization and its civil servants. As mentioned previously,[135] because organizations have privileges and immunities that exempt them from domestic jurisdiction, the most direct way for individuals to lodge complaints against them is if the organizations themselves provide for such mechanisms. Many international organizations have some kind of judicial organs with the task of settling disputes between the organization and its civil servants. These judicial organs are very important for the protection of the civil servants' labor rights. In contrast, individuals who have suffered other types of losses due to the international organizations' activities receive weak legal protection because of the organizations' immunities. Examples include disputes, e.g. between deliverers of goods and organizations arising from business

[135] See supra, Sect. 1.6.7.

transactions between private companies and organizations.[136] The ILO's administrative court is a welcomed exception, for it has jurisdiction over commercial treaties entered into with private persons.

There is a growing need to grant individuals and corporation legal protection and thus access to courts due to the expansion of the international organizations' activities insofar as they increasingly interfere with the rights of individuals, i.e. natural persons or private corporations. An example are resolutions of the UN SC as part of its main tasks, i.e. its responsibility to preserve international peace and security, that sanction individuals by, e.g. freezing their assets or limiting their freedom to move. Against these measures there is no access to an independent court.

A particularly important impact on the legal status of individuals and corporations have the legal acts of supranational organization. The transfer of powers from the member states to the organization, which includes the organization's power to legislate and to make formal decisions affecting the rights and duties of private persons and entities, necessarily entails—at least from a rule of law point of view—the right to challenge the legality of the organization's laws and acts in court. The EU as supranational organization has a well-developed legal protection system for the citizens of its member states. This is the natural consequence of the fact that the EU, like a national parliament, enacts norms directly applicable to individuals and companies. Every addressee of a decision by the EU, as well as anyone directly and individually affected by a decision, can bring a claim against the EU. This procedure necessarily accounts for the fact that the organs of the EU are both legislators and enforcers, and exercise jurisdiction over competences that previously belonged to member states.

d) Conclusion

Judicial organs as part of the institutional architecture of international organizations may serve important purposes. They ensure that the laws of international organizations are coherently applied. They also enjoy a so-called interpretation monopoly on an organization's primary and secondary law. Moreover, they can exercise jurisdiction over multilateral treaties that were created in relation to an international organization and where such treaties provide for it. However, in practice, the process of judicialization in the framework of international organizations has not gone very far. The most advanced is the EU, the prototype of a supranational organization. Most organizations, in contrast, are equipped with merely rudimentary judicial structures and processes.

---

[136]The UN Model Contract for Procurement of Goods and the Model Contract for Goods and/or Services Between the United Nations Development Programme and a Company or Organization provide, however, for arbitration under UNCITRAL rules.

1.8.3 Creation of Organs and Institutions by an IO

Organs are generally regulated in an IO's constitution. Therefore, the establishment of new organs requires usually an amendment to the treaty establishing the organization. Subsidiary organs, however, may be created by an IO's organ based either on specific provisions of the IO's constitution[137] or based on an implied power. The question is whether this power is more or less unlimited or restricted to those necessary for the functioning of the organ and the organization.

In practice, this power is quite unlimited. The UN SC has established the international criminal tribunals for Ex-Yugoslavia and Rwanda and thus created not only new organs, but independent international institutions with own international legal personality. As the Chamber of Appeals of the International Criminal Tribunal for the former Yugoslavia (ICTY) in the Tadic case held did the UN Security Council not act ultra vires; the establishment of the ICTY is covered by the wide discretion based on Article 41 UN Charter as a measure "to maintain or restore international peace and security".[138] Thus, it seems that organs of international organizations have wide discretion to create other organs or even independent international institutions at least as long as the powers of the other statutory organs are not adversely affected, and the creation of these organs is in line with an organization's purpose.

1.8.4 Decision-Making Process

In the practice of international organizations, there is a broad variety of decision-making methods at the disposal of the organizations' organs. The most common ones are the *unanimity vote* and the *majority vote*. Historically, the unanimity vote was the usual method of decision-making in all the organs, in particular in the plenary organs in which all member states participated, because it best respected the sovereignty of each member state. This was particularly true for the organizations created in the second half of the nineteenth century which required unanimity for most, if not all, of their important decisions. Therefore, each member state possessed a *de facto* veto power. The rule, while protecting national sovereignty, substantially hindered the development of international organizations because the will of the organization could never be more than the *lowest common denominator of all the member states' wills*. This was largely the case with the League of Nations. Despite this, the principle has survived and still remains a method of decision-making, particularly in some regional organizations with relatively few members. Examples

[137] See, e.g., the general power regulated in Art. 7(2) UNCh and the respective powers of the UN General Assembly (UN GA) (Art. 22 UNCh) and of the UN Security Council (SC) (Art. 29 UNCh).

[138] ICTY, *Prosecutor v. Duško Tadić*, Case No. IT-94-1, Decision on the Defence Motion for Interlocutory Appeal on Jurisdiction, 2 Oct 1995.

include the NATO, the EU with regard to some decisions, and the former Western European Union (WEU). In contrast, the OSCE may in some instances abandon the unanimity rule and may use a quasi-unanimity rule (consensus minus one).[139] A way of overcoming the rigidity of the unanimity rule is by stipulating that abstention by a member state does not amount to an objection to a decision. The abstention is merely interpreted as acquiescence in that case. At some organizations, a member state's abstention to a proposed resolution means that the member state is not bound by it.[140]

In global organizations like the UN and its special agencies with almost 200 member states, strict adherence to the unanimity rule would severely impede their functioning. Consequently, majority voting is common in these organizations. This voting system comes in different shapes and forms. The statutes sometimes prescribe an exact number of votes needed for majority; e.g.; according to Article 27 UN Charter, nine votes out of fifteen are needed for the adoption of an UN Security Council resolution. However, it is more common to set out a specific fraction needed, e.g. simple majority or qualified majority (usually two-thirds). For the IMF, in order to change its statutes, a qualified majority of three fifths of the member states is needed, which taken together have to amount to over 85% of the votes (every member state has a different proportion of votes).

The IMF example shows that, sometimes, not all the states' votes bear the same weight. This is despite the general principle of sovereign equality enshrined in, e.g., Article 2 of the UN Charter. The idea is that every state has an equal vote regardless of its size or economic power, etc. The *one-state-one-vote-principle* is applied in most international and regional organizations, e.g. in the UN General Assembly, in the OECD, in the OSCE and in the Arabic League. There are, however, derogations from this rule, the most well-known of which is the veto power of the permanent members in the UN Security Council. In addition, some organizations implement a system of so-called weighted votes of their member states. The weight of the states' individual votes may reflect, e.g., population and/or economic strength of the member state. This is the case in, e.g., the EU, where the vote of the individual states depends on their size and economic power. Some financial organizations such as the IMF and the World Bank weight the votes of their member states according to how much capital they provide which is again dependent on a country's economic power.[141] Vote weightage also varies in the Parliamentary Assembly of the CoE and in the European Parliament in accordance with the size of a member state's population. In such situations, according to the organizations' constitutions, the smaller countries are usually favored vis-a-vis the bigger ones when it comes to determining

---

[139] See Conference on Security and Co-operation in Europe, Second Meeting of the Council, *Prague Document on Further Development of CSCE Institutions and Structures* (1992), 4 whereby 'appropriate action may be taken by the Council or Committee of Senior Officials, if necessary, in the absence of the consent of the State concerned, in cases of clear, gross and uncorrected violations of relevant CSCE commitments'. For more information see Bloed (1993), 21 s.

[140] See e.g. Charter of the Organization of American States, Art. 57.

[141] Art. XII(5) IMF Articles of Agreement; Art. V(3) IBRD Articles of Agreement.

the number of votes in order to avoid a permanent domination of such organizations by large, powerful states. Vote quotas naturally only matter when unanimity is not required.

Apart from the unanimity and the majority rules, there is also a so-called *consensus rule* either as a political practice of an organization or as a formal legal rule according to the treaty establishing an organization. It means that negotiations in an organ are to continue until there are *no formal objections and a uniform opinion is formed.* This method of decision-making is often used because a decision by majority is harder to execute when particularly important states or state groups lose in the majority vote. It is therefore pragmatic to strive for a decision that every state consents to or at least tolerates because then there are better chances for observance and implementation by the member states. Most resolutions of the UN General Assembly base on consensus.

The effect and binding nature of international organizations' decisions depend on their constitutions or secondary law. Internal decisions, e.g. decisions on the budget, elections as well as internal regulations are usually binding.[142] External decisions, on the other hand, are often legally non-binding recommendations. For example, the resolutions by the UN General Assembly or by the Committee of Ministers of the CoE are non-binding. However, resolutions by the UN Security Council under Chapter VII UN Charter, as well as the decisions by the EU Council, are generally binding.

1.9 Powers of International Organizations; External Representation

1.9.1 Explicit Powers

International organizations need the requisite powers to achieve their specific purposes; adequate powers and competences are pre-conditions for an international organization's existence and success. The concrete competences of an international organization and its organs are usually dependent on the common will of the (founding) member states. This is usually expressed in the constituent instruments as well as in subsequent regulations and is reflected in the international organization's practice. As already mentioned, some organizations have narrowly prescribed competences, whereas others, like the UN, have broad competences due to their broadly defined goals and purposes. For instance, according Articles 1 and 2 UN Charter, the UN can conceivably develop activities in practically all policy fields.[143]

[142] See infra, Sect. 1.10.4.

[143] Art. 1(3) in particular provides that the UN's purpose is to "achieve international co-operation in solving international problems of an economic, social, cultural, or humanitarian character".

Starting point of the interpretation of the provisions in the constituent instrument regulating the organization's and its organs powers are the interpretation rules of the Vienna Convention on the Law of Treaties.[144] Apart from the powers explicitly regulated by the primary law of organizations, the practice of international organizations further shows that they often exercise competences not explicitly mentioned in the founding treaty or secondary law. These powers are based on particular doctrines of interpretation of the international organizations' constituent instruments.

1.9.2 *Implied and Inherent Powers*

a) Implied Powers

One of these doctrines is the doctrine of implied powers. Implied Powers are *powers not explicitly mentioned in a treaty*. Explicitly attributed powers are often not enough for an international organization to perform its tasks properly; implied powers are needed too, i.e. powers that are necessary for fulfilling the organization's purposes, but which are not explicitly mentioned in the organization's constitution either because the founders regarded it as obvious, or because the founders did not foresee the necessity of those powers. The gaps that arise subsequently in the constituent documents are thus filled by so-called implied powers because they are considered necessary or at least important for the organization's proper performance. The ICJ exemplifies the necessity of power implication by highlighting the essence of this element to the UN's performance in the Reparations for Injuries case.

The doctrine of implied powers was originally developed by the US Supreme Court as a method of constitutional interpretation. It helped to fill the lacunas created by an old, difficult-to-amend constitution so as to enable the US authorities to cope with the current requirements of statecraft. Similarly, in ICJ's *Reparations* case, the principle of implied powers got applied when the ICJ ruled that the UN could hold a non-member state liable for paying reparations to the UN even though the statutes did not grant such a right. The majority opinion in the case supported a flexible formula, i.e.

> *under international law, the organization must be deemed to have those powers which, though not expressly provided in the Charter, are conferred upon it by necessary implication as being essential to the performance of its duties. This principle of law was applied by the Permanent Court of International Justice to the International Labour Organization in its Advisory Opinion No. 13 of July 23rd, [p183] 1926 (Series B., No. 13, p. 18), and must be applied to the United Nations.*[145]

---

[144] Art. 31–38 VCLT.

[145] *Reparation for Injuries Suffered in the Service of the U.N.*, Advisory Opinion, ICJ Rep. 174 (1994), 182.

This means that *all powers necessary for achieving an international organization's purpose* should be allowed as long as they can be derived from the provisions of an organization's constitution.

An example of an explicit regulation of implied powers of an international organization is Article 352 TFEU, the so-called flexibility clause. This provision regulates decision-making regarding measures based on implicit powers of the European Union:

> *1. If action by the Union should prove necessary, within the framework of the policies defined in the Treaties, to attain one of the objectives set out in the Treaties, and the Treaties have not provided the necessary powers, the Council, acting unanimously on a proposal from the Commission and after obtaining the consent of the European Parliament, shall adopt the appropriate measures. Where the measures in question are adopted by the Council in accordance with a special legislative procedure, it shall also act unanimously on a proposal from the Commission and after obtaining the consent of the European Parliament.*

The doctrine of implied powers infringes on the otherwise widely recognized principle of state sovereignty in international law. However, the implied powers doctrine does not—at least theoretically—harm state sovereignty, since it is assumed that the states were willing to grant the organization the means to fulfill its purposes when the organization was founded or subsequently joined by non-founding states. There is also a presumption that if there were a specific competence that states did not want to grant to the international organization, it would have been expressly stated in the founding treaty.[146] Implied powers must be distinguished from *acts ultra vires* which are acts going beyond what could reasonably be construed as an organization's (implied) powers.[147] In theory, the distinction is quite clear, in practice, however, it is sometimes very difficult draw a clear line.

b) Inherent Powers

Inherent powers, closely related to the doctrine of implied powers, are powers that international organizations possess *owing to their status as an international organization vested with international legal personality*. Unlike implied powers, the doctrine of inherent powers does not interpret the organization's constitution but derives powers quite generally from the nature and/or general purpose of an organization. An organization, once established, would possess all the powers to perform all those acts which it needs to attain the organization's aims, simply because these powers are inherent to organizationhood. Although strongly contested, this doctrine has remained somewhat relevant.

---

[146] As an example, cf. Art. 1(d) of the Statute of the Council of Europe: "Matters relating to national defence do not fall within the scope of the Council of Europe."

[147] As to acts ultra vires see infra, Sect. 1.8.4.

1.9.3 Conflicts of Powers

Conflicts of powers within an organization and how they are resolved is a difficult issue, and neither legal doctrine nor practice is very clear. One reason for this is that most organization do not have an organ competent to decide on these conflicts. Such conflicts may arise within international organizations regarding what powers the organization and/or its organs should have. These conflicts may arise between the organization and a member state, or between the organs of the same organization. Who decides such conflicts of powers? Who has the respective decision-making powers, the "Kompetenz-Kompetenz"?

As just mentioned, many organizations lack rules and procedures to resolve such conflicts, especially when there is no organ that can give an authoritative interpretation of the law to resolve such conflicts what is very often the case.[148] Absent such an organ, the plenary organs as the highest, most representative bodies may try to adjudicate power disputes even without an explicit power of authoritative interpretation. This power could be based on the uncontested and usually explicit, sometimes implicit power of organizations to establish rules that are binding on the internal organization. However, if there is a conflict between the organization and one or several member states, it would be difficult for the plenary organ to issue an authoritative interpretation because such controversies usually go beyond issues of mere internal organization. Notwithstanding, the plenary organ might be able to issue an authoritative interpretation in cases where an organ's action clearly contradicts the statutes and is thus *ultra vires*.

Some organizations have courts that can decide on competency conflicts between the organization and its member states. This is true for the EU. The CJEU has comprehensive powers to adjudicate such conflicts and has done so also in landmark cases. It is disputed as to whether, under what circumstances and to which extent the ICJ also has that power. If it did, it would be only an implicit power because the ICJ's jurisdiction is limited to adjudicating controversies between states or to render advisory opinions upon the request of organizations and organs empowered to make such a request. The ICJ avoided a respective decision in the *Lockerbie* case between Libya, the US and UK over the Lockerbie bombing in 1988. The question was whether the ICJ can determine that the UN Security Council has exceeded its powers in relation to the sovereignty of member states. The court did not have to answer this question because it held that the Security Council acted within the powers conferred to it by the UN Charter.

The question has also been addressed by the ICTY. The Appeals Chamber ruled that

> *the Security Council is [...] subjected to certain constitutional limitations, however broad its powers under the constitution may be. Those powers cannot, in any case, go beyond the limits of jurisdiction of the Organization at large, not to mention other specific limitations or those which may derive from the internal division of powers within the Organization. In any*

[148] Examples include the WTO and the IMF, for details see infra, Sects. 5.2.4.4 and 5.3.6.2.

case, neither the text nor the spirit of the UN Charter conceives of the UN Security Council as legibus solutus,[149]

The real value of this statement is unclear, since the ICTY does not have the formal power to review UN Security Council resolutions and judgments rendered by the ICJ.

If there are no organs with the competence to make authoritative decisions, then the organs themselves decide on their own powers. This was held in the ICJ's *Certain Expenses* Advisory Opinion, where the ICJ stated that *"when the organization takes action which warrants the assertion what it was appropriate for the fulfilment of one of the stated purposes of the United Nations, the presumption is that such an action is not* ultra vires *the organization."*[150] The power to make such a self-judgment is an implied one and is binding on all member states. Otherwise, the member states could practically nullify the competences or acts of the organs by questioning such a power and challenging their decisions and resolutions.

There is, however, an exception to this: acts *ultra vires*. These are acts that are *clearly outside the scope or purposes of the international organization or an organ*. It can sometimes be difficult to distinguish between permitted implied powers and acts *ultra vires*. That is because the decision as to whether an act constitutes an act *ultra vires* lies with the individual member states in cases where there are no official mechanisms for such procedures at the international organization.

1.9.4 External Representation

The international organization's international legal personality is based on the recognition of the organization as legal subjects by its member states; this recognition, in turn, is implied in their membership in the organization. In relation to third party states, this international legal personality is accepted when these states recognize the organization as international legal subjects, either expressly or implicitly by practice. There is one notable exception to this requirement of third-party recognition: in the *Reparations case*, the ICJ held that the UN enjoy objective legal personality, which means that the status of its legal personality does not depend on recognition by third party states.[151]

The capacity to act internationally is inherent in the legal personality of international organizations. This also entails the power of external representation, which is an important consequence of an organization's international legal personality. The

---

[149] See ICTY, *Prosecutor v. Duško Tadić*, Case No. IT-94-1, Decision on the Defence Motion for Interlocutory Appeal on Jurisdiction, 2 Oct 1995, para. 28.

[150] *Certain Expenses of the United Nations (Art. 17, Paragraph 2, of the Charter)*, Advisory Opinion, ICJ Rep. 151 (1962), 168.

[151] *Reparation for Injuries Suffered in the Service of the U.N.*, Advisory Opinion, ICJ Rep. 174 (1994).

organization's external representation is exercised by the organ endowed with this power as stipulated in the founding treaty. Usually, the secretariat or the Secretary General has that task, though this varies from organization to organization. Plenary and internal organs such as general assemblies have no power to represent an organization externally.

In the EU, the subject matter in issue determines which organ represents the EU externally. Usually, the Commission is the main organ representing the EU. A special case is representation in international organizations as the example of the WTO shows. The EU was a founding member of the WTO, and the Commission represents the Union. At the same time, the EU member states are WTO members. The Union and its members have to coordinate representation and participation in the WTO as it is clear that the Union and the member states cannot vote together on the same subjects. Apart from this, it can sometimes be difficult for the EU to become a party to multilateral treaties even if these treaties, as to their ratione materiae, refer to the competencies of the EU only and not its member states' powers. Although the situation is about to change, external representation in international organizations or acceding to multilateral treaties is difficult because very often membership in international organization or becoming party of treaties is limited to states. This used to be the case for the ECHR, but with the 14th protocol to the ECHR, the European Union can join as well.[152]

1.10 The Law Governing the Activities of International Organizations; Law-Making

1.10.1 Basics

International organizations are both *law-based and law-makers*. The laws of international organizations include the constituent instrument, the rules, decisions and resolutions adopted by the organs, and the established practice of international organizations.[153] In addition, general international law may apply within an organization, i.e. in the relation between the organization and its member states or between its member states if and when the organization's rules are not conclusive, or in the relation between an organization and third parties such as non-member states or other international organizations.

[152] Art. 59 para. 2 ECHR.

[153] This is explicitly stated so in a definition in the ILC-Draft Articles on the Responsibility of IO: *"Art. 2(b) "rules of the organization" means, in particular, the constituent instruments, decisions, resolutions and other acts of the international organization adopted in accordance with those instruments, and established practice of the organization".*

1.10.2 The Organization's Own Law: Primary and Secondary Law

International law doctrine and practice distinguish between the organization's primary and secondary laws. Primary law includes *constituent instruments and other norms that have equivalent authority to the founding treaty*. These norms, particularly the founding treaty, are sometimes referred to as the constitution of an international organization. Secondary law includes all those *norms and rules which have been enacted by the organs of an international organization based on the constituent instruments*; they can be found in regulations, resolutions and decisions adopted by the organization's organs, and in treaties concluded by the organization. Both, primary and secondary laws govern an organization's activities.

Primary law consists of treaties concluded between states and, therefore belongs to the category of general international law. Secondary law, in turn, is based on primary law. Although it is closely intertwined with primary law and this with international law, it usually does not—with the exception of treaties concluded by the organization—form part of general international law. It has no general application, but rather, is particular to an international organization and is thus only valid within the organization. Therefore, secondary law is *not a formal source of international law* as defined, e.g. by Article 38 of the statute of the ICJ, which confines these sources to the classical triad: international treaties, customary international law, and the general principles of law. Generally, the primary and secondary law of each organization forms its own legal order, which is only binding on the organization itself and its member states. In particular, secondary law regulates above all an organization's internal matters.

Exceptionally, an international organization's legal norms or its organs' practice may become *part of customary international law*. The most familiar examples of this are some norms of the UN Charter that have partially become international customary law and are thus binding also on non-member states. These norms include the right of self-determination,[154] the prohibition on the use of force,[155] the protection of the territorial integrity and political independence of states,[156] and other fundamental norms underpinning the international system such as those contained in the Friendly Relations Declaration.[157] The same is true for some important resolutions of the UN General Assembly. These resolutions generally only have internal effect because the General Assembly does not have the power to enact legal norms binding for members, let alone non-member states. However, important declarations such as the aforementioned Friendly Relations Declaration or the Declaration on the

[154] Art. 1(2) UNCh.

[155] Art. 2(4) UNCh.

[156] Ibid.

[157] A/RES/1625 (XXV) (1970).

Granting of Independence to Colonial Countries and People[158] have become customary international law, based on their general acceptance by the states and their consistent application in the practice of the UN and of the states. Otherwise, the *pacta tertiis rule* applies: Primary and secondary law of an organization bind only the organization and its the organs and the member states, but not third parties.

1.10.3 Relation to Other Sources of Law

a) Preliminary Remark

Not only an organization's primary and secondary law determines its activities. As subjects of international law, they are bound by the treaties that they conclude, and further must observe international law in general, including customary international law. It follows that an organization's primary and secondary law may, e.g., not contradict *jus cogens* principles.

b) Treaties

Treaties concluded by an international organization are part of that organization's law. The organization's law then decides on the treaties' place in the organization's general legal hierarchy. This is similar to states making decisions regarding the place of international law in their domestic legal system. Independent of that place, international organizations must of course comply with the treaties concluded by them as these treaties belong to the organization's own (usually secondary) law; noncompliance would result in an organization's international liability. Such treaties may have an important impact on the organization. An example is the impact of the WTO's rules, and the judgments rendered by the WTO-panels, on EU law. The EU as founding member is directly bound by WTO law and practice, and provisions of the EU's primary and secondary law have to be construed in light of the pertinent law and practice of the WTO organs.[159] This is an example that an international organization, the supranational EU, has—as part of the membership status—to observe the law of another international organization.

c) Customary International Law

International organizations as subjects of international law are further bound by customary international law. For instance, UN troops are bound by humanitarian law as customary international law during their peacekeeping operations despite the fact that the UN cannot ratify the Geneva Conventions and their additional protocols because these treaties are only open for ratification by states. Likewise, the EC as predecessor of the EU used to be bound by the principles of the ECHR when they exercised jurisdiction over competences that previously belonged to the states. That

---

[158] A/RES/1514 (XV) (1960).

[159] For more information on the impact of WTO law and practice on EU law and policies, see e.g. Dee (2015); Young (2012), 23 ss.; De Ville (2012), 700 ss.

said, because the EC was a non-state actor and therefore not a party to the ECHR, it was bound only by those principles which had become regional customary law in Europe. Today, the EU has its own bill of rights which contains rights similar to those granted by the ECHR, and the CJEU considers the judgments of the ECtHR.

The relationship between customary international law and the law of international organizations is, however, complex as customary international law can modify the rules of an international organization. A good example is Article 27(3) UN Charter, which states:

Decisions of the Security Council on all other matters shall be made by an affirmative vote of nine members including the concurring votes of the permanent members; provided that, in decisions under Chapter VI, and under paragraph 3 of Article 52, a party to a dispute shall abstain from voting.

Despite its wording, it has been held and has become general practice that, when a permanent member of the UN Security Council abstains from voting, it does not amount to an exercise of the veto right. This means that customary law can derogate from international treaty law. Generally, customary international law and the general principles of law may supplement or amend the law of the organizations.

Not only does customary international law have an impact on the law of international organizations, but the international organizations' practice may contribute to the creation of customary international law as well. An example is the UN General Assembly's Friendly Relations Declaration and other important resolutions of the GA relating to the process of decolonization. They contributed to the construction of self-determination as one of the basic norms of international law, thereby concretizing Article 1(2) UN Charter. International organizations' decisions and resolutions often contribute to the development of general international law, especially customary law. Initially non-binding decisions by international organizations, in particular the UN, have substantially developed the international legal order. Such decisions are mainly soft law, which progressively transforms into customary international law to be codified.

d) UN Law; Article 103 UN Charter

Another relevant article regarding the relationship between different sources of international law is Article 103 UN Charter. It states:

In the event of a conflict between the obligations of the Members of the United Nations under the present Charter and their obligations under any other international agreement, their obligations under the present Charter shall prevail.

The UN Charter, and the binding decisions of UN organs, thus take precedence over other international legal instruments adopted by member states or the law and resolutions of other international organizations. This is due to the UN's specific status as a universal organization with a general purpose equipped with the powers to enforce coercive measures, as well as the UN Charter being something like the *constitution of a state-based international system*. However, Article 103 does not regulate the concrete relations between the states' obligations as UN members and their other international obligation or their domestic legal order. Therefore, one may not infer from the provision, e.g. that conflicting international obligations or national law or decisions by national authorities conflicting with UN membership obligations are null and void. The provision simply states that UN law and membership obligations precede. Thus, in case of a conflict between, e.g., a resolution of a regional organization and the obligations of the UN members resulting from binding UN SC resolutions, the latter take precedence for the member states of the regional organization. Any conflicting norm is simply not applied.

1.10.4 Law-Making by International Organizations

International organizations are not only bound by law; they also make law. International organizations can regulate and create norms on different subject matters. All organizations adopt regulations of internal matters which are legally binding. Moreover, some organizations can make laws that bind their member states. Only very few organizations enact laws that are directly applicable to individuals and confer rights and/or obligations on them. This is a feature of supranational organizations.

1.10.4.1 Internal Law-Making

All international organizations have the power to regulate their own internal matters even if the founding treaty does not provide for it; it is an implied or inherent power. Internal rules include rules of procedure, budget and election of organs and offices, rules applicable to the organization's officers, the creation of new organs and the limitation of the organs' powers. While these matters may already be regulated in the founding treaty, the organization, usually its General Assembly, may still concretize these rules in more detailed secondary regulations. An example is the UN General Assembly. Although Article 10 UN Charter provides generally that it cannot make binding decisions, it can nevertheless still make binding decisions regarding, e.g., the budget (Article 17 UN Charter). The same applies for other internal matters of the organization. An important internal regulation of the UN General Assembly is the Uniting for Peace Resolution which regulates relations between the UN Security Council and the UN General Assembly if there is a deadlock in the UN Security Council over conflict management. In such cases,

> *the General Assembly shall consider the matter immediately with a view to making appropriate recommendations to Members for collective measures,*

including...the use of armed force when necessary, to maintain or restore international peace and security.[160]

To date, eleven emergency special sessions have been convened, the most recent being an emergency session in February/March 2022 on the Russian aggression against the Ukraine. The UN Security Council also has powers to regulate internal matters as long as these regulations refer to the Council's primary task to preserve international peace and security, and its internal functioning.

1.10.4.2 Rules Directed to the Member States

It is *exceptional that international organizations can make laws binding their members*. The general principle in international law is that states are bound by international legal rules only when they have consented to the rules. This is a necessary consequence of the principle of sovereignty. International treaties are an example of this as a state only becomes a party if it agrees and ratifies or accedes to the treaty. This is different for decisions by international organizations: In most organizations, decisions are made based on the majority principle. If such decisions were binding, states would be legally bound without their consent. In most cases, the states that founded international organizations were not prepared to provide for this consequence, Hence, most international organizations' resolutions are non-binding and are *mere recommendations*. Examples include the resolutions by the UN General Assembly and the CoE's Parliamentary Assembly. However, in some instances legal rules directed to member states are binding, as will be seen just below.[161]

1.10.4.3 Norms Binding Member States Without Their Consent

Binding norms that do not require formal acceptance by member states and thus are generally legal binding are an exception. Examples include the UN Security Council's resolutions under Chapter VII of the UN Charter, and law-making by the EU. With regard to the UN Security Council's resolutions, given that these resolutions require only a majority vote in the Security Council, they are thus also binding on states that have not explicitly consented to the decision, which is the vast majority of the UN membership. The obligation that decisions by the UN Security Council, where only 15 of the 193 member states are represented, have to be adhered to by all member states without a chance to vote, is based on Article 25 of the UN Charter.[162]

[160] A/Res/377 (V), para. 1.

[161] See infra Sect. 1.10.4.3.

[162] Art. 25 reads: "The Members of the United Nations agree to accept and carry out the decisions of the Security Council in accordance with the present Charter."

As for the EU, it has in the international arena the broadest scope to enact binding laws. There are two main forms of binding legislative acts in the EU: directives and regulations. Regulations are general legislative acts, the entirety of which is binding and directly applicable in all member states. Like domestic laws, the adoption of regulations by the EU organs is a form of substantive law-making by an international organization for its member states and the legal and natural persons living in the territory of the member states.[163] Directives, on the other hand, only determine in a legally binding way the goal to be achieved, and the member states which are obliged to implement the directives into their domestic legal order, can freely choose what measures they take to achieve the desired effect.[164] Directives are mainly addressed to member states, whereas regulations are addressed to states *and* all individuals, whether natural or legal. These forms of lawmaking are atypical for international organizations, as they stem from the fact that the EU is a supranational organization with powers in subject matters necessarily requiring binding regulations.

1.10.4.4 Norms Directly Binding Individuals

The rules and norms that international organizations create are usually directed at member states and not individuals, regardless of whether they are legally binding. This is due to the veil of sovereignty that protects the relation between states and individuals from outside interference. Therefore, decisions of international organizations generally take the form of a duty of or a recommendation to all or some member states. It is then up to the states themselves to implement the decision on the national level in a manner of their choosing and in accordance with their own legal system. This is also the case if an international organization's resolutions should produce effects on individuals: As a general rule, it is up to the states to give these resolutions an internal effect, as only national legal rules are directly applicable on individuals, not the rules of the international organization. It is only in exceptional cases, most notably the EU, that the organization's rules and decisions are directed at individuals and confer on them rights and duties. A more recent practice of the UN Security Council's resolutions contains provisions directly addressed to individuals. This is particularly the case with resolutions managing specific conflicts, as well as resolutions combating the terrorist activities of groups and individuals. This special practice of the UN Security Council is analyzed in more detail below.[165]

---

[163] For details see infra, Sect. 4.9.1.

[164] For details see infra, Sect. 4.9.2.

[165] See infra, Sect. 2.9.3.

1.10.4.5 Amendments to the Constitution of an International Organization

Another kind of law-making are amendments to an organization's constitution. Such amendments are often adopted by a decision of the plenary organ, or, depending on an organization's amendments' rules, by a special state conference. As a general rule, which stems from the principle of state sovereignty, amendments only enter into force after all states have ratified the treaty amending the constitution, even if they have already unanimously or by a qualified majority consented to them in the plenary organ. However, many organizations require only ratification by (usually a qualified) majority. For example, Article 108 of the UN Charter provides that amendments take effect when two-thirds of the UN General Assembly have consented, and when two-thirds of the member states have ratified it. The amendments thus also apply to member states that have not consented to it. In some organizations, the amendments do not apply to non-consenting states. This is pragmatic but at the same time may lead to fragmentation within an organization's legal order.

1.10.4.6 Drafting of Treaties Within an International Organization

Treaty drafting within international organizations is also a kind of law making even though the adoption of a draft by the plenary organ of an organization is formally a mere recommendation to the member states to ratify it. De facto, however, drafts may have an impact on the member states' conduct as they would be in force.[166] The CoE's Parliamentary Assembly and Committee of Ministers, e.g., have drafted numerous treaties. Similarly, the UN and the ILO have also drafted many treaties, some more successful than others in being ratified by a majority of member states. Particularly important are the treaties prepared by the International Law Commission, a special organ of the UN General Assembly, and subsequently adopted by the UN General Assembly which then recommends member states to ratify them. These drafts are sometimes applied by courts as expressions of customary international law.

A few organizations allow member states to contract out or opt out of some legally binding legislation. This is e.g. the case for the WHO[167] and the ICAO.[168] Their legal acts or an agreement adopted by the member states may become binding for all member states without the need for a unanimous consent or ratification by the member states. However, in such cases states can make a unilateral declaration that they will not be bound by such decisions (opting out) or by an agreement

[166] Such treaties do not belong to the internal law of the organization but are merely treaties that have been created in the organization's committees.

[167] Art. 59, International Health Regulations.

[168] Art. 38, Convention of international Civil Aviation.

(contracting out). A state can in this way declare a law to be non-binding for itself although the law is binding on the rest of the member states. The reason for doing so are often conflicts with as state's internal law and political difficulties to change the national provisions in conflict with the organization's new binding rule.

1.10.4.7 Limits to Law-Making; Domaine Réservé

International organizations have only limited law-making powers. Apart from the explicit rules in an organization's constitution regulating its law-making powers, one obvious limit is *jus cogens* norms, i.e. peremptory norms. According to Article 53 VCLT

> *"a peremptory norm of general international law is a norm accepted and recognized by the international community of States as a whole as a norm from which no derogation is permitted and which can be modified only by a subsequent norm of general international law having the same character."*

This applies not only to treaties but to legal acts at large, i.e. international or national acts. Therefore, international organizations cannot make laws that infringe these norms. Such law would be null and void.

In addition, organizations may only enact such laws that are compatible with the organization's goals and purposes. Law-making that falls outside these goals and purposes could lead to acts *ultra vires*. International organizations further have to observe the principle of sovereignty, even in times of ever-increasing interdependencies, and therefore respect the subsidiarity principle in their law-making and in exercising their competences. According to this principle, the competences and regulations of the organization should not go further than what is required, broadly understood, to fulfill its purposes so as to ensure that the autonomy of member states is duly respected.

Part of this autonomy to be respected is the so-called *domaine réservé*, i.e. the powers that are *pure domestic matters* and therefore *beyond the realm of international interventions*. To the domaine réservé belongs, e.g., a state's internal administrative structure, the organization of its administration, and usually also how its political system is regulated.[169] General international law acknowledges that certain subject matters are exclusively for states to regulate. In particular, Article 2(7) of the UN Charter protects member states from such interventions.[170] Resolutions or decisions of an international organization infringing the *domaine réservé* are null and void and simply not applicable to the member states. Thus, in their activities, in

[169]This is the case as long as these regulations observe international minimum requirements regarding human rights and popular political participation.

[170]However, it has been argued that Art. 2(7)'s limiting effects are shrinking; cf. Alvarez (2006).

particular norm-setting ones, the international organization always needs to ascertain what belongs to the *domaine réservé*.

This is the traditional view, but only one perspective. Another perspective is that international organizations are created exactly for the purpose of *internationalizing certain national competences*, i.e. to limit or remove certain responsibilities previously exclusive to the member states. Pertinent examples are human rights and environmental issues, but also social problems or implementing democratic standards in national political systems. In recent times, the *domaine réservé* has therefore shrunken more and more as a result of international organizations' expanding norm-setting capacities.[171] The UN's practice, in particular, has led to this shift. That said, it is still common practice for states to expressly reserve some of their domestic competences in the founding treaties of some international organizations. This is almost always the case for issues concerning national security.

1.10.5 The Impact of the Law of International Organizations on the Domestic Legal Order

What is the impact of the law of international organizations on the domestic legal order? This inter alia depends on the *rank of international law in the domestic legal system*: As better as international law and henceforth the law of international organizations as part of it is integrated in the domestic legal system, the higher usually is its impact in a state. However, international organizations usually do not and cannot regulate the position of their legal order in the legal system's hierarchy of their member states as the states would consider this as an illegitimate intervention into their constitutional system. The main concern of international organizations is that their rules and decisions *are properly implemented and observed*. The place of the norms enacted by international organizations in domestic legal systems is therefore regulated by member states' specific constitutional provisions. It is thus the domestic legal system that primarily determines how the laws of international organizations are incorporated in a state.

The norms of international organizations often create rights and obligations of member states and sometimes for individuals, corporations and civil society organizations, too. Member states' rights and duties are usually regulated in the treaties establishing organizations, i.e. in an organization's primary law. But secondary law, too, may establish entitlements and obligations, but not only of the member states but also of individuals such as human rights obligations of states and the respective rights of the individuals. The execution of these rights and obligations needs participation by state institutions. It depends on the concrete norms whether and to which extent implementation by the member states of norms of international organizations in their national legal and political systems is required. Very often, national

[171] For a discussion on this, see Wood et al. (1993), 553 ss.

implementation is crucial for the effectiveness of some of an international organization's laws and recommendations. Here, too, is it up to the member states to decide on how to give effect to these norms in their national legal systems.

An easy way to give norms of an international organization domestic legal effect is *to allow direct application by state authorities and courts*. Whether this is possible depends also on whether a state has a dualist or monist system as to the in relation between national and international law, i.e. whether the state applies the adoption or transformation theory.[172] In the dualist theory, any international law requires a special national act transforming international to national law and integrating it into the domestic legal system whereas under adoption theory no such special transformation is required as international law simply becomes part of the national law.

Well, as has already been mentioned, norms created by international organizations are usually only directed towards states. There is a presumption that these norms are not self-executing and thus not directly applicable to individuals or companies but need to be implemented by the national legislator. In order that they become legally enforceable, the member states are obligated to make the appropriate domestic legal adjustments as a consequence of their membership. Thus, very often, a transformation is required also in countries that follow the monist theory. In these countries, it depends on the interpretation of an organization's norm at stake whether it is fit for direct application or not.

All this is different with supranational organizations such as the EU. They have the power to make directly applicable laws. Such laws do not require national implementation but become part of the national legal order immediately as a member states of a supranational organizations has to allows the direct applicability of supranational norms.

For international organizations with the power to make directly applicable laws, it is essential to distinguish between norms that are self-executing and those that are not. Whether a norm is self-executing or not depends on the will of the organization as norm creator. When they are self-executing, states must ensure their general priority over any conflicting present or future national law. Otherwise, the state may be in breach of its membership duties, as it would end up not implementing the organization's regulations in its national legal order. All this does not necessarily amount to a general supremacy of the inter- or supranational organization's laws in the national legal order; in most states, international law such as treaties does not enjoy general supremacy.

EU law differs also on this point. The ECJ has expressly stated already in the *ENEL* case that EU law enjoys supremacy over national law as a consequence of its supranational character.[173] The laws of other organizations would theoretically also

[172] According to the transformation theory, international norms are transferred into the national legal order by the creation of parallel norms of municipal law. The adoption theory applies domestically directly the international norm without transforming it into the national legal order.

[173] ECJ, *Case 6/64, Costa v. Enel*, ECR 585 (1964), para. 593.

enjoy supremacy over national law if the organization in question had the power to make binding laws upon its member states, but such power is still the exception. If a member state does not respect this supremacy, it is violating its membership duties, which can lead to sanctions.

1.11 Interpretation of the Law of International Organizations

1.11.1 Preliminary Remarks

Constituent instruments of international organizations are usually treaties. The VCLT contains general rules for treaty interpretation in its Articles 31–33. These rules of interpretation also apply to their founding instruments, as stated in Article 5 VCLT. In addition, there are specific rules that have been developed in the practice of international organizations and courts which are widely used to interpret the international organizations' constituent instruments. These rules take into account that legal instruments establishing an institution are a living and constantly developing body. They thus allow a more expansive, evolutionary interpretation of an international organization's constitution. The sovereignty of member states plays no general role when it comes to interpretation.

1.11.2 VCLT: Textual Approach and Teleological Interpretation

Every interpretation starts with the text. Therefore, article 31 VCLT states that a treaty is to be interpreted

> *in good faith in accordance with the ordinary meaning to be given to the terms of the treaty in their context and in the light of its object and purpose.*

In this provision, the textual approach is combined with the contextual as well as the teleological interpretation method. Article 32 VCLT provides for recourse to be made to supplementary modes of interpretation, including the "preparatory work of the treaty and the circumstances of its conclusion" to determine the object and purpose of a provision. Also, the preamble can be used to determine the goals of the constitution and to interpret the provisions in that light.

The teleological method of interpretation is particularly important. This method interprets a treaty in light of the goals of the organization and has served as the basis for a dynamic interpretation of treaties establishing international organizations, taking into account that international organizations are dynamic, living institutions.

In that sense, the teleological method is not only focused of the goal to be achieved by a particular provision but follows also a *holistic approach* by taking account of the institutional context and the organization's purpose at large.

1.11.3 Special Interpretation Rules

There are some special doctrines and rules for interpreting founding treaties that have developed just because of the fact that founding treaties create an institution, i.e. a living organism with its own dynamics. These rules are not contained in the VCLT but are deduced from the teleological interpretation,

One is the so-called *"effet utile" doctrine* which originally has been developed by the ECJ. 'Effet utile' is the French term for 'convenient effect' (literally), better known as the *principle of effectiveness*, meaning that the interpretation of a treaty provision has to suit the intended purpose of the concerning treaty in the best possible way. As a dynamic interpretation method, it allows to construe provisions and powers of an organization and its organs in a way to adapt to changing needs and circumstances. In the ICJ judgment of Fisheries Jurisdiction Case (Spain v Canada), ICJ affirmed this method: *"The Court was addressed by both Parties on the principle of effectiveness. Certainly, this principle has an important role in the law of treaties and in the jurisprudence of the Court……"* In his dissenting opinion to the advisory opinion on the international status of South-West Africa, Judge de Visscher made it clear that, that *"This rule is particularly applicable to the interpretation of a text of a treaty of a constitutional character like the United Nations."*

Other doctrines to interpret founding instruments and to construe powers of an organization not explicitly mentioned in the founding documents are the already mentioned *doctrines of implied powers and inherent powers.*[174] Implied powers refer to those *powers that are not explicitly mentioned, but which are required to enable the organization to perform its functions*. Inherent powers are powers that are neither explicit nor implied but *emanate from the international legal personality of an international organization.*[175]

1.11.4 The Impact of Norm Hierarchy

There is also the hierarchy of norms regulating the activities of international organizations which needs to be taken into consideration when interpreting the law. This means that secondary law should be interpreted in light of primary law, so that the secondary law is also in conformity with the organization's constitutional law. Other

[174] See supra, Sect. 1.9.3.

[175] See also supra, Sect. 1.9.3.

factors to be considered when interpreting norms of an international organization are general international law, general practices and general principles of international law. If, e.g., a provision of an organization's constitution mentions the right of self-determination or sovereignty of states, then these notions are to be interpreted in conformity with their understating in international legal doctrine and practice.

1.11.5 Authority of Interpretation

States in their quality of mere members have no authority to interpret an international organization's law in a generally binding way; only the organization's organs have this authority and responsibility. When disputes as to interpretation occur, the organization's rules will establish how the dispute is to be resolved. It can either be settled politically by an organ or sometimes by adjudication or on the basis of an advisory opinion. Adjudication is the main method to settle interpretation disputes in the EU where the CJEU has very broad respective powers. The ICJ may upon request by an organ of the UN render advisory opinions also in interpretation disputes.

In some organizations the constituent instruments vest organs with the *explicit power to make authoritative interpretations that are legally binding*. An example is Article XXIX of the IMF Agreement on interpretation. Article XXIX(a) provides that *"[any] question of interpretation of the provisions of this Agreement arising between any member and the Fund or between any members of the Fund shall be submitted to the Executive Board for its decision"*. Also, the WTO's Ministerial Conference and the General Council have this power with regard to the WTO agreements.[176]

Somewhat different is the situation as to the UN General Assembly which has made several interpretations of the UN Charter's articles. The most important is the UN Declaration of Friendly Relations,[177] which sets out fundamental norms for the relations between states. These declarations are not authoritative interpretations of Charter provisions because the General Assembly lacks formally this power. Nonetheless, these interpretations by the UN General Assembly sometimes have arguably led to de facto amendments of the UN Charter without invoking the normal rules of treaty amendments.

If there are no concrete rules as to how to decide on controversies regarding the interpretation of an international organization's law, it is most probably up to the *highest organ, the General Assembly, to make a political decision*.

[176] Art. IX (2) WTO Agreement.

[177] *Declaration of Principles of International Law concerning Friendly Relations and Cooperation among States in accordance with the Charter of the UN*, A/RES/2625 (XXV) (1970).

1.12 Other Aspects

1.12.1 Funding of International Organizations

International organizations primarily rely on annual contributions by their members to finance their activities. The membership fees are usually calculated based on the size of the state's populations and/or its economic strength based on the state's gross national product (GNP). Quite often, states also make voluntary contributions to support the organization's activities.

The evaluation of the states' financial strength for the purpose of determining membership fees may sometimes lead to problems. Since voting power is usually equal between states, some states consider it unfair to pay higher membership fees than others. Financially powerful states have consequently sometimes tried to gain more political influence over the organization. A example is the US which accounts for 22% of the UN budget. The US, for many years failed to pay their complete UN membership fee, and during the 1990s President Clinton managed lower the US' debt to the UN and to get a reduction of the assessment rate ceiling from 25% to 22%. The US has also caused financial crises to the ILO and the UNESCO by temporarily exiting the organizations.

Another way of financing international organizations is to take loans available on the capital markets. This is done, e.g., by the institutions of Bretton Woods. Member states are not directly liable for payments on the loans as long as this is not required by the loan conditions, and there exists an agreement with member states. Organizations may also finance themselves through their own resources. The EU finances itself through custom duties, though of the general value added tax (VAT) and member states' contributions based on the gross national income, which have become the largest source of the EU budget. The IMF and the World Bank finance themselves by charging for the services they offer. The World Intellectual Property Organization (WIPO) charges fees for registrations of patents.

The expenses that international organizations incur include the lease or rent of offices, salaries, travels, office equipment and infrastructure, its publications, communication and IT services. International organizations sometimes spend a lot of resources on special projects such as peacekeeping, fact-finding missions and special envoys.

References

Alvarez JE (2006) International organizations as law-makers. Oxford University Press, Oxford

Amerasinghe CF (2005) Principles of the institutional law of international organizations, 2nd edn. Cambridge University Press, Cambridge

Armstrong D (1982) The rise of the international organisation: a short history. Palgrave Macmillan, London

Beetz JP, Rossi E (2017) The EU's democratic deficit in a realist key: multilateral governance, popular sovereignty and critical responsiveness. Transnatl Leg Theory 8(1):22–41. https://doi.org/10.1080/20414005.2017.1307316

Bellamy R (2017) A European Republic of Sovereign States: sovereignty, republicanism and the European Union. Eur J Polit Theory 16(2):188–209. https://doi.org/10.1177/1474885116654389

Bloed A (1993) The Conference on Security and Co-operation in Europe: analysis and basic documents, 1972–1993. Kluwer Law International, Dordrecht

Blum YZ (1992a) UN membership of the "New" Yugoslavia: continuity or break? Am J Int Law 86(4):830–833

Blum YZ (1992b) Russia takes over the Soviet Union's seat at the United Nations. EJIL 3:354–362

Blum YZ (2007) Was Yugoslavia a Member of the United Nations in the years 1992–2000? Am J Int Law 101(4):800–818

Boas G et al (eds) (2012) International criminal justice. Edward Elgar, Cheltenham

Bono M (2023) The dark side of the BRICS: the lack of a legal definition. Opinio Juris Comparatione 1(1):464–487. https://www.opiniojurisincomparatione.org/wp-content/uploads/2023/12/13.-Bono1.pdf. Accessed 8 Mar 2025

Brand RA (1976) Security council resolutions: when do they give rise to enforceable legal rights: the United Nations Charter, the Byrd Amendment and a self-executing treaty analysis. Cornell Int Law J 9(2):298–317

Brölmann CM et al (eds) (2018) Special issue: exiting international organizations. Int Organ Law Rev 15(2):243–263. https://doi.org/10.1163/15723747-01502001

Butler WE (ed) (2009) On the history of international law and international organization: collected papers of Sir Paul Vinogradoff. Lawbook Exchange, Pennsylvania

Çakmak C (2017) A brief history of international criminal law and international criminal court. Palgrave Macmillan, New York

Cassese A (2012) The legitimacy of international criminal tribunals and the current prospects of international criminal justice. Leiden J Int Law 25(2):491–501. https://doi.org/10.1017/S0922156512000271

Closa C (ed) (2017) Secession from a Member State and withdrawal from the European Union. Cambridge University Press, Cambridge

Coughlan A (2004) Nation, state sovereignty and the European Union: some democratic principles. Studies: an Irish. Q Rev 93(369):33–43

Darcy S (2015) Retaliation and reprisal. In: Weller M (ed) The Oxford handbook of the use of force in international law. Oxford University Press, pp 886–891

De Hoon M (2017) The future of the international criminal court: on critique, legalism and strengthening the ICC's legitimacy. Int Crim Law Rev 17(4):591–614

De Ville F (2012) European Union regulatory politics in the shadow of the WTO: WTO rules as frame of reference and rhetorical device. J Eur Public Policy 1(5):700–718

Debuf E (2016) Tools to do the job: the ICRC's legal status, privileges and immunities. Int Rev Red Cross 97(897/898):319–344

Dee M (2015) The European Union in a multipolar world: world trade, global governance and the case of the WTO. Palgrave Macmillan, Basingstoke

Elrod RB (1976) The concert of Europe: a fresh look at an international system. World Polit 28(2):159–172

Falk RA (2007) The costs of war: international law, the UN, and world order after Iraq. Routledge, New York

Fassbender B (2009) The United Nations Charter as the constitution of the international community. Martinus Nijhoff, Leiden

Giegerich T (2020) Retorsion. In: Max Planck encyclopedias of international law. Oxford University Press, Oxford

Gifkins J (2012) The UN Security Council divided: Syria in crisis. Glob Responsibility Protect 4(3):377–393

Greer S (2008) What's wrong with the European Convention on Human Rights? Hum Rights Q 30(3):680–702
Helfer LR (2008) Redesigning the European Court of Human Rights: embeddedness as a deep structural principle of the European human rights regime. EJIL 19(1):125–129
Henkin L (1999) Kosovo and the law of "humanitarian intervention". Am J Int Law 93(4):824–828
Huysmans M (2019) Enlargement and exit: the origins of Article 50. Eur Union Polit 20(2): 155–175
International Administrative Law Centre of Excellence (2016) Internal Justice Systems of International Organisations Legitimacy Index 2016. https://rm.coe.int/internal-justice-systems-of-international-organisations-legitimacy-ind/16808b35a1. Accessed 9 Mar 2025
Islami I, Istrefi R (2018) Consolidation of statehood through membership in the UN: some remarks on Kosovo, democracy and international law. Rev Central East Eur Law 43(3):331–349
Ivaldi G (2018) Contesting the EU in times of crisis: the Front National and politics of Euroscepticism in France. Politics 38(2):278–294
Javits JM (2013) Internal conflict resolution at international organizations. ABA J Labor Employ Law 28(2):223–253
Jovanovic V (1997) The status of the Federal Republic of Yugoslavia in the United Nations. Fordham Int Law J 21(5):1719–1736
Klabbers J (2009) The United Nations Charter as the constitution of the international community. Int Organ Law Rev 6(2):667–673
Knapton EJ (1941) Historical revision no. XCVIII: the origins of the Treaty of Holy Alliance. History 26(102):132–140
Kock K (1969) International trade policy and the GATT 1947–1967. Almqvist & Wiksell, Stockholm
Krasner SD (ed) (1983) International regimes. Cornell University Press, Ithaca
Kratochvíl P, Sychra Z (2019) The end of democracy in the EU? The Eurozone crisis and the EU's democratic deficit. J Eur Integr 41(2):169–185
Krisch N (1999) Unilateral enforcement of the collective will: Kosovo, Iraq, and the Security Council. In: von Bogdandy A, Wolfrum R (eds) Max Planck Yearbook of United Nations Law, vol 3. Brill Nijhoff, Leiden, pp 59–103
Lentner GM (2019) The UN Security Council and the international criminal court: the referral mechanism in theory and practice. Edward Elgar, Cheltenham
Mangone GJ (1954) A short history of international organization. McGraw-Hill, New York
McGoldrick D (2004) From '9-11' to the 'Iraq War 2003': international law in an age of complexity. Hart, Oxford
McGoldrick D et al (eds) (2004) The permanent international criminal court: legal and policy issues. Hart, Oxford
Müller JW (2016) The EU's democratic deficit and the public sphere. Curr Hist 115(779):83–88
Osiander A (2001) Sovereignty, international relations, and the Westphalian myth. Int Organ 55(2): 251–287
Paolini AJ et al (eds) (1998) Between sovereignty and global governance: the United Nations and world politics. Palgrave Macmillan, Houndmills
Pirro ALP, Van Kessel S (2018) Populist Eurosceptic trajectories in Italy and the Netherlands during the European crises. Politics 38(3):327–343
Reinalda B (2009) Routledge history of international organizations: from 1815 to the present day. Routledge, London
Reinisch A (2008) The immunity of international organizations and the jurisdiction of their administrative tribunals. Chinese J Int Law 7(2):285–306
Reinisch A (2009) International organizations before national courts. Cambridge University Press, Cambridge
Reinisch A, Weber UA (2004) In the shadow of Waite and Kennedy – the jurisdictional immunity of international organisations, the individual's right of access to the courts and administrative tribunals as alternative means of dispute settlement. Int Organ Law Rev 1(1):59–110

Roach SC (2013) Legitimising negotiated justice: the international criminal court and flexible governance. Int J Hum Rights 17(5–6):619–632
Santhanam K et al (2003) Iraq War 2003: rise of the new 'unilateralism'. Institute for Defense Studies and Analyses, New Delhi
Singh N (1958) Termination of membership of international organisations. Praeger, London
United Nations Department of Peacekeeping Operations (2003) Handbook on United Nations multidimensional peacekeeping operations. United Nations, New York
Visoka G (2018) Acting like a state: Kosovo and the everyday making of statehood. Routledge, New York
Vitucci MC (2006) Has Pandora's box been closed? The decisions on the legality of use of force cases in relation to the status of the Federal Republic of Yugoslavia (Serbia and Montenegro) within the United Nations. Leiden J Int Law 19(1):105–127
Walling CB (2013) All necessary measures: the United Nations and humanitarian intervention. University of Pennsylvania Press, Philadelphia
Wheeler NJ (2000) Reflections on the legality and legitimacy of NATO's intervention in Kosovo. Int J Hum Rights 4(3–4):144–163
White ND (2006) The ties that bind: the EU, the UN and international law. Netherlands Yearb Int Law 37:57–107
Wood MC (1997) Participation of Former Yugoslav States in the United Nations and in multilateral treaties. Max Planck Yearb United Nations Law 1:231–257
Wood DP et al (1993) Theme IV roundtable: the internationalization of domestic law: the shrinking domaine réservé. Proc ASIL Annual Meeting 87:553–575
Yoo J (2003) International law and the war in Iraq. Am J Int Law 97(3):563–576
Young AR (2012) Less than you might think: the impact of WTO rules on EU policies. In: Costa O, Jørgensen KE (eds) The influence of international institutions on the EU. Palgrave Macmillan, Basingstoke, pp 23–41
Zweifel TD (2002) …Who is without sin cast the first stone: the EU's democratic deficit in comparison. J Eur Public Policy 9(5):812–840

Selected Bibliography

International Organizations in General

Archer C, Marsden L (2015) International organizations, 4th edn. Routledge, London
Barkin SJ (2013) International organization: theories and institutions, 2nd edn. Palgrave Macmillan, Hampshire
Boas G et al (eds) (2012) International criminal justice: legitimacy and coherence. Edward Elgar, Cheltenham
Boisson de Chazournes L (2017) Interactions between regional and universal organizations: a legal perspective. Brill Nijhoff, Leiden
Boisson de Chazournes L (2016) Relations with other international organizations. In: Cogan JK et al (eds) The Oxford handbook of international organizations. Oxford University Press, Oxford, pp 691–711. https://doi.org/10.1093/law/9780199672202.003.0032
Cogan JK et al (eds) (2016) The Oxford handbook of international organizations. Oxford University Press, Oxford
Davies M, Woodward R (2014) International organizations. Edward Elgar, Coventry
David É (2016) Droit des Organisations Internationales. Bruylant, Bruxelles
Delanty G (ed) (2017) Routledge handbook of cosmopolitan studies. Routledge, London
Devin G (2016) Les organisations internationales, 2nd edn. U Science Politique, Paris
Dixon M (2007) Textbook on international law, 6th edn. Oxford University Press, Oxford

Do Nascimento e Silva GE (1978) Privileges and immunities of permanent missions to international organizations. German Yearb Int Law 21:9–26
Dupuy RJ (1998) Manuel sur les organisations internationales – a handbook on international organizations, 2nd edn. Martinus Nijhoff, Dordrecht
Fassbender B (2009) The United Nations Charter as the Constitution of the International Community. Martinus Nijhoff, Leiden
Fassbender B (1986) Die Völkerrechtssubjektivität internationaler Organisationen. Österreichische Zeitschrift für öffentliches und internationales Recht 37:17–49
Fisher K (2008) Handbook on international organisations. Springer, Berlin
Sinclair GF (2017) To reform the world: international organizations and the making of modern states. Oxford University Press, Oxford
Hurd I (2020) International organizations: politics, law, practice, 4th edn. Cambridge University Press, Cambridge
Karns MP, Mingst KA (2015) International organizations: the politics and processes of global governance, 3rd edn. Lynne Rienner, Boulder
Kirton JJ (ed) (2009) International organization. Routledge, London
Klabbers J (2015a) The transformation of international organizations law. EJIL 26(1):9–82
Klabbers J (2015b) Advanced introduction to the law of international organizations. Edward Elgar, Cheltenham
Lagrange É, Sorel JM (eds) (2013) Droit des organisations internationales. LGDJ, Paris
MacKenzie DC (2010) A world beyond borders: an introduction to the history of international organizations. In: International themes and issues, vol 1. University of Toronto Press, Toronto
Meng W (1979) Das Recht der internationalen Organisationen: eine Entwicklungsstufe des Völkerrechts. Nomos, Baden-Baden
Mràzek J (2018) The responsibility of international organizations. Czech Yearb Int Law 9:171–196
Pease KKS (2011) International organizations, 5th edn. Routledge, New York
Peters A (2011) The constitutionalisation of international organisations. In: Walker et al (eds) Europe's constitutional mosaic. Oxford University Press, Oxford, pp 253–285
Rama-Montaldo M (1970) International legal personality and implied powers of international organizations. Br Yearb Int Law 44:111–155
Reinalda B (ed) (2013) Routledge handbook of international organization. Routledge, London
Reinisch A (2008) The immunity of international organizations and the jurisdiction of their administrative tribunals. Chinese J Int Law 7(2):285–306
Reinisch A, Weber UA (2004) In the shadow of Waite and Kennedy – the jurisdictional immunity of international organisations, the individual's right of access to the courts and administrative tribunals as alternative means of dispute settlement. Int Organ Law Rev 1(1):59–110
Reuter P (1972) Institutions internationales, 7th edn. Thémis, Paris
Rittberger V et al (2019) International organization, 3rd edn. Red Globe Press, London
Ruffert M, Walter C (2015) Institutionalized international law. C.H. Beck, Baden-Baden
Sands P, Klein P (2009) Bowett's law of international institutions, 6th edn. Sweet & Maxwell, London
Scharf MP, Williams PR (2013) The law of international organizations: problems and materials, 3rd edn. Carolina Academic Press, Durham
Schermers HG, Blokker NM (2018) International institutional law, 6th edn. Brill Nijhoff, Boston
Shaw MN (2021) International law, 9th edn. Cambridge University Press, Cambridge
Trifunovska S (2018) The law of international organizations: documents and cases, 3rd edn. Eleven International Publishing, The Hague
Weiss TG, Wilkinson R (2023) International organization and global governance, 3rd edn. Routledge, London

White ND (2017) The law of international organisations, 3rd edn. Manchester University Press, Manchester
Wood MC (1997) Participation of Former Yugoslav States in the United Nations and in multilateral treaties. Max Planck Yearbook of United Nations Law 1:231–257
Yi-Chong X, Weller P (2018) The working world of international organizations: authority, capacity, legitimacy. Oxford University Press, Oxford

International Organizations: Specific Issues

Abbott KW et al (2015) International organizations as orchestrators. Cambridge University Press, Cambridge
Álvarez JE (2017) The impact of international organizations on international law. Brill Nijhoff, Leiden
Anderson S (2007) EU, NATO, and CSCE responses to the Yugoslav crisis: testing Europe's new security architecture. Eur Secur 4(2):328–353
Bailes AJK (2006) The politico-military dimension of OSCE. Helsinki Monitor 17(3):214–225
Barros AS (2017) International organizations and Member State responsibility: critical perspectives. Brill Nijhoff, Leiden
Block-Lieb S, Halliday TC (2017) Global lawmakers: international organizations in the crafting of world markets. Cambridge University Press, Cambridge
Blokker N, Schrijver N (eds) (2015) Immunity of international organizations. Brill Nijhoff, Leiden
Boisson De Chazournes L, Sands P (eds) (1999) International law, the International Court of Justice and nuclear weapons. Cambridge University Press, Cambridge
Bolton J, Holbrooke R (2008) Reforming the United Nations. Brown J World Aff 14(2):11–21
Borchardt KD (1987) European unification: the origins and growth of the European community, 2nd edn. Office for the Official Publications of the European Communities, Luxembourg
Bortloff J (1996) Die Organisation für Sicherheit und Zusammenarbeit in Europa: eine völkerrechtliche Bestandesaufnahme. Drucker & Humblot, Berlin
Bossong R, Hegemann H (eds) (2015) European civil security governance: diversity and cooperation in crisis and disaster management. Palgrave Macmillan, London
Brand RA (1976) Security council resolutions: when do they give rise to enforceable legal rights: the United Nations Charter, the Byrd Amendment and a self-executing treaty analysis. Cornell Int Law J 9(2):298–317
Brownlie I (1998) The rule of law in international affairs – international law at the fiftieth anniversary of the United Nations. Springer, Netherlands
Cabranes JA (1978) Reflections on the Belgrade Meeting (1977–78) of the Conference on Security and Cooperation in Europe. Yale Stud World Public Order 4:274–290
Cannizzaro E, Palchetti P (2011) Ultra vires acts of international organizations. In: Klabbers J, Wallendahl J (eds) Research handbook on the law of international organizations, Cheltenham, pp 365–397
Chan S (2017) Plural international relations in a divided world. Polity Press, Cambridge
Charnovitz S (2006) Nongovernmental organisations and international law. Am J Int Law 100(2): 348–372
Chayes A, Chayes AH (1995) The new sovereignty: compliance with international regulatory agreements. Harvard University Press, Cambridge
Cornish P (1996) European security: the end of architecture and the new NATO. Int Aff 72(4): 751–769
Crawford J (2019) Brownlie's principles of public international law, 9th edn. Oxford University Press, Oxford
Crawford J (2006) The creation of states in international law, 2nd edn. Clarendon Press, Oxford
Da Conceição-Heldt E et al (eds) (2015) Internationale Organisationen: Autonomie, Politisierung, interorganisationale Beziehungen und Wandel. Nomos, Baden-Baden

Deen-Racsmany Z (2000) A redistribution of authority between the UN and regional organizations in the field of the maintenance of peace and security? Leiden J Int Law 13(2):297–331

Droesse G (2020) Membership in international organizations: paradigms of membership structures, legal implications of membership and the concept of international organization. T.M.C. Asser Press, The Hague

Döll B (1967) Völkerrechtliche Kontinuitätsprobleme bei internationalen Organisationen. De Gruyter, Berlin

Fenaux R (1978) The Transnational Family of Associations (INGOs) and the new world order. Transnatl Assoc 30(4):192–199

Ferstman C (2017) International organizations and the fight for accountability: the remedies and reparations gap. Oxford University Press, Oxford

Freeman J (1991) Security and the CSCE process: the Stockholm conference and beyond. Palgrave Macmillan, London

Fukuda-Parr S (2004) Millennium development goals: why they matter. Glob Gov 10(4):395–402

Furtak FT (2015) Internationale Organisationen: Staatliche und nichtstaatliche Organisationen in der Weltpolitik. Springer VS, Wiesbaden

Galbreath DJ (2007) The Organization for Security and Co-operation in Europe. Routledge, London

Gasbarri L (2017) The dual legality of the rules of international organizations. Int Organ Law Rev 14(1):87–119

Gazzini T (2001) NATO coercive military activities in the Yugoslav Crisis (1992–1999). EJIL 12: 391–435

Gold J (1996) Interpretation: the IMF and international law. Kluwer Law International, Boston

Goldberg AJ (1979) The Belgrade conference and international human rights. National Black Law J 6(2):179–182

Harsch MF (2015) The power of dependence: NATO-UN cooperation in crisis management. Oxford University Press, Oxford

Hartwig M (1993) Die Haftung der Mitgliedstaaten für internationale Organisationen. Springer, Berlin

Henig R (2010) The league of nations. Haus Publishing, London

Henkin L (1999) Kosovo and the law of "humanitarian intervention". Am J Int Law 93(4):824–828

Hénon S et al (2014) The changing role of NGOs and civil society in financing sustainable development. OECD Development Co-operation Report:109–119

Higgins JR (1997) The reformation in international law. In: Rawlings R (ed) Law, society and economy: centenary essays for the London School of Economics and Political Science 1895–1995. Yale University Press, Oxford, pp 125–145

Hollis S (2015) The role of regional organizations in disaster risk management. Palgrave Macmillan, London

Job BL (2004) The UN, regional organizations, and regional conflict: is there a viable role for the UN? In: Price RM, Zacher MW (eds) The United Nations and global security. Palgrave Macmillan, New York, pp 217–243

Kaufman JP (2002) NATO and the former Yugoslavia: crisis, conflict, and the Atlantic alliance. Rowman & Littlefield, Lanham

Keck ME, Sikkink K (1998) Activists beyond borders: advocacy networks in international politics. Cornell University Press, Ithaca

Kelsen H (1950) The law of the United Nations: a critical analysis of its fundamental problems. Stevens & Sons, London

Killham EL (1984) The Madrid CSCE conference. World Aff 146(4):340

Klabbers J (2016) Theorizing international organizations. In: Orford A, Hoffmann F (eds) The Oxford handbook of the theory of international law. Oxford University Press, Oxford, pp 618–634

Kolb R (2010) An introduction to the law of the United Nations. Hart, Oxford

Kratochvíl P, Sychra Z (2019) The end of democracy in the EU? The Eurozone crisis and the EU's democratic deficit. J Eur Integr 41(2):169–185
Krisch N (1999) Unilateral enforcement of the collective will: Kosovo, Iraq, and the Security Council. In: von Bogdandy A, Wolfrum R (eds) Max Planck Yearbook of United Nations Law, vol 3. Brill Nijhoff, Leiden, pp 59–103
Lachowski Z (2004) Confidence- and security-building measures in the new Europe. Oxford University Press, Oxford
Liskofsky S (1979) The Belgrade conference. Am Jewish Year Book 79:152–159
Liskofsky S (1978) Human rights: from Helsinki to Belgrade. Am Jewish Year Book 78:121–145
Lodgaard S (1987) The Stockholm CSBMs and the future of the CDE. Arms Control 8(2):155–168. https://doi.org/10.1080/01440388708403865
Magliveras KD (2015) Legal aspects of competition between international organizations. In: Jalloh CC, Elias O (eds) Shielding humanity: essays in international law in honour of Judge Abdul G. Koroma. Brill Nijhoff, Leiden, pp 242–260
Marro P-Y (2021) Rechtsstellung internationaler Organisationen: Grundlagen und Grenzen ihrer Sonderstellung. Dike Verlag, Zürich
Martens K (2003) Examining the (non-)status of NGOs. Indiana J Glob Leg Stud 10(2):1–24
McGoldrick D et al (eds) (2004) The permanent international criminal court: legal and policy issues. Hart, Oxford
Niezen R, Sapignoli M (eds) (2017) Palaces of hope: the anthropology of global organizations. Cambridge University Press, Cambridge
Olonisakin F (1996) UN co-operation with regional organizations in peacekeeping: the experience of ECOMOG and UNOMIL in Liberia. Int Peacekeeping 3(3):33–51
Paliwal S (2010) The primacy of regional organizations in international peacekeeping: the African example. Virginia J Int Law 51(1):185–230
Pataut É (2015) Les Organisations Internationales et le Droit International Privé: Droit International Privé Universel et Droit International Privé Régional. In: Vellano G (ed) Il Futuro delle Organizzazioni Internazionali: Prospettive Giuridiche = L'Avenir des Organisations Internationales: Perspectives Juridiques: XIX Convegno, Courmayeur, 26–28 giugno 2014. Editoriale Scientifica, Naples, pp 501–514
Patel BN (2013) Responsibility of international organizations towards other international organizations: law and practice of the United Nations, the World Bank, the European Union (EU) and the International Atomic Energy Agency (IAEA). Eastern Book Company, Lucknow
Perry V, Keil S (2013) The OSCE Mission in Bosnia and Herzegovina: testing the limits of ownership. Nationalities Papers 41(3):371–394
Peters C (2016) Praxis internationaler Organisationen – Vertragswandel und völkerrechtlicher Ordnungsrahmen. Springer, Berlin
Ragazzi M (ed) (2013) Responsibility of international organizations: essays in memory of Sir Ian Brownlie. Brill Nijhoff, Leiden
Ritsch FF (1970) Origins of the Council of Europe: Part one: the post-war unity movements to the Hague Congress. Il Politico 35(1):69–94
Ruffert M (2000) Zuständigkeitsgrenzen internationaler Organisationen im institutionellen Rahmen der internationalen Gemeinschaft. Archiv des Völkerrechts 38(2):129–168
Rühle M (2013) Reflections on 9/11: a view from NATO. In: Hallams E et al (eds) NATO beyond 9/11: the transformation of the Atlantic alliance. Palgrave Macmillan, London, pp 54–66
Ryngaert C (2015) The responsibility of Member States of international organizations: concluding observations. Int Organ Law Rev 12(2):502–517
Ryngaert C et al (eds) (2016) Judicial decisions on the law of international organizations. Oxford University Press, Oxford
Saksena KP (1974) The United Nations and collective security. D. K. Publishing House, Delhi
Sato C (2004) Immunität internationaler Organisationen. Schriften zum internationalen und zum öffentlichen Recht, vol 53. Peter Lang, Frankfurt a. M

Schmalenbach K (2004) Die Haftung internationaler Organisationen: im Rahmen von Militäreinsätzen und Territorialverwaltungen. Kölner Schriften zu Recht und Staat, vol 18. Peter Lang, Frankfurt a. M
Shestack A (1978) The economics of nonprofit institutions: studies in structure and policy. Oxford University Press, Oxford
Sica M (1996) The role of the OSCE in the former Yugoslavia after the Dayton Peace Agreement. Helsinki Monitor 7(2):5–12
Sidhu WPS (2020) Regional organizations. In: Weiss TG, Daws S (eds) The Oxford handbook on the United Nations, 2nd edn. Oxford University Press, Oxford, pp 345–362
Simma B (1999) NATO, the UN and the use of force: legal aspects. EJIL 10(1):1–40
Simma B et al (2024) The Charter of the United Nations - a commentary, 4th edn. Oxford University Press
Spandler K (2020) UNAMID and the legitimation of global-regional peacekeeping cooperation: partnership and friction in UN-AU relations. J Intervention Statebuilding 14(2):187–203
Sperling J, Webber M (2017) NATO and the Ukraine crisis: collective securitisation. Eur J Int Secur 2(1):19–46
Suter D (2015) The Shanghai Cooperation Organisation. A Chinese practice of international law. Schulthess Juristische Medien AG, Zürich
Szasz P (1998) The law on economic sanctions. In: Schmitt MN, Green LC (eds) International law studies, vol 71. Naval War College, Newport, pp 455–481
Tertrais B (2016) Article 5 of the Washington Treaty: its origins, meaning and future. Research paper no. 130, NATO Defense College, Rome
Thomas DC (2001) The Helsinki effect: international norms, human rights, and the demise of communism. Princeton University Press, Princeton
Van Den Bossche P, Zdouc W (2017) The law and policy of the World Trade Organization, 4th edn. Cambridge University Press, Cambridge
Villiger ME (2009) Commentary on the 1969 Vienna Convention on the Law of Treaties. Martinus Nijhoff, Leiden
Virzo R, Ingravallo I (eds) (2015) Evolutions in the law of international organizations. Brill Nijhoff, Leiden
Walling CB (2013) All necessary measures: the United Nations and humanitarian intervention. University of Pennsylvania Press, Philadelphia
Walter C (2009) Regional arrangements and the United Nations Charter. In: Wolfrum R (ed) Max Planck encyclopedia of public international law. Oxford University Press, Oxford
Webb P (2014) Treaties and international organizations: uneasy analogies. In: Tams C et al (eds) Research handbook on the law of treaties. Edward Elgar, Cheltenham, pp 255–275
Weiss N (2009) Kompetenzlehre internationaler Organisationen. Springer, Dordrecht
Willetts P (2011) Non-governmental organizations in world politics. Routledge, Abingdon
Wessel RA, Dekker IF (2015) Identities of states in international organizations. Int Organ Law Rev 12(2):293–318
Wood M (2014) Do international organizations enjoy immunity under customary international law? Int Organ Law Rev 10(2):287–318
Yi-Chong X, Weller P (2018) The working world of international organizations: authority, capacity, legitimacy. Oxford University Press, Oxford
Zaum D (ed) (2013) Legitimating international organizations. Oxford University Press, Oxford

Chapter 2
United Nations

2.1 Before the Establishment of the League of Nations: The Heydays of National Sovereignty

2.1.1 Old Alliances, Kant's Perpetual Peace Concept and the European Peace Conferences

2.1.1.1 Kant's Peace Concept

Securing and maintaining global peace has always been pivotal in international relations. Since the Peace of Westphalia international law as well as international relations have been traditionally centered on issues referring to war and peace. One of the solutions to secure peace is to establish an international institution for that purpose. This is an idea with a very old tradition. Already alliances in Ancient Greece, the Hanseatic League of Low German merchants (from thirteenth century to seventeenth century) and the Old Swiss Confederation (from fourteenth century to eighteenth century) were (also) based on that idea. After the late Medieval Times and before the modern times, there was already a quest for an organization that had clear powers to sanction and coerce to create and uphold peace and stability.[1]

Among all the doctrinal ideas for a world organization during this period, Immanuel Kant's idea expressed in his work entitled 'Toward Perpetual Peace' (Zum ewigen Frieden) of 1795 was the most influential as to the idea to establish a political world organization. Kant pointed out that there are two conditions of state between nations: the natural state and the civilized state. The reign of force dominates the former, while the reign of law directs the latter. To change from a natural to

---

Special thanks to He Jiawei and Steven Rüttimann for their important contribution to the elaboration of this chapter.

---

[1]For more details, see Kolb (2010), p. 1 s.

U. Saxer, *The Law of Global and European Organizations*, Springer Textbooks in Law, https://doi.org/10.1007/978-3-032-00067-5_2

civilized state and to have reign of law between nations, the best solution is to establish a world government. However, this goal is difficult to realize. An alternative is to form an alliance, namely the 'Community of the States' in which the rule of law takes the place of the rule of force. All states are required to settle controversies in a peaceful manner, based on legal rules. Though Kant does not give a precise description of the power distribution and the structure of such a kind of World confederation, this idea was at the origin of the League of Nations after the end of World War I.

2.1.1.2 The Impact of Sovereignty; First International Organizations

Kant's developed this concept almost 150 years after the peace of Westphalia in 1648 which put an end to the Thirty Years' War and which was the birth hour of the sovereignty concept, conceived earlier by French jurist Jean Bodin.[2] After the peace of Westphalia, organizational political structures made a shift from a power system based on a hierarchy of personal feud relations headed by a sovereign king or ruler to a more general and more abstract state-based system. Sovereignty as a quality of states, not as a quality of a ruler, was a main principle in the relations between nations and ensured that every state was treated equally and possessed large autonomy. This conception of sovereignty included - although not explicitly mentioned in the Westphalian peace treaties—the option for states to go to war (ius ad bellum). War was therefore a licit method for a state to advance its interest. There were thus two aggregation states between nations: War or Peace. Hence, the title of Hugo Grotius' masterwork which established for the first time a system of legal rules applicable between sovereign states was *"De iure bellis ac pacis"*. This so-called classical understanding of the Law of Nations persisted until the Vienna congress in 1815. Following the Vienna congress, the Law of Nations—since the mid-nineteenth century also dubbed "international law"—underwent some elementary changes, thus turning into what we nowadays understand under the expression, namely a traditional body of legal rules applicable to the relations between nations regulating coexistence and cooperation between these nations based on a traditional understanding of the principle of sovereignty.

The nineteenth century was very sovereignty-oriented. *Ius ad bellum*, the sovereign right to resort to war remained dominant. Since the state has the 'absolute power' (Hegel), wars were not only allowed but also necessary so as to meet the national interest. States were entitled to switch freely from peace to war, for 'war is a continuation of policy by other means'(Clausewitz).[3] Thus, Kant's idea of a

[2] Kant I (1795) Zum ewigen Frieden: Ein philosophischer Entwurf. Originally published in 1795; Bodin J (1576) Les Six Livres de la République. Originally published in 1576.

[3] Hegel GWF (1820) Elements of the Philosophy of Right, §331–340. Originally published in 1820; Clausewitz C (1832) On War. Originally published in 1832.

community of states based on the rule of law had no impact on the political and legal realities in Europe and in the world.

Nonetheless, for very practical reason, in the course of the nineteenth century, increasingly institutions were created by the states with the purpose to deal with foremost technical issues of common concern. Such organizations were, e.g. the International Telecommunication Union (1865) or the Universal Postal Union (1874) which both had a mere technical purpose and no political mandate.[4] Both are now United Nations specialized agencies. As part of this process of institutionalization, also the conception in international law started to move modestly from the perception of 'legal coexistence' to 'legal cooperation'.

2.1.1.3 European Conferences as Precursors of International Organization; the Road to the League of Nations

In contrast, matters of war and peace were not handled in the framework of an institution, but politically at European conferences organized and attended by the important European powers which assumed the power to decide on the shape of Europe. These congresses of the nineteenth century, like the 1814–1815 Vienna Congress, the 1856 Paris Congress, and the 1878 Berlin Congress were devoted to setting up rules to balance the powers, to regulate the outcome of wars in the common European interest, and to prevent states going to war whenever possible. The 'Concert of Europe System' laid solid foundation for what later became real international organizations devoted to the concept of 'collective security'. However, these *congresses lacked permanent institutions*. Moreover, the principle of unanimity made it even harder to respond efficiently and effectively to political crises. Admittedly, the temporary peace maintained was to a large extent derived from a balance-of-power system based on alliances. The system may make states think twice before they start a war, but it may, at the same time, enlarge the scale of war.

In the nineteenth century, international law applied foremost to a *club of states consisting of the European, American and only some African and Asian states*, not to other state entities. *Colonialism and Imperialism* had just arrived at their peaks, leaving no place on the map unclaimed. With the beginning of WWI, this old, Europe-centered order broke down. The end of the Great War, as World War I was labelled at that time, gave an important impulse to reorganize the international system. 1919 saw the signing of the peace treaties of Versailles which formally ended the war. In addition to the documents declaring the end of war, the agreements also included the *Covenant of the League of Nations*, thus officially establishing the League.[5] The establishment of the League was a consequence of the steady

---

[4] See supra, Sect. 1.2.2.3.

[5] The term 'League of Nations' goes back to an essay by Immanuel Kant 'Idee zu einer allgemeinen Geschichte in weltbürgerlichen Absicht' (1784) where Kant advocated the establishment of a League of Nations.

institutionalization of international relations. The League of Nations was a special case insofar as it was the *first international organization devoted to international security* and thus the *first international organization with a genuine political purpose* whereas the organizations established earlier had non-political, technical purpose. The most important and persistent supporter of the idea of a League were the United States which then, however, did not become a member state because of the U.S. Senate's refusal to give its consent.

Thus, there was a consent shared by both the ordinary people suffered most in the outrageous war and the elites like politicians and diplomats that a *political World Organization on the basis of collective security* should be set up. The League of Nations, conceived in Paris Peace Conference in 1919 and formally established in 1920 according to *the Treaty of Versailles*, marked the birth of the first world organization for political matters, having some power of coercion.

2.1.2 The Concept of Collective Security

One of the basic issues in international relations is how to secure international peace and stability in an anarchic world of sovereign states seeking foremost their own benefit and security. To have rules designed to guide states' conduct does not suffice. Required are institutions with the purpose to secure peace and stability. Already Kant developed the idea of an organized state system based on the rule of law and securing peace. The League of Nations was the first attempt to create such an organization. It was the *first time that a collective security system was created.*

The concept of collective security is to be distinguished from alliances as a well-known phenomenon in the history of international law. Alliances are usually based on treaties between states which seek to advance common goals, in particular common security and stability goals in the framework of the alliance. Collective defense alliances are a subgroup of alliances. These are arrangements, usually formalized by a treaty which establishes a common structure, among participating *states that commit to militarily support the defense of a member state if it is attacked by another state outside the organization.* A good example is NATO.[6] Modern defense alliances are created to exercise the right to collective self-defense as enshrined in Article 51 of the UN Charter. The idea is that this has a deterrent effect against potential aggressors because an *attack against an alliance member amounts to an attack against all the members of the alliance.*

Collective security arrangements are different. These are usually treaty-based and often international organizations in which the *participating states cooperate collectively to provide security for all by their common actions against any states within or outside the security arrangement which might challenge the existing order by using force.* Collective security is to be understood as an instrumental "...*proposition that*

[6]For derails see infra, Sect. 3.5.

aggressive and unlawful use of force by one nation against another will be met by the combined strength of all nations. All will co-operate in controlling a disturber of the peace. They will act as one for all and all for one. Their combined strength will serve as a guarantee for the security of each."[7] It is a measure to disincentivize warfare or a threat thereof by the threat of or by taking actions against any member of the institution by the entire institution. Compared to defense alliances, collective security is more ambitious in that it seeks to encompass the *totality of states within a region or indeed globally*, and to address a wide range of possible threats to security and provide for dispute settlement mechanisms. Instead of using force should the *states use the methods of the settlement of disputes and available as part of the collective security system.* This is the main difference to collective defense systems. This idea was already generally reflected in the 14 points of US President, Woodrow Wilson, principal driving force behind the League of the Nations.[8]

Collective security systems have thus the following features: (1) Limits on national sovereignty, in particular as to national defense, as security issues are partly discussed and decided within an international institutions; (2) a common institution established by states and concerned with peace and security between them; (3) legal limitations or a ban of the unauthorized use of force in the relations between states; (4) the will of the institution and the member states to identify an aggressor and to enforce the limitations or the prohibition to use force also by military means (collective sanctions); (5) dispute settlement mechanisms as part of the security system and available to states to find ways for an amicable solutions of their controversies and tensions. Hence, the collective security organization becomes an arena for diplomacy, balance of power and exercise of soft power instead of using hard power. The use of force by states, unless legitimized by the Collective Security organization, is considered illegitimate, reprehensible and calls for remediation of some kind. The success of a collective security system, however, largely depends on the extent to which is supported by the member states.

[7] Saksena (1974), p. 4 s.

[8] Wilson, *Fourteen Points,* Speech to the United States Congress, 8 Jan 1918; Henig (2010), p. 15 ss.

2.2 The League of Nations as First Collective Security Organization

2.2.1 Goals, Organs and Fundamental Features of the League of Nations

2.2.1.1 Establishment, Goals

The League of Nations was established in 1920. Its constitution, the Covenant of the League of Nations, was signed on 28 June 1919 as Part I of the Treaty of Versailles, and it became effective with the entire Versailles Treaty on 10 January 1920. As is stated in the Covenant, the major task of the organization is to *"promote international co-operation and to achieve international peace and security."*[9] In pursuit of this goal, the League set up three main organs and series of rules on which the system of peaceful settlement of disputes and collective security rested. These three main organs of the League were: the Assembly, the Council and the Secretariat.[10] In addition, the Permanent Court of International Justice (PCIJ) was established as well as some special organizations such as the International Labour Organization and countless agencies and commissions. Furthermore, the League called a number of other bodies into life in order to ensure particular missions.

2.2.1.2 Assembly

The Assembly was the plenary organ, which could address *"any matter within the sphere of action of the League or affecting the peace of the world."* (Article 3(3) LoN Covenant). It consisted of up to three representatives of every member state which together held one vote in the Assembly.[11] Its main function was to coordinate the League's business on a legislative level, discussing and deciding issues such as the admission of new permanent and non-permanent members to the Council, budget management and the election of judges for the Permanent Court of International Justice (in cooperation with the Council). Usually taking place at the Leagues Head Office in Geneva, the Assembly typically met once a year or additionally upon request of a member state, if approved by the majority of member votes. Each member state had one vote. For the Assembly to make non-binding 'recommendations', and 'resolutions' *unanimity* was required.[12] To decide procedural issues, a majority of votes was sufficient.

[9] Preamble, LoN Covenant.

[10] Art. 3 LoN Covenant.

[11] Art. 3(3) LoN Covenant.

[12] Art. 5(1) LoN Covenant.

2.2.1.3 Council

Second most important organ of the LoN was the Council. Being the executive body of the League and handling the legislative directives of the Assembly, the Council was formed through four permanent[13] as well as four non-permanent members which were elected to office on a tri-annual cycle. The number of non-permanent seats has later been increased four times to a total of 11 seats. The Council met several times a year - nearly every other month—totaling in 107 sessions in the time between 1920 and 1939. Although the executive character of the Council may imply differently, the tasks of the Council and the Assembly were similar. In general, both organs were authorized to handle any matter concerning the League's peace-related tasks. However, both shared the problematic concept of unanimity in their decision-making process: Like in the Assembly, the Council's decisions required unanimity even when they were non-binding.[14] Only *"matters of procedure at the meeting of Assembly or of the Council, including the appointment of Committees to investigate particular matters……may be decided by a majority of the Member of the League represented at the meeting"* (Article 5(2) LoN Covenant). The idea behind unanimity was that the League did not seek solutions by dictate but by consensus, thus respecting the principle of state sovereignty.

2.2.1.4 Secretariat

The Secretariat, based in Geneva, completed the three main organs of the LoN. Its purpose was the administrative management of the League under the lead of the General Secretary. Focused on the preparation of the Council's and Assembly's agenda, the Secretariat was in charge of the political, financial and legal framework of the League.

2.2.1.5 Permanent Court of International Justice (PCIJ)

In addition to these organs, it is noticeable that the Permanent Court of International Justice, though operated as an independent organ, had strong ties with the League. States had no obligation to submit disputes to the PCIJ, the Council did, however, encourage the states to solve problems in a legal way instead of using military force.

[13] These permanent members were the representatives of the Principal Allied and Associated Powers of WW 1; Art. 4 (1) LoN Covenant.

[14] Art. 5(1) LoN Covenant.

2.2.2 The League of Nation's System of Collective Security

The Covenant of the League of Nations established the first institutionalized system of collective security. It further introduced a procedure of peaceful conflict management and ultimately the possibility of calling upon sanctioning measures by declaring in Article 11(1) LoN Covenant that:

> *"Any war or threat of war, whether immediately affecting any of the Members of the League or not, is hereby declared a matter of concern to the whole League, and the League shall take any action that may be deemed wise and effectual to safeguard the peace of nations [..]"*

Although warfare was not completely banned under the Covenant of the League of Nations, it was effectively limited when the Covenant of the LoN was put into action. The *ius ad bellum*, i.e. the right to go to war, was constrained to very limited situations because of the imposition of the legal restraints in Article 12 et seq. LoN Covenant. The logic of it was that no war is allowed without meeting certain procedural requirements set by the League. This included procedures before resorting to war and institutionalized decision-making as main features of the League's system of collective security.

Core provision was Article 12 LoN Covenant which stated the following: "*The Members of the League agree that, if there should arise between them any dispute likely to lead to a rupture they will submit the matter either to arbitration or judicial settlement or to enquiry by the Council, and they agree in no case to resort to war until three months after the award by the arbitrators or the judicial decision, or the report by the Council. In any case under this Article the award of the arbitrators or the judicial decision shall be made within a reasonable time, and the report of the Council shall be made within six months after the submission of the dispute.*"

The Council would contribute to a settlement of the dispute through a recommendation.[15] If such an endeavor failed to solve the dispute, because e.g. one party to the disputes disagreed, the Council could make and publish a report containing the facts and the recommendations about the problem.[16] If the report was unanimously agreed by the members other than the disputed parties, war was prohibited.[17] If the report failed to gain unanimous agreement without counting the disputed parties, the parties could resort to war three months after the report.[18] The three months were set as buffer time to enable the parties to cool off in the hope no war would occur. Furthermore, this was connected with the option to impose sanctions as part of the collective security system. Article 16 Covenant states: "*Should any Member of the League resort to war in disregard of its covenants under Article 12, 13 or 15, it shall*

---

[15] Art. 15(3) LoN Covenant,

[16] Art. 15(4) LoN Covenant.

[17] Art. 15(6) LoN Covenant.

[18] Art. 15(7) in conjunction with Art. 12(1) LoN Covenant.

ipso facto be deemed to have committed an act of war against all other Members of the League." An aggressor could face embargoes and even military sanctions on the recommendation of the Council. These mechanisms went hand in hand with the Leagues main task of promoting international cooperation and achieving international peace and security, as stated in the preamble to the Covenant.

2.2.3 Why the League of Nations System of Collective Security Failed

The system of collective security established by the LoN Covenant was very innovative at that time. It was unique as there were absolutely no precursors. In addition, it had an important impact on shaping the UN system of collective security established after WW 2. As will be explained[19] the organizations share the main purpose, i.e., the maintenance of peace and security. In addition, the main organs are the same: a plenary organ (Assembly), an executive organ with only some members ([Security] Council), and an administrative Secretariat.[20] However, the League's system of collective security was a failure because it contained some basic deficiencies which were largely eliminated by the drafters of the UN Charter.

2.2.3.1 No General Ban on Wars

First, the Covenant of the League did not offer a general ban on wars.[21] Instead, it demanded all parties of the disputes to go through peaceful settlement and 3-months period to cool off. The assumption that states would observe a cool-off period was not realistic and did not sufficiently take into account the dynamics of severe conflicts between state at the brink to war. The UN Charter, after the catastrophe of WW 2, made a historic step by prohibiting war in general (Article 2(4) UN Charter). The use of military force should simply not anymore be a method available to states in case of tensions with other states. The only exceptions to the total ban on wars are self-defense and authorization by the UN Security Council.[22]

---

[19] See infra, Sect. 2.5.2.

[20] For more details, see Kolb (2010), p. 10 s.

[21] It was the Briand-Kellogg-Pact of 1928, i.e. the General Treaty for Renunciation of War as an Instrument of National Policy that banned wars of aggression generally. In this agreement, the states promised not to use war to resolve "disputes or conflicts of whatever nature or of whatever origin they may be, which may arise among them".

[22] See more: Dixon (2007), p. 312 ss.

2.2.3.2 Limited Membership

Another problem was the limited membership of the LoN. One of the most innovative ideas of American President Wilson in his Fourteen Points on the post-war order was the establishment of a world organization guarding peace under a collective security system. Paradoxically, USA, as a main promoter, did not join the League due to the disapproval by the U.S. Senate. Though the membership of the League reached its peak during 1937 till 1938, it never enjoyed universality. Japan and Germany withdrew from the League in 1933, and Italy in 1937. Japan and Italy started wars at that time which were clearly illegal. The USSR, another great power at that period, enjoyed membership only from 1934 to 1939. There were altogether 17 countries that withdrew from the League. Lacking universalism and the lacking support of powerful states, the League was deemed to fail in face of many challenges to world peace and security. In contrast, the UN accomplished almost universality in its membership.

2.2.3.3 Unanimity Requirements in the Decision-Making

A further, basic problem was the unanimity requirement in the decision-making of the organs of the LoN. This was, before the establishment of the LoN, the usual practice at international political conferences and in intergovernmental organizations, and therefore it was also the rule in the League's decision-making.[23] The principle protected national sovereignty almost absolutely and gave de facto each member state a veto power. An efficient conflict management by an international institution is under such circumstances extremely difficult and confined to internationally uncontested cases. The problem was and is however, that instances giving rise to decisions of a collective security system are often very contested. On contrary, in terms of UN, only a two-thirds majority in the General Assembly is demanded for decisions on special issues while a simple majority vote is required for decisions on other matters.[24] In the Security Council, the affirmative vote of 9 out of 15 members is required with only the permanent members of the UN (USA, UK, France, Russia, China) vested with a veto power.

Another problem was that the state representatives in the organs of the LoN, in particular the Council were *not* permanently present in Geneva and therefore not prepared for an immediate respond to threat to peace or breach of peace. Rather, the Council met for four ordinary sessions annually before 1928, while met only three sessions after that. On contrary, the Security Council requires permanent representative of its member states to gather in New York. In addition, have the power to be kept pace of the latest information about certain region or crisis with the assistance of the Secretariat. Moreover, the LoN Council could not make binding decisions but

[23] Art. 5 LoN Covenant.

[24] Arts. 18, 27, 67 and 89 UNCh.

only recommendations in case a state started a war.[25] This is completely different in the UN. The Charter gives the Security Council in Chapter VII the power to make decisions and to impose sanctions as well as any other measures in resolutions binding all the member states.

2.2.3.4 Unclear Distribution of Powers Between the Assembly and the Council

A further problem was the very unclear distribution of powers between the Assembly and the Council of the LoN as to peace and security. One example were the parallel functions on issues relating to maintaining peace of both, the Assembly, which had in addition to peace and security many other policy fields to cover and to monitor, and the Council. This could lead to either contradicting, different decisions from each of the two organs, or the 'buck-passing' condition. Under the UN Charter as well, the General Assembly and the Security Council have some parallel powers relating to peace and security. However, there is a clear distribution of power in the UN insofar that it is mainly the Security Council which is as the executive organ responsible for any matter relating the threat or breaches of the peace (Article 24 of the Charter), in particular as to the management of concrete conflicts[26] and may make binding resolutions including sanctions while the General Assembly may discuss issues of peace and security generally and has no power to make binding decisions in concrete conflicts.

2.2.3.5 Decentralized System of Sanctions

Finally, the LoN system of sanctions was decentralized, contrary to the system under the UN Charter. Though Article 16(1) of the Covenant provided seemingly 'automatic' economic sanctions like the severance of all trades or financial relations against an aggressor, it were the individual states instead of the Council that had the ultimate right of decision on an embargo against the aggressor. Hence, likewise, though Article 16(2) adds that *"It should be the duty of the Council ......to recommend to the several Governments concerned what effective military, naval or air force......shall contribute to the armed force"* to punish the aggressor, it were in the very end the states that had the ultimate say as to whether the conditions for use of force were fulfilled and whether they were to follow the recommendation by the Council. All in all, the economic and military coercion powers laid in the hands of individual states. They made their unilateral assessment of a situation or a conflict and decided on the measures to be individually taken by them. As a result, the League could not fulfill its role in banning wars with its non-binding procedures and

[25] Art. 16 LoN Covenant.

[26] Chapters VI and VII UNCh.

decisions. In comparison, the Security Council of UN has the centralized power to impose binding measures on the aggressor and all the member states are obliged to execute these measures.[27]

The complicated and non-binding system of collective security of the League therefore failed before World War II and then totally collapsed. The most important reason for the failure of the League, however, was the lack of support by the great powers as to the peaceful settlement of conflicts and collective security measures. Giving priority to their own national interest, states did not hesitate to withdraw or simply knock the system down when the League restricted their political goals. Nazi Germany, Japan and Italy withdrew from the League one after another in pursuit of their aggressive ambition. The USSR, likewise, simply withdrew from the League when its invasion in Finland could arouse blame in the League. Even UK and France, the pillars of the League, turned to the policy of appeasement to ensure their own safety and 'illusion' for peace. The dismissal of the League may be best illustrated by the word of Sir Winston Churchill: *"a failure of the nations of the League more so than a failure of the League of the Nations."*[28]

In 1946, a resolution carried out by the Assembly finally declared the dismissal of the 'shell organization.' Thus, the first attempt in human history to build an ambitious political world organization aiming at maintaining peace and security failed.

2.2.4 Achievements of the League of Nations

2.2.4.1 Special Organizations and Agencies

Despite all this, there were also important achievements by the League. The League made great contributions in economics, social, health, labor and other technical areas, foremost through its special organizations and agencies. These included the International Labour Organizations, the Disarmament Commission, the Health Organization, the Mandates Commission, the International Commission on Intellectual Cooperation (precursor to UNESCO), the Permanent Central Opium Board, the Commission for Refugees, and the Slavery Commission. Other important achievements were the Mandate System and the system protecting minorities.

2.2.4.2 Mandate System

The Mandate System applied to former colonies of the German Empire and to many territories of the former Ottoman Empire. Its legal basis was Article 22 of the Covenant of the League of Nations:

---

[27] Cf. Arts. 25 and 41 UNCh.

[28] Churchill (1948), p. 108.

> *To those colonies and territories which as a consequence of the late war have ceased to be under the sovereignty of the States which formerly governed them and which are inhabited by peoples not yet able to stand by themselves under the strenuous conditions of the modern world, there should be applied the principle that the well-being and development of such peoples form a sacred trust of civilisation and that securities for the performance of this trust should be embodied in this Covenant. The best method of giving practical effect to this principle is that the tutelage of such peoples should be entrusted to advanced nations who by reason of their resources, their experience or their geographical position can best undertake this responsibility, and who are willing to accept it, and that this tutelage should be exercised by them as Mandatories on behalf of the League …*

The basic idea was an international, institutionalized responsibility for these territories as "a sacred trust of civilization" to develop the peoples inhabiting these territories until they were able to govern themselves or attain another chosen status. The mandate status rested on the *principle of non-annexation of the Mandate territories* and was also designed to prevent any colonialist-type of exploitation of the peoples in the mandated territories. The idea was exactly not to simply transfer these territories from one colonial power to another, but to *prepare the peoples of these territories for self-government* and, in the very end, self-determination even though the LoN Covenant did not provide for a right to self-determination. Thus, developed states should, as mandatory powers, be responsible for the inhabitants and act in the best interest of the inhabitants based on agreements concluded between these states and the League of Nations. There were three different types of mandates: *A mandates* were established over territories formerly belonging to the Ottoman Empire which had reached a stage where they could be provisionally recognized as independent states but needed some help to get full independence. *B mandates* were installed over the former German colonies in Africa which were quite far away to govern themselves. The *C mandates* referred to territories for which it was considered to be the best that they were administered as integral part of the mandatory power but nonetheless would have a special, internationalized status. The treaties concluded between the metropolitan states and the League of Nations established the legal status as a mandate and contained constitution-like provisions such as minority rights clauses and the right of petition. The mandatory powers were accountable to the League of Nations, were controlled by the organization's organs and had regularly to report to them.

The mandate system was a precursor of the UN trusteeship system and was followed by the successful decolonization activities of the UN under the umbrella of the right of self-determination as one of the most important rights granted by the UN Charter which led to the establishment of more than one hundred new states. From a legal point of view, the mandate system was interesting as it internationalized status issues of many territories. It made their status an international concern, thus limiting the sovereignty of the mandatory powers in the interest of the international community as well as of these territories' inhabitants.

2.2.4.3 Minority Rights Protection

National minority protection occupied a very prominent place on the League's activities. As part of the agreements concluded after World War I to regulate the political outcome of the war, in particular territorial and other status issues, a system of the protection of minorities was established. That system was mainly built on bilateral and multilateral treaties, mostly concluded between the victorious Allied Powers and states newly established as the result of the dismemberment of the Austrian and the Ottoman Empires. The creation of these states was monitored by the Paris Peace Conference, and formal recognition of these states was made dependent on the ratification of minority treaties by these states as a precondition of their collective recognition. The reason for this was that there were important national and other minorities in these states as well as in other states due to territorial changes. The status of these minorities was considered to be an international concern because their discrimination and other kinds of unjust treatment could become a *potential source of regional conflicts and adversely affect the stability of these new states*. There were not only bilateral and multilateral treaties but also unilateral declarations by some states.[29] Multilateral treaties were concluded between the Allied Powers and Poland, Czechoslovakia, the Kingdom of Serbs, Croats and Slovenes, Greece, Romania and Turkey. Bilateral treaties included the Austrian–Czechoslovak treaty and the German-Polish Accord on East Silesia.

Minority protection was in substance above all a *prohibition of discrimination of persons belonging to minorities*. This was carried out by establishing in the treaties that all nationals shall be equal before the law in areas such as the right to life, personal liberty and free exercise of any creed, religion or belief and shall enjoy the same civil and political rights without distinction as to race, language or religion. Thus, the regulations did not really grant group rights to minorities but foremost *individual rights to persons belonging to minorities*. Other provisions referred to the right to use a minority's language and the entitlement of primary school instructions in minority languages.

All these provisions were insofar important as they *internationalized the relation between the affected states and parts of their inhabitants by setting normative limits to national sovereignty* which was then considered to protect against any international interventions in the relations between a state and its inhabitants. At that time, the concept of international human rights standards did not exist yet. The rights established in the minority protection treaties were, however, precursors of the human rights declarations and treaties concluded after World War II.

Observance and implementation of the minority treaties was controlled by the organs of the League of Nations. Thus, the League performed a function typical for international organizations: *to monitor treaty compliance by member states*. As part of this, the League introduced a petition procedure. Members of minorities as well as groups and associations representing minorities could claim in petitions that their

---

[29] Such unilateral statements were made by Albania, Latvia, Lithuania, Bulgaria, and Greece.

rights under a minority protection arrangement were violated by a state. These complaints were first handled by the Minority Section of the LoN Secretariat. The Secretariat then tried a mediation. The main organ responsible for monitoring compliance was, however, the Council which established a special committee of three which had to decide on complaints or to submit the issue to the Council for decision. Moreover, each member of the Council had the right to bring to the Council's attention any infraction, or any danger of infraction, of a treaty provision. Finally, any Council member could refer a case to the Permanent Court of International Justice.

This too was an important innovation in international law because for the first time individuals as well as Civil Society institutions gained access to an international institution to protect their rights against a state. This scheme was a precursor to the international human rights protection mechanisms established after World War II, in particular under the Optional Protocol of the International Covenant on Civil and Political Rights (ICCPR) of 1966.

In sum, the Minority Rights Protection System was a milestone in the evolution of international law and the law of international organizations and certainly one of the most important legacies of the League.

2.3 The Establishment and Development of the United Nations

2.3.1 The Path to the Establishment of the UN

2.3.1.1 The Atlantic Charter and the Moscow Conference

The first phrase in establishing the UN started with the Atlantic Charter, on August 14th, 1941 declared jointly by American President Roosevelt and British Prime Minister Churchill. In point 8 of the Atlantic Charter, the course was set to achieve the *"establishment of a wider and permanent system of general security"*.[30] Though at that time, the League of Nations had not dissolved yet, it was widely accepted that a stronger collective security system should be established. Less than half a year later, a total of 26 governments signed *The Joint Declaration by United Nations* in Washington on D.C on January 1, 1942 which endorsed the Atlantic Charter at the Arcadia Conference in January of 1942 in Washington. Created as a formal outline of the Atlantic Charter, the Declaration came to be the basis of the UN as we know it today. Greatly associated with the idea of general security is Franklin D. Roosevelt's foreign affairs policy of a 'One-World' concept. Therein Roosevelt highlighted the need for cooperation of all nations to achieve global peace and socioeconomic growth.

[30] Atlantic Charter, 14 Aug 1941; Churchill (1950), p. 602 s,

At the Moscow Conference in 1943, the four nations USA, UK, USSR and China reached a consensus that the League should be replaced. *The Moscow Declaration* pointed out *"the necessity of establishing at the earliest practicable date a general international organization, based upon the principle of sovereign equality of all peace-loving states, large and small, for the maintenance of international peace and security."*[31]

2.3.1.2 Dumbarton Oaks and Yalta Conference

At the subsequent Dumbarton Oaks Conference, held from August to October in 1944, the *Proposals for the Establishment of a General International Organization*[32] were adopted on October 9, 1944. Though criticized by many small countries, the proposal was indeed a great compromise while *"the more lofty ideas, like utopian versions of the world government, had disappeared, while another, more pragmatic, tendency, like regional agencies to preserving peace, prevailed."*[33] It covered almost all the important points in the Charter we see today. However, it was not until the *Yalta Compromise* when the foundation of the UN was completed. Special mention should be made to the agreement on the veto power of the permanent members of the Security Council, for it had been highly disputed at the previous conference. Moreover, two of the republics of the USSR - the Ukraine and Byelorussia- enjoyed separate membership, though they were not 'sovereign state'. This was a compromise to relieve Stalin from the doubt that USSR may be isolated by the majority vote of the western States.

2.3.1.3 San Francisco Conference

The founding conference took place in San Francisco from April 24th to June 25th in 1945, when the wars in Europe were over while the battles in Asia and Pacific were still marching to the closing stage. Several amendments approved, the UN Charter was unanimously adopted on its penultimate plenary on June 25, 1945, sponsored by USA, UK, USSR and China[34] and signed by 50 participating nations without reservation.[35] The United Nations officially came into existence on 24 October 1945, when the Charter was ratified by all the powerful allies of World War II

[31] Moscow Conference: Joint Four-Nations Declaration (1943).

[32] These Proposals outlined the structure, purposes, and functions of what would become the United Nations, focusing on maintaining international peace and security, developing friendly relations among nations, achieving international cooperation, and being a center for harmonizing the actions of nations.

[33] Simma et al. (2024), p. 16 s.

[34] France refused to join the sponsoring governments for not being invited to Yalta.

[35] Poland signed the Charter in Washington on 15 Oct 1945, as the 51st member State.

including the permanent five (USA, UK, France, USSR and China). United Nations Day is celebrated on 24 October each year.

2.3.2 *Basic Features of the United Nations*

The United Nations was established as an international organization committed to maintaining international peace and security, developing friendly relations among nations and promoting social progress, better living standards and human rights. It started with 51 Member States and has now 193 members, covering almost all the countries in the world. Due to its universal membership, the UN can take action on a wide range of issues. It has six main organs: the General Assembly, the Security Council, the Economic and Social Council, the Secretariat, the Trusteeship Council (suspended now), and the International Court of Justice. The United Nations System also contains many specialized agencies, funds and programs, touching every corner of the globe. Although best known for peacekeeping, peace-building, conflict prevention and humanitarian assistance, the Organization also works on a broad range of fundamental issues, from sustainable development, environment and refugees protection, disaster relief, counter terrorism, disarmament and non-proliferation, to promoting democracy, human rights, gender equality and the advancement of women, governance, economic and social development and international health, clearing landmines, expanding food production, and more, in order to achieve its goals and coordinate efforts for a safer world for this and future generations. All this was the result of important historical developments which will be highlighted under the aspect of the main goal of the UN - to secure international peace and security.

2.3.3 *Cold War (1945–1953)*

2.3.3.1 Beginning of the Cold War

The common will and collaboration of the great powers is a prerequisite for peace and security of the world. It was expected that the permanent five of the Security Council would continue to bear this responsibility together after World War II. However, the once united Allies soon separated by two groups, namely the socialist group of countries under the leadership of the USSR and the western group pf countries headed by the U.S.A. This was the beginning of the so-called Cold War. By 1949, the disunity between the East and the West resulted in many vetoes in the Security Council, leaving many decisions aborted, many duties untaken. The UN Security Council could only function when there was no clash of interest, for example, unanimity in the Resolution to establish Israel in 1947.[36] Otherwise, the Council could not really perform. A very peculiar exception happened at the beginning of the Korean War in 1950. It was due to a temporary boycott of the Council by the USSR, protesting the UN's refusal to accept the People's Republic of China as state representing China, that the Council was able to authorize a military intervention lead by the U.S.A. in the Korean War to combat the invaders from North Korea. This was the last instance that the Security Council was boycotted by a veto power!

2.3.3.2 Uniting for Peace Resolution

The Cold War had a major impact on the UN, since it vastly jeopardized the Security Council's decision-making process through western members and the Soviet Union interposing their vetoes on respective matters. For the UN, this meant a factual loss of many of its powers as the SC requires no veto to pass binding decisions. Therefore, the UN crisis management activities were gravely jeopardized despite that the UN Charter provided as a principle and contrary to the League of Nations for majority voting. Trying to overcome this issue, the western members launched Resolution 377 of the UN General Assembly—titled 'Uniting for Peace'—which gave the General Assembly additional powers, such as the ability to make recommendations in order to maintain peace and security when the Security Council was blocked by a veto and brought the matter, in a pure, not vetoable procedural decision to the attention of the General Assembly. Arguably this resolution is difficult to reconcile with Article 12(1) of the UN Charter, providing: *'While the Security Council is exercising in respect of any dispute or situation the functions assigned to it in the present Charter, the General Assembly shall not make any recommendation with regard to that dispute or situation unless the Security Council so requests'*. The main problem is that the General Assembly as non-executive, plenary organ was not designed to conduct concrete conflict-management activities. In the meantime, however, the Uniting for Peace mechanism has been applied several times, e.g. also in the Ukraine War 2022.[37]

2.3.3.3 Human Rights Achievement of the UN

Even though the UN had struggled with its powers in early days, in particular as to its role regarding peace and security and its impact on concrete conflicts, it managed to accomplish enormous breakthroughs in international relations and politics that were of great importance for the coming decades. The *Universal Declaration of Human Rights*, adopted in 1948, the reconstruction plans of post-war Europe, or the

[36] S/RES/181 (1947).

[37] A/RES/377 A(V) (2022).

enormously important impact of the UN in the process of decolonization period are just some examples of such influence.

2.3.4 Decolonization and the Beginning of Peacekeeping Operations (PKO) (1953–1964)

The period from 1953 to 1964 witnessed a booming of the newly independent countries. Under the auspices of the UN, especially with the adoption of GA Resolution 742(VIII) in 1953 and of the *Declaration on the Granting of Independence to Colonial Countries and Peoples* in 1960,[38] more than 100 states were created from once colonized territories in Asia and Africa. Even though resolution 1514 was a mere recommendation, it had much more impact than Article 22 of the LoN Covenant which was the legally binding basis of the Mandate System. By the year 1962, 50 newly independent states had joined the UN, and an additional 50 new states until the 80ies. This was not only a push for the UN's influence in general, but also the beginning of a shift of power dominance from Western Europe to the Third World, bringing along a focus on development and human rights issues. The Third World desired to self-organize and launched the Non-Aligned Movement in 1961. It gradually became an independent and important force on the global stage.

Along with the success of the decolonization, 1953 also witnessed the end of Korean War, which was seen as a proxy war/conflict[39] between the USA and USSR as well as communist China, and the pass away of Stalin. The UN's performance in matters of peace and security improved. During the Suez Crisis (1956–1957), a UN peace-keeping troop was established around Suez and the Sinai Peninsula. This was the origin of peace-keeping operations (PKO) of the UN. The aim of these neutral troops, titled as 'Blue Helmet', is to stop hostilities and to maintain peace in troubled regions. Although they are widely accepted, PKOs have no explicit basis in the UN Charter as the power to establish them was derived from implied powers of the Charter. Likewise, in Congo from 1960 to 1964, when civil war burst out shortly after the independence of Congo from Belgium, the UN SC authorized a military enforcement to make peace in the region. Similar actions were later taken e.g. in Yugoslavia, Somalia, Rwanda, etc. However, the UN had only a subsidiary function or even no function in other crisis such as the 1956 military intervention of USSR in Hungary, and the 1962 Cuba Missile Crisis. It revealed the fact again that the UN could not fill up its responsibility whenever USSR and USA were unable to reach an agreement on the course of action to be taken in a particular conflict.

---

[38] Adopted by A/RES/1514(XV) (1960).

[39] Proxy wars are military conflicts carried out by other parties on behalf and with the backing of the main parties in conflict. In times of the Cold War, these were foremost the superpowers U.S.A. and USSR.

2.3.5 *Increasing Domination of Third World Issues (1965–1986)*

The period from 1965–1989 was still dominated by the Cold War, in which peace between the East and the West was maintained through a fragile balance of military power. Proxy Wars between the two sides were carried out around the globe, which made it difficult for the UN to have an impact, since veto powers were tied to most conflicts in some manner. In the Vietnam War from 1961–1973, e.g., the UN did not play a role since the USA and USSR were involved on opposite sides. In the Middle East Crisis, however, agreement after a period of veto vote of the two great powers endowed the UN Security Council with capacity of action. In 1967, Israel and Arab states accepted S/Resolution 242 and agreed to cease fire, with a PKO being stationed along the front line between the adversaries.

One year later, in 1968, the General Assembly approved the *Treaty on the Non-Proliferation of Nuclear Weapons,* an international treaty between the USSR, USA, UK, France and China as nuclear powers. The treaty was signed to make it for other states impossible to become nuclear powers and to promote the peaceful use of nuclear energy. There are 189 states to date who have ratified the treaty, not including India, North Korea (who opted out of the treaty in 2003), Pakistan and Israel.

The leading topic on the agenda of the UN of this phrase was, however, development. In 1967, the Group of 77, established on 15 June 1964 by developing countries at the end of the first session of the *United Nations Conference on Trade and Development (UNCTAD),* held its first Ministerial Meeting in Algiers (Algeria) on 10–25 October 1967 and adopted the *Charter of Algiers*. This largest network of developing countries provides the means for the countries of the South to articulate and promote their collective economic interests and enhance their joint negotiating capacity on all major international economic issues within the UN system. With the founding of UNDP (United Nations Development Program) and UNIDO (United Nations Industrial Development Organization), the UN gradually served as a platform for multilateral development. For a while, 80% of the UN financial resources were put in these programs.

From 1970s to 1980s, there were increasing conflicts between the developing countries and the developed countries, or 'the South and the North' within the UN. The developing countries seized every opportunity to impose their views in accordance with their national goals. This had an impact also on non-economic issues. Thus, Israel got isolated in various organs of UN by Arabian countries with the support of many developing countries. In 1974, South Africa was at the edge of expulsion from the UN due to its racial segregation policy ('Apartheid'). Under the pressure of the Third World, the General Assembly deprived South Africa of the right to attend the General Assembly meetings. Special mention should further be made to the replacement of Republic China by People's Republic China of UN membership in 1971. Long-term effort of mainland China to regain its permanent membership status finally took effect under the support of developing countries.

Since Taiwan authority also admitted there is only one China, the only representative of China was now the RPC, which further strengthening the power of the developing countries in UN.

From 1974 to 1975, two special General Assemblies were held to discuss a 'New International Economic Order'. In December 1974, the General Assembly approved the *Charter of Economic Rights and Duties of States*[40] which affirmed a new concept for a new international economic order involving more participation and interest of the developing countries. However, ambitious as the Charter of 1974 may seem, the goals by Third World were seldom accomplished, for the socialist trend in nationalizing key industries and generally to control the economy contradicted sharply with the liberal, market-oriented views of the developed countries. The overwhelming pressure of the Third World on the Western states made the developed countries rather reluctant to support the UN, which further widened the gap. In this period, socialist countries under the leadership of the USSR tried to represent also the developing countries to give them a greater voice within the UN and the international community.

Fundamentally different views between the developed countries on one side and the socialist and developing countries on the other side extended also to the field of human rights. After the adoption of the European Convention for the Protection of Human Rights and Fundamental Freedoms in 1950 which reflected the classical liberal human rights concept as advocated by western states, discussions arose about the social dimension of human rights as well as about group or collective rights such as self-determination or rights for indigenous peoples. This lead to the adoption of the *International Covenant on Economic, Social and Cultural Rights (ICESCR)* in 1966 by the UN General Assembly, together with the *International Covenant on Civil and Political Rights (ICCPR).* The ICESCR reflects the needs of the developing and socialist countries and their emphasis not only on social rights, but also on people's rights, the right of self-determination, national wealth and resources, work, living and education, whereas the ICPSR contains the guarantees of classical individual fundamental rights. The adoption of these two fundamental human rights treaties by the UN General Assembly was a great achievement of the UN.

2.3.6 End of Cold War and Revival of UN Security Council; Involvement in National Conflicts (1987 until 1998)

When Mikhail Gorbachev was elected the president of USSR in 1985, the relationship between the East and the West changed fundamentally, which had a tremendous impact on the UN. Cooperation among the permanent members of UN was enhanced, the duty of Security Council in maintaining peace and security was invigorated and the use of vetoes decreased. The Security Council played a vital

[40] A/RES/3281(XXIX) (1974).

role in the settlement of various regional conflicts. In 1987, S/Res 598 was adopted to call upon Iraq and Iran to cease fire immediately, and to end the Iraq-Iran War. In 1988, after a UN mediation resulting in the Geneva Agreement, the USSR's armed forces finally withdrew from Afghanistan. With the Fall of the Berlin Wall in 1989, the Cold War ended. Two years later, the USSR dissolved giving way to the Russian Federation which succeeded the USSR's UN membership. However, regional ethnic conflicts, vastly originating from confronting narratives began to emerge.

The most prominent turning point of the Security Council's operation were the UN Security Council's conflict management activities following Iraq's Invasion and annexation of Kuwait in 1990. Only a couple of hours after the invasion the Security Council adopted unanimously a resolution indicating that the actions of Iraq constituted a breach of international peace and security.[41] The UN SCs Resolution 678 consequently authorized any member state to use *"all means necessary"* to get Iraq to comply with the resolution and withdraw from Kuwait. The UN Security Council's revival was significantly marked by authorizations to use military force as part of a conflict management under the auspices of the UN system of collective security. In addition, the UN Security Council, based on a *much broader understanding of the notion of peace* as used in the UN Charter, gradually enlarged its methods and instruments to address challenges to international peace and security by paving the way for *preventive diplomacy, peace enforcement* and *post-conflict peace building*.

Iraq's abortive attempt to forcefully annex Kuwait was an exception insofar as most conflicts in the 1990s were internal, national conflicts. Previously the UN had focused on peacekeeping in conflicts between states. Indeed, the provisions of Chapter VI and VII of the UN Charter refer explicitly or tacitly to interstate conflicts, not intrastate. In spite of this, the UN Security Council shifted the focus and put its policy of non-involvement into national conflicts into new perspective. The spillover of national armed conflicts and their adverse impact on regional peace and security necessitated an involvement of the UN Security Council as the UN organ with the main responsibility for peace and security. Therefore, the UN Security Council got heavily involved in national conflicts. This went so far that, from time to time, the UN as part of a peacekeeping operation took over roles similar to a government in countries and territories like Namibia, Cambodia and East Timor. E.g., based on a peace agreement after the civil war in Cambodia, the UNTAC (United Nations Transitional Authority in Cambodia) was established to administrate the country and to prepare elections of a new government.[42] Though the UNTAC had met some difficulties, its activities cannot be seen as a failure. In Somalia, however, the activity of UN could hardly be viewed as successful. Also experiencing an ongoing civil war, Somalia has not had a stable and internationally recognized government nor a fully functioning and recognized state with corresponding geographical borders since the ending of the Siad Barre regime in 1991. Furthermore, the Rwanda Crisis—as

[41] S/RES/660 (1990).

[42] S/RES/745 (1992).

former Secretary General Kofi Annan stated—marked the biggest failure in UN history. Due to the lack of a mandate and a shortage of troops, the 1994 Rwandan Genocide, causing 800'000 casualties could not be prevented.

Another difficult chapter was UN involvement in the former Socialist Federal Republic of Yugoslavia which attracted international criticism. During the beginning of the 90s, this country fell apart splitting the former socialist federation of Yugoslavia into its constituent entities. There was an intense conflict management by the UN Security Council, but failing to foresee cultural and ethnic diversity of the Yugoslav nations, the UN was completely overwhelmed with this conflict. Most importantly, the UN failed to prevent a large number of civil casualties which pushed the civil war and the dissolution process of the country further.[43] Retrospectively, the internal difficulties to bring up sufficient funds and the inability to organize the own peace-keeping missions (due to a flood of different programs) as well as structural issues are considered the main reasons for this outcome of the UN's involvement.

On the other side, thanks to the improved international environment, the General Assembly paid more attention to cooperation and development. It performed as a center for stimulating sustainable development and for protecting human rights. In 1993, after the World Conference on Human Rights in Vienna, a *High Commissioner for Human Rights (UNHRC)* was established to strengthen and harmonize the monitoring capacity of the UN system. In addition, the establishment of the *ICTY (International Criminal Tribunal for the former Yugoslavia)*[44] and *ICTR (International Criminal Tribunal for Rwanda)*[45] marked the UN's determination to establish a global rule of law where no one who commits crimes that shock the conscience of humanity is above the law. These huge leaps made a great contribution in the protection of basic human rights, life and dignity. Furthermore, it pushed its peace-keeping missions to a new level by doubling the number of missions and significantly increasing the budget.

2.3.7 The UN in the Twenty-First Century

Peace and security have dominated as top issues also the UN's agenda in the twenty-first century. After Kofi Annan became Secretary General in 1996, the UN started to rethink their operational business. In the year 2000, Annan called for the *Report of the Panel on United Nations Peace Operations*, also known as the *Brahimi report*. It was issued to evaluate the UN's efficiency in conducting operations and pinpointed

[43] Among these casualties was the massacre of Srebrenica, a town controlled by the UN and rendered a "Safe Haven" for civilians. Protection of Srebrenica could not be guaranteed after the UNPROFOR mission failed to deter the Bosnian Serb attacks, giving way for General Ratko Mladic's Troops to take control of Srebrenica. What followed was the most severe carnage in the Yugoslav Wars.

[44] S/Res 827 (1993).

[45] S/Res 955 (1994).

specific recommendations for changing strategy and operation. The report also highlighted the UN's policy of the non-use of force. Troops and resources provided by the developed states had previously been drastically reduced and moved to NATO missions, further weakening the UN's position. Therefore, the report called for permanent troops established under the UN framework.

Following this pursuit of improvement of the UNs operations, the *Millennium Declaration* was adopted. In September 2000, Member States, represented at the highest level—including 147 Heads of State and Government—expressed their collective vision in this declaration which sets out measurable goals in every area of UN endeavor—the *Millennium Development Goals*. The catalogue of the declaration consists of 8 precisely formulated goals centering around better implementation of human and humanitarian rights as well as sustainable and ecological development. In September 2008, world leaders renewed commitments to achieving those Goals by 2015 and set out concrete plans and practical steps for action.

In the twenty-first century, the activities of the UN have been characterized by achievement, challenges, and setbacks. as well. Generally, however, the UN lost much of the optimism and activism that characterized the 90s. *The Rome Statute of the International Criminal Court,* entering into force on 1 July 2002, established the International Criminal Court (ICC), which can investigate and prosecute the core international crimes (genocide, crimes against humanity, war crimes and the crime of aggression) in states that signed the statute. This was a major achievement. It was the UN General Assembly which initiated the drafting process of the statute. However, the UN also experienced serious drawbacks. Unilateralism as to the use of force returned to the world stage step by step from Kosovo (1999), Afghanistan (2001), to Iraq (2003). If the former two have some reasons like protection of human rights and self-defense in face of terrorism, the unilateral use of force by USA and UK against Iraq in 2003 was generally criticized. The USA failed to acquire UN authorization for its mission in Iraq which moved the question of the UNs effectiveness right back into focus. Over the following years, the organization's effectiveness remained one of its key issues, with, e.g., another in 2010, when 101 UN personnel died in the Haitian earthquake. In addition, the UN Security Council's activities in national conflicts were inconsistent and controversial. In particular, the inability of the SC to intervene in the conflict in Syria as from 2012 was very critically commented.

A key challenge for the UN system was the Russian attack on Ukraine on February 24, 2022. This blatant violation of the most fundamental principles of international law, which the UN exists to protect, began as a military invasion during a Security Council meeting on the situation in Ukraine. This extreme disrespect shown by a permanent member of the Security Council for these fundamental principles and for the mechanisms of peaceful conflict resolution, and thus for the Security Council, is unprecedented. It was condemned by a large majority of UN members in several UN General Assembly resolutions.[46] However, because of

[46] The resolutions were adopted during the eleventh emergency special session of the UN GA, based on the Uniting for Peace resolution. Cf. A/RES/ES-11/1 (2022). with 141 voting in favour, 5 against,

Russian vetoes in the Security Council, the UN was unable to manage the conflict effectively.

2.4 The UN Charter: Status, Interpretation and Amendments

2.4.1 Status of the UN Charter

The Charter of the United Nations is the UN's constituent instrument. It is a multilateral treaty among sovereign states to establish an international organization for an unlimited time. Scholars often refer to it as the "World Constitution", giving special mention to the constitutional character of the Charter, despite being a multilateral treaty. It is much more detailed than the Covenant of the League of the Nations. Despite high expectations by the international community and its unique status in the international law system, it was, is and always will be a treaty among sovereign states and not really a constitution. This nature of the Charter as a treaty has the following consequences: (1) Despite the fact that almost all states have joined the UN and the absence of a withdrawal clause, it is still a voluntary treaty based on international consent that a state can decide to withdraw from. (2) Likewise, according to the principle of *pacta tertiis nec nocent nec prosunt,* those states which have not joined will have no obligation directly derived from the treaty, though they will still be bound by UN principles as far as they are customary international law of general principles international law, and by the UNs duty to maintain international peace and security even among and in the relation to non-members (Article 2(6) UNCh). (3) The UN, as a creation of the Charter, remains a political organization without supranational authority. Its competence rolls back e.g. when matters are 'within the domestic jurisdiction of any States.' Its law is not directly applicable in member states and does not have general precedence, for Article 103 of the UN Charter only states that *"[i]n the event of a conflict between the obligations of the Members of the United Nations under the present Charter and their obligations under any other international agreement, their obligations under the present*

---

and 35 abstentions; the resolution deplores Russia's invasion of Ukraine and demands a full withdrawal of Russian forces and a reversal of its decision to recognize the self-declared People's Republics of Donetsk and Luhansk. A/Res/ES-11/2 (2022), confirming ARES/ES-11/1. A/RES/ES-11/3 (2022) and suspending the membership of Russia in the United Nations Human Rights Council over "grave concern at the ongoing human rights and humanitarian crisis in Ukraine [...] including gross and systematic violations and abuses of human rights" committed by Russia. A/RES/ES-11/4 (2022) with 143 in favour, 5 against and 35 abstaining declares that Russia's so-called referendums in the Donetsk, Kherson, Luhansk and Zaporizhzhia oblasts and the subsequent attempted annexation are invalid and illegal under international law. It calls upon all states to not recognize these territories as part of Russia. Furthermore, it demands that Russia "immediately, completely and unconditionally withdraw" from Ukraine as it is violating its territorial integrity and sovereignty.

Charter shall prevail." (4) The widely acknowledged interpretation method as enshrined in the Vienna Convention on the law of Treaties applies to the Charter as well even though the methodology in construing Charter provisions, as generally provisions of treaties establishing international organizations, sometimes is similar to the methodology applied to national constitutions.[47]

Though not accurate, the comparison of the Charter to a constitution and the label 'World Constitution' coined by many scholars may reflect its special position in the world order. At the end of World War II, the world was shocked by the degree of violence which nobody wanted to experience again. Therefore, the Charter enjoys a somewhat superior status compared to other international treaties. This significant *constitutional aspect of the Charter* reflects in the following key points: (1) The UN has a *quasi-universal membership*. Its basic principles as established, e.g., in *Articles 1 and 2 UN Charter constitute customary international law* and to a considerable extend even jus cogens. (2) The Charter enjoys a somewhat *'superior' status* than other treaties. This can be evidenced by the aforementioned Article 103 of the Charter as well as by Article 2(6) UN Charter which states the Organization's duty to ensure non-member states act with the principles in Article 2 'so far as may be necessary for the maintenance of international peace and security.' This implies that the principle of *pacta tertiis nec nocent nec prosunt* may derogate in face of threat of peace and security. (3) The Security Council may *make resolutions binding all the member states* (Chapter VII UN Charter) and benefits from a prioritization of its enforcement powers in regional arrangements (Article 53) as well as the duty to monitor and register treaties and agreements between member states (Article 102). Considering this, the Charter may be seen as an expression of the post-war spirit, seeking to prevent wars such as the two World Wars. The principles laid in Article 2 lie in the heart of the current international law. (4) Though the UN is created by states, its aims do not only focus on inter-state issues. Fundamental (human) rights, dignity, and wellbeing of individuals as well as peoples, e.g., have been recognized in the Charter. The history of UN thus has witnessed the increasing role in inner-state issues like human rights, economic and social development, civil wars, and so on. Consequently, the once sacred doctrine of non-intervention in the internal affairs of states, based on a very extensive interpretation of national sovereignty, has been largely weakened by the global concern on individual rights and welfare as well as world peace and security. (5) In order to enable the UN to keep pace in an ever-changing world, also interpretation methods found common in the interpretation of national constitutional law has been used in construing Charter provisions. The dynamic-evolutionary methods of the effet-utile rule and the implied-powers doctrine are important reference point of the interpretation of the Charter.[48]

---

[47] Cf. the implied powers and the inherent powers doctrines; see supra, Sect. 1.9.2.

[48] Simma et al. (2024), p. 76.

2.4.2 Interpretation of the UN Charter

Considering that the UN Charter is the basis of the UN system and enjoys a fundamental status in international law at large, the methodology of its interpretation is of great significance. This methodology reflects the dual nature of the Charter as a treaty and as a constitutional document. In addition, the time dimension is important:

International society now is different from that of e.g. 1940s. At the center of attention of the comprehensive changes since the inception of the Charter in 1945 are especially semantic shifts. Words can easily change their meaning throughout time. This automatically poses the question whether, in case of such a semantic shift, the meaning of a term should be interpreted historically, as it was meant when the Charter was created, or whether it is to be interpreted as the term stands at the time of interpretation. The ICJ answered this question in its 1972 advisory opinion on *Namibia*: *"Moreover, an international instrument has to be interpreted and applied within the framework of the entire legal system prevailing at the time of the interpretation."*[49] Generally, all the methods regulated in the VCLT are applicable to the Charter as an international treaty. In addition, the International Court of Justice as the judicial organ of the UN applies the *effet-utile* rule[50] as well as the implied power rule[51] which both mirror the constitutional character of the Charter. Therese rules are particularly important in the context of Charter interpretation and have made it possible to adapt Charter practice to changed circumstances without the necessity to formally amend the Charter.

2.4.3 Amendments to and Review of the UN Charter

Amendments to the Charter are regulated in Chapter XVIII, Articles 108 and 109. According to Article 108, an amendment comes into force for all member states equally, should they have formally adopted it with the approval of a two thirds majority in the General Assembly. Furthermore, a ratification quote by two thirds in accordance with the members' constitutional processes, including the Security Council's permanent members, is required. Article 109 of the Charter sets the regulations for the review process. The Charter can be reviewed by a General Conference established by a majority of once again two thirds of the members of the GA and by a vote of any of the SC members. Alterations to the Charter following the review process demand a two thirds majority in the assembly as well as a ratification by a two thirds majority, including all permanent members of the SC. The conference was expected to be held before the tenth annual session of

[49] *Legal Consequences for States of the Continued Presence of South Africa in Namibia* (Advisory Opinion), ICJ Rep. 16 (1971), para. 53.

[50] See supra Sect. 1.11.3.

[51] See supra Sect. 1.9.2.

General Assembly when the Charter came into effect or at an agreed upon time. It never took place.

The rules provided by Article 108 and 109, which mark a detachment from classic unanimity, stand as examples for the creation of a sort of international legislation based on the Charter itself.[52] Cumbersome as they may seem, they have a great share in establishing more legitimate procedures regarding the political interests of states. Obviously, the attitude of the permanent five members of the Security Council is crucial to the Charter's status. No amendment or revision can take place without their consent. Only four amendments have been adopted so far, most of which concern an increase in the number of member states in some UN organs.[53]

These formal requirements to amend the UN Charter are obstacles to necessary changes. With the expanding role of the UN in the course of the years, there is strong need to adopt the 1945 UN Charter to the practice of twenty-first century. On one hand, the geographic balance of power has been altered ever since the end of World War II. Many clauses, like the World War II enemy clause in Article 107, are obviously old-fashioned and have become obsolete. On the other hand, obstacles have not been removed between the States. The reform of the Security Council, in particular changes in its composition and in the attribution of veto power to states, is very difficult to achieve for it depends on the consensus of the permanent five.[54]

In spite of this, the UN Charter remains a flexible and vigorous instrument. This is foremost due to the particular ways of interpretation applied to Charter provision: The dynamic evolutionary method, the implied power doctrine, the *effet-utile* rule and subsequent practices of UN have been explaining, developing, and supplementing the context of the Charter to keep pace with the changeable world.

2.5 Purposes and Aims of the United Nations

The UN is a world organization which derives its legitimacy from almost universal membership. From the very beginning, the UN's scopes were defined broadly, much broader than those of the League of Nations. The scope was then further expanded in the practice of the organs throughout the organization's history. Therefore, the UN has been *playing a crucial role in almost every aspect of the relations between states, but also of human existence*, aiming to provide the world with a system that promotes peace, but also human rights, social progress and the advancement of the

[52] Conforti and Focarelli (2010), p. 20.

[53] These four amendments were: (1) Expansion of the SC from 11 to 15 members, 31 Aug 1965; (2) Expansion the ECOSOC from 18 to 27 members, 31 Aug 1965; (3) Expansion of the ECOSOC from 27 to 54 members by an amendment to Art. 61 of the Charter, 24 Sep 1973; (4) Adjustment of the supermajority required for action being increased from 7 to 9 votes, following the enlargement of the council, 12 Jun 1968.

[54] As to attempts to reform the UN see infra, Sect. 2.11.3.

standard of live. This chapter will focus on the main goals of the organization on the basis of the pertinent provisions of the UN Charter after analyzing its preamble.

2.5.1 Preamble

The UN Charter's preamble has a rather moving and morally sound tone due to the completely devastating effects and humanitarian horrors of the two World Wars. The preamble clearly shows the international community's will to maintain peace and security on the one hand and the urge to reaffirm human rights and promote social progress on the other. The latter is driven by *"the scourge of war"* and the associated rampant and extreme violations of human rights. This reference to human rights constitutes one of the basic differences to the LoN; in the interwar period there was not yet an international human rights discourse. The League was only concerned with minority rights.[55]

From a legal point of view, the preamble is an *auxiliary instrument to interpret the main aims of the Charter*. These very general aims are carried out in more detail in Article 1of the UN Charter. This provision states four aims of the UN: a) to maintain international peace and security, b) to develop friendly relations among nations, c) to achieve international co-operation, and d) to be a center for harmonizing the actions of nations.

2.5.2 To Maintain International Peace and Security (Article 1(1) UN Charter))

This goal is probably the most important one. Closely related to the general prohibition of the use of force in article 2(4) UNCh, Article 1(1) obliges the United Nations to *"take effective collective measures for the prevention and removal of threats to peace and the suppression of acts of aggression or other breaches of peace."* Therefore, the Charter confers to the UN the power to take preventive and repressive measures in order to ensure the territorial and political status quo and strengthen international relations among states. To attain this goal, Chapters VI and VII provide, depending on the nature of a conflict, for two methods: peaceful dispute settlement, or enforcement measures of the Security Council. These activities include preventive diplomacy, peacemaking, peace keeping and peace building.[56] The SC has the power to scrutinize conflicts and determine whether they constitute a threat to or even a breach of international peace or not. Absent a threat or a breach of peace, the SC can, under Chapter VI of the UN Charter, recommend a

---

[55]For more details supra, Sect. 2.2.4.3.

[56]Boutros-Ghali (1992). For details infra, Sects. 2.9.2 and 2.9.3.

suitable method or process for dispute settlement, should the dispute in question fall under its jurisdiction, or, in case of a threat or breach, decide on binding measures, including sanctions, under Chapter VII.[57]

The Security Council is empowered to act in international issues relating to '*peace*'. A core question is how to interpret this notion in the UN Charter. Historically, the definition was reverse engineered from the opposing term 'war' which gives it a somewhat negative connotation. According to this understanding, peace refers to the *absence of war between states*. War can thus only exist between states, and indeed, when the UN was established, the Security Council's main task was to prevent inter-state war from happening. This is the result of the aforementioned 'negative' interpretation of 'peace', referring to the absence of wars between states.

Such an understanding is too narrow given the many challenges to international peace, security and stability which have as source not (only) interstate tensions. These challenges include inter alia armed conflicts within states, severe natural disasters, massive violations of human rights and humanitarian law, terrorist or cyber-attacks, epidemies and pandemics, or non-compliance with nuclear non-proliferation obligations. The UN bodies have increasingly directed their activities in a way that the *positive and negative understanding of peace are both relevant.* This means that, based on a positive understanding, peace does not only mean the absence of war between states but also includes *the responsibility of the UN for conditions which make international peace and security possible*. This positive understanding of the notion of peace, thus '*positive peace*'[58] gradually started to direct the activities of UN since the beginning of the 90ies of last century. The resolutions of the Security Council adopted under Chapter VII in Yugoslavia,[59] Somalia,[60] Libya,[61] Rwanda[62] show that inter-state conflicts or civil wars can also be considered as a 'threat of peace', for the large number of refugees and massive violation of human rights. Since then, this has become a steady practice of the Security Council.

2.5.3 *To Develop Friendly Relations Among Nations (Article 1(2) UN Charter)*

As has been proven by history repeatedly, wars occur more often under conditions of distrustful and fragile relationships between states. Thus, developing friendly

[57] See ibid.

[58] See more: Kolb (2010), p. 29 ss.

[59] E.g. S/RES/713 (1991); S/RES/757 (1992); S/RES/816 (1993).

[60] E.g. S/RES/733 (1992); S/RES/751 (1992); S/Rees/794 (1992).

[61] E.g. S/RES/1970 (2011); S/RES/ 1973 (2011); S/RES/ 2009 (2011).

[62] E.g. S/RES/918 (1994); S/RES/925 (1994); S/RES/929 (1994).

relations is vital to create a stable world based on mutual trust. As better the relations between states are, the more stable the world is.

The very important *Friendly Relations Declaration* of 1970, UN General Assembly Resolution 2625 (XXV) , carries out in detail the meaning and substance of this goal and the respective obligations of the states to secure it. Most of the provisions of this declaration have become customary international law. The principle of equal rights and self-determination of peoples as laid down in Article 1(2) UN Charter belongs to the basis of the goal to develop friendly relations and must be observed and implemented by the UN. But what does the reference in Article 1(2) of the Charter *"[..] based on respect for the principle of equal rights and self-determination of peoples [..]"* practically mean?

This reference was the *normative basis of the entire process of decolonization.* It was the UN General Assembly which partly initiated and steered this process by adopting some basic resolutions which gave colonial peoples and territories a right to establish their own state.[63] Outside the colonial context however, the impact of the principle is highly contested, in particular as to a right to secede, i.e. to establish unilaterally a new state by disrupting the political and territorial integrity of the metropolitan state. Steps have been taken to turn the poorly defined political principle into legal practice. These include the reference to self-determination in the common Article 1 of the two UN Covenants on Human Rights of 1966, and the jurisprudence of the ICJ[64] in several cases,[65] without any conclusive result. Can it, e.g., be considered as a right for an ethnic minority to secede from a sovereign state? A universally accepted view has not been formed.[66] The prevailing opinion, which is also supported by state practice, is, however, that *there is no right for an (ethnic) group to secede unilaterally from a state so long as internal self-determination is respected.* Internal self-determination in this context means meaningful political participation and the respect of human rights. The Supreme Court of Canada was quite clear when it stated in the case *Reference re Secession of Quebec* Case (1998): *"A state whose government represents the whole of the people or peoples resident within its territory, on a basis of equality and without discrimination, and respects the principles of self-determination in its own internal arrangements, is entitled to the protection under international law of its territorial integrity."*[67]

In the processes of the dissolution of the USSR and of the Socialist Federal Republic of Yugoslavia (SFRY) there was a certain impact of self-determination on the formal recognition by third states of the states newly established as a

---

[63] Cf. in particular the *Declaration on the Granting of Independence to Colonial Countries and Peoples* in 1960, adopted by A/RES/1514 (XV) (1960).

[64] Kolb (2010), pp. 28 ss. and 100 ss.

[65] *Legal Consequences for States of the Continued Presence of South Africa in Namibia* (Advisory Opinion), ICJ Rep. 16 (1971), para. 52; *Western Sahara,* Advisory Opinion, ICJ Rep. 12 (1975), paras. 25 ss.; *East Timor*, Advisory Opinion, ICJ Rep. 102 (1995), 29.

[66] Simma et al. (2024), p. 330 s.

[67] Reference re Secession of Quebec 2 S.C.R. (1998), 217 ([1998] 37 ILM 1340ss.).

consequence of the dismemberment of the USSR and the SFRY, but rather in requiring these newly established states to observe democracy as well as human and minority rights as a precondition for their recognition and not in the sense of supporting a unilateral right to secede.[68] According to a widespread but not uncontested opinion, self-determination may culminate in *a right to secede under extreme circumstances*, including extreme and systemic violation of human rights and/or extreme case of denial of internal self-determination.[69]

2.5.4 To Promote International Co-operation (Article 1(3))

Closely related to friendly relations among nations and part of it is the goal to promote international cooperation. This objective is extremely broad, embracing, e.g. economic, social, cultural, and humanitarian issues, with a special focus on human rights and fundamental freedoms. It is interconnected with Article 55 UNCh which states that the UN,

> *"[w]ith a view to the creation of conditions of stability and well-being which are necessary for peaceful and friendly relations among nations based on respect for the principle of equal rights and self-determination of peoples, [..]shall promote: higher standards of living, full employment, and conditions of economic and social progress and development; solutions of international economic, social, health, and related problems; and international cultural and educational cooperation; and universal respect for, and observance of, human rights and fundamental freedoms for all without distinction as to race, sex, language, or religion."*

Practically, there is no issue area that could not be internationalized based on Article 1(3). Thus, the UN gained competence over almost all topics concerning human life and international society. The principle of non-intervention in domestic jurisdiction enshrined in Article 2(7) may only modestly limit the UN's scope with regard to international cooperation.

2.5.5 Center for Harmonizing the Actions of Nations (Article 1(4))

Last but certainly not least is the UN's clearly obvious goal to become a *"center for harmonizing actions of nations in the attainment of these common ends."* The UN

[68] Crawford (2006), p. 390 ss.

[69] Ibid.

has come a long way since its founding, especially when considering that many systemic errors were avoided after the experiences with its predecessor, the League of Nations. The LoN's failure has pushed the UN's own development and made it possible for the UN to act as an open, fair and effective global institution that can give impulses to the world economy, social progress and war prevention.

2.5.6 *Article 1 as Basis to Internationalize Issues of Global Concern*

In conclusion, Article 1 of the Charter shows that the organs of the UN may deal with *all international issues and that they can internationalize almost whatever they want*. With the pace of interdependences throughout the world, the power of UN has been increasing as ever more issues got internationalized. Since there is no clear normative limit to the powers of the UN, it is rather easy to construe concrete powers on the basis of *effet-utile* and the implied-powers rule. Important is further a shifting emphasis from the rights of states to that of individuals. Coexistence and cooperation are the keywords setting the course of the UN's work. However, article 1 does not regulate enforceable rights and duties of the UN and its Member States. These rights and obligations are specified in Article 2 of the Charter.

2.6 Fundamental Principles of the UN

2.6.1 *Overview*

Article 2 contains in para. 1 to 7 basic principles in pursuit of the purposes stated in article 1. Their major addressees are the UN member states, but some of them also apply to the UN as an organization. They impose *enforceable rights and duties to the member states* and some even apply to non-member states for most of these principles have become customary international law and some even *jus cogens*. Conceived in the subsequent practice of states and the organs of the UN, a quasi-authentic interpretation of these principles was concretized and further developed in the aforementioned UN General Assembly's '*Declaration on Principles of International Law concerning Friendly Relations and Cooperation among States in accordance with the Charter of the United Nation*' (Friendly Relations Declaration) of 1970.[70] These interpretations are only 'quasi-authentic' because the GA has not the power to adopt such a resolution with legally binding effect.

[70] A/Res/2625 (XXV).

2.6.2 Principle of Sovereign Equality (Article 2(1))

Article 2(1) states that, *"[t]he Organization is based on the principle of sovereign equality of all its Members."* The principle of sovereign equality contains at least three dimensions. On the domestic level, all states are vested with the superior authority to choose and develop their own political, economic and cultural system. On the international plain, each state has the obligation to respect the other states' rights and legal personalities under international law. Finally, each state has the equal right to participate in international affairs and global order, enjoying rights and bearing obligations under international law. Thus, very generally Article 2(1) is a *guarantee of basic rights of states*.

In addition, this provision refers basically to two principles: sovereignty of states, and equality of states. Sovereignty remains *a cornerstone of the international system*. Many other principles are constructed on this basic principle such as the principle of non-use of force (Article 2(4) UN Charter), the respect for territorial integrity and the principle of non-intervention into state's domestic affairs (Article 2(7) UN Charter). However, the principle has a decreasing normative impact since interdependencies increasingly reduce the scope of action of states in modern international affairs. Therefore, the field of application of the principle is shrinking. Generally, a *relative understanding of sovereignty nowadays prevails* against the background of the rapidly increasing interdependencies in the globalized world.

Equality of States as a genuine legal standard is now laid more emphasis on. As *Kolb* very appropriately puts it: *"Sovereignty is Hobbes; equality is Kant; through "sovereign equality under the law", Kant rolls back Hobbes."*[71] Equality is thus the other important principle implying that, from a legal point of view, there is *no hierarchy among states* and that states, e.g. as members of international organizations, are basically vested with the same rights and duties. Equality is, however, not an absolute but relative standard. E.g., the annual contributions of an international organization's member states may of course vary according to the states' size, population, and economic strength. On the other side do factual inequalities among states not derogate the legal quality in the international society.

Given that sovereign equality is not *jus cogens*, it is possible, with the consent of the affected states, to deviate from it for various reasons. The veto power of the permanent five in Security Council may serve as a very good example to illustrate the factual as well as legal inequality in the area of peace and security. *More power, more responsibility:* This realistic formula, stemming from the failure of the League, presumes that the effective function of the UN should be built on the consensus among great powers, otherwise it will not work. Though disputed, the balance between power politics and the universal goal of the UN[72] clearly shows that it is the sovereign equality that guarantees states to reach an agreement on bearing

[71] Kolb (2010), p. 40.

[72] Taylor and Curtis (2011), p. 313.

different rights and responsibilities under the post-war order. Such is also the case, e.g., in the weighted voting in the International Monetary Fund.[73]

2.6.3 *Fulfillment of Obligations in Good Faith (Article 2(2))*

Article 2(2) UNCh requires Member States to fulfill the obligations assumed by them in good faith and in accordance with the UN Charter. In essence, this article is a consequence of the membership status. Non-fulfillment of membership duties by UN member states violates also Article 2(2) UN Charter so that, based on this provision, sanctions against a non-complying member state may be adopted. The obligation refers however not only to the commitments under the UN Charter. According to the GA resolution 2625, the principle applies also to general international law and duties under treaties as well. Vertically, the principle regulates the relationship between member states, between various UN organs, and between the UN and its member states, i.e. to the execution of international legal obligations at large.[74]

The principle is further mentioned in some international agreements such as the *Vienna Convention on the Law of Treaties* 1969[75] and the *UN Convention on the Law of the Sea* in 1982[76] but has, based on Article 2(2), universal application. Due to lack of a general supranational authority, the good faith of states to stick to their commitment and fulfill their obligation under treaties is indispensable to international law and the stability of the international system. Good faith thus plays a leading role in directing States' acts and the interpretation of treaties, covering almost all areas.

2.6.4 *Duty to Settle Disputes Amicably (Article 2(3))*

According to Article 2(3) UNCh, member states

> *"shall settle their international disputes by peaceful means in such a manner that international peace and security, and justice, are not endangered."*

Derived from the prohibition of the use of force, this obligation belongs to the basics of a collective security system. Collective security is made up of *two basic and interconnected parts: Settling disputes peacefully, and non-use of force*. Article 2(3) is therefore closely linked to the prohibition to use force according to Article

[73] For details see infra, Sect. 5.3.7.

[74] For details see Simma et al. (2024), p. 169.

[75] Arts. 26 and 31 VCLT.

[76] Art. 309 s. UNCLOS.

2(4) UNCh. Peaceful settlement performs as both a prerequisite and a consequence of the obligation to abstain from using force. Only if the UN provides the states with sufficient and effective methods to solve disputes peacefully can it pave way for a world free of inter-state military conflicts.

Article 2(3) has to be clarified in the following four points: (a) The wording 'shall' suggest that States are obliged to resort to peaceful settlement to their disputes. However, non-respect of this obligation may not be sanctioned unless it violates Article 2(4). (b) The wording 'international disputes' means that normally the situation must reach an extent to which a 'dispute' takes place. A simple hostile relationship between two countries does not meet the requirement. Moreover, the dispute is usually between 'States' which has international impact. However, though having limits, internal disputes may also arouse a recommendation for peaceful settlement in practice of Security Council like *East Timor* (Resolution 389, 1976), *Kosovo* (Resolution 1160, 1998), or *Congo* (Resolution 1304, 2000). (c) The wording 'peaceful means' refers to those means referred to in GA Resolution 2625 and Article 33 of the Charter. The use of force is obviously excluded. In addition, it is the peaceful 'means' that demand emphasis, for there is no specific requirement for the result. (d) The wording 'justice' connotes that these

> *"disputes shall be settled on the basis of the sovereign equality of States and in accordance with the principle of free choice of means."*

As has mentioned supra,[77] the LoN knew certain legal procedures for settling dispute and a 3-month 'cool off' system. As a successor, the UN further developed peaceful settlement methods. Chapter VI UNCh is a specification of its contribution to this area.

2.6.5 *Prohibition of the Threat or the Use of Force (Article 2(4))*

Article 2(4) states a general prohibition on the use of treat or force:

> *"All Members shall refrain in their international relations from the threat or use of force against the territorial integrity or political independence of any state, or in any other manner inconsistent with the Purposes of the United Nations."*

This is the *core rule of the system of collective security*. The drafters of the Charter made up their mind to replace the loopholes of relative ban on war in the Covenant of the League with a general ban on all unilateral use of force. Though it was the Briand-Kellogg Pact in 1928 that first prohibited to resort to war, it was the

[77] See Sect. 2.2.2.

UN Charter that extended the prohibition to a 'threat of force' and first centralized the coercion power to the Security Council to punish an offender.

Over the years this article has been subject to much debate and interpretative efforts. The following points are important: (a) 'Members' and 'of any state' mean that the addressees are States. Since it does not only restrain use of force against member States, the non-member States benefit as well. The prohibition is not directly applicable to non-state actors and thus in armed internal conflicts. However, the Security Council in resolutions based on Chapter VII has the power to direct parties to internal conflicts to halt hostilities. In S/Resolution 1190, e.g. the Security Council *"demands that all parties, groups and individuals immediately cease hostilities and maintain a ceasefire in Kosovo."* The ban on Kosovo Liberation Army's use of force may thus be cited as an example. (b) 'International relations' suggests that the article applies to inter-border military conflicts, without jurisdiction in internal conflicts. As already mentioned, there is a steady practice of the Security Council in internal conflicts to demand the parties to refrain from or stop the use of military force. Basis of this type of the prohibition to use force is, however, not Article 2(4) UNCh but the respective resolutions of the UN SC. (c) 'Force' does not have a precise definition under the current international law. However, the prevailing interpretation, supported by the wording 'armed force' used in the Para.7 of the Preamble and Article 44 of the Charter is that it should be 'armed force'. It should be mentioned that 'indirect force' may also be considered a forbidden force. As has shown in *the Friendly Relations Declaration* of GA and later supported by the ICJ judgment *Military and Paramilitary Activities in and against Nicaragua,* an armed attack includes *"the sending by or on behalf of a State of armed bands, groups, irregulars or mercenaries, an actual armed attack, or its substantial involvement therein."*[78] (d) 'Threat or use of force' clearly shows that also the threat to use force is impermissible. However, in the Advisory Opinion on the *Legality of the Threat or Use of Nuclear Weapons*, the ICJ decided, with some judges dissenting, that, if a threatened retaliatory strike was consistent with military necessity and proportionality, it would not necessarily be illegal.[79] (e) The wording "against the territorial integrity or political independence of any state, or in any other manner inconsistent with the Purposes of the United Nations' might give rise to some doubt claiming that the use of force not directed against 'the territorial integrity or political independence' of any states while consistent 'with the Purposes of the United Nations.' is not prohibited. Such being the case, the Pandora's Box may be opened. States usually try to justify their unilateral use of force by referring to international legal norms. This was even the case when Russia started the military invasion of the Ukraine in February 2022. Difficult cases were the unauthorized 1999 NATO air strikes in Serbia during the Kosovo conflict and the unilateral 2003 USA military action in

[78] A/RES/2625 (XXV) (1970); *Military and Paramilitary Activities in and against Nicaragua (Nicaragua v. United States of America)*, ICJ Rep. 14 (1986), 103 para. 195.

[79] *Legality of the Threat or Use of Nuclear Weapons*, Advisory Opinion, ICJ Rep. 226 (1996), 245 para. 96.

Iraq. Even then, arguments based on international law were forwarded as a justification. Generally, one should avoid this slippery slope and stick to the meaning, purpose, and function of the prohibition to use force: There is a general ban on use of force and a clear relation between broad application of the general rule and the narrow understanding of the exceptions. According to the restrictive view on the permissibility of the use of force, mainly supported by *Kelsen* and *Brownlie*, "*the effect of the disputed words (territorial integrity and political independence) were not intended to qualify the obligation not to use force but merely to describe the totality of a state's existence under international law.......Likewise, the final words (prohibiting use of force against the purpose of the UN) were not intended to allow force to achieve those purposes, but rather as a safety net to ensure that force could never be used against non-state entities, such as colonies and protectorates.*"[80]

Since the prohibition of use of force is general, the only *exceptions to the principle are self-defense and authorization by the UN Security Council.* The unilateral use of force by NATO in Kosovo 1999 and by the US and UK in Iraq 2003 challenged the system of collective security and the legitimacy of the UN at large. They gave as deliberately misunderstood examples the pretext to Russia to justify its war of aggression against the Ukraine.

2.6.6 Collective Security (Article 2(5))

The Charter determines in Article 2(5) that all members shall give the United Nations every assistance in any action it takes in accordance with the present Charter, and shall refrain from giving assistance to any state against which the United Nations is taking preventive or enforcement action.

This Article symbolizes the nature of UN's collective security system: Facing a disturber of peace, "*they will act as one for all and all for one.*"[81] It is a kind of alliance clause imposing the binding obligation to member states to execute the SC's resolutions in the context of collective security. The provision is therefore strongly linked to Chapter VII of the Charter. In the advisory opinion of ICJ on *Certain Expenses of the United Nations*,[82] the ICJ made it clear that, enforcement measures generally refer to measures under Article 41 and 42 of the Charter.[83] Likewise, the

[80] Dixon (2007), p. 314.

[81] Saksena (1974), p. 4 s.

[82] *Certain Expenses of the United Nations (Art. 17, Paragraph 2, of the Charter)*, Advisory Opinion, ICJ Rep. 151 (1962), para. 54.

[83] Art. 41: The Security Council may decide what measures not involving the use of armed force are to be employed to give effect to its decisions, and it may call upon the Members of the United Nations to apply such measures. These may include complete or partial interruption of economic relations and of rail, sea, air, postal, telegraphic, radio, and other means of communication, and the severance of diplomatic relations.; Art. 42: Should the Security Council consider that measures provided for in Art. 41 would be inadequate or have proved to be inadequate, it may take such

wording 'action' in the first part should also be understood as the 'enforcement measures'.

2.6.7 Non-member States (Article 2(6))

According to Article 2(6) UNCh, *"[t]he Organization shall ensure that states which are not Members of the United Nations act in accordance with these Principles so far as may be necessary for the maintenance of international peace and security."*

For a state not to seek UN membership is an abnormality: States, as soon as they get independent, are very eager to become UN members immediately. They consider this membership as the corollary of their newly acquired independence. And indeed: those state-type political entities which are not UN members are almost all special cases: Kosovo, Taiwan, the Turkish Republic of Northern Cyprus, or the Vatican, just to mention some of them. They are either mini-states or political entities with contested statehood and/or stabilized de facto regimes. How should the UN deal with them? How is it possible to ensure that these entities do not undermine the UN's efforts as to its main purpose, i.e. the maintenance of peace and security? And how to protect them against member states' acts violating the Charter?

From a legal point of view, it is quite clear: the UN Charter is an international treaty and therefore binding only on the member states. A treaty cannot impose obligations to states which have not ratified it. Article 34 VCLT states: *"A treaty does not create either obligations or rights for a third State without its consent."* And Article 35 VCLT declares as to treaties providing for obligations of third states: *"An obligation arises for a third State from a provision of a treaty if the parties to the treaty intend the provision to be the means of establishing the obligation and the third State expressly accepts that obligation in writing."* All this goes back to the famous rule of Roman law that *pacta tertiis nec nocent nec prosunt*.

Kelsen had a broad understanding as to the power of the UN to enforce basic Charter rules against non-member states: *"If the Charter attaches a sanction to a certain behavior of non-members, it established a true obligation of non-members to observe the contrary behavior."*[84] However, this broad interpretation of Article 2(6) as an exception to the *pacta tertiis* rule did not get general recognition. Indeed, the wording of Article 2(6) is cautious. It avoids conveying the impression of directly imposing legal obligations on non-member states. But it gives the UN's organs the power and imposes an obligation on them to ensure a conduct of non-member states in conformity with the principles of Article 2. This is not a problem as these principles are customary international law, and some of them even

---

action by air, sea, or land forces as may be necessary to maintain or restore international peace and security. Such action may include demonstrations, blockade, and other operations by air, sea, or land forces of Members of the United Nations.

[84] Kelsen (1950), p. 100.

jus cogens. Therefore, the UN could, as an international organization, impose sanctions on non-member states as countermeasures in response to violations of these customary international law principles. It is less clear whether the UN may impose sanctions against non-member states not complying with important resolutions of the SC. The SC has sometimes imposed such sanctions but foremost against non-recognized entities qualified by the SC as illegal.

Usually, non-member states comply with SC resolutions adopted under Chapter VII UNCh. The practice of the non-member state to observe and to implement such decisions reflects that they consider these resolutions as quasi-obligation under international law and seek to preserve their political credibility by complying with them.[85]

2.6.8 Non-intervention/Domaine Réservé (Article 2(7))

The non-intervention principle is a consequence of sovereign equality of states. Its goal is to *protect States from external incursions*. The wording of Article 2-(7) imposes the obligation to respect member states' domestic affairs, or the *domaine réservé*,[86] only on the UN bodies. However, the principle of non-intervention is a *rule of customary international law with general application* and thus also and foremost in the relations between states. GA Resolution 2625 make this clear by stating that, *"[n]o State or group of States has the right to intervene, directly or indirectly, for any reason whatever, in the internal or external affairs of any other State."* Addressees are therefore the UN as well as the member states.

However, in this interdependent world and under the practice of UN more involved in the once 'domestic affairs', the *domaine réservé* is considerably shrinking. Therefore, questions may be asked: Is this principle of empty content today? If not, what is the exact realm of it? There are two approaches to clarify the scope of the principle: one from the interpretation of the wording 'to intervene', while another is to circumscribe what is 'essentially within the domestic jurisdiction'. The latter approach is the one preferred, for *"the application of Article 2(7) ultimately depends on the concrete substance of the issue concerned and not on the abstract form of the action."*[87] In the case of the *Nationality Decrees in Tunis and Morocco*, the PCIJ made the following statement: *"The question whether a certain matter is or is not solely within the jurisdiction of a State is an essentially relative question; it depends on the development of international relations."*[88] Therefore, the practice of the UN is decisive in determining the scope of the principle.

---

[85] Same opinion see: Simma et al. (2024), p. 147.

[86] This French term is very often used to denote the powers of the states protected against external intrusions.

[87] Simma et al. (2024), p. 290.

[88] PCIJ, Series B, no. 4, 7 Feb 1923, 24.

Human rights are an excellent example for the changing scope of the principle. Though once claimed to belong to the domestic jurisdiction of states, basic human rights as enshrined in *Universal Declaration of Human Rights* in 1948, the UN Human Rights Covenants of 1966 as well as many further human rights conventions adopted by the UN General Assembly, many resolutions of the GA and the SC as to the human rights situations in certain countries are clearly an international concern and therefore do not belong to the *domaine réservé*. Human rights are only one of many examples which include also civil wars, internal conflicts, environmental issues, terrorism, extreme poverty, global health crises such as an epidemic or even a pandemic, social problems, economic development, disasters and catastrophes, minority rights and rights of indigenous peoples, even the violent overthrow of an elected government. It depends on the acts of the organs of the UN, in particular of the GA, the SC and the ECOSOC, whether an issue is an international concern in a way that it evades the exclusive domestic jurisdiction of states. Whether an issue is an international concern depends largely on whether there are any international rules stipulated in legal, soft law or political documents, as a basis for internationalization. Given that the goals of the UN are defined very broadly and against the background of the extremely dense web of global legal rules in numerous policy areas, there are ever less *"matters which are essentially within the domestic jurisdiction of any State"*. These matters include most likely the basis of the political system, such as the basic principles regulating (democratic) decision-making, the organization of state power, the choice of the economic and social system, the language and culture, etc. The UN as well as other states must respect the most important attributes of national self-determination and sovereignty. But even in this regard there are international limits and rules which apply to the states' political system such as human rights, minority protection and democratic self-determination.

The last part of the Article stipulates an exception to the rule of non-intervention: The conflict management activities of the SC based on Chapter VII UNCh do not have to observe the domestic jurisdiction clause. To preserve or to reestablish international peace and security is more important than the rights of certain states in situations where there is a threat to or a breach of peace in the sense of Chapter VII UNCh. Therefore, as long as the Security Council regards a certain issue as within the scope of Article 39, it can and should take action even if the conflict's roots are internal in nature or if the SC's decisions intrude domestic jurisdiction. This means that the SC may request from a state measures which normally would be protected by the domestic jurisdiction clause such as granting autonomy to a minority[89] or amendments to the constitution[90] or other political decisions referring to the basis of a state's political system.[91]

Despite this, the UN as well as the other states have, as just mentioned, to respect important aspects of a state's self-determination and autonomy. In that sense

[89] S/RES/1244 (1999).

[90] S/RES/1373 (2001).

[91] Shaw (2021), p. 197 ss.

contains Article 2(7) together with Article 2(1) UNCh an *international guarantee of autonomy which protects the basic rights of states*. This autonomy is not absolute but depends on the circumstances. The UN, especially the SC, must consider this autonomy. In the very end the main point is whether the involvement of UN in the once 'domestic areas' lives up to the *requirement of proportionality*. Hence, who will decide if the measures are necessary and proportionate? Should the ICJ be endowed with the power of judicial review? These are all questions to be clarified through the reform and further development of the UN.

2.7 UN-Membership

2.7.1 Members and Observers

Established on the basis of state sovereignty, the United Nations is an 'inter-state club', whose members are states only. These states could be categorized into two groups: the original members (51 nations including the permanent five) and the subsequent admitted members. With 193 members throughout the world is the UN now the by far most important global institution with an almost universal membership.

Besides member states, there are also other entities that make contribution to the UN activities without enjoying a formal membership status. These include the very few non-member states, other intergovernmental organizations, and NGOs (non-governmental organizations). Two entities enjoy permanent observer state status, namely the Holy See and the State of Palestine. Special mention should be made to the State of Palestine. By UN General Assembly Resolution A/RES/67/19 of 29 November 2012, the General Assembly accorded non-member observer 'state' status to Palestine, which equates Palestine with that of the same status of Holy See in the UN. Apart from these permanent state observers, some intergovernmental organizations and entities have received a standing invitation to participate as observers in the sessions and the work of the General Assembly. Regarding intergovernmental organizations, the African Union, the European Union, the League of Arab States, the International Criminal Court and the Shanghai Cooperation Organization are among them. There is also a large number of non-governmental organizations participating in a wide variety of activities of the UN.[92] The most eminent ones are the International Committee of the Red Cross, Inter-Parliamentary Union and the International Olympic Committee. All in all, the UN is an organic entity of ties with various entities, whose roles cannot be underestimated.

[92] For more details see infra, Sect. 6.4.2.

2.7.2 *Admission (Article 4 UN Charter)*

2.7.2.1 Preconditions

Similar to the League of Nations, the victorious nations in the World War II, which either signed the 1942 'United Nations Declaration' or declared war on the Axis Ally before March 1st, 1945, were regarded as the original founding members. By ratifying the UN Charter, 51 members of the so-called 'wartime United Nations' automatically joined the UN without further examination on their qualities. Strictly speaking, Ukraine and Byelorussia did at that time, as constituent republics of the Soviet Union, not share the state status under the international law. Nevertheless, they were permitted to join the UN under a political compromise to ease Stalin from doubting the numerical advantage of Western seats in the UN.

Membership of the UN *"is open to all peace-loving States that accept the obligations contained in the United Nations Charter and, in the judgment of the Organization, are able to carry out these obligations"* (Article 4(1) UNCh). These states are admitted to the UN by a decision of the General Assembly upon the recommendation of the Security Council (Article 4(2) UNCh). What is a 'peace-loving' state? There are no clear criteria. At the beginning of the Cold War, the membership admission issue was utilized by both superpowers, U.S.A and Soviet Union, to strengthen their respective stance in the communist and liberal Western block. This led to a deadlock because each superpower blocked the admission of countries of the opposite block. In this situation, the ICJ, in its *Conditions of Admission of a State to Membership in the UN* (1948) advisory opinion,[93] clearly stated that only the requirements of Article 4(1) are relevant. It is not allowed that a member state makes his agreement to admission dependent of the admission of other states.

2.7.2.2 Organs Deciding on Admission

It is up to the political organs of the UN, i.e., the SC and the GA, to judge whether a state is capable and willing to respect the obligations of the Charter. In practice, an applicant state submits with the application to the Secretary-General a letter formally stating that it accepts the obligations under the Charter. After the positive recommendation of the Security Council (affirmative votes of 9 of the 15 members of the Council, no veto from the permanent five is exercised) and the 2/3 votes of the General Assembly, membership becomes effective as from the date when the resolution for admission is adopted by the GA, usually with the declaration of the candidate state expressing its willingness to carry out the obligations of the Charter. In the early days of the Cold War and facing the deadlock in the Security Council,

[93] *Conditions of Admission of a State to Membership in the UN Advisory Opinion*, ICJ Rep. 57 (1948), para. 10.

the Western states argued that a vetoed admission application was equal to a 'negative' recommendation but was still a 'recommendation' within the context of Article 4(2). Thus, the General Assembly could still vote on such a 'recommendation' and admit the applying state. Again, the ICJ, in its *Competence of the GA for the Admission of a State to the UN* (1952) advisory opinion, pointed out that it is not possible to bypass the SC; a favorable SC recommendation is required.

2.7.2.3 Admission and International Recognition of a State

What is the relationship between admission of the state to the UN and this state's international recognition as a subject of international law? Recognizing a state is an - often but not always formal - act of other states expressing acceptance of a newly established state as subject of international law. The amount and extent of international recognitions by states constitutes a vital element for deciding whether an entity, a body politic, is accepted by the international community as a new state or not. Usually states or groups of states decide unilaterally and therefore decentralized on recognition. However, *admission to the UN as a collective act* of the most important and universal international organization *de facto equates to the decentralized recognition of a new state* by other states. This is so because the UN, by accepting a state as a member, guarantees the entity the uncontestable status as a 'state' since the Charter protects, through the UN's system of collective security, the territorial integrity and political independence of its member states. From a legal perspective, statehood of a newly admitted state may not be legally contested anymore.[94]

Although the requirements listed in Article 4 were mostly considered as a formality during the process of decolonization beginning in 1960s, the significant legal and political weight of being a member of the UN upon being a genuine 'state' still makes it a priority for all newly established states to apply for membership. They consider the application as a corollary of the newly gained independence, for UN membership of the state reflects the global opinion and has decisive legal consequences. There were, however, some instances where the application of a state was rejected, because, e.g., it got vetoed in the SC. An example is Kosovo which, as a unilaterally independent state outside the colonial context, remains non-member of the UN due to a Russian veto, which reflects a controversial attitude of the international community as to Kosovo's statehood.

[94] An example is Bosnia-Herzegovina which was admitted 1992 as member during an ongoing internal war with a fragmented territory partly under the power of local leaders rejecting Bosnia-Herzegovina Bosnia-Herzegovina's independent statehood and a very weak central government.

2.7.2.4 Admission and Issues of Identity and Continuity of States

Admission of a new state is the general rule applied in case of absence of identity and legal continuity of statehood between the applying state and another states. This is, however, sometimes controversial, and there were instances where political considerations played an important role on deciding whether there was identity and continuity or not. When Czechoslovakia broke up into the two states Slovakia and Czech Republic, it was clear that both states had to apply for membership. This was less clear with the Federal Republic of Yugoslavia consisting of Serbia and Montenegro which considered itself as continuing the legal existence of the Socialist Federal Republic of Yugoslavia. Its representatives were not accepted as the legitimate representative of former Yugoslavia by the UN. Therefore, the Federal Republic of Yugoslavia was considered by most states as a new state and had to apply for membership. On the contrary, Russia succeeded the permanent member status of the USSR in the Security Council after the consensus reached among the members in the UN that Russia would continue the legal existence of the USSR.[95] Therefore, the ultimate criterion for admission in controversial cases is the recognition by the majority in the UN. In case of incorporation and fusion of states, however, sometimes a simple notification is sufficient, such as in the case of the incorporation of the GDR Germany, and no other procedural requirement is needed.

2.7.3 Suspension, Expulsion and Withdrawal (Article 5 and 6 UN Charter)

2.7.3.1 Suspension

Article 5 of the Charter provides that,

> *"[a] Member of the United Nations against which preventive or enforcement action has been taken by the Security Council may be suspended from the exercise of the rights and privileges of membership by the General Assembly upon the recommendation of the Security Council. The exercise of these rights and privileges may be restored by the Security Council."*

No state has ever been suspended according to this article. There were, however, instances in which some states were de facto suspended based on other reasons.[96]

[95] Crawford (2006), p. 667 ss.

[96] E.g. South Africa due to its apartheid policies, see A/RES/3207 (XXIX) (1974); Yugoslavia, when it claimed to continue the membership of the former state after the breakup of the Socialist Federal Republic of Yugoslavia, see S/RES/757, 30 May 1992 and A/RES/47/1 (1992); Cambodia, as the UN continued to recognize the Khmer Rouge regime as the legitimate government of Cambodia following the Vietnamese invasion of Cambodia and the establishment of the People's

2.7.3.2 Expulsion

According to Article 6,

> *"[a] Member of the United Nations which has persistently violated the Principles contained in the present Charter may be expelled from the Organization by the General Assembly upon the recommendation of the Security Council."*

The conditions for expulsion thus are: (a) persistent violations which means that occasional violations are not sufficient; (b) a violation of principles of the Charter, which means that violations irrelevant to principles of the Charter do not count; (c) a recommendation of the Security Council; the recommendation is an indispensable prerequisite and needs an affirmative 9 out of 15 votes of the SC without a veto exercised by one or more of the permanent five.

Expulsion is an ambivalent sanction and not always the most adequate measure to protect the UN principles: Although expulsion will deprive the norm-violating state of all the benefits and contacts of the UN, it will also free the state from any obligation and sanctions under the UN framework. No formal expulsion of a state has ever taken place. There were attempts to expel Israel and South Africa from the UN, but the according resolutions were vetoed in the Security Council by the U.S.A. The exclusion of the Taiwan Government of China and of the representatives of former Yugoslavia were no formal expulsions. In the former case, the issue was which government is the legitimate government to represent China, the communist government in Beijing or the national government in Taiwan. Since most Chinese population and territory are under the jurisdiction of the Beijing government and that Taiwan regime also admit that 'there is only one China', GA Resolution 2758 (XXVI) passed on October 25, 1971, recognized the People's Republic of China (PRC) as *"the only legitimate representative of China to the United Nations"* and excluded *"the representatives of Chiang Kai-shek from the place which they unlawfully occupy at the United Nations."*[97] In the latter case, since the Social Federal Republic of Yugoslavia had been effectively dissolved into five independent states, the claim of Federal Republic of Yugoslavia (Serbia and Montenegro) to be a legal continuation of the Socialist Federal Republic of Yugoslavia in the UN has not been generally accepted. On 22 September 1992, UN General Assembly Resolution A/Res/47/1 decided that *"the Federal Republic of Yugoslavia (Serbia and Montenegro) should apply for membership in the United Nations and that it shall not participate in the work of the General Assembly"*.[98] This is an issue about admission of a new state that lacks the legal continuity of its predecessor in UN.

Republic of Kampuchea, see A/RES/32/22 (1979); Afghanistan during the Taliban regime, see *Credentials of Representatives to the Fifty-Sixth Session of the General Assembly: Report of the Credentials Committee*, 2001.

[97] A/RES/2758 (XXVI) (1971), 1.

[98] A/RES/47/1 (1992).

2.7.3.3 Withdrawal

The Charter does not contain any clause regulating the withdrawal of a member. This might have been a lesson learned from the failure of the League of Nations, which permitted a voluntary withdrawal of a state in Article 1(2) of the Covenant and left space for the (future) aggressors in World War II to be free from obligations and pressure of the League.

The prevailing opinion is that withdrawal is possible even without an explicit norm regulating it, but not with immediate effect. Article 56 VCLT,[99] the general clause of withdrawal from a treaty without withdrawal provision, can be applied.[100] In history, only Indonesia had 'withdrawn' from the UN for one year and a half (1965–1966) in dissatisfaction with Malaysia's being elected as a non-permanent member of the SC. However, when it returned to the UN, it was accepted by the GA and the Secretary-General that Indonesia had only 'suspended' from the UN instead of denouncing its membership. Therefore, it simply resumed all its rights and obligations of the UN.

2.8 Organs of the UN

2.8.1 Preliminary Remark

The United Nations have six principal organs: the General Assembly (GA), the Security Council (SC), the Secretariat, the Economic and Social Council (ECOSOC), the Trusteeship Council, and the International Court of Justice (ICJ).

To better fulfill their functions, the principal organs are entitled to create subsidiary organs. This is based on an implied power of each organ under the UN Charter. Generally, subsidiary organs are under the authority of its principal organs. However, they may also enjoy a certain degree of independence.

[99] Which also applies to treaties establishing international organizations; see Art. 5 VCLT.

[100] Art. 56 VCLT: Denunciation of or withdrawal from a treaty containing no provision regarding termination, denunciation or withdrawal

1. A treaty which contains no provision regarding its termination, and which does not provide for denunciation or withdrawal is not subject to denunciation or withdrawal unless:
   (a) it is established that the parties intended to admit the possibility of denunciation or withdrawal; or
   (b) a right of denunciation or withdrawal may be implied by the nature of the treaty.
2. A party shall give not less than twelve months' notice of its intention to denounce or withdraw from a treaty under paragraph 1.

2.8.2 *The General Assembly (GA)*

2.8.2.1 Features

The General Assembly is the main deliberative and policymaking and the *only plenary organ of the UN*. It is sometimes labelled 'parliament of nations'. Each of the 193 members of the UN is entitled one equal seat and one equal vote with at most five representatives for each state. The Assembly is empowered to discuss almost all issues including international issues as well as internal affairs of the organization. However, there are important and obvious differences between GA and a true parliament. The individuals represent the states in GA, not parties and they are therefore official representatives appointed by the governments and not elected by the people. Further, the GA is not a legislator, having no general power to enact laws. Its powers as the plenary organ of an international organizations are, except of internal matters, confined to recommendations. However, the GA is a unique forum for multilateral discussion at the universal level. It played and still plays an important role in decolonization, development, economic and social issues, codification and promotion of International Law and so on. It is well recognized that GA possesses moral authority of the UN community. The GA meets in regular session from September to December annually. Special or emergency sessions are convoked by the Secretary-General at the request of the Security Council or of a majority of the Member States of UN.

2.8.2.2 Voting

According to Article 18(1) UNCh, each member state has one vote in the GA. As to the adoption of decisions and resolutions, a two-third majority is required for 'important issues' listed in Article 18(2) like recommendations on peace and security and the election of SC members. A simple majority is required on 'other issues'. In case of those issues lack clarity, a simple majority vote may decide on the preliminary question of whether the issue should be regarded as 'important'.

It is a common practice of the GA that many of its resolutions get adopted by consensus without a vote and an objection, thus gaining more weight in GA's decisions. Based on the agreement of delegates, a resolution without a vote can be proposed by the president of GA.

2.8.2.3 Subsidiary Organs

The GA debates and decides on almost countless issues each year. For example, the agenda of the seventy-fifth session of the GA, adopted at its 2nd plenary meeting, on 18 September 2020, contained 183 agenda items. Usually, these items are pre-discussed and prepared in permanent subsidiary committees of the GA. Otherwise, the GA could not handle the workload.

There are six main committees:

- First Committee: Disarmament and International Security Committee
- Second Committee: Economic and Financial Committee
- Third Committee: Social, Humanitarian and Cultural Committee
- Fourth Committee: Special Political and Decolonization Committee
- Fifth Committee: Administrative and Budgetary Committee
- Sixth Committee: Legal Committee

All Member states are represented in these committees. The result of the discussions in specific committees are reported back to the GA. Besides these major committees, the GA is also entitled under Article 22 to establish *"such subsidiary organs as it deems necessary for the performance of its functions."* There are many other committees and subsidiary organs such as Disarmament Commission, the International Law Commission (ILC), the United Nations Commission on International Trade Law (UNCITRAL), the United Nations Peace-building Commission, the Committee on Contributions, and many committees in the area of human rights such as the Committee against Torture, the Committee on the Rights of the Child, the Human Rights Committee etc. The GA has the authority to decide and modify the power of these subsidiaries. Thus, there is a comprehensive and dynamic GA system, consisting of various commissions, committees and boards, which is, however, also quite bureaucratic.

A legal issue is whether the GA can establish organs with power beyond the scope of the GA. The creation of the United Nations Administrative Tribunal (UNAT)) may give an affirmative answer. Despite the GA's lack of judicial power, UNAT enjoys the power to render binding judgments on disputes between the UN and its staff members as this power refers to the UN's internal affairs where the GA has uncontested regulatory power. According to the opinion of the ICJ on *Effect of Awards of Compensation Made by the UNAT* (1954), the judicial independence is *"essential to ensure the efficient working of the Secretariat, and to give effect to the paramount consideration of securing the highest standards of efficiency, competence and integrity. Capacity to do this arises by necessary intendment of the Charter."*[101] In other words, subsidiary organs created by the GA within the latter's regulatory power may be vested with instruments and means not available to the GA, because these powers are derived from the Charter itself in compliance with the doctrine of implied powers.

[101] *Effect of Awards of Compensation Made by the UNAT*, Advisory Opinion, ICJ Rep. 57 (1954).

2.8.2.4 Functions and Powers of the GA

a) Generally

The principal functions of GA are: to receive and consider reports from SC and other organs of UN (Article 15 UNCh);[102] to consider and approve the budget of the UN (Article 17 UNCh); to participate in elections and other internal issues of the organization; and, as most fundamental function of GA, to considerate and thus make recommendation to issues within the scope of the Charter (Article 10 UNCh). Thus, the GA may, in the words of Article 10 UNCh, deal with *"any questions or any matters within the scope of the present Charter or relating to the powers and functions of any organs provided for in the present Charter, and, except as provided in Article 12, may make recommendations to the Members of the United Nations or to the Security Council or to both on any such questions or matters."* The only two limitations to the vast recommendation power of GA are matters *"which are essentially within the domestic jurisdiction of any state"* (Article 2(7) UNCh) and disputes or situations which *"the Security Council is exercising the function assigned to it"* (Article 12 UNCh). However, these two limitations have minor impact in reality. In terms of Article 2(7) UNCh, matters without any international concern are shrinking in this interdependent world. When it comes to Article 12, the seemingly 'exclusive' authority of Security Council does not impede the GA to express its opinion on conflicts in which the SC is involved.

As has been pointed out earlier,[103] the GA usually merely makes recommendations. However, it is clearly an oversimplification to argue that it has no binding power at all. The legal nature of its resolutions depends on the concrete resolutions. There are resolutions which may create direct obligations for member states, such as approval of budget (Article 17), elections to different organs (Article 4, 23 and 61), admission to membership (Article 4), the interpretation of the Charter by the GA, and binding directions to all subsidiary organs except those that have independent powers like UNAT or which were established by the SC. In other words, the GA has, as all plenary organs of international organizations have,[104] *internal law-making power and thus to make binding decisions*. Another type of recommendations in form of *formal declarations adopted by consensus may be viewed as 'soft law'*, which contain a consensus of the world community and will become evidence of new rules of international law first *in statu nascendi*, and later, if there is a consistent practice, of customary international law. This can be illustrated with the examples of the Universal Declaration of Human Rights (1948) and the Declaration on Principles of International Law concerning Friendly Relations and Co-operation among States (GA Res 2625 XXV 1970). Contents in these declarations relating to human rights, the right of self-determination and non-intervention principle are crucial in

---

[102] In earlier times to perform functions with respect to the now inactive trusteeship system as required by the Charter (Art. 16).

[103] See supra, Sect. 2.8.2.1.

[104] See supra, Sect. 1.10.4.

identifying the development of customary international law. Moreover, the GA may also play a kind of *legislative role in drafting and adopting treaties and conventions* such as the Law of the Sea Conventions (1982) or the UN Framework Convention on Climate Change (1992). The adoption of these treaties by the GA, however, only means that they are open to ratification by states. The adoption itself in the GA does not create legal obligations of the states.[105]

Despite the non-binding nature of most recommendations made by GA to states on international issues, the GA is involved in numerous aspects of human society. Four specific functions of the GA shall be described in more details.

b) International Peace and Security[106] (Article 11 and Article 14):
The GA is entitled to *"consider general questions concerning the maintenance of peace"* (Article 11(1) UNCh), and *"to discuss all questions in this context"* (Article 11(2) UNCh). In a larger sense, the GA is entitled to recommend, when required, solutions for the peaceful settlement of disputes or other situations *"of a nature likely to impair the general welfare or friendly relations among States"* (Article 14 Charter). Bearing in mind that the main responsibility of maintaining international peace and security lies in the hand of the Security Council, based on Chapter VI and VII of the Charter, the respective powers of the GA are concurring or subsidiary. The basic difference is that the GA's focus is foremost to adopt *general principles on the maintenance of peace and security* like disarmament issues (Article 11(1) UNCh), and *not concrete conflict management* which is the task of the SC. However, also the GA often makes recommendations in specific conflicts, but these recommendations are usually not binding. There are, however, two practices developed within the UN that deviate from is principle:

aa) Uniting for Peace Resolution The first practice is the Uniting for Peace Resolution.[107] At the end of the 1940s, the Western States dominated in the UN. As a reaction, the Soviet Union very often used its veto power in the Security Council. Frustrated by the deadlock of the Security Council caused by the veto, Western States pushed the GA to adopt the resolution Uniting for Peace (Resolution 377(V)) on November 3, 1950.[108] Under this resolution, when the Security Council is paralyzed by a veto, the GA may be convoked in the form of an emergency session through *a simple procedural vote of the SC* (a vote of affirmative 9 states, which cannot be turned down by veto) and put the situation on the GA's agenda. The GA then holds the power to determine a threat to the peace, breach of the peace or act of aggression and to make recommendations, but not binding measures, to the member states in the concrete conflict, *thus acting as a conflict manager at the place of the SC. This may include to legitimize member states to use force.*

---

[105] See supra, Sect. 1.10.4.6.

[106] <https://www.un.org/en/global-issues/peace-and-security> (accessed 9 March 2025).

[107] See supra, Sect. 2.3.3.2.

[108] See supra, ibid.

After the adoption of the resolution, the Soviet Union strongly opposed the resolution, doubting its legality. It contended that the Security Council, according to Article 12(1), possesses as a conflict manager absolute priority over specific actions, especially military actions. Article 11(2) also suggests, according to the Soviet Union, that the Security Council enjoys 'exclusive responsibility' of specific form of concrete decisions. In contrast, the Western states asserted that the resolution was lawful. They argued that the Security Council only has 'primary responsibility' of maintaining peace and security. They proved it with the fact that 'primary' is used in Article 24(1), which means that the GA has a subsidiary responsibility in this regard. Concerning article 11(2), they believed that 'recommendation' is not 'actions' implied in Article 11(2).

Though the controversies remain, the subsequent practice has confirmed the legality of the resolution. The Suez question (1956) was referred to the GA after the veto of UK and France against the resolution proposed by US, in which suspension of military sanctions against Egypt was requested. Likewise, the Congo Conflict (1960/1961) was transferred to GA after the veto of USSR. Moreover, despite the opposition of Israel, the ICJ was requested by the GA in an emergency session to provide an advisory opinion on the *Legal Consequence of the Construction of a Wall in the Occupied Palestinian Territory* (2004). The most recent instance of calling for an emergency meeting of the GA based on the Uniting for Peace Resolutions took place in February 2022 after the military attack of Ukraine by Russian armed forces which started the Russian-Ukrainian war. The adoption of Uniting for Peace can be viewed as a *de facto* amendment to the UN Charter.

bb) Peacekeeping Operations established by the GA The second practice are the UN peacekeeping forces established by the GA. During the Suez crisis in 1956, the United Nations Emergency Force (UNEF I), the first peacekeeping force operation,[109] was proposed by Dag Hammarskjold, the then Secretary-General of UN, and approved by General Assembly through Resolutions 997, 998 and 1000 (ES-1) to separate the confronting parties in the region. The establishment of the UNEF force based on resolutions of the GA met the strong opposition of USSR. The Soviet Union opined that an UN force established by the GA violated Article 11(2) and 12, which protect the sole competence of SC to take military action. In response to that, the ICJ implicitly confirmed the GA's power to establish a UN peacekeeping force in the advisory opinion on *Certain Expenses of the United Nations.*[110] The Court advised that the SC has only 'primary' responsibility for maintaining peace and security, which does not preclude the capacity of GA to make recommendations under Article 10 and 14. In addition, 'actions' in Article 11(2) refers to 'enforcement action' which has a nature of coercion against a certain state. The UNEP 'action'

---

[109] There are different understandings regarding the first peacekeeping operations. Some hold that the United Nations Truce Supervision Organization is the first peacekeeping mission.

[110] *Certain Expenses of the United Nations (Art. 17, Paragraph 2, of the Charter),* Advisory Opinion, ICJ Rep. 151 (1962), 163.

does not amount to an 'enforcement action'. Rather, it was only a 'measure' recommended under Article 14, which complies with the purposes and principles of the UN.

Ever since then, many similar peacekeeping operations have been launched in different parts of the world, but in most cases by the SC. In fact, peacekeeping operations authorized by GA are only exceptions to the common practice of peacekeeping operations decided by SC. It was under a SC resolution that the UNEF was re-established in the Middle East in 1973. Likewise, there were many SC-authorized peacekeeping forces in places such as the former Yugoslavia, Rwanda, East Timor, Cyprus, Darfur, and in other conflicts.[111]

c) General International Co-operation (Article 13 UNCh)

According to Article 13(1), the GA shall initiates studies and make recommendations for the purpose of

> *"a) promoting international co-operation in the political filed and encouraging the progressive development of international law and its codification; b) promoting international co-operation in the economic, social, cultural, educational, and health fields, and assisting in the realization of human rights and fundamental freedoms for all without distinction as to race, sex, language, or religion."*

Most of the powers of the GA as well as of the UN at large addressed by Article 13(1) (b) UNCh are also regulated in the Chapters IX (International Economic and Social Cooperation) and X (the Economic and Social Council) of the UNCh.

Since the founding of the UN, abundant resolutions targeted at almost all aspects of human society have been adopted. Aside from general issues listed in the Charter, the GA has spared no effort in giving impetus to issue areas not explicitly mentioned in the Charter such as environmental issues, development, terrorism, drug trafficking, refugees, and migration. The milestone Millennium Declaration (2000) and the World Summit Outcome Document (2005) reflect the determination of member states to reach specific goals to attain development and eliminate poverty; protect human rights and promote rule of law; preserve the environment; and strengthen the UN.

d) Advancement of International Law (Article 13(1) (a) UNCh)

Article 13(1) (a) provides that the GA shall encourage *"the progressive development of international law and its codification."* In pursuit for a more peaceful and dynamic world determined by the rule of law, the GA has established several bodies like the General Assembly Sixth Committee (Legal), the International Law Commission (ILC), and the United Nations Commission on International Trade Law (UNCITRAL).

---

[111] See infra, Sect. 2.9.4.2 for more details.

Among them, the *International Law Commission (ILC)*[112] is perhaps the most significant body as to the advancement of international law. It is a *subsidiary organ with an own statute* established by GA resolution 174(II) in 1947. It is composed of recognized international law experts who sit in their own knowledge and capacity and not as representatives of their governments. Article 1(1) of the Statute of ILC provides that the *"Commission shall have for its object the promotion of the progressive development of international law and its codification."* Many of the important global codifications were drafted by the ILC including the Vienna Convention on the Law of Treaties, Diplomatic and consular relations, State responsibility, State succession, Law of the Sea, Immunity of States etc. The recent topics on the program of work of ILC include: Immunity of State officials from foreign criminal jurisdiction, formation and evidence of customary international law, protection of the environment in relation to armed conflicts, and protection of the atmosphere.

e) Protection of Human Rights:*[113] *(Article 13(1) (b) UNCh)

Article 13(1)(b) provides that the GA shall assist in *"the realization of human rights and fundamental freedoms for all without distinction as to race, sex, language, or religion."* Human rights, highlighted in the preamble, Article 1(2), Article 13(1) and Article 55 of the UNCh, belong to the priorities of the UN: No sustainable protection of human rights, no long-term peace. Evidently, the protection of human rights is part of the 'positive peace' approach of the UN.

The GA made a great contribution to human rights development by adopting series of pivotap conventions and declarations such as the Universal Declaration of Human Rights (1948), the International Covenant on Economic, Social and Cultural Rights (1966), the International Covenant on Civil and Political Rights (1966), the International Convention on the Elimination of All Forms of Racial Discrimination (1965), the Convention on the Elimination of All Forms of Discrimination against Women (1979), the Convention against Torture and Other Cruel, Inhuman or Degrading Treatment or Punishment (1984), the Convention on the Rights of the Child (1989), the International Convention on the Protection of the Rights of All Migrant Workers and Members of Their Families (1990), the International Convention for the Protection of All Persons from Enforced Disappearance (2006), and the Convention on the Rights of Persons with Disabilities. These treaties, documents, and declarations (some of them are created by subsidiary organs of the GA and/or the ECOSOC) touch areas involving minorities, indigenous peoples, self-determination of peoples, prevention of discrimination, rights of women, rights of children, rights of older persons, rights of migrants, rights of stateless persons, asylum and refugees and so on. Without doubt, *the GA plays the leading role in global human rights standard setting.*

[112] <http://www.un.org/law/ilc/> (accessed 9 March 2025).

[113] <https://www.un.org/en/our-work/protect-human-rights> (accessed 9 March 2025).

In 2006, the Human Rights Council was created by GA to replace its predecessor, the Human Rights Committee. The Committee was a subsidiary organ of ECOSOC. Its main task was to ensure the respect and protection of universal human rights by standard setting, confidential consultation procedure with member states accused of gross and systemic violations of human rights, and making recommendations to states according to its reporting system. However, it had been criticized by Western countries due to the ineffectiveness of its activities and the presence of member states with little regard to human rights. Therefore, the Council reformed in three ways. First, the Council is a subsidiary organ of the GA, reflecting the elevated status of the institution. Second, the number of member states got reduced from 53 to 47. States will not become members unless they are elected by a (simple) majority of the GA and keep the highest standards in human rights. Crucially, if a member state commits gross and systemic violations of human rights, it can be suspended by a two-thirds majority of the GA.[114] Third, a universal periodic review mechanism was established to ensure the fulfillment of human rights obligations of all UN member states. Though the Council marked a new start in the UN supervision on human rights, the Council, due to its role of offering unbinding recommendations, may still do little in a world divided on human rights issues.

The Human Rights Council is not to be confused with the United Nations Human Rights Committee, which is a treaty-based body composed of 18 experts established by the 1966 International Covenant on Civil and Political Rights (ICCPR). This body considers the periodic reports on human rights compliance submitted by the parties to the Covenant and decides on individual petitions referring to concrete human rights violations, based on the First Optional Protocol to the ICCPR.

2.8.3 The Secretary General (SG) and the Secretariat (Article 97–101 UN Charter)

2.8.3.1 Overview

The SG heads the Secretariat which is an international staff that carries out the daily work of the UN. Currently, it has approximately 43,000 staff members around the world.[115] The SG is the Chief Administrative Officer of the UN (Article 97). He or she is elected by the GA on the recommendation of the SC. Since 2017 António Guterres is the ninth Secretary-General of the United Nations. As international civil servants, the SG and its staff are solely responsible to the UN for their activities. They shall not seek or receive instructions from any government or external

[114] This happened to Russia after the 2022 military invasion of the Ukraine: see A/ES-11/L.4 (2022).

[115] *Composition of the Secretariat: staff demographics*, Report of the SG, A/78/569 (2023).

authority. Moreover, they are also protected accordingly by the Convention on the Privileges and Immunities of the UN (1946).

2.8.3.2 Functions and Powers

The SG has administrative and political functions. In terms of administrative functions, the SG is responsible for the entire UN administration. Internally, he shall coordinate the work of the Secretariat and that of the other UN organs. Externally, he is the representative of the UN. The SG is also in charge of the budget and other financial aspects of the UN, the agenda setting for the principal organs, the preparation and implementation of resolutions of the principal organs, and the registration of the treaties (Article 102 UNCh). Moreover, he shall elaborate the annual report to the GA on the work of UN (Article 98 UNCh).

Besides the main bureaucratic functions, the SG also has important political power. In particular, he *"may bring to the SC any matter which in his opinion may threaten the maintenance of international peace and security"* (Article 99). Literarily, this power, which also member states and the GA have, seems limited. However, the political function of SG goes beyond the limit of mere signaling potential crisis to SC. These powers include responsibility for peacekeeping forces, mediation efforts made in various crises like the lengthy Palestinian crisis by several SGs, and the prevention of crisis by preventive diplomacy advocated in Secretary General Boutros Boutros-Ghali's report termed 'An Agenda for Peace' (1992). In addition, the SG shall also perform all the other activities entrusted to him by principal organs. This can be illustrated with the example of international civil presence in Kosovo after 1999, which was established by the SG under the authorization of SC. Generally, it is often up to the SG to execute the decisions of the SC.

2.8.4 The Security Council (SC)

2.8.4.1 Overview

The Security Council (SC) is *the key executive organ of the UN*. It bears the primary responsibility for the maintenance of international peace and security (Article 24 UNCh) and is thus in charge with the *concrete conflict and crisis management*. In contrast to the Council of the LoN, the SC was given greater power to react efficiently to emergencies and to threats of international peace and security. First, there is no strict limit of its competence. The only limit of its capacity is that it shall *"act in accordance with the Purposes and Principles of the UN"* (Article 24(2) UNCh). Second, it is a permanent organ, which can be called into session at any moment in case of the need for a quick reaction to a crisis. A permanent representative of each SC member state shall be present at the UN headquarter in New York City at all times. Third, it is equipped with a variety of means and options for measures, including recommendations, provisional measures, enforcement measures etc. In fact, the SC has the freedom to choose among these measures or adopt new measures beyond those listed in Chapter VI, VII, VIII and XII. Unlike the universal membership in GA as the plenary organ of the UN, the SC as *non-plenary organ* is composed of 15 member states, 5 permanent members with veto power and 10 non-permanent members without veto power (Article 23). Reflecting the political status of states at the end of WW II, the five permanent members are: USA, UK, France, Russia, and China. In 1971, the government of People's Republic of China replaced the seat of Taiwan. In 1991, Russia continued the seat of the Soviet Union. The 10 non-permanent members have been elected for a two-year term, with 5 replaced each year. The geographic distribution should be respected: 3 from African; 2 from Asian States, 1 from Eastern European States, 2 from Latin American States; and 2 from Western European and other States.

2.8.4.2 Procedure, Decision-making, and Voting

The veto power is given to the five permanent SC members (P-5). According to the realistic theory in International Relations, the SC or even the UN would not function well if the great powers were not given more rights and privileges. It is difficult to imagine that an activity of the UN operates well if the great powers fundamentally disapprove it. Since these great powers are given more responsibility for international peace and security, it seems reasonable to give them more political power than others.[116] This at least was the prevailing opinion when the UN were established. Thus, because based on the agreement by all member states, the special status does not violate the principle of sovereign equality conferred in Article 1(1) UNCh.

According to article 27(1) UNCh, each SC member has one vote. Procedural matters, narrowly defined, require 9 affirmative votes. The veto is not available (Article 27(2) UNCh). Non-procedural matters require 9 affirmative votes with no veto from one or more permanent members (Article 27(3) UNCh). This steady practice of the SC does not correspond to the wording of Art, 27(3) UNCh which states that *"[d]ecisions of the Security Council on all other matters shall be made by an affirmative vote of nine members including the concurring votes of the permanent members."* The practice thus is that an abstention of a permanent member does not amount to a veto. This is an example of a tacit modification of a treaty establishing an international organization through a steady practice of an organ of the organization recognized by the member states as lawful. If the nature of an issue, procedural or non-procedural, is in controversy, a preliminary decision, subject to veto, shall be voted. This so-called *'double veto' is designed to prevent bypassing a veto simply through a majority vote of 9.*

There is no general rule in the Charter that a state which is a party e.g. in a dispute shall not vote in the GA or the SC. Thus, the rule *nemo iudex in re sua* is not observed. This is why Russia could prevent the SC from taking any decisions after the Russian invasion of the Ukraine - an invasion that was a flagrant violation of

[116] Another issue is whether the right states are vested with the veto power and whether veto power should (also) be given to regional organizations such as AU or the OAS.

basic Charter principles as well as of basic rules of international law such as the prohibition to use force and the obligation to respect a state's territorial integrity and political independence. The duty of a SC member which is a party to a dispute under consideration of the SC to abstain from voting refers only to *"decisions under Chapter VI, and under paragraph 3 of Article 52"* (Article 27(3) UNCh). This obligation thus is limited to dispute settlement attempts of the SC or of regional arrangements.

Along with the unique voting requirement, the procedure and decision-making process reveals the character of SC as well. Though there are regular meetings, numerous informal meetings and consultations play a significant role in the bargaining and decision-making process. To avoid a veto, there are often consultations among the P-5 prior to a formal SC meeting. Some criticize that this practice lacks transparency and leaves the public deliberation a mere formality. Others believe that it is understandable to have this type of decision-making process which reflects the practices of international diplomacy and international politics, and which allows to reach negotiation-based compromises.

2.8.4.3 Subsidiary Organs

Maintenance of international peace and security is a comprehensive and dynamic task demanding different political and administrative actors from different levels to make their contribution in different phases and at different places. To better support the SC decision-making, the SC has established various subsidiary organs based on Article 29 UNCh. These include: Committee concerning Peacekeeping Operations (PKOs); sanctions Committees for special conflicts; several Working Groups; Tribunals for Ex-Yugoslavia and Rwanda; committees dealing with counter-terrorism; etc.

Sanctions committees created by SC[117] oversee the daily administration of sanctions the SC imposes. The member states in the sanction committees are usually the same as those in SC. Typical sanction committees were Al-Qaida/ Taliban (Resolution 1267, 1999), fight against terrorism (Resolution 1373, 2001), and Iraq (Resolution 1533, 2004).[118] Though the ultimate power to alter the sanction is seized by SC, sanction committees are empowered to examine the reports submitted by the Secretary General, regional organizations or states on how to put sanctions into practice. Moreover, they also have a decision power relating to the execution of the sanctions.

In addition, *ad hoc international criminal courts* such as the International Criminal Tribunal for the former Yugoslavia (ICTY) are other examples for—*albeit very untypical - subsidiary organs of the SC*. These courts are international institutions

---

[117] See the overview under <https://www.un.org/securitycouncil/content/repertoire/sanctions-and-other-committees> (accessed 9 March 2025).

[118] See for an overview on the many sanction committees of the SC, ibid.

vested with *international legal personality*.[119] They act, as courts, basically independent of the SC. The power of the SC to establish these courts is considered *an implied power as well as the power of the SC to define the crimes to be judged by the courts*. This implied power which includes the power to create institutions with international legal personality and to legislate is derived from the general power of the SC to make legally binding decisions under Chapter VII in instances of a threat to the peace or of a breach of peace. This practice which goes far beyond of the usual powers of an executive organ of an international organization reflects almost unlimited powers of the SC.

2.8.4.4 Functions and Powers

a) Functions

The SC has mainly two sorts of functions, *organizational* and *political*. To the organizational functions belongs the involvement of the SC in decisions regarding membership status like the admission, suspension, and expulsion of states to be decided by the GA upon the indispensable recommendation of SC (Article 4–6 UNCh). In addition, the Secretary General is appointed by the GA upon the recommendation of the SC (Article 97 UNCh), and the ICJ judges are elected by the GA and the SC together (Article 2 of ICJ Statute).

As for political functions, the SC is given the *"primary responsibility for the maintenance of international peace and security"*. The member states agree that the SC can *"act on their behalf"* (Article 24(1) UN Charter). Then, what are the criteria for 'international peace and security'? In its practice, especially those in the recent 30 years, the SC has developed a very broad understanding of the notion of peace. Internal conflicts within a certain state, in the eye of SC, may also affect overall international peace. Relevant issues for international peace include human rights, terrorism, ecological problems, health, poverty, development etc. Moreover, the SC plays a role as *the guardian and executor of international law*. The non-observance of international law may constitute a problem of international peace as well. The extensive interpretation of international peace and security can be proved not only by the actual practice of the SC but was conceptionalized in reports and documents of UN such as the Report 'A More Secure World' (2004) and the Report 'In Larger Freedom' of the UN Secretary General (2005). Despite the guidance and limitation from the purposes and principles of the UN (Article 24(2)), the power of the SC inevitably expanded based on the broad view on notion of peace.

b) Powers

The basic powers of the SC are two-fold: *pacific settlement of disputes under Chapter VI*, and *action with respect to threat to the peace, breaches of the peace, and acts of aggression under Chapter VII*. Compared to the powers of the SC under

---

[119] See supra, Sect. 1.8.2.7.

Chapter VII, powers directed to a pacific settlement of disputes are relatively limited. It is common for the SC to make non-binding recommendations to the parties of the dispute. In contrast, the actions under Chapter VII may consist of mere recommendations, provisional measures, binding obligations, enforcement measures not involving or involving the use of force. The measures are taken in the form of resolutions which are binding on member states according to Article 2(5), Article 25, Article 48, Article 49 and Article 103. A more general legal basis in the Charter as to binding decisions of the SC are Article 24 and 25.

Therefore, a resolution may consist of *paragraphs of different (legal) nature*. It is thus necessary to examine the resolution paragraph by paragraph even if a resolution is in its entirety adopted under Chapter VII. The starting point of an analysis are the *wording* and the *legal basis mentioned in the resolution*. To begin with, procedural resolutions and those pertaining to UN-internal matters are legally binding.[120] Resolutions based on Chapter VI are usually non-binding recommendations. On the contrary, resolutions based on Chapter VII are usually binding except for those recommendations provided in Article 39. In addition, provisional measures based on Article 40 are binding. Lastly, there are still some binding decisions directly based on Article 24 and 25. According to the advisory opinion of ICJ on *Legal Consequences for States of the Continued Presence of South Africa in Namibia* (1971), the SC could exercise its coercive power directly based on Article 25 when it determines to do so.[121]

2.8.5 The Economic and Social Council (ECOSOC)

2.8.5.1 Overview

The Economic and Social Council is a non-plenary organ created to coordinate economic, social, cultural, environmental, human rights and other activities of the UN and its affiliated organizations. Since ECOSOC shares overlapping competence with GA and is under the overall authority of the GA (Article 60), it is *de facto* a subsidiary organ of the GA regarding economic and social issues. The establishment of a principal organ devoted to economic and social issues is rooted in the idea that peace cannot be achieved simply by coercive measures against aggressive states but that sustainable peace requires also social and economic cooperation and integration. Moreover, it is also inspired and pushed by the lesson of the Bruce Committee of the League of Nations in 1939[122] and the establishment of Bretton Wood System in 1944, which shows that more attention should be paid in this field and that a

[120] E.g. the establishment of a PKO as a subsidiary organ of the SC.

[121] *Legal Consequences for States of the Continued Presence of South Africa in Namibia* (Advisory Opinion), ICJ Rep. 16 (1971), para. 115.

[122] The Special Committee made a report in Aug 1939 suggesting reforms to the League's organization regarding the dealing with economic and social issues.

specialized organ of UN should be responsible for the coordination work within and outside the UN principal system.

ECOSOC consists of 54 delegates from 54 respective member states elected by the GA. The government delegates, serving a three-years term, come from various continents so as to represent a wider range of economic, social and cultural interests. ECOSOC holds the longest ordinary meeting in July while it also holds several short sessions a year. The session is divided into 5 segments: High-level; Coordination; Operational Activities; Humanitarian Affairs; and General. Among them, the High-level segment often attracts top-ranking policymakers. Focusing on themes from the UN's Millennium Development Goals, the segment's Annual Ministerial Review (AMR) and biennial Development Cooperation Forum (DCF) have been a remarkable success.

2.8.5.2 Voting

The equality of member state is respected in ECOSOC, where each member state has one vote (Article 67(1) UNCH). Decisions of the ECOSOC are based on a simple majority of the members present and voting (Article 67(2) UNCh).

2.8.5.3 Subsidiary Organs

In pursuit to fulfill its broad task, the ECOSOC established a variety of subsidiary organs, the activities of which may be finally decided by ECOSOC:

- *ECOSOC Functional Commissions*: Statistical Commission, Commission on Population and Development, Commission for Social Development, Commission on the Status of Women, Commission on Narcotic Drugs, Commission on Crime Prevention and Criminal Justice, Commission on Science and Technology for Development, Commission on Sustainable Development, United Nations Forum on Forests.
- *ECOSOC Regional Commissions*: Economic Commission for Africa (ECA) Economic and Social Commission for Asia and the Pacific (ESCAP), Economic Commission for Europe (ECE), Economic Commission for Latin America and the Caribbean (ECLAC), Economic and Social Commission for Western Asia (ESCWA).
- *ECOSOC Standing Committees*: Committee for Programme and Coordination, Committee on Non-Governmental Organizations, Committee on Negotiations with Intergovernmental Agencies.
- *Other*. For instance, expert bodies composed of governmental experts like United Nations Group of Experts on Geographical Names.

2.8.5.4 Functions and Powers

Chapter IX of the Charter, i.e. Articles 55–60, is devoted to international economic and social cooperation. The ECOSOC bears, together with the GA, the main responsibility for developing the respective policies and rules (Article 60 UNCh). It is responsible for some 70% of the human and financial resources of the entire UN system. Though ECOSOC is set up with a wide range of tasks (Article 55 and 56), it is not given the power of legislation and enforcement. Rather, it can only make recommendations to states, to the GA and to the specialized agencies (Articles 58 and 62 UNCh), receive annual reports from specialized agencies (Article 64 UNCh) and coordinate the UN activities with more than 5000 NGOs. However, in its role as a coordinator the ECOSOC is indispensable.

a) General competence
Article 62 UNCh regulates the general functions and powers of the ECOSOC. Based on this provision it *"may make or initiate studies and reports with respect to international economic, social, cultural, educational, health, and related matters and may make recommendations with respect to any such matters to the General Assembly to the Members of the United Nations, and to the specialized agencies concerned."* The ECOSOC also has the power to make recommendations to promote and protect human rights and fundamental freedoms and to prepare draft conventions in all the policy areas covered by its activities, to be adopted by the General Assembly.

b) Relationship with other organs, states and special agencies
ECOSOC further assists in matter falling in its competence the SC, the GA (Article 65 and 66 UNCh), member states and specialized agencies with the approval of the GA (Article 66 UNCh). The UN Development Program (UNDP), established by GA Res 2029 (XX) in 1966, e.g., is the major channel for providing developing countries with technical and investment assistance. The financial source is mainly originated from the contribution of governments. The supervision power lies in the hand of an Executive Board. The program is closely associated with financiers, receivers and international financing institutions.

On balance, programs and funds are principally subject to the supervision of the GA and can be modified by GA resolution. With the advent of new issues such as the spread of AIDS, Covid-19, climate change, population growth, the rights of women and children, new programs and funds emerged. Aside from UNDP, the following programs and funds are also of great significant in respective areas: UN International Drug Control Program (UNDCP), UN Environmental Program (UNEP), World Food Program (WEP), UN Population Fund (UNPF), and UN Children's Fund (UNCF).

c) Coordination with Specialized Agencies
Contrary to programs and funds, specialized agencies are legally, financially and politically independent from GA and ECOSOC. Specialized agencies are special organizations belonging to the UN family but with their own international legal

personality. According to Articles 57 and 63 UNCh, after entering an agreement with these specialized agencies, ECOSOC may coordinate the activities by ways of consultations with and recommendations to these specialized agencies. Moreover, ECOSOC may also make recommendations to the GA and the member states. The most well-known specialized agencies include: the World Health Organization (WHO), the Food and Agriculture Organization (FAO), the International Labour Organizations (ILO), the United Nations Educational, Scientific and Cultural Organizations (UNESCO), the International Atomic Energy Agency (IAEA), etc.[123]

d) Relations with other IOs
Compared to the formal arrangements between specialized agencies and the UN, informal arrangement is dominant in the relationship between other intergovernmental organizations, including regional organizations, and the ECOSOC. It is a common practice that the ECOSOC occasionally invites regional organizations and other international organizations to observe certain sessions on related issues. Further, exchange of documents and information may also take place between the ECOSOC and other international organizations on an ad hoc basis.

e) Relations with NGOs
The interaction between the ECOSOC and non-governmental organizations (NGOs) is regulated in 'suitable arrangements' based on Article 70 UNCh and ECOSOC resolution 31 of 1996.[124] In practice, the NGOs are categorized into three types: one with a 'general consultative status', one with a 'special consultative status' and 'the Roster'. The first category refers to those which have a fundamental interest in most activities of the ECOSOC. They can make oral presentations or even motion agendas on the sessions. The second category is those which have a special interest and competence in several areas of the ECOSOC. They generally have the right to submit written documents to member states of ECOSOC. The last category is usually composed of those could make occasional contribution to specific issues. It is noteworthy that under no circumstances will the NGOs enjoy the same status as state and specialized agencies in the ECOSOC. Nevertheless, the significance of the link between UN and the civil society can hardly be neglected.[125]

---

[123] See also infra Sect. 2.10.

[124] *Consultative relationship between the United Nations and non-governmental organizations*, E/RES/1996/31.

[125] For more details see infra, Sect. 6.4.3.

2.8.6 *The International Court of Justice (ICJ)*

2.8.6.1 Overview

The International Court of Justice (ICJ) is the main judicial organ of the UN and regulated in Chapter XIV UNCh. The seat of the ICJ is at the Peace Palace in the Hague, Netherlands. Compared to other UN courts like UNAT, ICTY and ICTR, the ICJ is the central instrument in legal dispute settlement within the UN legal framework. It is composed of 15 independent judges elected for 9 years by the GA and the SC. The two organs vote independently at the same time. A candidate should acquire a two-third majority of the votes in both organs.

There are three defining characters of ICJ: the high legal status, the universality of potential (state) parties, and the overall source of international law. To start with, the Statute of International Court of Justice forms an integral part of the Charter (Article 92), which means that the Statute shares the equal status as provisions in the Charter. The Statute and Chapter XIV UNCh together constitute the legal foundation of the Court. This is different from the Statute of the Permanent Court of International Justice, for the Statute of PCIJ was a separate treaty to the Covenant of the League of Nations. Moreover, it is open to UN members and non-members (Article 93 UNCh). Since the universality of UN is nearly accomplished, the ICJ is now the court of the entire state system constituting the international community. Furthermore, based on Article 38 of the Statute of ICJ regarding the source of international law, the ICJ is the only judicial body empowered to apply general international law without restriction to a specific treaty or area like the European Court of Human Rights is.

Over 80 years, the ICJ has contributed to the development of public international law through its case law and advisory opinion. Therefore, an understanding of ICJ is a must in understanding rule of law within and outside UN.

The ICJ has two major functions: *contentious cases* and *advisory opinions*. The former refers to legal disputes between states, while the latter are legal opinion on legal questions referred to it by UN organs and specialized agencies. Since the two functions have different characters, they need separate examination.

2.8.6.2 Functions and Powers: Contentious Cases

a) Parties

Only states may be the parties to the contentious cases (Article 4(1) ICJ Statute). These states include the member states of the UN, other States which have become parties to the Statute of the Court, and states that have accepted ICJ's jurisdiction under certain conditions laid down by the SC (Article 93 UNCh; Article 35 of ICJ Statute). International organizations, NGOs, corporations, individuals, and other private entities have no standing at the ICJ.

b) Jurisdiction and admissibility

Jurisdiction of the ICS basically *rests on the consent of the parties*. That is because the ICJ has no mandatory jurisdiction for and over the member states of UN. The states still have the freedom to choose whether to submit the dispute and which tribunal to submit (Article 95 UNCh). Therefore, without the consent of parties, the ICJ lacks the power to examine a dispute. There are several ways that states agree to the ICJ's jurisdiction:

- A special agreement entered into between the parties accepting ICJ's jurisdiction in a particular controversy.
- A compromissory clause in treaties between the parties, i.e. a treaty provision regulating the Courts mandatory jurisdiction under the treaty.
- A unilateral declaration by a state. However, the declaration should be reciprocal, which means that declarations have once been made by both parties, whether simultaneously or not, to accept the jurisdiction of the ICJ as compulsory in an event of a dispute. However, a clear insight into these declarations is essential, for they may contain all sorts of reservations, whether they limited to certain states, certain categories of dispute, or certain time periods (Article 36(2) ICJ Statute).

Another question crucial to consider is whether the dispute submitted by the parties is a legal dispute. The ICJ is not empowered to give judgment on pure political or technical issues. Then, as numerous international disputes have both a legal side and a political one, how can one determine whether it is a legal dispute or not?

In practice, a subjective approach may be helpful. In other words, it is necessary to examine whether the parties, through a special agreement or the applicant party in a unilateral suit, frame their disputes based on legal rights and arguments or not. If the answer is affirmative, then the dispute is a legal one; if not, the dispute is a political one. For instance, State A may claim that State B should change its foreign policy. If State A claims that the foreign policy actually violated a certain provision in an existing treaty between the two, the dispute is legal. If, on the contrary, State A argues that the foreign policy is immoral or inappropriate without producing any legal argument, then the dispute is political.

c) Proceeding

In contentious proceedings, when a dispute is brought before the Court by a unilateral application filed by one State against another State, the names of parties in the official title of the case are separated by the abbreviation v. for the Latin versus (e.g., India v. Pakistan). When a dispute is submitted to the Court on the basis of a special agreement between two States, the names of the parties are separated by an oblique stroke (e.g., Vietnam/Thailand).

Under Article 31(2) (3) of ICJ Statute, a state party may choose a person to sit as judge if there is a judge of the nationality of the other party on the Bench. Moreover, if there is no judge of the nationalities of the parties, each of the parties may appoint a judge to the Bench. These *ad hoc* judges chosen by the parties need not have the nationality of the appointing state. Yet they share equality with their colleagues. Though controversies exist, the majority of states believe that it is helpful to have an "own" judge more familiar with the situation to be on the court. The practice of the ad hoc judges also shows that these judges may decide regardless of what 'their states' stand for.

d) Sources of Law

Article 38(1) of ICJ Statute regulates the sources of law to be applied by the ICJ.[126] The article reads as follows:

> *"The Court, whose function is to decide in accordance with international law such disputes as are submitted to it, shall apply:*
> a. *international conventions, whether general or particular, establishing rules expressly recognized by the contesting states;*
> b. *international custom, as evidence of a general practice accepted as law;*
> c. *the general principles of law recognized by civilized nations;*
> d. *subject to the provisions of Article 59, judicial decisions and the teachings of the most highly qualified publicists of the various nations, as subsidiary means for the determination of rules of law."*

The article mentions the classical three categories of legal sources of international law relevant for and to be applied by the ICJ: *international treaties and conventions* in force; *customary international law*; and the *general principles of law* recognized by the states. The three are different. International treaties and conventions are agreements between states or international organizations on their respective rights and obligations. Customary international law requires an *opinio juris* and state practice. State practice should be consistent, long-term, and general, and it should be conducted by the states out of a sense of obligation (*opinio juris*). The general principles are more controversial, because they lack definition and do not have a clear boundary with customary international law. It is the task of ICJ, which is composed with *"representatives from the main forms of civilization and of the principle legal systems of the World"*,[127] to define and develop international law in this respect. It is commonly believed that there is no hierarchy among the three, but the order of the three in the article implies a certain order of application for the ICJ. But this has more to do with the legal quality of these three sources: treaty provisions are much more specific than customary international law or the general principles of law. It is therefore not surprising that treaty law plays a dominant role in ICJ judgments.

"Judicial decisions and the teachings of the most highly qualified publicists of the various nations" are subsidiary means to identify international legal rules. In addition, Article 38(1) of ICJ Statute does not list resolutions of international

---

[126] Art. 38(1) of ICJ Statute does not preclude the possibility of ICJ to decide a case ex aequo et bono if the parties agree. However, no case has been decided without referring to legal principles and rules yet.

[127] Art. 9 Statute ICJ.

organizations as a source of international law. And indeed, these *resolutions display legal force only within the organization* and are therefore not generally applicable. Nonetheless, ICJ judgments regularly refer to resolutions, e.g., of the UN GA and/or SC, but rather as an expression of an international practice and/or as evidence for the existence of a rule of customary international law but not as an independent source of law.

e) Judgment and Execution

The judgment of the ICJ on contentious case is final and without appeal. The binding effect only exists between the parties and in respect of that particular case (Article 59 of the ICJ Statute). However, in practice ICJ judgments are very important and have as leading cases an impact far beyond the concrete case.

In terms of execution of the judgment, the judgments are usually honored. The reasons are three-fold: First, according to Article 94(1) UNCh, a member state, by signing the Charter, promised to comply with any decision of the Court in a case to which it is a party. Further, ICJ can only issue judgment when the parties have agreed to the jurisdiction of the ICJ, which means that they had evaluated the possible outcome of the case and that they are ready to accept that. More importantly, if any party fails to perform the obligations incumbent upon it by the judgment of ICJ, the other party may refer the matter to the SC, which has power to make recommendations or decide upon measures to give effect to the judgment (Article 94(2) UNCh). An exception is the *Military and Paramilitary Activities in and against Nicaragua* Case (Merits, 1996). The US vetoed the execution of the judgment in SC. This demonstrates that loopholes exist in the ICJ judicial and enforcement system.

2.8.6.3 Advisory Opinions

According to Article 96 UNCh, UN organs and specialized agencies are entitled to request an advisory opinion from the ICJ. As for GA and SC, they may request the ICJ to give judicial statements on "any legal questions." When it comes to other organs and specialized agencies, they are only allowed to request an advisory opinion on "legal questions arising within the scope of their activities" based on an authorization by the GA. In general, the ICJ, as a principal judicial organ within the UN, should and does not refuse a request for an opinion, unless *"compelling reasons would justify refusal of such a request."*[128] Also abstract legal issues can be submitted to the ICJ for an advisory opinion. The ICJ answered in an advisory opinion that such an opinion is a *"legal advice to organs and institutions requesting the opinion…, The fact that the question put to the Court does not relate to a specific*

[128] *Application for Review of Judgment No. 273 of the United Nations Administrative Tribunal*, Advisory Opinion, ICJ Rep. 347 (1982), para. 22.

dispute should consequently not lead the Court to decline to give the opinion requested."[129]

However, the Court is sometimes compelled to distinguish legal questions from political ones and to focus on the legal issues. The ICJ did not directly respond to that question, but it underlined again in its advisory opinion on *Legality of the Threat or Use of Nuclear Weapons* (1996) that the fact that a question had a political aspect could not deprive it of its character of a legal nature, because the ICJ was asked to give opinion on the compatibility of the use of nuclear weapon with international law. This is somehow the 'subjective approach' as has been introduced in the counterpart of 'contentious cases.' Another question is whether the consent of a state concerned is a prerequisite to enable the ICJ to render an advisory opinion. The ICJ replies with a negative answer. That is because the advisory opinion has no binding effect. It is given to an organ to enable that organ to conduct its activities in accordance with law. The reply to a request represents ICJ's participation in the UN to which it itself belongs as an organ.[130]

Advisory opinions, unlike the ICJ judgments, have no binding force. Therefore, the organs and specialized agencies still have the freedom to decide what they can draw from the opinions. However, the advisory opinion may be binding if certain instruments and regulations so provide.

2.8.6.4 The ICS's Role and Impact

There is little doubt that the ICJ, as the leading judicial body of the world, has made important contributions to the development of international law by its contentious case judgments and advisory opinions. Clarifying significant international customs and general principles, many of the judgments and opinions serve as the cornerstone of current international law and of peaceful dispute settlement. Despite these achievements, criticism has been raised against several aspects of the ICJ. For instance, some argue that parties are restricted to 'states' will deprive victims suffering from crimes against humanity of their opportunities to access to ICJ, for their states may not back up them. Moreover, the restrictive regulation as to the standing before the ICJ makes it for the Court impossible to play a role as a kind of constitutional court of the UN comparable to the CJEU's role as main court of the EU securing the rule of law within the Union. Additionally, since the ICJ has no supervisory jurisdiction for a great number of international tribunals and courts like ICC, ICTY, ICTR and Tribunal for the Law of the Sea, there may be uncertainties and conflicts in parts of the international law system, this because of an incoherent international case law.

---

[129] *Legality of the Threat or Use of Nuclear Weapons*, Advisory Opinion, ICJ Rep. 226 (1996), para. 13.

[130] *Interpretation of Peace Treaties with Bulgaria, Hungary and Romania, First Phase,* Advisory Opinion, ICJ Rep. 65 (1950), 71 s.

2.8.7 *The Trusteeship Council (TC)*

2.8.7.1 Overview

The International Trusteeship System goes back to the mandate system of the League of Nations as regulated in Article 22 LoN Covenant.[131] The drafters of the UN Charter picked up the idea of the LoN mandate system that the internationally monitored administration of certain non-self-governing territories should lie in the hand of developed countries *acting as trustees for the international community in the interest of the inhabitants of these territories.*

The UN's International Trusteeship System is regulated in Chapter XII UNCh. Its main goal is to

> *"promote the political, economic, social, and educational advance of the inhabitants of the trustee territories, and their progressive development towards self-government or independence as may be appropriate to the particular circumstances of each territory and its peoples and the freely expressed wishes of the peoples concerned, and as may be provided by the terms of each trusteeship agreement"* (Article 76(b) UNCh).

This phrasing was later used by the GA in modified versions in the most important resolutions on self-determination of colonial territories.[132]

The Trusteeship Council is regulated in Chapter XIII UNCh. 1945, the Council consisted of the five permanent members of the Security Council and was established as one of the main organs of the UN to supervise 11 territories that were placed under trusteeship administered by seven States. The 11 territories could be divided into three categories according to Article 77 of the UN Charter:

a) 'territories now held under mandate'. These territories referred to those colonial territories that have been detached from their defeated powers (Germany, Austrian-Hungary Empire, and the Ottoman Empire) in the First World War. These territories were placed under the supervision of Mandatory States, which should keep the League of Nations informed of the territories in accordance with Article 22 of the League of Nations.
b) Territories which may be detached from enemy states as a result of the Second World War'. Italian Somalia was the only case in this category.
c) 'Territories voluntarily placed under the system by states responsible for their administration.' Some Pacific Islands, first under a Japanese mandate, then occupied by US, fitted into this category.

---

[131] See supra, Sect. 2.2.4.2.

[132] See, e.g. *the Declaration on the Granting of Independence to Colonial Countries and Peoples*, A/RES/1514 (XV).

2.8.7.2 Functions and Powers

According to Article 87 and 88 UNCh, the main functions and powers of the Trusteeship Council are to consider reports from the Administering Authorities on the political, economic, social and educational advancement of the people of Trust Territories. Moreover, in consultation with the administering authorizes, the Trusteeship Council could accept petitions and undertake periodic visit to the trust territories. Lastly, the Trusteeship Council was empowered to take any other actions on the basis of the trusteeship agreements signed between the administering authority and the Trusteeship Council.

2.8.7.3 Current Status

On 1 November 1994, with the independence of the last trust territory—Palau on 1 October 1994—the operation of the Trusteeship Council was suspended. On 25 May 1994, the Trusteeship Council agreed to meet occasionally by its decision or the decision of its President, or, at the request of a majority of its members or the GA or the SC. Since then, the Council has been inactive.

The trusteeship system was no doubt a success, with all Trust Territories' attainment of self-government or independence, either as separate states or by joining neighboring independent countries. This marked an end to colonialism.

2.9 UN System of Collective Security: Crisis and Conflict Management

2.9.1 Preliminary Remark

The maintenance of international peace and security is the UN's most important goal. The Charter-based system of collective security as regulated in Chapters VI to VIII UNCh provides the political tools and mechanisms to maintain, to build and to enforce peace as a multi-facet task. *The SC plays the most vital role, for it is this organ that has the necessary enforcement powers, but the GA and SG also make their contribution.*

The subsequent analysis of the overall UN framework for maintaining peace and security focuses on the following aspects: Pacific Settlement of Disputes; the Collective Security System; Peacekeeping Operations; and the role of Regional Arrangements.

2.9.2 *Pacific Settlement of Disputes (Chapter VI UNCh)*

2.9.2.1 Disputes and Situations

There are two parts of the UN Charter that carry out the UN system of pacific settlement of disputes: the general obligation of states to settle disputes peacefully according to Article 2(3);[133] and the detailed regulation in Chapter VI of measures and instruments available to states to settle a concrete dispute with the support of the UN, in particular of the SC.

According to Article 2(3) and Article 33, all states are obliged to settle a dispute in an amicable way. 'Dispute' in this context refers to tensions between states, concretely to circumstances adversely affecting positive (economic, historical reasons which may give rise to conflicts) or negative peace (tensions short of a threat to peace). It must have a character that *"its continuance must be likely to endanger the maintenance of international peace and security"* (Article 33 UN Charter). Internal conflicts with mere domestic concern do not belong to this type, otherwise the interference into the dispute could violate the *domaine reservé* principle of Article 2(7) UN Charter. However, in practice, the UN tends to get involved also in internal conflicts based on Chapter VI, not only on Chapter VII, for also an internal situation may give rise to tensions between states and thus become a dispute. But even absent a dispute between states the SC may get involved by referring to the notion of "situation" used in Articles 34 and 35 UNCh if there is an international concern.

2.9.2.2 Powers of the SC

In a dispute, the SC may, where it deems necessary, call upon the parties to settle their controversy by means like negotiation, inquiry, mediation, conciliation, arbitration, judicial settlement, resort to regional agencies or arrangements or other peaceful means (Article 33 UNCh). The SC may also launch its own investigation into the dispute or situation by setting up a subsidiary organ (Article 34 UNCh). This decision of investigation is subject to a non-procedural vote. Though no explicit obligations are laid upon states to permit the access of the investigation group into their territory under Chapter VI, the states generally will accept the group on the basis of the implied effect of Article 25 and international pressure. Particularly, if the investigation is undertaken under Chapter VII, serving as a fundamental basis to the solution of a threat of peace, member states are obliged to accept the investigation group.

If the parties to the dispute cannot solve the problem in a traditional way on their own, all member states have the right to direct the attention of the SC or the GA to the dispute or situation (Article 35(1) UNCh). Moreover, non-member states (Article 35(2)), the GA (Article 11 and 12), and the SG (Article 99) also have a right to call

[133] For details see supra, Sect. 2.6.4.

the attention of the SC to the dispute or situation. After the referral of the dispute, a procedural vote of a majority of nine is required to decide whether to put the dispute on the agenda of SC.

Once the dispute is on the agenda, the SC may react to it in various ways. The first way is to remind the parties to solve the dispute by using the traditional methods listed in Article 33(2) UNCh. The second way is that the SC makes recommendations regarding the procedure or methods to settle the dispute (Article 36). The *Corfu Channel* dispute between the UK and Albania in 1947 was a salient case which the SC recommended the parties to refer the dispute to the ICJ for a judicial settlement. Moreover, the SC also created subsidiary organs to deal with disputes, as happened in the Dutch-Indonesian dispute in 1947 when the Commission of Good Offices was established by the SC to help solve the problem. The third way is to make recommendations directly to the substance of the dispute

> *"[i]f the Security Council deems that the continuance of the dispute is in fact likely to endanger the maintenance of international peace and security"* (Article 37(2) UNCh).

The most well-known case may be Resolution 242 (1967) on the Israeli-Arab conflict. To establish a long-lasting peace in this region, two major principles were outlined: a) Israeli shall withdraw *"from territories occupied in the recent conflict."* b) the right of every state to live in this region with secure and recognized frontiers shall be acknowledged and all claims of belligerencies should be terminated.[134] One tempting question to ask is whether the SC can only make recommendations to the dispute when the dispute is referred to it by the parties. In practice, the SC refers the matter to itself and make recommendations to the substance. In other words, the SC separates Article 37(2) from Article 37(1), extending its power to seize disputes according to its will. The fourth way is to provide a specific settlement plan for the disputed parties but only if the parties request so.

2.9.2.3 Role of the GA

The GA has a subsidiary responsibility for the maintenance of international peace and security. So long as the SC is not dealing with the same matter, the GA may discuss any matters within the scope of the Charter and make recommendations to the member states and SC regarding peace and security (Article 10, 11 and 12 UNCh). Moreover, it can also *"recommend measures for the peaceful adjustment of any situation regardless of origin, which it deems likely to impair the general welfare or friendly relations among nations"* (Article 14 UNCh). This can be proved, e.g., by the recommendations relating to the Israeli-Arab conflicts

[134] S/RES/242 (1967).

(GA Resolution 47/118. 1992, for instance) and the GA's resolutions referring to the Russian/Ukrainian conflict.[135]

2.9.2.4 Role of the SG

The SG has the already mentioned power to *"bring to the attention of the SC any matter which he thinks may threaten the maintenance of international peace and security"* (Article 99 UNCh). In practice, the function of SG in this respect has greatly expanded thanks to the effort made by several SGs and by the special representatives nominated by the SG for specific conflicts. Good offices and mediation activities of SG and their special representatives made and make unique contributions to the peaceful settlement of disputes.[136]

2.9.3 Binding Measures and Sanctions (Chapter VII)

2.9.3.1 Collective Security, the Prohibition to Use Force and Its Exceptions

Collective security structures can be understood as (regional or global) security arrangements, usually an international organization, not only a treaty, which provide for mechanisms of the peaceful settlement of disputes. As part of this system, all states cooperate collectively to provide security for all by the actions of all against any states within or outside the group which might challenge the existing order by using or threatening to use force.[137]

The normative framework of the collective security system of UN is based on Articles 2(4) and 2(5) UNCh and on Chapter VII. The prohibition to use force according to Article 2(4) UNCh is pivotal for the entire system, for an essential purpose of the collective security system is to enforce this provision. Accordingly, based on Article 2(5) UNCh, UN member states are obliged to support the actions of UN organs, in particular the SC, when the collective security system is applied. The Charter assumes that the SC has virtually a monopoly on the use of force at the international level. Therefore, subject to the right of self-defense, the *legitimate and legal use of military force can only come from the Security Council.* There are only two exceptions to this: self-defense and authorization by the SC. Other attempts to legitimize the unilateral use of force such as humanitarian interventions or preemptive and preventive strikes are not recognized as legitimate exceptions to the prohibition to use force.

---

[135] A/RES/ES-11/1-6 (2022).

[136] See supra, Sect. 1.8.2.4.

[137] See supra, Sect. 2.1.2.

2.9.3.2 Justified, but Institutionally Embedded Unilateralism: Self-Defense

Self-defense as the only exception allowing the unilateral use of force by a state is regulated in Article 51 UNCh: *"Nothing in the present Charter shall impair the inherent right of individual or collective self-defense if an armed attack occurs against a Member of the United Nations, until the Security Council has taken measures necessary to maintain international peace and security."* This preserves a right that predated the Charter under customary international law. However, this Charter provision legitimizes the use of force only until the Security Council has made the necessary decisions in the framework of the collective security system. This concept of self-defense thus does not depart from the logic of the collective security system. It is embedded in that system. Therefore, to ensure the primacy of the Security Council's decisions and its monopoly on the use of force, the legal exercise of the right of self-defense is made dependent on compliance with certain legal requirements.

First, self-defense is *only legitimate against an 'armed attack'*. Force below that level does not trigger the right. Whether the attack needs to be conducted by a state has become unclear. The USA undertook a large military operation against the Taliban regime in Afghanistan, claiming to execute self-defense to the terrorist attack on Sept. 11, 2001. The extent of the governmental involvement of Taliban in the terrorist attack, however, was unclear; the Taliban regime certainly did not directly participate in the attack which was executed by a terrorist organization on the territory of the U.S.A. When Hamas attacked Israel in Fall 2023 and took and highjacked more than one thousand hostages, Israel based its counterattack against the Gaza Strip on the right to self-defense. This justification was accepted by many states, but most of them considered the extent of the use of military in exercising self-defense to be excessive. Another, second requirement is that the *armed attack is 'ongoing' and the use of force immediate to counter the attack*. This again makes the armed self-defense against Afghanistan seems dubious. That is because there was one month between the attack of terrorists (2001/9/11) and the military action against the Taliban (2001/10/7). A third requirement is the *principle of necessity and proportionality of the use of force*, which was first developed in the famous Caroline Case (1837). Necessity tests whether there are peaceful alternatives, such as making diplomatic efforts. Proportion is somehow more assessed by the result to be achieved by the defensive action, and not on the forms or strength of the action itself. The final requirement is that *states must notify the Security Council right after they operate self-defense*.

Here again the SC plays the dominant role. However, if the SC is deadlocked due to vetoes the SC may bring a conflict to the attention of and recommendations or decisions by the GA.

2.9.3.3 Prerequisites to Apply Chapter VII According to Article 39 UNCh

The system of collective security according to Chapter VII applies in case of *"any threat to the peace, breach of the peace, or act of aggression"* (Article 39 UNCh). Therefore, before the SC takes any measures according to Chapter VII, a *determination of the SC on at least one of the above three instances must be made, based on Article 39.*

In specific, *'breach of peace'* refers to the outbreak of an armed conflict. The well-known cases include the 1950 Korean War, the 1982 Argentina's invasion in Falkland, the 1987 Iran-Iraq War, the 1990 Iraq's invasion of Kuwait, and the Russian war against Ukraine beginning in March 2022.

'Act of aggression' is broader defined than 'breach of peace' is. Any *concrete military action independent of whether there is an armed conflict* may qualify as an act of aggression. In 1974, the GA adopted Res 3314 (XXIX) 'Definition of Aggression'. This resolution, some parts of remained contested, states in Article 1, that

> *"aggression is the use of armed force by a state against the sovereignty, territorial integrity or political independence of another state, or in any manner inconsistent with the UN Charter."*

Article 2 of the resolution provides that

> *"[t]he first use of armed force by a State in contravention to the Charter shall constitute* prima facie *evidence of an act of aggression…"*

However, it should be noted that the resolution is not binding for the SC, but it helps the SC in making an assessment of a concrete situation and to identify certain acts of aggression by states.

Lastly, *'threat to the peace'* is the most broadly defined and most widely used basis of the SC's activities under Chapter VII. Originally, it referred only to *interstate tensions short of war*. Nowadays, a much broader understanding of this term prevails in the practice of the SC. There seems to be unanimity that also *internal conflicts without transnational spill-over* may qualify as 'threat of peace'. This is reflected, e.g., in considerations of the Appeal Chamber of the ICTY in the *Tadic* Case according to which *"[i]t can thus said that there is a common understanding, manifested by the "subsequent practice" of membership of the United Nations at large, that the "threat of peace" of article 39 may include, as one of its species, internal armed conflict."*[138] Since 1990s, also a *humanitarian crisis* may qualify as a threat to peace, as evidenced, e.g. by Res 794 (1992) (Somalia), Res 955 (1994)

[138] ICTY, *Prosecutor v. Duško Tadić*, Case No. IT-94-1, Decision on the Defence Motion for Interlocutory Appeal on Jurisdiction, 2 Oct 1995, para. 29.

(Rwanda) and a series of resolutions (1998/1999) on Kosovo.[139] Beginning with Res 748 (1992) on Libya, also *international terrorism* may be a threat of peace. According to Res 873 (1993) on the situation in Haiti, the *violent overthrow of an elected government* together with other deteriorating situations may constitute a 'threat of peace.'

If one of the above three circumstances is identified by the SC, the domestic jurisdiction clause in Article 2(7)[140] does not apply. Moreover, a broad notion of peace as well as a broad understanding of threat to peace expanded the powers of SC enormously in the last thirty years. The SC now enjoys very broad discretion as to the assessment of the circumstances. *The decision on the application of Chapter VII is not subject to any control, neither political nor legal.*

2.9.3.4 Provisional Measures (Article 40)

According to Article 39, the SC can choose either to make recommendations or to decide on enforcement measures in case of a threat of peace, breach of the pace, or act of aggression. However, before all these, the SC may also, according to Article 40, call upon the parties to comply with provisional measures, which *"shall be without prejudice to the rights, claims, or position of the parties concerned"*. It should be noted that these provisional measures can also be directed to non-state parties. Since these provisional measures have a binding nature, non-observance of them may give rise to sanctions under Chapter VII.

2.9.3.5 Enforcement Measures

Contrary to the decentralized coercion pattern of the League of Nations, the SC has the *ultimate authority and power to adopt binding resolutions providing for coercive measures*. The main 'teeth' of the SC are enforcement measure not involving the use of force according to Article 41 UNCh, and enforcement measure involving the use of force as provided for in Article 42 UNCh.

a) Without the Use of Force (Article 41)

Measures according to Article 41 UNCh include, as explicitly mentioned in this provision, economic sanctions, interruption of sea, rail, air, postal and other communications, arm embargoes, and the severance of diplomatic relations. Besides these traditional measures, the SC has created numerous other non-military measures within the realm of Article 41: ad hoc tribunals like the ICTY according to S/Res 808, 1993 and the ICTR based in S/Res 955, 1994; interim administrative presence like those in East Timor (S/Res 1272, 1999) and Kosovo (S/Res 1244, 1999); quasi-

[139] S/RES/1160 (1998); S/RES/1199 (1998); S/RES/1203 (1998); S/RES/1244 (1999).

[140] See supra, Sect. 2.6.8.

legislative measures like the fight against terrorism (S/Res 1373); the freeze of assets; travel restrictions etc. Important are so-called *targeted sanctions which are directed against particular groups and individuals*. Very often *sanctions committees* are established to monitor and execute the imposition of sanctions.

One criticism regarding S/Res 1373 on fighting terrorism by imposing a duty on member states to enact laws to prevent financing terrorist activities is that the SC has overstepped its function and power as an executive organ of the UN by acting as a legislator. The wording of the resolution was drafted after the provisions of conventions fighting terrorism. Thus, SC ordered all states to *"freeze without delay funds and other financial assets or economic resources of persons who commit, or attempt to commit, terrorist acts or participate in or facilitate the commission of terrorist acts' and call upon all states to 'ensure that terrorist acts are established as serious criminal offences in domestic laws and regulations and that the seriousness of such acts is duly reflected in sentences served."*[141] Moreover, a Counter Terrorism Committee [CTC] has been established to monitor state compliance with the resolution. This law-making capacity may give rise to doubts about the legality of the resolutions and the status of SC. However, in practice there was no serious opposition in the UN membership against these activities of the SC.

b) Involving the Use of Force (Article 42)

Enforcement measures involving the use of force are the core of the collective security system of the UN. When the SC finds that the non-military enforcement in Article 41 is insufficient to cope with the circumstances, collective measure including the use of force become the *ultimate measure available to the SC* to uphold or re-establish peace and security and to settle any "threat to the peace, breach of the peace, or act of aggression".

Arts 43 ss. UNCh provide that agreements should be concluded between UN and member states to establish armed forces under the control of the UN Security Council with the advice and assistance of a Military Staffs Committee composed of the Chiefs of Staff of the five permanent members or their representatives (Article 43, 45, 46 and 47). However, these provisions remained dead letters for no state was willing to accept that an UN organ would decide on the deployment of its own troops. To overcome the dilemma of inability to act with collective military force at the disposal of SC, a *system of authorization to use force* has been developed. The Korean War 1950 was the first example when the SC authorized the US and other countries to defend South Korea against the military invasion from the north. This is *a kind of outsourcing of military enforcement to willing states*. In the eye of some countries, the authorization to individual states to use force marks a decentralization of the powers of SC and a circumvention of Article 42. One might argue that states will utilize the authorization of the UN to hide their true motives and to legalize their action which otherwise may violate international law. However, the UN chose the authorization mode of military enforcement because the inability to act in the face of

---

[141] S/RES/1373 (2001), paras. 1(c), 2(e).

vast crises is far more unacceptable than the hidden motives of certain states. This is also reflected in the legal opinion of the ICJ on *Certain Expenses of the United Nations* (1962),[142] in which the court held that *"an argument which insists that all measure taken for the maintenance of international peace and security must be financed through agreement concluded under Article 43, would seem to exclude the possibility that the Security Council might act under some other Article of the Charter"*.

Since the beginning of the 90ties, such authorizations were granted on many occasions. A leading case was the universally accepted S/Res 678 (1990) to combat Iraq's invasion of Kuwait in 1990. Facing the invasion of Kuwait by Iraq on August 2, 1990, the SC adopted S/Res 678 (1990) on Nov. 29, 1990, to provide Iraq with a "final opportunity" to comply with relevant resolutions and to withdraw from Kuwait. It was stated in the resolution that member states cooperating with the Government of Kuwait were authorized to use *"all necessary means"* to give effect to S/Resolution 660 (1990) and to restore international peace and security in this region. Consequently, armed forces from several countries under the leadership of the US defeated the Iraqi troops. Other instances of the authorization to use force followed. *Usually, the "all necessary means" – formula was used to express the authorization.*[143]

Authorization is conferred to states or groups of states like NATO. Usually there is no implicit authorization in the wording of resolutions of SC; the SC generally uses the 'all necessary means' formula originated from S/Res 687. The main goal of the authorization is often *to implement or enforce resolutions of the SC*. An important principle applicable to the use of military force is *the principle of proportionality* which is generally to be observed during an enforcement involving the use of force. This principle is not always respected. The powers and abilities of the SC to control military operations are quite limited. As an executive, strategic organ of the UN it is institutionally not fit and not designed to control and direct military operations. It is the authorized leading power that solely decides the scale, the period and the extent of the enforcement measures.

It is clear that states willing to use force to, e.g. enforce resolutions, are under the obligation to request an SC authorization as legal legitimation. *A unilateral, unauthorized military enforcement violates the prohibition to use force according to Article 2(4) UNCh.* This rule got challenged several times. An example is the US-UK invasion of Iraq in 2003 which also undermined the credibility of the SC. The main justification for the military attack was the alleged existence of weapons of mass destruction in Iraq. The UK-US coalition could, however, not sufficiently convince the SC, so that no authorization to use force was granted. And indeed, no evidence for the existence of weapons of mass destruction was found in Iraq after the invasion. From a legal point of view, can a state or groups of states act

[142] *Certain Expenses of the United Nations (Art. 17, Paragraph 2, of the Charter)*, Advisory Opinion, ICJ Rep. 151 (1962), 168.

[143] Cf., e.g., S/RES/794 (1992); S/RES/940 (1994); S/RES/1973 (2011); S/RES/2216 (2015).

unilaterally to use of force to give effect to the resolution, especially when the resolution does not involve an authorization of SC to use force? It usually cannot. Such operations violate the multilateralism that is the basis of the system of collective security. The failure of the SC to react to Iraq's 'non-compliance' with the *"combined effect of S/Res 678, 687, 1441"*[144] and to stop the USA and the UK from using force without SC authorization further raised serious doubts as to the effectiveness of the prohibition on use of force and of collective security system. The same is true as to the unilateral, non-authorized use of force in Kosovo (1999) and in Afghanistan (2001) even though these military interventions had under the given circumstances at least some legitimacy.

Another issue as to states seeking a SC authorization to use force is the problem of instrumentalization of the SC by such states. The rationale why states seek to intervene militarily is not always clear. Behind the assertion, e.g., that the intervention aims to enforce resolutions of the SC could be illicit motives and goals not in a global, but just in a national interest. This was discussed when the use of force by states ended in a forced regime change not explicitly covered by an authorizing resolution. Particularly Russia and China considered the overthrowing of the Khaddaffi regime in Libya in 2011 as a consequence of the authorized use of force by Western states as not backed by the pertinent SC resolutions. According to Russia and China, the violent overthrow of a government is usually not a legitimate goal of SC authorized military interventions.

2.9.3.6 Conclusion

The SC has very broad powers under Chapter VII. As to parties of the conflict, the SC tends to hold a *position of limited neutrality and does very often not comment the parties' position.* Admittedly, against the background of a duty of the UN to take into consideration the sovereignty of the states involved also in situations of an UN-led conflict management, *it is usually up to the parties to find a solution to a conflict.* Yet, if the conflict constitutes a threat of peace, breach of peace or act aggression, then the SC will not hesitate to resort to recommendations, binding directives, non-military enforcement measures and the military sanctions to restore international peace and security. Generally, *regarding violations of international law or the resolutions of the SC, there is usually no neutrality of the SC,* to the contrary: the SC often imposes sanctions against parties violating important rules of international law or resolutions of the SC. It is noteworthy that the principle of proportionality applies when sanctions are imposed. It should also be noted that no unilateral use of force is permitted without satisfying the requirement of self-defense or authorization of the SC.

[144] UK Attorney General (2003) Written Answer to a Parliamentary Question, 17 Mar 2003. Hansard HL vol. 646, col WA2.

2.9.4 The UN Conflict Management; Peace-Keeping Operations (PKO)

2.9.4.1 Broad Understanding of the Role of the UN

After the end of Cold War, the UN international peace and security activities increased enormously. Once paralyzed functions in these era due to the conflict between East and West revived and developed. Under these circumstances, Boutros Boutros-Ghali, then UN Secretary General developed in his report *An Agenda for Peace* (1992) a new, broad understanding of the role of the UN about the core responsibility for global peace and security. This overall picture of the function and power of the UN distinguished different phases of the maintenance of peace and security. These included: conflict prevention and mediation; traditional peace-keeping; peacemaking; peace enforcement; and peace-building.[145]

Conflict prevention involves diplomatic measures to keep intrastate or inter-state tensions and disputes from escalating into violent conflicts. The tasks involve early warning, information gathering and a careful analysis of the factors driving the conflict. The activities may include the use of the Secretary-General's good offices, preventive deployment of UN missions, or conflict mediation led by the UN Department of Political Affairs.

Peacekeeping is the most traditional and original form of UN involvement in the management of conflicts. It refers to the deployment of a UN force or observer presence in a certain area with the consent of all parties. Its main goal is to help reduce tensions, separate confronting forces, and stimulate a calm environment in which peaceful settlement may be sought.

Peacemaking generally includes peaceful measures to address conflicts in progress and usually involves diplomatic action to bring hostile parties to a negotiated agreement. The UN Secretary-General may exercise his or her good offices to facilitate the resolution of the conflict. Peacemakers may also be envoys, governments, groups of states, regional organizations or the United Nations. Peacemaking efforts may also be undertaken by unofficial and non-governmental groups, or by a prominent personality working independently.

Peace enforcement involves the application of a range of coercive measures, including the use of military force authorized by the Security Council. It is used to restore international peace and security in situations where the Security Council has decided to act in the face of a threat to the peace, breach of the peace or act of aggression. It is also used when all peaceful means have failed. The Council may utilize, where appropriate, regional organizations and agencies for enforcement action under its authority and in accordance with the UN Charter.

Peacebuilding aims to reduce the risk of lapsing or relapsing into conflict by strengthening national capacities at all levels for conflict management. Its main goal is to lay the foundation for sustainable peace and development. It is a complex,

[145] The following explanations are partly based on the UN homepage.

long-term process of creating the necessary conditions for sustainable peace. Peacebuilding measures address core issues that affect the functioning of society and the state and seek to enhance the capacity of the state to carry out its core functions effectively and legitimately.

The comprehensive report of Boutros Boutros-Ghali on the role of the UN in maintaining peace and security concluded the former experience of the UN activities and pointed out the future direction of peacekeeping operations as well. Importantly, while UN peacekeeping operations are, in principle, deployed to support the implementation of a ceasefire or peace agreement, they are often required to play an active role in peacemaking efforts and may also be involved in early or post-conflict peacebuilding activities. Multidimensional peacekeeping operations facilitate the political process (UN Mission in Bosnia-Herzegovina (UNMIBH));[146] protect civilians (UN Assistance Mission in Rwanda (UNAMIR) 1994);[147] assist in the disarmament, demobilization and reintegration of former combatants (UN Force in Cyprus (UNICYP) 1964);[148] support the organization of elections (UN Observer Group for the Verification of Elections in Nicaragua (ONUVEN) 1992);[149] protect and promote human rights and assist in restoring the rule of law (UN peacekeeping operations in Kosovo (UNMIK))[150] 1999, making an undeniable contribution to the stability and development of certain regions.

2.9.4.2 Peacekeeping Operations (PKOs)[151]

Traditional PKOs are less ambitious. They are established with the consent of the parties to the conflict. Their main responsibility is to separate the parties, to be present in buffer zones and to monitor, e.g., a truce or any other arrangement between the parties.

a) legal basis

There is no explicit legal basis of PKOs in the UN charter. They are based on the general provisions regulating the powers of the SC and/or the GA and are an implied power of UN to maintain international peace and security. In the *Certain Expense* legal opinion (1962), the ICJ held that, "*[w]hen the Organization takes action which warrants the assertion that it was appropriate for the fulfillment of one of the stated purposes of the UN, the presumption is that such action is not ultra vires the Organization.*"[152] In particular, the SC may establish subsidiary organs as it

[146] S/RES/1035 (1995).

[147] S/RES/872 (1993).

[148] S/RES/186 (1964).

[149] S/RES/637 (1989).

[150] S/RES/1244 (1999).

[151] <http://www.un.org/en/peacekeeping/> (accessed 9 March 2025).

[152] *Certain Expenses of the United Nations (Art. 17, Paragraph 2, of the Charter)*, Advisory Opinion, ICJ Rep. 151 (1962), 168.

deems necessary for the performance of its function (Article 29) and has the power to make recommendations or decision to restore international peace and security (Article 39). Likewise, the GA may establish such subsidiary organs as it deems necessary for the performance of its function and has the power to recommend measures for the peaceful adjustment of any situations (Article 14). In practice, the establishment of a PKO is mostly based on the decision by the SC, and only once created by a resolution of GA in case of UNEF I in the Suez Crisis 1956.

PKOs have the legal nature of a subsidiary organ. As a method to contribute to peace and security, they are partly a contribution to peaceful settlements according to Chapter VI, and partly an enforcement measure under Chapter VII. Therefore, *some commentators label the legal basis as 'Chapter VI 1/2'*. Traditionally, a PKO lasts for 6 months. However, it is usually extended based on an SC Resolution. They are financed by voluntary contributions of member states of UN.

b) Principles applicable to PKO

In his *Supplement to an Agenda for Peace* in 1995, then UN Secretary General Boutros Boutros-Ghali emphasized three principles of PKOs[153] which reflect generally accepted international practice:

- *Consent of the parties*: The commitment by the parties to a political process is indispensable. Acceptance of a PKO provides the UN with the necessary freedom of action. In the absence of such consent, a PKO risks (1) becoming a party to the conflict, (2) being drawn towards enforcement action, and (3) leaving its fundamental role of keeping the peace. After the withdrawal of the host state's consent, the peacekeeping force should leave the territory of that state. This happened, e.g., in 1967 when Egypt withdrew its consent to UNEF I.
- *Impartiality*: It is crucial for the peacekeeping forces to maintain the consent and cooperation of the main parties. *Yet one should not mix impartiality with neutrality or inactivity.* United Nations peacekeepers should be impartial in their dealings with the parties to the conflict but not be neutral in the execution of their mandate.
- *Non-use of force except in self-defense*: PKOs are not an enforcement tool, and their mandates do not cover enforcement measures. However, they may use force at the tactical level, with the authorization of the Security Council, if acting in self-defense and to maintain their mandate. In certain volatile situations, the SC has given PKOs 'robust' mandates, authorizing them to 'use all necessary means' to deter forceful attempts to disrupt the political process, protect civilians under imminent threat of physical attack, and/or assist the national authorities in maintaining law and order. United Nations operations in Somalia II (UNOSOM II) in 1992 may serve as an early example of robust peacekeeping operation.

[153] *Supplement to an Agenda for Peace* in 1995.

c) Robust Peacekeeping

Traditional peacekeeping, robust peacekeeping and peace enforcement are different concepts. Robust peacekeeping involves the use of force at the tactical level with the authorization of the Security Council and the consent of the host state and/or the main parties to the conflict. Contrary to that, peace enforcement does not require the consent of the main parties and may involve the use of military force at the strategic or international level, which is normally prohibited for Member States under Article 2(4) of the Charter, unless authorized by the Security Council.

The Panel on UN Peace Operations[154] clarified some principles applicable to peacekeeping as outlined by then Secretary General Boutros-Ghali. Impartiality, e.g., must be taken into consideration in accordance with the UN Charter. To those who keep violating the principles of the UN Charter, equal treatment is not applicable. In addition, robust peacekeeping is only recommended in specific situations. It is therefore not a general concept. The panel advocated, however, *"robust rules of engagement against those who renege on their commitments to a peace accord or otherwise seek to undermine it by violence."*[155]

d) Typical PKO mandate

Typical mandates of PKOs include the following goals:

- Deployment of blue helmets to prevent the outbreak of conflict or the spill-over of conflict across borders;
- To stabilize conflict situations after a ceasefire and to create an environment for the parties to reach a lasting peace agreement;
- Assistance in implementing comprehensive peace agreements;
- To lead states or territories through a transition to stable government, based on democratic principles, good governance and economic development.

To realize their mandates, the PKOs may execute the following activities:

- Disarmament, demobilization and reintegration of ex-combatants;
- Mine action;
- Security sector reform and other rule of law-related activities;
- Protection and promotion of human rights;
- Electoral assistance;
- Support for the restoration and extension of State authority;
- Promotion of social and economic recovery and development.

---

[154] *Report of the Panel on United Nations Peace Operations* (the Brahimi Report), UN Doc. A/55/305-S/2000/809, 21 Aug 2000; 39 ILM (2000), 1432.

[155] Ibid., 55.

2.9.5 *UN Conflict Management: The Role of Regional Arrangements (Chapter VIII UN Charter)*

While creating a UN system for peaceful settlement of disputes, collective security, and peacekeeping operations, the UN Charter also provides for close interactions with regional organizations, arrangements, or agencies. Therefore, to maintain international peace and security, regional subsystems play a vital role:

- First, so long as the activities of regional arrangements or agencies are consistent with the Purpose and Principles of the United Nations, the existence and the appropriate pacific settlement measures of regional arrangements are welcomed and encouraged (Articles 52(1) and 52(3) UNCh).
- Second, if possible, the member states of UN should first refer to regional arrangements to settle their conflicts (Article 52(2) (UNCh).[156]
- Third, to use force, an SC authorization based on Chapter VII is required. Usually, there are simultaneous conflict managements on both regional and global level. This can be evidenced, e.g., by the activities of OSCE, NATO and UN in the Kosovo Crisis 1998/1999, though NATO has launched an air campaign against Serbian without the explicit authorization by SC.
- Fourth, regional arrangements play an important role in enforcing and implementing resolutions of the Security Council. They also play an important role in all the peace-related activities of the SC, such as conflict prevention and mediation, peace-keeping, peacemaking, peace enforcement, peace-building.[157]

2.9.6 *Typical Features of a Conflict Management of the SC*

There are often three stages of a typical conflict management of the SC: pre-conflict crisis management activities; conflict management based on Chapter VII; and post-conflict measures and activities.

Pre-conflict crisis management activities are usually based on Chapter VI or Article 24/25 UNCh. They start when a dispute or a situation has an adverse impact on peace, security and stability but does not (yet) constitute a Chapter VII conflict. These activities of the SC which often are conflict preventive in nature may include to encourage both parties to pacific settlement (Article 33 UNCh), to undertake investigation and go start a mediation (Article 34 UNCh), to dispatch a mission, to appoint special envoys or request the SG to use good offices (Article 36 UNCh), to

[156]This can be illustrated with the involvement of OSCE in the first period of the Kosovo Crisis in 1998/1999.

[157]This illustrates, e.g., the NATO-led Implementation Force (IFOR) in Bosnia and Herzegovina in 1995, when NATO was authorized to use of force by resolution 1031 to help the peacekeeping force in that region S/RES/1031 (1995).

set forth principles for a peaceful settlement (Article 37) and/or to develop a concrete settlement plan if the parties to the dispute agree (Article 38 UNCh). Most of these measures and activities refer to the methods to settle a dispute only, *not to the dispute's substance. This is a tribute to the principle of sovereignty, in particular that the UN has not the power to impose a settlement on the parties, but that is it up to them to come to a negotiated solution*. Therefore, the parties must agree if the UN intends to develop a concrete settlement plan based on Article 38 UNCh. Thus, the main function of the SC under Chapter VI is to remind and to recommend the parties a peaceful settlement by offering procedural methods, general principles or a concrete plan if so requested. It is, however, usually up to the states to finally solve the dispute.

Conflict management activities are usually based on Chapter VII UNCh. They foremost deal with peace-making and peace enforcement. They start with an assessment of the SC in a formal resolution based on Article 39 UNCh that a conflict or a situation is a threat to peace or that there was a breach of peace. The SC enjoys very broad discretion as to the qualification of a conflict or a situation to fall under Article 39 UNCh. This assessment is political in nature even if the SC refers to breaches of legal norms such as the prohibition to use force (Article 2(4) UNCh) as a reason for a breach of peace or a threat to peace. Based on this assessment, the SC may use all its powers under Chapter VII but does not have to do so. Sometimes SC resolutions contain a mix of measures based on Chapter VII, Chapter VI and Article 24/25 UNCh even if the resolution is explicitly adopted under Chapter VII. It therefore depends on the concrete interpretation of a resolution's paragraphs what their legal basis and thus their legal nature is. In case of military hostilities, the parties are usually called up to halt them and to negotiate a cease-fire. This request may be combined with a threat to sanction parties not complying with the resolution. These measures are usually provisional measures in the sense of Article 40 UNCh. At that stage of a conflict, the SC further often imposes an arms embargo on the parties to the conflict, to be implemented by the UN membership at large. The further concrete measures very much depend on the particular conflict. These measures may include economic sanctions, financial penalties and restrictions and travel bans and the severance of diplomatic relations as non-miliary sanctions based on Article 41 UNCh. These sanctions are imposed against states or, as targeted or so-called "smart" sanctions, against individuals or groups such as terrorist organizations. Military sanctions are based on Article 42 and adopted, e.g., to restore law and order in a failed state, or to enforce important rules of international law, or to execute SC resolutions against parties not complying with the binding measures of the SC in a conflict.

All these actions are often accompanied by humanitarian measures and attempts to mediate to bring the conflict to a negotiated solution. The humanitarian measures refer to refugees, internally displaced persons, and the observance of international humanitarian law by the parties to the conflict. As to the mediation efforts, the SG often nominates a special envoy. There is further often involvement of third parties acting as mediators in the conflict such as states, groups of states and regional agencies. These international actors exercise pressure on the parties to the conflict to start meaningful negotiations. The SC or the SG often coordinates and supports the international peace efforts and the efforts of others. Sometimes, the SC delineates a framework of an agreed political solution.[158] As part of the negotiations or of a cease-fire, the SC may decide on dispatching military observers or a peacekeeping force to reduce tensions, to separate opposing forces and to establish the precondition for peaceful settlements. A negotiated agreement sometimes is adopted by the SC in a resolution based on Chapter VII. This corresponds to an *international, UN sponsored guarantee of the agreement in a way that violations of the agreement's terms qualify as threat to or even breaches of peace and may give reason to the SC to impose sanctions against a perpetrator.*

The last stage, *post-conflict measures and activities*, varies depending on the concrete conflict. The measures include post-conflict multifunctional peacebuilding, complex peace-keeping operations and similar activities to address and to eliminate the roots of the conflict and to re-establish state institutions and a functioning society.

2.10 Specialized Agencies and Organizations

2.10.1 Independent Organizations, but Part of the UN Family

There are many well-known specialized agencies in the UN system. These include: the Food and Agriculture Organization of the United Nations (FAO), the International Civil Aviation Organization (ICAO), the International Labour Organization (ILO), the International Maritime Organization (IMO), the International Monetary Fund (IMF), the International Telecommunication Union (ITU), the United Nations Educational, Scientific and Cultural Organization (UNESCO), the United Nations Industrial Development Organization (UNIDO), the Universal Postal Union (UPU), the World Bank Group (consisting of the International Bank for Reconstruction and Development (IBRD), the International Centre for Settlement of Investment Disputes (ICSID), the International Development Association (IDA), the International Finance Corporation (IFC), and the Multilateral Investment Guarantee Agency (MIGA)), the World Health Organization (WHO), the World Intellectual Property Organization (WIPO), the World Meteorological Organization (WMO), the World Tourism Organization (UNWTO) etc.

Specialized agencies and organizations are independent from the UN but *belong to the UN family based on agreements concluded with the UN.* They have separate legal personality, purpose, membership, and budgetary powers. The reason why these specialized agencies are not merged into UN organs is the fear of over-centralization and the risk of politicization of these functional organizations. The first reason is based on the belief that, due to decentralization, these functional

[158] See e.g. S/RES/242 (1967); S/RES/1244 (1999); S/RES/2202 (2015).

organizations can develop an institutionalized expertise, will be closer to the problems and will perform better. In addition, and based on the experience of the League of Nations, the benefits of this separation into independent functional organizations would help these less politized organizations to continue their activities even in case of a political stalemated in the main political organization.

However, the hope for a pure technical feature of these specialized agencies is sometimes an illusion. As the topics of a certain specialized agency become controversial, the organizations may inevitably be 'politicized'. This can be illustrated by the request of WHO for an ICJ advisory opinion on the *Legality of the Use of Nuclear Weapons*, which was opposed by some states. This can also be confirmed by the withdrawal of US from International Labour Organization in 1977, the US withdrawal from UNESCO in 2018 due to the 'politicization', and the US withdrawal from WHO in 2020. Nevertheless, the specialized agencies, through the cooperation with ECOSOC, make very important contributions in their activity fields which are important for various aspects of human society.

2.10.2 Legal Basis

Specialized agencies are regulated in Articles 57 and 63 UNCh. They have, according to Article 57 UNCh the following features: they are established by international agreements, have wide international responsibilities as defined in their constituent instruments in "economic, social, cultural, educational, health and related fields" (Article 57 UN Charter) and are 'inter-governmental'. All these requirements preclude NGOs, regional organizations and organizations with a general political purpose to become specialized agencies in the sense of these provisions.

The formal status as specialized UN agency is regulated in an agreement between the agency and the ECOSOC. This agreement is subject to the approval of the UN General Assembly (Article 63(1) UNCh) and defines the concrete terms of the cooperation between the UN and the agency. As for affiliation, there are the following forms of interactions:

- *Cooperation in work:* To make the work between the UN and the specialized agencies coherent, the ECOSOC makes recommendations for the policies and activities of the specialized agencies (Article 58). The power of discharge the functions of the specialized agencies lies in the hand of the GA. Moreover, the specialized agencies have to respect and also give effect to pertinent resolutions of the UN. In addition, the exchange of information and documents between UN and the specialized Agencies are important as well.
- *Membership association:* Many specialized agencies have the same membership as the UN.
- *Budgetary and financial coordination:* The UN controls the budgetary of the specialized agencies, as provided in Article 17(3) of the Charter. Moreover, the

UN may also receive voluntary contributions from the states and distribute these financial contributions to various specialized agencies.

Under the Millennium Development Goals Framework, a more coherent approach was adopted among different agencies and the ECOSOC.

2.10.3 Selected Specialized Agencies

2.10.3.1 International Labour Organization (ILO)

The International Labour Organization is a unique tripartite organization set up by Pt. XIII of the Treaty of Versailles in 1919. *Tripartite structure means that the organs are not only composed of the member states' governments, but also of representatives of the employers and employees.* This is a departure from the general principle that states are represented in international organizations only by their governments. This tripartite structure makes ILO a unique forum for its 187 members to debate not only horizontally among states, but also to have dialogues vertically among governors, employers, and workers.

The ILO became the first specialized agency of the UN after an amendment of its constituent instrument in 1946. Its main goals are to promote rights at work, create decent employment opportunities, enhance social protection, and strengthen social dialogue. To realize these goals, the ILO formulates international policies and programs, creates international labour standards supported by a supervision system, and provides training, education, and research activities. Under the ILO framework, approximately 200 international labour conventions were adopted in pursuance of conditions of employment, rights of children and women and safety regulations. The ILO has developed a Decent Work Agenda for the community to put into practice. It defines the priorities and aims of national development with the support through integrated Decent Work Country Programs in coordination with its constituents.

The ILO is composed of three main bodies: The International Labour Conference, the Governing Body, and the International Labour Office. The international Labour Office is the organization's secretariat, the Governing Body an executive non-plenary, and the International Labour Conference the plenary organ. The organs, except for the Labour Office, have as mentioned a unique composition as they comprise governments', employers' and workers' representatives. The conference as plenary organ has the power to adopt international conventions, to recommend to member states and to supervise the implementation of conventions and recommendations. A two-third majority is needed in the Conference. The Governing Body as an organ of limited membership holds a three-year term. It consists of 56 representatives, 28 of which are representatives of governments, 14 of employers and 14 of employees. 10 of the 28 government representatives should come from states of "chief industrial importance" (Article 7(2) of the Constitution). The Governing Body is responsible for formulating policies and programs, supervising the Office and appointing the Director General. Except for a two-third majority required by the constitution, simple majority suffices. The Office is in charge of assistance to the Conference, the Governing Body and governments. More importantly, according to article 22, member states should make annual reports to the Office. When a complaint of non-observance of a certain state is brought before ILO by employees, workers, or member states (Article 24 and 26), it may also establish a commission of inquiry or even refer the complaint to ICJ (Article 26(3) and 29).

2.10.3.2 Food and Agricultural Organization (FAO)

The FAO was established by the UN Conference on Food and Agriculture in 1943 already.[159] Its main objectives are to help eliminate hunger, make agriculture, forestry, and fisheries more sustainable, reduce rural poverty, build inclusive and efficient agricultural and food systems, and increase the resilience of livelihoods from disaster. To achieve these goals, FAO implements various programs and projects, which are funded by the FAO Technical Cooperation Program (TCP) and the Special Program for Food Security (SPFS) and many more voluntary contributions. Moreover, the World Food Program (WFP) was created jointly by the UN and FAO in 1961, with an aim to provide best use of food surpluses for the developing countries and establish a secure system for emergency food needs.

The FAO has a structure typical for an international organization. It consists of three main organs, namely the Conference), the Council), and the Director-General). The main tasks of the biennial FAO Conference are to review global governance policy issues and international frameworks, to evaluate work carried out and to approve the budget. The Council is composed of 49 members elected by the Conference. The Council, with a three-year term, is the executive body of programs and other activities. The Director-General is the chief administrative officer under the supervision of the Conference and the Council. The European Union is one of the FAO's members. This is unique among nearly all specialized UN agencies.

2.10.3.3 United Nations Educational, Scientific, and Cultural Organization (UNESCO)

UNESCO was established at the London Conference in 1945.[160] Its purpose is to mobilize education, build intercultural understanding, pursue scientific cooperation, and protect freedom of expression. It created the idea of World Heritage to protect natural and historical sites of extraordinary charm and common value for all human

[159] *Constitution of the Food and Agriculture Organization of the United Nations*, adopted on 16 Oct 1945.

[160] *Constitution of the United Nations Educational, Scientific and Cultural Organization*, adopted on 16 Nov 1945.

beings. It also helped to establish early warning systems for tsunamis or transboundary water management agreements to strengthen the ability of nations in face of natural disasters. Moreover, there are abundant published materials produced by UNESCO to provide people from different parts of the world with new knowledge and ideas. Therefore, it is something like the 'intellectual' agency of the UN.

The main organs of UNESCO are the General Conference, the Executive Board and the Secretariat. The General Conference meets every two years, and is attended by Member States and Associate Members, together with observers of non-Member States, intergovernmental organizations and non-governmental organizations. It determines the policies and main lines of work, the programs and the budget, and elects the Members of the Executive Board and the Director-General. Many conventions have been adopted by the two-third majority of the members of the Conference, among which the 1972 Convention concerning the Protection the World Cultural and National Heritage is one of the most well-known. The Executive Board, made up of 58 members elected by the Conference, prepares the work of the Conference and ensures the implementation of its decisions. It also performs functions derived from agreements concluded between UNESCO and the UN and other specialized agencies. The distribution of its seats pays attention *"to the diversity of culture and a balanced geographical distribution"* (Article V (3) of the Constitution). A simple majority is the basic mode of voting in the Executive Board.

One distinguished feature of the UNESCO is its National Committees, which are national governmental or non-governmental bodies with the work of the Organization. Though they are organs established by member state instead of the UNESCO, they have a positive impact on the implementation of UNESCO's policies at the national level.

2.10.3.4 World Health Organization (WHO)

The WHO was established in 1946.[161] Its main purpose is *"[t]he attainment by all peoples of the highest possible level of health"* (Article 1 of the WHO Constitution). To this end it is responsible for providing leadership on global health matters, shaping the health research agenda, setting norms and standards, articulating evidence-based policy options, providing technical support to countries, and monitoring and assessing health trends. The activities of the WHO were particularly important during the Covid-19-pandemia.

The main organs of the WHO are the World Health Assembly), the Executive Board) and the Secretariat). The World Health Assembly is the plenary organ of the WHO. The annual meetings in Geneva are attended by all its 194 members. Its main function is to determine the policies of the Organization, supervise the financial policies, review and approve the program budget. The Executive Board is composed of 34 'technically qualified' member states' representatives. The main functions of

[161] *Constitution of the World Health Organization*, adopted on 22 Jul 1946.

the Board are to give effect to the decisions and policies of the Health Assembly, to advise it and generally to facilitate its work. The Secretariat of WHO has a staff of more than 8000 health and other experts and support staff on fixed-term appointments around the world. The Director-General), who is appointed by the Health Assembly on the nomination of the Executive Board, is the main director of WHO.

Since health is a shared concern particularly in neighboring states, six regional offices are established in six regions. Together with each office, there is also a committee made up of respective members and associated members in that region.

2.11 Problems and Reforms

2.11.1 Preliminary Remarks

After ups and downs in the past 80 years, the United Nations remains the most important international organization. It has made its unique and far-reaching contribution to almost all areas of the human society including traditional aspects like international peace and security, interstate operation, economic and cultural development, human rights and newly emerged issues like environment, disease, refugees, population, terrorism, etc. On the other hand, it inevitably has its defects. There is too often inaction of the UN when the world is asking for help. There are also undesirable or insufficient results of the UN performance. Too often states bypass the UN to realize their interest. Indeed, the UN has its inherent flaws in procedures and structures, whereas it is unwise and misleading to criticize the UN itself solely for all the unsatisfactory conditions, because the UN necessarily reflects also geopolitical realities which set limits to its activities. Nonetheless, there has been already for years for good reasons a UN reform debate.

2.11.2 Problems

2.11.2.1 Legitimacy of the UN SC and UN at Large

After the establishment of the UN, the organization with its increasingly universal membership was regarded as a source of legitimacy to act on an international sphere, this based on the *UN Charter as the Constitution of the International Community of States*. The Security Council, the powerful executive body, was viewed as a guard of international peace and security as well as international law. However, its status has been permanently challenged.

a) Composition of the SC

An important issue is whether the composition of the SC is representative enough to reflect changed geopolitical realities regarding global power distribution. Though it was enlarged from 11 to 15 in 1965, the pattern of the permanent five and non-permanent ten have been criticized for lack of geographic balance, and true reflection of economic and military powers. The incentives of some states to join the SC as permanent members are extremely strong. These include Germany, Japan, India, Brazil, Nigeria, and others. Also, permanent membership of regional organizations is debated.

b) Limits of the Powers of the SC

Another issue are the limits of the powers of the SC. Does the SC sometimes surpass its powers and even act *ultra vires*? As to be seen in the case of various resolutions related to combat terrorism after 9*11, the SC has acted as a kind of lawmaker. The Council has sanctioned individuals suspected of terrorist activities and requested concrete mandatory financial and immigration measures to be adopted by each state and expected concrete anti-terrorist measures to be enacted by the legislators of all the member states. Moreover, the establishment of international criminal courts like ICTY and ICTR also raised the question of what the limits of the Security Council's power are. Admittedly, the UN charter is a flexible legal basis. Yet measures must be found to ensure the extensive power of SC to issue resolutions comply with the rule of law. Therefore, some voices request that ICJ should have, like a national constitutional court or like the CJEU, the power to review resolutions of SC.

2.11.2.2 Conflicts Between Obligations Under a SC Resolution and Other International Legal Instruments

An important problem is what will happen if the obligation under a SC resolution clashes with the obligation under other conventions. This concerns Article 103 of the UN Charter which provides that "[i]n the event of conflict between the obligations of the Members of the United Nations under the present Charter and their obligations under any other international agreements, their obligations under the present Charter shall prevail." In the *Lockerbie* case, the ICJ affirmed that all member states were obliged to accept and carry out the decision of the SC in accordance with Article 25 of the Charter, and this obligation extended to resolution 748 (1992). Therefore, in accordance with Article 103, the resolution prevailed over the Montreal Convention.[162]

However, what if these resolutions lead to the violation of human rights, e.g., under the European Convention of Human Rights? Will European Courts like the Court of Justice of the European Union (CJEU) and European Court of Human Rights (ECtHR) admit that obligations under SC resolutions prevail the obligations of states under ECHR to respect human rights of individuals? The European courts did not directly answer the question, leaving this norm conflict open to discussion.

[162] *Case Concerning Questions of Interpretation and Application of the 1971 Montreal Convention Arising from the Aerial Incident at Lockerbie (Libya v. United States)*, Provisional Measures, ICJ Rep. 114 (1992), para. 42.

One way of them to solve the problem is the 'presumed non-conflict' approach as in the ECtHR Grand Chamber judgment of *Al-Jedda v United Kingdom*. The ECtHR held that, *"there must be a presumption that the SC does not intend to impose any obligation on Member States to breach fundamental principles of human rights. In the event of any ambiguity in the terms of a Security Council Resolution, the Court must therefore choose the interpretation which is most in harmony with the requirements of the Convention and which avoids any conflict of obligations [..] it is to be expected that clear and explicit language would be used were the Security Council to intend States to take particular measures which would conflict with their obligations under international human rights law."*[163] However, the court did not answer how to proceed when the pertinent SC Resolution is explicitly contradictory to the obligations under ECHR.

Another way adopted is the 'all possible measures to adapt' approach. This can be revealed in the Grand Chamber Judgment of the ECtHR on *Nada v Switzerland* (2012): *"[T]he Court finds that the respondent State could not validly confine itself to relying on the binding nature of Security Council resolutions, but should have persuaded the Court that it had taken – or at least had attempted to take – all possible measures to adapt the sanctions regime to the applicant's individual situation"*'[164] The court, however, did not answer the condition when the state had already done its best to avoid violating the ECHR.

The way to answer the question implicitly is the judgment of ECJ of *Kadi and Al Barakaat International Foundation v. Council of the European Union* (2008); *"[T] he review by the Court of the validity of any Community measure in the light of fundamental rights must be considered to be the expression, in a community based on the rule of law, of a constitutional guarantee stemming from the EC Treaty as an autonomous legal system which is not to be prejudiced by an international agreement."*[165] *"[T]he Community judicature must … ensure the review, in principle the full review, of the lawfulness of all Community acts in the light of the fundamental rights forming an integral part of the general principles of Community law, including review of Community measures which, like the contested regulation, are designed to give effect to the resolutions adopted by the Security Council under Chapter VII of the Charter of the United Nations."*[166] It seems from the judgment that the EU Charter of Fundamental Rights and the ECHR, in the view of ECJ, still prevails over SC resolutions in case of direct clashes.

[163] ECtHR, *Al-Jedda vs United Kingdom*, Application no. 27021/08 (2011), para. 102.

[164] ECtHR, *Nada v. Switzerland*, Application no. 10593/08 (2012), para. 196.

[165] *Kadi and Al Barakaat International Foundation v. Council and Commission*, Joined Cases C-402/05 P and C-415/05 P (2008) ECR I-6351, para. 316.

[166] Ibid., para. 326.

2.11.2.3 Further Exceptions to the Prohibition to Use Force?

Another very serious problem is whether there are other exceptions to the prohibition of use of force besides self-defense and collective enforcement measures under Chapter VII. In other words, does any state or groups of states have the legal authority to resort to use of force without the authorization of the SC? Is, e.g., the so called 'preemptive self-defense' a legitimate exception of use of force? In the past 25 years, there were several instances of an unauthorized use of force, among them the air campaign of NATO in Kosovo (1999), the unilateral use of force by US and UK in Iraq (2003), the threat of use of force in Syria (2011–2013), and Russia's war against the Ukraine (2022, ongoing). In fact, when Secretary General Kofi Annan asserted that the SC is the sole source of legitimacy for the use of force in the world, US Senator and later US President Joe Biden said: *"Nobody agrees with the secretary-general on that point."*[167] As unilateralism gradually reinforces its place in international sphere, will the international community continue to insist on the prohibition of use of force under Article 2(4) and the collective security system under the framework of UN?

2.11.2.4 Effectiveness of the UN Procedure and Activities

If legitimacy is the primary concern of the comparatively smaller, less developed and 'conservative' southern and eastern countries, ineffectiveness is more complained by the more powerful, developed and liberal western countries.

Both the SC and the GA is criticized for the ineffectiveness of the voting procedure. In terms of the SC, the frequent use of veto power had paralyzed the SC during the Cold War for a long time. This gave rise to the creation of peacekeeping operations and the 'Uniting for Peace' resolution. The Gulf War in 1990 marked the rebirth of SC activities under chapter VII. However, the veto seems to come back since the times of the Syria Crisis (2011–2013), and the Russian veto with regard to the war in Ukraine is responsible that the SC is completely paralyzed in this military conflict with geopolitical ramifications. According to some commentators, it is the veto power of the P5 and the inability of SC to act that somehow caused some states to circumvent the collective security system of UN.

As for the GA voting, some have argued that unrealistic conventions and declarations with little impact on the human society have been passed by the two-third majority vote of GA. In contrast, some valuable resolutions have been turned down by the majority of GA. John Bolton, the US permanent representative to the United Nations from August 2005 to December 2006, once illustrated this phenomena with the example that, *"[u]nder the system of contributions the United Nations has, the fifty-plus who voted in favor of these very modest reforms contribute 90 percent of the budget of most UN agencies. The 120 countries that voted against the reform*

---

[167] Bolton and Holbrooke (2008), p. 14.

contribute less than 10 percent. And that tells you an awful lot about the problems in the United Nations and why the United States' voice is not heard more effectively."[168]

Another problem is the (in)effectiveness of functions of organs like ECOSOC and Human Rights Council. ECOSOC serves as a coordinator of the economic and social work of the UN and the specialized agencies, with no power of management. In consequence, the performance of ECOSOC is incoherent, inefficient while time-consuming. Similarly, though the Human Rights Council has replaced the Human Rights Committee as the main UN body to supervise the observance of human rights condition of state, the impact of it is limited. This is because the views on human rights remain divided.

2.11.3 Reforms

Realizing the problems of the UN, the UN and its member states have kept the process of reforming since the 1990s. After the 9*11 and the Iraq War in 2003, other issues are taken into consideration.

2.11.3.1 Appeals for Reform

On the overall facet, three voices from different entities need to be examined. One is the report titled *'A more secure world: Our shared responsibility'* (2004)[169] by the High-Level Panel (HLP) on Threats, Challenges and Changes. The report deals with the new, transnational threats to international peace and security. Five specific threats were analyzed: Poverty, infectious disease, and environmental degradation; war between states and violence within states; nuclear, radiological, chemical, and biological weapons; terrorism and transnational organized crime.

Another Report titled *'In Larger Freedom: Towards Security, Development and Human Rights to All'* (2005)[170] was published by Secretary-General. In comparison to the HLP-Report, the report of the former Secretary-General Kofi Annan is more optimistic. Cornerstones of Kofi Annan's report are the three freedoms: a) Freedom from want: 0.7% target of gross national income for official development assistance, development cooperation in return to good governance, and environmental sustainability. b) Freedom from fear: Preventing terrorism, nuclear, chemical and biological weapons, reducing the prevalence and risk of war. c) Freedom to live in dignity: Rule

---

[168] Ibid., 15 s.

[169] Note of the SG, *A More Secure World: Our Shared Responsibility*, Report of the High-level Panel on Threats, Challenges, and Change, A/59/565 (2004).

[170] *In Larger Freedom: Towards Security, Development and Human Rights for All*, Report of the SG, A/59/2005 (2005).

of law, human rights, and democracy. Kofi Annan says in his report further reforms are indispensable for strengthening the UN. As the HLP-Report, Kofi Annan also concludes that the membership of the Security Council needs to be changed in order to reflect today's reality.

The Heads of States gathered at the UN Headquarters in New York from 14 to 16 September 2005 for the World Summit. On September 15, they adopted the outcome document: *2005 World Summit Outcome*.[171] In the outcome document, the world leaders expressed their collective will to strengthen the UN system and support UN reforms in SC, GA, ECOSOC, and Secretariat. They also committed to giving impetus to the following areas:

- Peace and collective security: Terrorism, peacekeeping, peace-building and creation of a peace-building commission and targeted sanctions.
- Human rights and rule of law: Internally Displaced Persons (IDP), 'Responsibility to Protect' (R2P), refugees, democracy, civilization, religions and dialogues between different cultures.
- Sustainable development: Global partnerships, education and empowerment of women.

All these documents were adopted more than 20 years ago. Current Secretary-General António Guterres' focus is on three areas: development; management; and peace and security. Generally, the reform proposals are by far less ambitious than they used to be.

2.11.3.2 Reform of the Security Council

The discussions about a reform of the Security Council enjoy wide support among the state community. The Security Council has constantly expanded its competences. More frequently, the Security Council is active in legislative manners. The SC is creating new ad-hoc institutions (war crime tribunals) and is probably exceeding sometimes its competences by for example, granting immunity to troops from the ICC (Chapter VII resolutions 1422, 1487).

All permanent members of the Security Council need to agree to the reform according to Article 108 of the UN Charter. Therefore, the reform process is extraordinarily difficult. For the reform of the Security Council, the following starting points are being discussed: widening of the composition of the Security Council; widening participation in the Security Council for a better reflection of the changes that have taken place in the international context since its establishment. Some proposals for a new SC composition are as follows:

- Germany, India, Japan and Brazil (G4) proposed an increase in members from 15 to 25 by creating 6 seats for permanent members without right of veto and four

[171] A/RES/60/1 (2005).

seats for non-permanent members. The new permanent members would be Germany, India, Japan, Brazil, Nigeria, South Africa.
- The "Uniting for Consensus' coalition (Italy, Spain, Canada, Mexico, Argentina, Pakistan, Columbia and Rep. Korea) wants the increase of non-permanent members to 20 seats, no new permanent members, and the deletion of the re-election prohibition for non-permanent members. Thereby new rotation circles could be created.
- African Union (AU) proposed 11 new seats, 6 with right of veto and 5 for non-permanent members.
- The USA and China insistently opposed against all proposals.

Besides composition of the SC, the Small 5 (Costa Rica, Jordan, Switzerland, Liechtenstein and Singapore, S5) prioritize an improvement of the working methods of the Security Council. They suggest more frequent reporting of the Security Council to the General Assembly (Article 24 para. 3 of the UN Charter), increase transparency of the decision-making process and reasoning of the use of a veto. This has been partly implanted after the Russian attack against Ukraine and the use of the veto by Russia in this context. In a resolution with the title *"Standing mandate for a General Assembly debate when a veto is cast in the Security Council"* the GA adopted on April 26, 2022 a resolution that its President shall convene a formal meeting within 10 working days of the casting of a veto by one or more permanent members of the Council and hold a debate on the situation as to which the veto was cast. Further, the Assembly invited the Council, in accordance with Article 24(3) of the Charter of the United Nations, to submit a special report on the use of the veto in question, to the Assembly at least 72 hours before the relevant discussion is to take place.[172]

As has been discussed, the decision-making of the SC is not very transparent. Moreover, the resolutions of the SC after 9*11 sometimes contradicted the protection of individual human rights. Thus, the 'Targeted Sanctions and Due Process' was initiated by Germany, Sweden and Switzerland. Afterwards, the Watson Institute of the Brown University drew up the study 'Strengthening Targeted Sanctions through Fair and Clear Procedures'. It is advocated that the legitimacy and acceptance of SC-resolutions could be improved, if they were Executed in accordance with human rights.[173]

---

[172] *Standing mandate for a General Assembly debate when a veto is cast in the Security Council*, A/RES/76/262 (2022), para. 2 s.

[173] Watson Institute for International and Public Affairs (2006) *Strengthening Targeted Sanctions through Fair and Clear Procedures*. Brown University, Providence.

2.11.3.3 Peace-Building Commission (PBC)[174]

The Commission, established by the SC and the GA, comprised of 31 members, was tasked with addressing a critical gap within the UN and global system by providing a coordinated, coherent and integrated approach to post-conflict peace-building and facilitating dialogue among key actors.[175] The PBC started working in June 2006. The Peace-building Commission is a consultative board for the SC, for the ECOSOC if the SC is not concerned with the matter, and the SG. The PBC has been engaged with several conflicts.[176]

2.11.3.4 Responsibility to Protect (R2P)[177]

As has been discussed, the nature of armed conflicts has changed. Inter-state conflicts were replaced by internal conflicts, and civilians now make up most casualties. In the 1990s, a devastating famine occurred in Somalia. The UN intervened on the basis of a Chapter VII SC-Resolution (S/RES/794). Therewith, Chapter VII of the Charter was given a new interpretation. Such a resolution would principally have violated article 2(7) of the UN Charter. Nevertheless, the genocides in Cambodia, Rwanda, and Bosnia, as well as crimes against humanity in Kosovo, East Timor and Darfur have demonstrated massive failures of the international community. After these failures, there was a recognized need to shift the debate about crisis prevention and response: the security of the community and the individual, not only the state, must be priorities for national and international policies. That is the way the concept of Responsibility to Protect (R2P) developed.

The first report on this matter was published by the International Commission on Intervention and State Sovereignty (ICISS) in September 2000 (www.iciss.ca). According to the Commission, the following responsibilities exist:

- Responsibility to Prevent;
- Responsibility to React;
- Responsibility to Rebuild

This was taken up by the states: In paragraphs 138–139 of the World Summit Outcome Document in 2005, the governments agreed to the following:

- Each individual state has the primary responsibility to protect its populations from genocide, war crimes, crimes against humanity and ethnic cleansing, including a responsibility for prevention of these crimes.

---

[174] <www.un.org/peacebuilding> (accessed 9 March 2025).

[175] A/RES/60/180 and S/RES/1645 (2005), para. 4.

[176] E.g. Burundi, the Central African Republic, Guinea-Bissau and Sierra Leone.

[177] https://www.globalr2p.org/about/ (accessed 9 March Aug 2025).

- The international community should encourage or assist states to exercise this responsibility.
- The international community has the responsibility to use appropriate diplomatic, humanitarian and other peaceful means to help protect populations threatened by these crimes. When a state fails to protect and peaceful means are inadequate, the international community must take stronger measures, including collective use of force authorized by the Security Council under Chapter VII.

'The Responsibility to Protect any Population from Genocide, Ethnic Cleansing, War Crimes and Crimes against Humanity' is an international commitment of governments to prevent and react to grave crises, wherever they may occur. On 30 January 2009, then Secretary-General Ban Ki-moon issued a report on the implementation of the Responsibility to Protect.

Opposition to the new concept of R2P comes mainly from the southern hemisphere. States fear a further decrease of their sovereignty and interferences in their internal affairs. Though the operation in Libya 2011 can be viewed as the first implementation of the R2P, many states became more cautious on the concept afterwards.

2.11.3.5 Revitalization of the General Assembly

The revitalization of the General Assembly is a permanent element in the agenda of the UN since 1991 and has resulted in many resolutions on the matter. The topics covered include: Working methods and documentation; GA's role in the selection of the UN Secretary-General; the role and authority of the GA; and its visibility.

However, progress is very slow. In the 62nd Session, the Working Group 'only' evaluated the implementation status of the existing provisions on GA Revitalization. On September 15, 2008, the GA adopted the draft report of the AHWG and its recommendation, deciding to establish the Working Group for another year (Res 62/276). Since then, there were annually reports of the Working Group as well as resolutions of the GA[178] stating the necessity of a revitalization of the GA. However, there has been almost no concrete outcome.

References

Bolton J, Holbrooke R (2008) Reforming the United Nations. Brown J World Aff 14(2):11–21
Boutros-Ghali B (1992) An agenda for peace. United Nations, New York

[178] See A/RES/55/285 (2001), 56/509 (2002), 57/301 (2003), 58/126 and 58/316 (2004), 60/286 (2006), 61/292 (2007), 62/276 (2008), 63/309 (2009), 64/301 (2010), 65/315 (2011), 66/294 (2012), 67/297 (2013), 68/307 (2014), 69/321 (2015), 70/305 (2016), 71/323 (2017), 72/313 (2018), 73/341 (2019), 74/303 (2020), 75/325 and 77/335 (2023).

Churchill W (1948) The gathering storm. Cassell, London
Churchill W (1950) The grand alliance. Cassell, London
Conforti B, Focarelli C (2010) The law and practice of the United Nations, 4th edn. Martinus Nijhoff Publishers, Leiden
Crawford J (2006) The creation of states in international law, 2nd edn. Clarendon Press, Oxford
Dixon M (2007) Textbook on international law, 6th edn. Oxford University Press, Oxford
Henig R (2010) The league of nations. Haus Publishing, London
Kelsen H (1950) The law of the United Nations: a critical analysis of its fundamental problems. Stevens & Sons, London
Kolb R (2010) An introduction to the law of the United Nations. Hart Publishing, Oxford
Saksena KP (1974) The United Nations and collective security. D. K. Publishing House, Delhi
Shaw MN (2021) International law, 9th edn. Cambridge University Press, Cambridge
Taylor P, Curtis D (2011) The United Nations. In: Baylis J et al (eds) The globalization of world politics: an introduction to international relations, 5th edn. Oxford University Press, Oxford, pp 312–329
Watson Institute for International and Public Affairs (2006) Strengthening targeted sanctions through fair and clear procedures. Brown University, Providence
Wilson W (1918) Fourteen Points. Speech to the United States Congress, 8 Jan 1918

Selected Bibliography

Blum YZ (1992a) Russia takes over the Soviet Union's seat at the United Nations. EJIL 3:354–362
Blum YZ (1992b) UN Membership of the "New" Yugoslavia: continuity or break? Am J Int Law 86(4):830–833
Blum YZ (2007) Was Yugoslavia a member of the United Nations in the years 1992–2000? Am J Int Law 101(4):800–818
Bolton J, Holbrooke R (2008) Reforming the United Nations. Brown J World Aff 14(2):11–21
Brand RA (1976) Security Council resolutions: when do they give rise to enforceable legal rights: The United Nations Charter, the Byrd Amendment and a Self-Executing Treaty Analysis. Cornell Int Law J 9(2):298–317
Cassese A (2012) The legitimacy of international criminal tribunals and the current prospects of international criminal justice. Leiden J Int Law 25(2):491–501. https://doi.org/10.1017/S0922156512000271
Deen-Racsmany Z (2000) A redistribution of authority between the UN and regional organizations in the field of the maintenance of peace and security? Leiden J Int Law 13(2):297–331
Droesse G (2020) Membership in international organizations – paradigms of membership structures, legal implications of membership and the concept of international organizations. Asser Press/Springer
Fassbender B (2009) The United Nations Charter as the constitution of the international community. Martinus Nijhoff, Leiden/Boston
Gifkins J (2012) The UN Security Council Divided: Syria in crisis. Global Responsib Prot 4(3): 377–393
Harsch MF (2015) The power of dependence: NATO-UN cooperation in crisis management. Oxford University Press, Oxford
Henig R (2010) The league of nations. Haus Publishing, London
Islami I, Istrefi R (2018) Consolidation of statehood through membership in the UN: some remarks on Kosovo, democracy and international law. Rev Central East Eur Law 43(3):331–349
Job BL (2004) The UN, regional organizations, and regional conflict: is there a viable role for the UN? In: Price RM, Zacher MW (eds) The United Nations and global security. Palgrave Macmillan, New York, pp 217–243

Jovanovic V (1997) The status of the Federal Republic of Yugoslavia in the United Nations. Fordham Int Law J 21(5):1719–1736
Kelsen H (1950) The law of the United Nations: a critical analysis of its fundamental problems. Stevens & Sons, London
Klabbers J (2009) The United Nations Charter as the constitution of the international community. Int Organ Law Rev 6(2):667–673
Kolb R (2010) An introduction to the law of the United Nations. Hart Publishing, Oxford
Lentner GM (2019) The UN Security Council and the International Criminal Court: the referral mechanism in theory and practice. Edward Elgar Publishing, Cheltenham
McGoldrick D et al (eds) (2004) The permanent International Criminal Court: legal and policy issues. Hart Publishing, Oxford
Olonisakin F (1996) UN co-operation with regional organizations in peacekeeping: the experience of ECOMOG and UNOMIL in Liberia. Int Peacekeep 3(3):33–51
Paolini AJ et al (eds) (1998) Between sovereignty and global governance: the United Nations and world politics. Palgrave Macmillan, Houndmills/Basingstoke/Hampshire
Patel BN (2013) Responsibility of international organizations towards other international organizations: law and practice of the United Nations, the World Bank, the European Union (EU) and the International Atomic Energy Agency (IAEA). Eastern Book Company, Lucknow
Saksena KP (1974) The United Nations and collective security. D. K. Publishing House, Delhi
Simma B (1999) NATO, the UN and the use of force: legal aspects. EJIL 10(1):1–40
Simma B et al (2024) The Charter of the United Nations - a commentary, 4th edn. Oxord University Press
Spandler K (2020) UNAMID and the legitimation of global-regional peacekeeping cooperation: partnership and friction in UN-AU relations. J Interv Statebuild 14(2):187–203
Vitucci MC (2006) Has Pandora's box been closed? The decisions on the legality of use of force cases in relation to the status of the Federal Republic of Yugoslavia (Serbia and Montenegro) within the United Nations. Leiden J Int Law 19(1):105–127
Walling CB (2013) All necessary measures: the United Nations and humanitarian intervention. University of Pennsylvania Press, Philadelphia
Walter C (2009) Regional arrangements and the United Nations Charter. In: Wolfrum R (ed) Max Planck encyclopedia of public international law. Oxford University Press, Oxford
Wood MC (1997) Participation of former Yugoslav states in the United Nations and in multilateral treaties. Max Planck Yearb United Nations Law 1:231–257

Chapter 3
European Organizations

3.1 Introduction

Regional organizations are intergovernmental organizations with a specific geographical focus. They were established after World War II[1] to promote and improve cooperation and political and economic integration among states within a region or a continent. The growing number of regional organizations points to the increasing need for closer cooperation between states in the same region in solving problems that, because of their transnational dimensions, exceed the problem-solving capabilities of individual states, and which are not sufficiently addressed by global institutions. Regional organizations thus serve as a forum for the states in the region to discuss common issues and devise solutions to those issues. The most common examples of regional organizations in Europe are the OSCE, the Council of Europe (CoE), the North Atlantic Treaty Organization (NATO), and the supranational European Union (EU). With the notable exception of the EU, regional organizations generally do not prescribe mandatory actions to be taken by their members but create space for a collective exchange of ideas and establish political guidelines and recommendations for member states on issues of common concern.

Special thanks to Ulrike Heinrich for her important contribution to the elaboration of this chapter.

[1] For a history of the formation of regional organizations, see Reinalda (2009), especially 361–372 and 443–496.

U. Saxer, *The Law of Global and European Organizations*, Springer Textbooks in Law, https://doi.org/10.1007/978-3-032-00067-5_3

3.2 Regional Organizations and the United Nations

3.2.1 Regional Organizations and Chapter VIII UNCh

The United Nations (UN) encourage the activities of regional organizations, particularly as to peace and security. The UN Security Council, responsible for the maintenance of international peace and security, often relies on regional organizations to take on part of its workload so that it can remain an oversight body. This idea dates back to the creation of the UN Charter. As it was considered to be insufficient to only adopt a universal approach to securing international peace and security, the idea of regionalism was put in place to complement the universalist approach.[2] It was generally agreed that one single globally acting entity—such as the Security Council—could not address all security issues simultaneously. As a result, the UN Charter provides for regional arrangements to play a role in maintaining international peace and security, as established in Chapter VIII, Articles 52–54. These articles did not result from a *"common understanding of all negotiating parties in 1945"*, but were a *"compromise between universalist and regionalist approaches to the maintenance of international peace and security"*.[3]

Chapter VIII regional arrangements are essentially treaty-based cooperations between two or more states in a specific geographical area focusing on issues concerning regional peace and security, including institutionalized dispute settlement. Several articles of the UN Charter regulate the relationship between regional arrangements and the UN system. Article 52(1) of the UN Charter states that

> *"nothing in the present Charter precludes the existence of regional arrangements or agencies for dealing with such matters relating to the maintenance of international peace and security as are appropriate for regional action provided that such arrangements or agencies and their activities are consistent with the Purposes and Principles of the United Nations."*

Article 52(2) invites the members of the UN entering such arrangements or constituting such agencies to

> *"make every effort to achieve pacific settlement of local disputes through such regional arrangements or by such regional agencies before referring them to the Security Council"*.

To ensure the efficacy of Article 52(2), Article 33(1) UN Charter states that parties to any dispute endangering international peace and security

---

[2] For an analysis of the interplay between the UN and regional organizations in peacekeeping, see Sidhu (2020).

[3] Walter (2009), para. 1.

"shall, first of all, seek a solution by...resort to regional agencies or arrangements, or other peaceful means of their own choice".

Thus, regional organizations and arrangements play an important role in the management of conflicts and threats to regional security. However, *Chapter VIII does not limit the Security Council's powers; a member state may always bring an issue forward to the attention of the Council.* Nonetheless, although the work of regional organizations complements the Security Council's work, *regional organizations should be the first port of call in cases of conflict.*[4] In addition to managing and solving security conflicts, Chapter VIII regional organizations also have an important role to play in, e.g., managing the aftermath of natural disasters and global pandemics.[5]

3.2.2 *What Are Regional Arrangements and Organizations?*

3.2.2.1 Regional Arrangements Under Chapter VIII of the UN Charter

In general, regional arrangements are *treaty-based structures established to enable cooperation between the nation states of a specific region in security, economic, social, cultural and other matters.* Such treaty-based structures often, but not always, develop into a legal framework of a regional organization as an international legal person. It seems, however, that the term 'Regional Arrangements' as used in Chapter VIII may include non-treaty-based structures. Indeed, it has been even argued that *"the modern understanding of ['regional arrangements or agencies'] foregoes the requirement of a binding treaty".*[6] An example is the OSCE: although it is not based on an international treaty, its Helsinki Summit Declaration of 10 July 1992 defines itself as an organization under Chapter VIII.[7] The UN, in turn, has accepted this self-definition by granting the OSCE observer status.[8] This, however, is an exception.

Under the UN Charter, regional arrangements are significant insofar as they play a substantial role in the maintenance of regional peace and security. *Regional organizations which have established mechanisms for collective security and internal dispute settlement mechanisms fall under Chapter VIII and are part of the UN system of collective security; other organizations without such mechanisms do not.*

---

[4] For a critical analysis of the relationship between regional organizations and the UN, including the larger role assumed by regional organizations in peacekeeping operations in the 1990s, see Job (2004).

[5] See e.g. Hollis (2015); Bossong and Hegemann (2015).

[6] Walter (2009), para. 7.

[7] OSCE, *Helsinki Summit Declaration*, 10 Jul 1992, para. 25.

[8] A/RES/48/5 (1993).

The UN Charter does not define regional organizations; further, Chapter VIII does not establish a procedure for formally recognizing regional organizations. It is therefore an unclear category. As the UN's implicit recognition of the OSCE as a regional organization under Chapter VIII shows, whether a regional arrangement is also a regional organization depends sometimes on the UN's actions, such as the granting of observer status. Other regional organizations recognized under Chapter VIII include the African Union (AU), the Organization of American States (OAS) and the Arab League.

3.2.2.2 Regional Arrangements and Organizations Outside of Chapter VIII

Regional arrangements can be found throughout the world. They take on a multitude of different responsibilities, as only a few are formed for the main purpose of security. Most organizations focus on other subject matters such as trade, social and cultural exchange, and development. In many political and economic fields regional organizations play a very important role independent and outside of Chapter VIII of the UN Charter. Some of the regional organizations cover subgroups of a region with closer ties (see, e.g., the EU in Europe). Some so-called regional organizations cover more than one region or continent such as the OECD.

Regional organizations formed for economic, social, cultural or other purposes do not fall under Chapter VIII if they were *not* established for collective security purposes and do not provide for common security and dispute settlement mechanisms. An example is the Council of Europe (CoE). Some regional organizations aimed primarily at economic integration also carry out peace enforcement activities, such as the Economic Community of West African States (ECOWAS) which was active in conflicts in Liberia and other African countries; such organizations may qualify as regional organizations under Chapter VIII.[9]

Defense alliances such as NATO do not fall under Chapter VIII. This is because their focus is on common defense and military cooperation but not on collective security and the settlement of disputes. Even if they engage in UN peace enforcement activities based on a Security Council authorization, their nature as defense alliances remain unchanged.

3.2.2.3 Scope of Regional Organizations Under Chapter VIII

Chapter VIII regional organizations can be understood as *subsystems of the UN-system*: There is the UN as global international organization with a very comprehensive, all-encompassing purpose on one side, and regional organizations

[9] ECOWAS, *Protocol Relating to the Mechanism for Conflict Prevention, Management, Resolution, Peacekeeping and Security* (1999), where ECOWAS's role in peace enforcement is outlined.

such as the OAS, AU, the Arab League and the OSCE on the other side. As far as the maintenance of peace and security is concerned, Chapter VIII UN Charter erects a *decentralized system of collective security with the UN Security Council as the main organ* responsible for global collective security, and regional security arrangements complementing the often-overstrained UN system of collective security on the regional level.

The UN, as the largest and most experienced international organization, takes a global approach to peacekeeping and dispute settlement which may not be the best approach in regional disputes which often require familiarity with the reasons and roots of the dispute as well as the relevant actors. Therefore, regional organizations may play an important role in peacekeeping and dispute settlement under the auspices of the UN Security Council. Regional organizations are able to mediate disputes and conflicts with a more regionally focused approach. They can take cultural, geographical and political issues more into account and provide an approach to mediation that is better suited to local conditions. Furthermore, regional organizations provide the first point of contact for dispute settlement and are a form of authority secondary to the UN.[10] This is why, according to Article 52(3) of the UN Charter, the Security Council may on its own initiative or on request of a state refer a dispute to a regional arrangement. Thus, Chapter VIII gives regional arrangements a genuine role in the maintenance of peace and security in a region.

The powers of regional arrangements in the framework of the UN system of collective security refer to *"local disputes"* (Article 2 (1) UNCh) if and when they have an adverse effect on regional peace and security. The term 'dispute' includes conflicts that fall under Chapter VI and VII of the UN Charter, but also situations affecting peace and security outside the scope of application of these two chapters of the UN Charter.

Parties to the local dispute are called up to consult regional arrangements.[11] There is, however, no UN Charter obligation of involved states to refer disputes that do not constitute a threat to international peace to regional dispute settlement mechanisms. As regards disputes involving an actual threat to international peace, i.e. conflicts in the sense of Chapter VII of the UN Charter, they fall under the purview and responsibility of the UN Security Council. Accordingly, it is not necessary to refer the dispute to regional dispute settlement mechanisms first before bringing it to the UN Security Council. *The Security Council arguably enjoys a certain superiority over other international, including regional, organizations due to the supremacy of the UN Charter in international law.* This also means that the responsibility for the maintenance of peace and security lies primarily with the Security Council. In practice, though, the Security Council, when managing regional and international conflicts, frequently calls upon regional arrangements to take coercive measures and to play an active role in the conflict management.

---

[10] For specific instances of UN and regional organizations' peacekeeping cooperation, see Olonisakin (1996), p. 33 ss.; Paliwal (2010), p. 185 ss.; and Spandler (2020), p. 187 ss.

[11] Cf. Arts. 33 and 52(2) UNCh.

Regional arrangements are bound by the UN Charter[12] and international law in general. In particular, there are legal limits on the methods to be used by regional arrangement in managing a dispute. According to Article 53(1) of the UN Charter,[13] enforcement action to be taken under regional arrangements or by regional agencies requires the prior authorization of the Security Council. This refers foremost to the use of military force. It is inconclusive from state and UN practice whether an authorization is also required for non-military sanctions, though in many instances states did not ask for a Security Council permit when imposing non-military sanctions.[14] Even with regard to a military involvement, regional organizations have sometimes and, contrary to the provisions of the UN Charter, also acted without UN Security Council explicit authorization and undertaken enforcement measures to maintain peace and security. For example, the ECOWAS intervened in the conflicts in Liberia and Sierra Leone, and NATO took unilateral action against Serbian targets in Kosovo in 1999. Such coercive measures by regional organizations without UN authorization usually violate the UN Charter.[15]

3.2.3 Relation Between Regionalism and Universalism

The practice of the UN Security Council regarding the relation between regionalism und universalism under Chapter VIII UN Charter is unclear. For disputes not involving a treat to international peace and which thus fall outside Chapter VII,

---

[12] In particular, Art. 103, which provides: "In the event of a conflict between the obligations of the Members of the United Nations under the present Charter and their obligations under any other international agreement, their obligations under the present Charter shall prevail." Therefore, member states of regional organizations have a duty, as UN members, to secure that these regional organizations observe the provisions of the UN Charter.

[13] Art. 53(1) reads: "The Security Council shall, where appropriate, utilize such regional arrangements or agencies for enforcement action under its authority. But no enforcement action shall be taken under regional arrangements or by regional agencies without the authorization of the Security Council, with the exception of measures against any enemy state, as defined in paragraph 2 of this Article, provided for pursuant to Article 107 or in regional arrangements directed against renewal of aggressive policy on the part of any such state, until such time as the Organization may, on request of the Governments concerned, be charged with the responsibility for preventing further aggression by such a state."

[14] See, e.g. as a recent example the sanctions imposed by the EU against Russia after the Russian military attack of the Ukraine. Russia as a a permanent member of the UN SC would have vetoed any authorization of economic sanctions of the EU. The right of individual states to unilaterally impose economic sanctions on other states is sill disputed. It has been argued that imposing such sanctions to apply political pressure on another state is allowed only when it is in the interest of the international community, and when the international community does not strongly oppose the sanctions in question. See Szasz (1998), p. 456 ss. This view is not confirmed by state practice and most probably outdated.

[15] For an analysis of the impact of these regional efforts on the UN's authority in the maintenance of international peace and security, see Deen-Racsmany (2000), p. 297 ss.

regional dispute settlement appears to be the first resort even though states have no obligation to refer the dispute to a regional arrangement. The provisions of Chapter VI of the UN Charter and Article 52(3)[16] show that a reference to regional dispute settlement is more a convenience than an obligation.

In situations and disputes involving an actual threat to peace and thus falling under Chapter VII UN Charter, primary responsibility for these disputes lies with the UN Security, not regional dispute settlements, even though states may first notify the situation to a regional organization in an attempt to trigger a regional conflict management.

Generally, therefore, due to the supremacy of the UN Charter, the UN Security Council enjoys a certain superiority of power. This is also due to the Security Council's general responsibility for the maintenance of international peace and security.

3.2.4 Regional Conflict Management

Conflict management activities of regional organizations are often embedded in the UN conflict management: They are regularly called upon by the UN Security Council to take coercive measures to restore peace and security in the region. On the other hand, regional arrangements often initiate their own conflict management activities, independent or in addition to the Security Council's activities. This includes regional peacekeeping operations which, however, usually require a Security Council authorization if the peacekeeping operation's mandate includes the use of force. Only if the host state consents to the use of force—for instance, when the peacekeeping force is intervening in an internal conflict—the Security Council's authorization to use force may not be required. More recently, joint peacekeeping operations of the UN and regional organizations have been established (e.g. in Liberia and Sudan). Generally, in practice and in the field, there is much more cooperation between regional arrangements and the UN than subordination. This is also reflected in a resolution of the UN General Assembly.[17]

---

[16] Art. 52(3) reads: "The Security Council shall encourage the development of pacific settlement of local disputes through such regional arrangements or by such regional agencies either on the initiative of the states concerned or by reference from the Security Council."

[17] See *Declaration on the Enhancement of Cooperation between the United Nations and Regional Arrangements or Agencies in the Maintenance of International Peace and Security*, A/RES/49/57 (1994).

3.3 Organization for Security and Co-operation in Europe (OSCE)

3.3.1 Main Goals of the OSCE

Consisting of 57 members from Europe, Central Asia and North America, the OSCE provides a platform for political dialogue on a wide range of security issues and aims to improve the lives of individuals and communities. Even though the organization covers many areas such as security, disarmament, human rights, protection of minorities, rule of law, democracy, and economic and ecological issues, its principal purposes are peace and security.

*"The OSCE has a comprehensive approach to security that encompasses politico-military, economic and environmental, and human aspects. It therefore addresses a wide range of security-related concerns, including arms control, confidence- and security-building measures, human rights, national minorities, democratization, policing strategies, counter-terrorism and economic and environmental activities. All 57 participating States enjoy equal status, and decisions are taken by consensus on a politically, but not legally binding basis."*380

The OSCE is a Chapter VIII UN Charter organization. However, given that its purpose is not confined to peace and security, the organization's activities often overlap with the activities of other European organizations such as the Council of Europe.

The OSCE approaches security from three angles:[18]

- politico-military;
- economic and environmental; and
- human rights and fundamental freedoms.

To create greater openness and transparency in military matters, the organization has developed the world's most advanced regime of arms control and confidence-building measures.[19] In economic and environmental matters, the OSCE promotes good governance, tackling corruption and environmental awareness. Regarding human rights and fundamental freedoms, two efforts must be emphasized: The organization's work in helping its participating states to build democratic institutions, and its work in helping participating states hold genuine and transparent elections. For instance, the OSCE was the principal organization that oversaw and facilitated elections in Bosnia after the Dayton Peace Agreement ended the Bosnian

[18] Factsheet: What is the OSCE, available at: <https://www.osce.org/whatistheosce> (accessed 9 March 2025).

[19] For an in-depth report on the OSCE's confidence- and security-building measures, see Lachowski (2004); For an analysis of the OCSE's politico-military achievements and flaws, see Bailes (2006), p. 214 ss.

War in 1995.[20] Lastly, respect for human rights has been pushed through these measures and is the fundamental basis of the organization's work.

3.3.2 Origin and Development of the OSCE

3.3.2.1 Establishment of the CSCE; the Helsinki Final Act

The idea of a "European Security Conference" to bring together the opposing superpowers U.S.A. and USSR under a common goal of security and cooperation in the Atlantic-Euro area[21] already existed in the 1950s. However, it was only in 1975 that the CSCE, the precursor of the OSCE, officially got established as an institutionalized conference The origin of today's OSCE, the world's largest regional security organization, can be traced back to the Conference on Security and Cooperation in Europe (CSCE) which started in Helsinki in 1973.[22] This conference was convened to improve cooperation and relations between Eastern and Western Europe as part of a policy of détente, or the easing of political tension. Initially, 35 states were involved, including the seven states of the Warsaw pact, 13 neutral or non-aligned countries and the 15 NATO countries.

In 1975, the participating Heads of State or Government signed the Helsinki Final Act. The Final Act envisaged further conferences, discussed below, and focused on questions relating to security, cooperation in the field of economics, science, technology and the environment, cooperation in humanitarian and other fields, confidence building measures in the military sector and human rights. The Final Act also established ten fundamental principles (the *Decalogue*) to govern both the behavior of states towards their citizens, as well as towards each other.[23] The Final Act was not a treaty but a political document belonging to the normative category of soft law, and it has become one of the most important soft law documents.[24] It accorded respect to the sovereignty of the participating states, as sovereignty was of particular importance to the socialist states of Eastern Europe. Nonetheless, it also contained principles referring to the states' domestic jurisdiction such as human rights which resulted in a certain limitation of the sovereignty of the participating states.

---

[20] For a breakdown of the OSCE's responsibilities in this regard, see Sica (1996), p. 5 ss.; For an assessment of the OSCE's work in Bosnia and Herzegovina, see Perry and Keil (2013), p. 371 ss.

[21] Galbreath (2007), p. 24.

[22] For the official transcript, see <https://www.csce.gov/publications/transcripts/> (accessed 9 March 2025).

[23] These are contained in Art. 1(a) of the Final Act. The principles include sovereign equality, territorial integrity of states, peaceful settlement of disputes and respect for human rights and fundamental freedoms.

[24] For an analysis of how the Helsinki Final Act has shaped international norms, including human rights norms, see Thomas (2001).

3.3.2.2 Follow-Up Conferences

Following the Helsinki conference, several follow-up conferences were held. After the first conference (Belgrade, 1977/78) failed due to a disagreement on human rights issues,[25] the next one held in Madrid (1980–1983) led to improvements in human rights.[26] At Madrid, the participating states also decided to hold a special conference relating to confidence-building measures and disarmament. Accordingly, the Stockholm conference (1984–1986) led to further confidence-building measures which included public notification of larger military trainings and the obligation to invite observers to such trainings/maneuvers.[27] Following these conferences, the Treaty on Conventional Armed Forces in Europe (CFE Treaty) was signed in 1990. This first disarmament treaty ever in Europe limited the number of conventional forces, i.e. the number of battle tanks, combat vehicles, pieces of artillery, combat aircraft and attack helicopters, as opposed to non-conventional weapons such as biological, chemical, nuclear and ballistic missiles. Further, the Vienna Document of 1992[28] elaborated on a number of confidence-building measures. For instance, paragraph 10 provides that

> *participating States will exchange annually information on their military forces concerning military organization, manpower and major weapon and equipment systems…in the zone of application for confidence- and security-building measures.*

Paragraph 12 obliges states to *"exchange data relating to their major weapon and equipment systems"*. The Document also lists specific major weapon and equipment systems for which states are required to provide data. Most of these arrangements broke down, due to the Russian attack against Ukraine in 2022.

3.3.2.3 Charter of Paris for a New Europe

Through the creation of several institutions such as a CSCE Secretary, the Council of Ministers, the Council of Senior Officials and the Office for Free Elections, a basis for the evolvement of the later OSCE was gradually created. All these institutions

---

[25] For more information and academic reflections on the Belgrade Conference, see e.g. Liskofsky (1978), p. 121 ss.; Liskofsky (1979), p. 152 ss.; Cabranes (1978), p. 274 ss.; and Goldberg (1979), p. 179 ss.

[26] For more information, see Killham (1984), p. 340 ss.

[27] For more information on the Stockholm Conference and its impact on security, see e.g. Freeman (1991) and Lodgaard (2007), p. 155 ss.

[28] OSCE (1992) *Vienna Document 1992 of the Negotiations on Confidence- and Security-Building Measures, adopted at the Helsinki Summit of the Conference on Security and Co-operation in Europe (CSCE).*

were established on the basis of soft law documents and not a treaty among the member states.

In 1990, with the end of the Cold War in Europe, the Paris Summit set the CSCE on a new course.[29] The CSCE participants adopted the Charter of Paris for a New Europe. The Charter stated that *"the era of confrontation and division of Europe has ended"*[30] and that *"Europe is liberating itself from the legacy of the past"*. This important document on the creation of a new peaceful order in Europe contributed to the reshaping of the European political landscape. The Charter contains several principles designed to guide cooperation in Europe. These include principles on human rights, democracy, rule of law, economic liberty and responsibility, friendly relations among states, security and cooperation in many areas. In addition, the Charter created new structures and institutions for the CSCE, such as a Foreign Affairs Council and a Conflict Prevention Center. Again, these institutions were created on the basis of soft law.

At the follow-up conference in Helsinki in 1992, the participants created mechanisms to settle all kinds of disputes. This made the CSCE the primary forum for regional conflict management and the prevention and settlement of conflicts. Since then, and as mentioned earlier, the CSCE has been deemed as a regional arrangement under Chapter VIII of the UN Charter.

3.3.2.4 Establishment of an International Organization

At the Budapest conference in 1994, the structure of the CSCE was changed from a series of conferences to an institutionalized international organization. The CSCE was renamed OSCE. Thus, the OSCE was successfully established as a regional organization just on the basis of soft law. Such a creation of an international organization based solely on soft law and not a legally binding treaty remains very exceptional.

3.3.3 Organs of the OSCE

3.3.3.1 Overview

The OSCE maintains a number of bodies and institutions through which the organization fulfills its mandate. The organigram of the OSCE's organization is as follows (Figs. 3.1 and 3.2):

---

[29] For more information, see <https://www.osce.org/event/summit_1990> (accessed 9 March 2025).

[30] OSCE (1990) *Charter of Paris for a New Europe,* Paris Summit, 3.

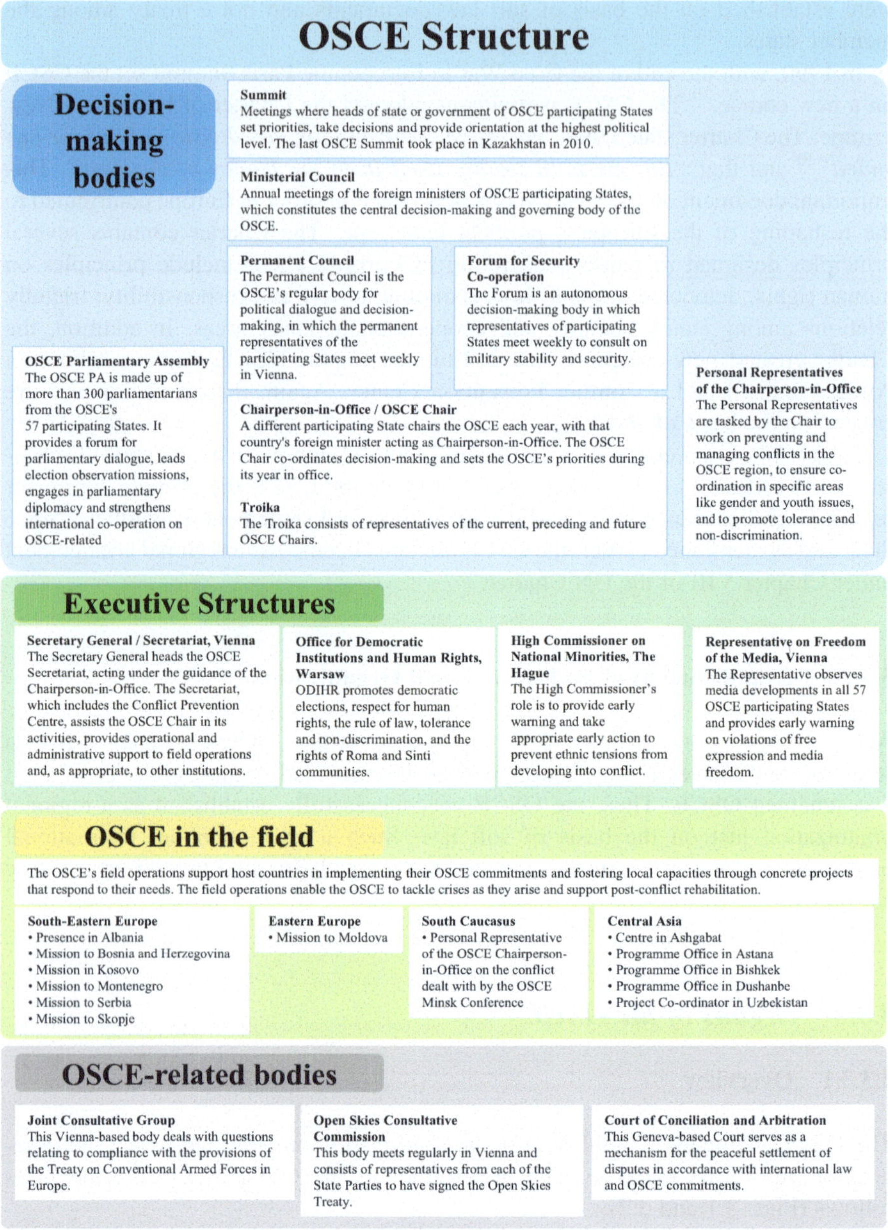

Fig. 3.1 The OSCE structure. Own graphic modeled after OSCE (n.d.) What is the OSCE?. 7. <https://www.osce.org/files/f/documents/d/d/35775_10.pdf> *(accessed 9 March 2025)*

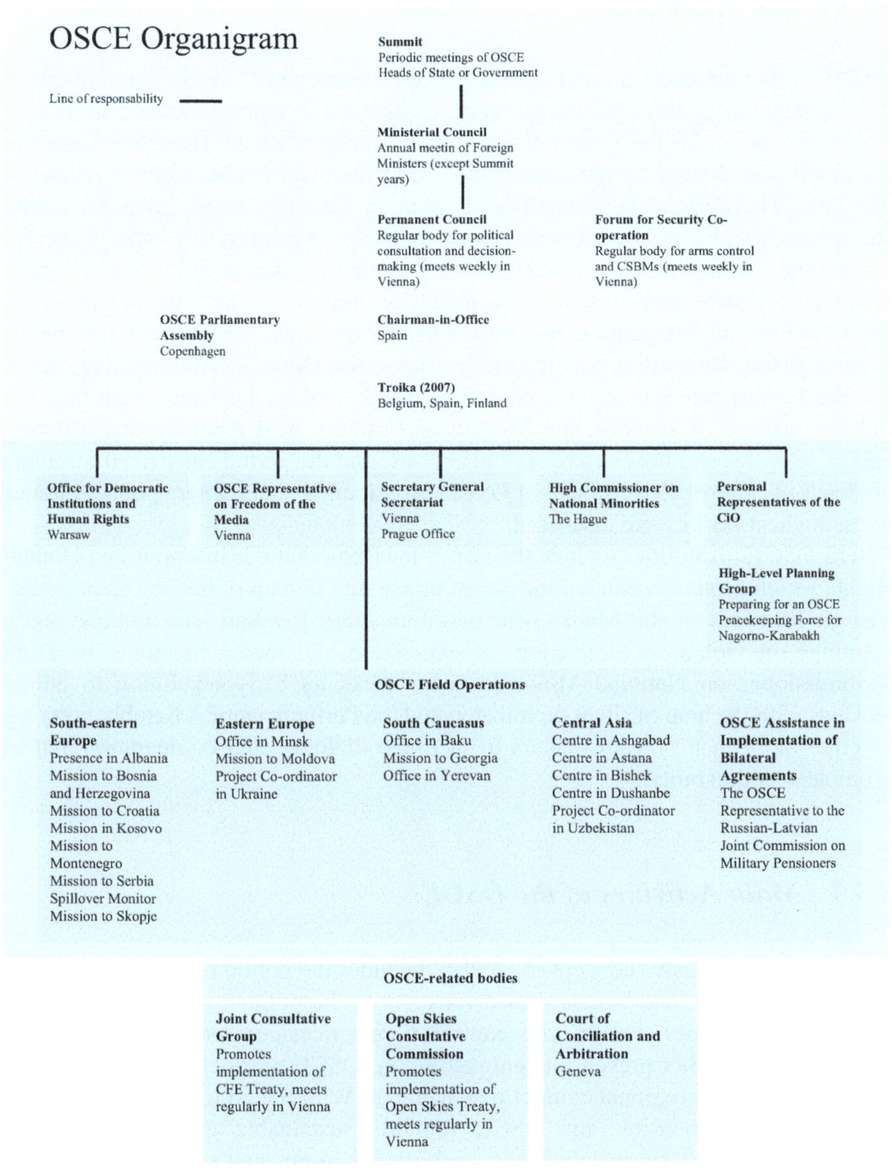

Fig. 3.2 OSCE Organigram. Own graphic modeled after OSCE (2008) (2008) OSCE Organigram. OSCE, Vienna: <https://www.osce.org/files/f/documents/d/8/31273.pdf> (accessed 9 March 2025)

3.3.3.2 Principal Bodies

OSCE's principal decision-making body is the Permanent Council which oversees the OSCE's day-to-day operational work. Composed of ambassadors of all 57 participating states, the Permanent Council meets once a week. These meetings are convened and chaired by the Chairperson-in-Office who is elected for a period of one year. The Permanent Council holds plenary meetings where all participating states hold regular political consultations and may also raise any other issue for discussion. During plenary meetings, all participating states enjoy equal rights. Given that OSCE decisions must be made by consensus, the Chairperson seeks approval from all delegations. It is only when all delegates agree that the decisions become politically binding for all participating states. Other decision-making bodies are the Forum for Security Co-operation which makes decisions regarding the military aspects of security; the Ministerial Council, held annually, that reviews OSCE activities and provides overall directions; and the periodically fixed Summits of Heads of State or Government of OSCE participating states where political issues of the highest priority are discussed.

The OSCE institutions include the Office for Democratic Institutions and Human Rights which promotes democratic development and human rights; the Representative on Freedom of the Media who monitors press freedom and provides early warnings on violations of freedom of expression and media freedom; the High Commissioner on National Minorities who seeks an early resolution to ethnic tensions with the help of silent diplomacy; and the Parliamentary Assembly bringing together more than 300 lawmakers to facilitate dialogue and co-operation and to promote accountability.

3.3.4 Main Activities of the OSCE

OSCE's comprehensive concept of security includes the politico-military, economic and environmental, and human dimensions. As to the politico-military dimension, the OSCE's activities include arms control, border management, counter-terrorism measures and conflict prevention and resolution. OSCE conducts many field operations as part of its regional conflict management. With regard to the economic and environmental dimension, the OSCE supports sustainable growth and fosters regional economic cooperation. It also supports environmental activities and assists states in establishing good governance. The human dimension focusses on the protection and observance of human rights, the strengthening of democratic institutions in the member states, the observance of elections and referenda, to ensure respect for media freedom, the rights of persons belonging to national minorities and the rule of law.

The Russian war against Ukraine has a very negative impact on the OSCE. The organization was very active in attempts to settle the strong tensions between Russia, the Russian-backed separatists and the Ukraine and to contain the military recounters between separatists and the Ukrainian army. It was the only international organization conducting a conflict management. The Russian attack which violated all important OSCE principles put an immediate and brutal end to all these endeavors of the OSCE. The organization is to a certain extent paralyzed because decision-making is largely dependent on the consensus of the member states. The Russian war of aggression makes it impossible to find a consensus on many important European security issues.

3.4 Council of Europe (CoE)

> The aim of the Council of Europe is to achieve a greater unity between its members for the purpose of safeguarding and realizing the ideals and principles which are their common heritage and facilitating their economic and social progress. This aim shall be pursued through the organs of the Council by discussion of questions of common concern and by agreements and common action in economic, social, cultural, scientific, legal and administrative matters and in the maintenance and further realization of human rights and fundamental freedoms.[31]

3.4.1 Origin and Establishment of the CoE

After World War II, several European NGOs had the ambition to establish a new, integrated Europe based on human rights and the rule of law and to create an institutionalized basis for a lasting peace within the continent. This idea had its precedent in a speech of the war time British Prime Minister Winston Churchill delivered at the University of Zurich on 19 September 1946, asserting that *"[w]e must build a kind of United States of Europe... The first step is to form a Council of Europe"*.[32]

On 20 July 1947, the International Committee of Movements for European Unity was set up by several European NGOs to coordinate the efforts of civil society associations and national councils seeking to promote European integration.[33] The Committee comprised the Independent League for European Cooperation, the Union of European Federalists (UEF), and Winston Churchill's United Europe Movement (UEM). Shortly afterwards, at the Congress of Europe held in The Hague on 10 May 1948 by the Committee, the idea of convening a European assembly was discussed in more detail. The Congress concluded with the participants adopting a political

[31] Art. 1 Statute of the Council of Europe.

[32] Winston Churchill, *Speech to the Academic Youth* (speech, University of Zurich, 19 Sep 1946).

[33] For a history of the International Committee of Movements for European Unity, see Ritsch (1970), p. 69 ss.

resolution[34] calling for the convening of a European assembly, the drafting of a charter of human rights and the establishment of a court of justice responsible for ensuring compliance with the charter.

Subsequently, on 5 May 1949, ten Western European countries signed the Draft Statute, basically pre-drafted by an NGO movement, of the CoE. These countries were Belgium, Denmark, France, Ireland, Italy, Luxembourg, Norway, the Netherlands, Sweden and the United Kingdom. By signing the draft statute, they agreed to *"accept the principles of the rule of law and of the enjoyment by all persons within [their] jurisdiction of human rights and fundamental freedom, and collaborate sincerely and effectively in the realization of the aim of the Council as specified in Chapter."*[35]

The ambition to create an organization as first attempt at political unification in Europe was thus given up in the favor of a pragmatic intergovernmental cooperation in issues of common European concern.[36] The CoE is essentially a regional organization in the classical sense, i.e. one *based on institutionalized cooperation between sovereign states* who voluntarily join the organization to work together in specific common areas. This is a functional approach to creating a regional organization that respects the sovereignty of member states. The more far-reaching concept, which was rejected, was the so-called federalist approach which advocated a political community of the European states. This went more in the direction of a supranational organization like the EU.

3.4.2 Membership of the CoE; Observers and the Role of Non-Member States

The Council was established by the 10 founding member states, listed above, on 5 May, 1949. According to Article 4 of the Statute of the CoE, *"any European State which is deemed to be able and willing to fulfill the provisions of Article 3 may be invited to become a member of the Council of Europe by the Committee of Ministers."* Following the Western European countries in the 1970s and early 1980s, all European Mediterranean countries became members of the CoE,[37] and by the end of the Cold War in 1989, the number of members increased to 23. Today, with the admission of the Eastern European countries and the Balkan countries and the expulsion of Russia (2022), the CoE has 46 member states, more than half of whom (27) are also members of the European Union. The Union itself is not member

---

[34] For the full text, see <https://www.cvce.eu/content/publication/1997/10/13/15869906-97dd-4c54-ad85-a19f2115728b/publishable_en.pdf> (accessed 9 March 2025).

[35] Art. 3 Statute of the CoE.

[36] For more on European unification, see Borchardt (1987).

[37] This was after the demise of the dictatorships in Spain, Portugal and Greece.

of the CoE because membership is only open to states.[38] Today, nearly every European country is represented in the CoE with the exception of Russia, Belarus, Vatican City and Kosovo. Belarus held an official special guest status after the country restored its moratorium on the death penalty,[39] but in March 2022 the CoE's Committee of Ministers decided to suspend all relations with *Belarus* because of the country's active participation in the Russian aggression against Ukraine. Vatican City is represented indirectly via the Holy See's observer status. Kosovo is not yet a member as it has yet to be recognized by the UN as a sovereign country due to its controversial declaration of independence.[40]

According to Article 3 of the CoE Statute, members are required to

> *"[...] accept the principles of the rule of law and of the enjoyment by all persons within its jurisdiction of human rights and fundamental freedoms, and collaborate sincerely and effectively in the realisation of the aim of the Council [...]"*

Based on Article 4, membership is awarded to a European State following an invitation of the Council of Europe if and when this state is able and willing to fulfill the provisions of Article 3. An important political prerequisite for membership in the CoE not mentioned in the Statute of the CoE is the applicant's adherence to the European Convention on Human Rights; this has become a *conditio sine qua non* for membership.

Article 5 of the Statute provides for the option of associate membership status to subjects of international law under certain special circumstances. This provision has become obsolete. The Council also grants observer status to several subjects of international law. The status is granted to

> *"[...] any state willing to accept the principles of democracy, the rule of law and the enjoyment by all persons within its jurisdiction of human rights and fundamental freedoms and wishing to cooperate with the Council of Europe [...]."*[41]

Currently, the status is granted to the Holy See, Canada, Japan, USA, and Mexico. The observer status grants rights to observe the workings of the Council and partake in the Committee of Ministers and any other intergovernmental

---

[38] This is due to Art. 4 of the Statute of the CoE, which provides: "Any European State which is deemed to be able and willing to fulfil the provisions of Article 3 may be invited to become a member of the Council of Europe by the Committee of Ministers. Any State so invited shall become a member on the deposit on its behalf with the Secretary General of an instrument of accession to the present Statute".

[39] For an analysis of whether Belarus should join the CoE, see Smok (2015).

[40] For a concise analysis of Kosovo's declaration of independence and why it is seen as controversial, see *CSS Analyses in Security Policy* (2008), available at <https://www.files.ethz.ch/isn/48155/css_analysen_nr29-0308_E.pdf> (accessed 9 March 2025).

[41] CoE, Statutory Resolution (93) 26 on Observer Status.

committees. Financial contributions remain voluntary for observers. In addition, Canada, Mexico and Israel have acquired observer status at the Parliamentary Assembly.

Lastly, a considerable number of treaties and partial agreements are drawn up by the CoE with non-member parties. Thus far, treaties and partial agreements with 45 non-member states have been adopted.[42] Generally, Council of Europe legal instruments are increasingly drawn up with the participation of interested non-member states. These states do, apart from their status as party to CoE agreements, not have any status in the organization.

3.4.3 Organs of the CoE

3.4.3.1 Introduction

The structure of the Council of Europe is quite different from traditional organizations; it has some unique organs. The organization consists of the Committee of Ministers as plenary organ, the Parliamentary Assembly as a parliamentarian body, the Secretariat, the Congress of Local and Regional Authorities of Europe, the European Court of Human Rights and the Commissioner for Human Rights. As it is based on the voluntary cooperation of sovereign states, the Council of Europe cannot enact laws with binding effect on the member states.

3.4.3.2 Committee of Ministers

The Committee of Ministers decides with binding effect all matters relating to the internal organization and arrangements of the Council of Europe.[43] In addition, the Committee of Ministers may, based on the recommendation of the Parliamentary Assembly or on its own initiative, take any steps required to further the aim of the Council of Europe, including the approval of draft conventions to allow ratification by member states and the adoption of a common policy about matters within its powers.[44]

These actions usually are recommendations to the member states' governments, but the Committee may request the governments to inform the Committee about the implementations of these recommendations.[45]

---

[42] Partial agreements are "a [treaty-based] particular form of co-operation within the Organisation" that allows CoE member states to "abstain from participating in a certain activity advocated by other member states"; CoE, *About Partial Agreements*, available at <https://www.coe.int/en/web/conventions/about-partial-agreements> (accessed 9 March 2025).

[43] Art. 16 Statute of CoE.

[44] Art. 15(a) Statute of CoE.

Each member state is entitled to one representative, usually its Minister for Foreign Affairs, on the Committee of Ministers, and each representative is entitled to one vote.[46] If a Minister for Foreign Affairs is unable to attend a committee meeting, an alternate representative may be nominated, and this alternate representative is usually the ambassador of the member state. The presidency on the Committee of Ministers changes twice a year.

3.4.3.3 Parliamentary Assembly (PACE)

The Parliamentary Assembly[47] provides the CoE with some democratic legitimacy, as well as with a link to the national parliaments of the member states. It consists of representatives of each member state who are elected or appointed by the respective parliament, and each member must be a national of the member state he or she represents.[48] The number of representatives from each state is determined by the size of the country. The biggest number is eighteen, the smallest two. The total number of members of the Assembly are 306 representatives and 306 substitutes[49] plus 30 observers from countries closely related to the CoE.[50] In addition, by its Resolution 1680 (2009) the Assembly decided to establish a "partner for democracy" status. This status aims at developing co-operation with parliaments of non-member States of neighboring regions.[51] Kosovo has a special status given its contested international position.

The tasks of the Parliamentary Assembly are open-ended. At its core, it is a *forum for debate*. Being the deliberative organ of the CoE, the Parliamentary Assembly debates issues within its competence and *presents its conclusions in the form of recommendations to the Committee of Ministers.*[52] The Parliamentary Assembly's powers include: demanding action from 46 European governments, who must jointly reply; conducting probes to uncover new facts about human rights violations; questioning Presidents and Prime Ministers on any topic it chooses; observing elections and sending delegations to mediate in crisis hot-spots; negotiating the terms on which states joining the Council of Europe; inspiring new national laws by proposing and giving opinions on treaties; requesting legal opinions on the laws and constitutions of member states; and sanctioning a member state by

---

[45] Art. 15(b) Statute of CoE.

[46] Art. 14 Statute of CoE.

[47] See <https://pace.coe.int> (accessed 9 March 2025).

[48] Art. 25 Statute of the CoE.

[49] Substitutes are replacement members of the Assembly who are allowed to speak and vote only if designated by the national delegation.

[50] These countries are Canada, Israel and Mexico.

[51] Currently, these countries are Jordan, Palestine, Morocco and Kyrgyzstan.

[52] Art. 22 Statute of CoE.

recommending its exclusion as it happened with Russia, or suspension. In addition, the Assembly scrutinizes the actions of organizations such as the UN, the EU, WHO, NATO or FIFA for their compliance with human rights standards.

The Assembly adopts three types of texts: *recommendations*, *opinions* and *resolutions*. Recommendations require a two-third majority vote. Opinions require a simple majority on issues such as membership and draft treaties submitted by the Committee of Ministers. Resolutions, in which the Assembly expresses its viewpoint on an issue, require also just a simple majority.

Apart from presenting political guidelines in the form of recommendations to the Committee of Ministers, the Parliamentary Assembly also appoints the Secretariat and the judges of the European Court of Human Rights.

3.4.3.4 Secretariat

Pursuant to the Statute of the CoE, the Committee of Ministers and the Parliamentary Assembly are assisted by a Secretariat.[53] The Secretariat is headed by the Secretary General who oversees the organization's operative activities and is responsible for both the strategic management of the CoE's work program and the budget.

3.4.3.5 Congress of Local and Regional Authorities

The Congress of Local and Regional Authorities[54] is a unique organ: it gives local and regional governments of the member states a say on the international level, which is exceptional in international organizations which are traditional state-based. By giving sub-state entities a voice within the institutional structure of the CoE, *the Congress protects and strengthens democracy at the local and regional level.*

The most important legal document regulating the activities of the Congress is the *European Charter of Local Self-Government*,[55] which was ratified by all the member states. The Charter regulates basic principles protecting meaningful local and regional self-government and securing political, administrative and financial independence of local authorities. It provides that the principle of local self-government shall be implemented in domestic legislation and, where practicable, also in the constitution.[56] In addition, local authorities are to be elected by universal suffrage.[57] The Congress monitors regularly the application of the Charter by each member state. It also oversees local and regional elections. Further, working as the consultative body, the Congress must be consulted by the Parliamentary Assembly and the

[53] Art. 10 Statute of the CoE.

[54] <https://www.coe.int/en/web/congress/home> (accessed 9 March 2025).

[55] CoE, *European Charter of Local Self-Government*, ETS No. 122 (1985).

[56] Art. 2 Charter of Local Self-Government.

[57] Art. 3(2) Charter of Local Self-Government.

Committee of Ministers before recommendations pertaining to local self-government are made.

3.4.3.6 Commissioner on Human Rights

On 7 May 1999, the Committee of Ministers adopted a resolution that created the office of the Commissioner on Human Rights[58] and elaborated on the Commissioner's mandate. According to Resolution (99) 50 of the Council of Europe, the Commissioner *"shall be a non-judicial institution to promote education, in awareness of and respect for human rights, as embodied in the human rights instruments of the Council of Europe"*.[59] Additionally, the Commissioner *"shall respect the competence of, and perform functions other than those fulfilled by, the supervisory bodies set up under the European Convention of Human Rights or under other human rights instruments of the Council of Europe."*[60] Thus, the Commissioner is mandated to foster the effective observance of human rights, and assist member states in the implementation of Council of Europe human rights standards; to promote education in and awareness of human rights in Council of Europe member States; to identify possible shortcomings in human rights law and practice; to facilitate the activities of national ombudsperson institutions and other national human rights structures; and to provide advice and information regarding the protection of human rights across the region.

The Commissioner's concrete activities consist primarily of country visits and dialogue with national authorities and civil society, thematic reporting and advising on human rights systematic implementation and awareness-raising activities. The role of the Commissioner is thus quite different from the role of the European Court of Human Rights. The Commissioner *does not act upon individual complaints* but is rather *concerned with the structural dimension of human rights protections* in the member states of the CoE.

3.4.4 Functions, Aims and Tasks of the CoE

3.4.4.1 General Activities

The CoE serves as *Europe's leading organization for human rights, democracy and the rule of law* but also concerns itself with many other issues. These include, among others, the media, social and economic issues, education, health and environmental

[58] <https://www.coe.int/en/web/commissioner/home> (accessed 9 March 2025).

[59] CoE, Art. 1(1) of Resolution (99)50 on the Council of Europe Commissioner for Human Rights (1999). For the full text, see <https://www.cvce.eu/content/publication/2003/5/14/f641de4f-6c15-40ec-9207-b436bcfed79b/publishable_en.pdf> (accessed 9 March 2025).

[60] Art. 1(2) of Resolution (99)50.

issues. Matters relating to national defense do, however, not fall within the CoE's scope.[61]

Regarding human rights, the CoE's activities focus on the protection and promotion of all human rights, including social rights and some group rights, e.g. minority rights. Democracy is very broadly understood by the organs of the CoE, and the respective activities embrace the standard setting and the promotion of democracy on all levels, the creation of a democratic culture etc. Worth mentioning is the protection of democracy through parliamentary scrutiny and election monitoring by the Parliamentary Assembly as well as assistance in democratic reforms, in particular by the Venice Commission.[62] As for the rule of law, the activities of the CoE refer to the efficiency of justice, development of legal standards and common policies as to, e.g., data protection, crimes and criminal sanctions, and measures combating threats to the rule of law such as corruption, terrorism, cybercrimes and money laundering.

3.4.4.2 Drafting Conventions

As part of its activities, the organs of the CoE have drafted more than 200 conventions,[63] most notably in area of human rights. Human rights are protected, inter alia, by the European Convention on Human Rights (ECHR),[64] social rights under the European Social Charter,[65] the Convention on Action against Trafficking in Human Beings,[66] the Convention on the Protection of Children against Sexual Exploitation and Sexual Abuse,[67] the Convention on Human Rights and Biomedicine,[68] protecting linguistic rights under the European Charter for Regional or Minority Languages,[69] granting minority rights under the Framework Convention for the Protection of National Minorities,[70] and securing media freedom under Article 10 of the European Convention on Human Rights and the European Convention on Transfrontier Television.[71]

The CoE's human rights activities are reflected not only in conventions but also in the *establishment of special bodies concerned with particular human rights issues*

---

[61] Art. 1(d) Statute of the Council of Europe.

[62] The Venice Commission meets regularly in Venice, <https://www.venice.coe.int> (accessed 9 March 2025), but its official label is European Commission for Democracy through Law. It is the Council of Europe's advisory body on constitutional matters. The role of the Venice Commission is to provide legal advice to its member states and, in particular, to help states wishing to bring their legal and institutional structures into line with European standards and international experience in the fields of democracy, human rights and the rule of law.

[63] See the full list at <https://www.coe.int/en/web/conventions/full-list> (accessed 9 March 2025).

[64] CoE, ETS no. 5 (1950).

[65] CoE, ETS no. 35 (1961).

[66] CoE, ETS no. 197 (2005).

[67] CoE, ETS no. 201 (2007).

[68] CoE, ETS no. 164 (1997).

such as the European Committee for the Prevention of Torture and the European Commission against Racism and Intolerance.

Noteworthy conventions beyond human rights are, inter alia, the Convention on Cybercrime,[72] the Convention on the Suppression of Terrorism,[73] the Conventions against Corruption and Organized Crime,[74] the promotion of cultural cooperation and diversity under the Council of Europe's Cultural Convention of 1954,[75] and the promotion of fairness in sports through the Anti-Doping Convention,[76] and the Convention against Spectator Violence.[77]

3.4.4.3 Categories of Agreements

There are several categories of agreements, depending on the states allowed to be party.[78] Some conventions are open for signature only to the member states or, as *Partial Agreements*, to some member states. However, the CoE also provides for agreements by some member states of the Council of Europe together with one or more non-member states (so-called *Enlarged Partial Agreement*), or by all member states together with one or more non-member states (so-called *Enlarged Agreement*). A member state of the Council of Europe may join any agreement by a simple declaration to the Secretary General whereas non-member states need an invitation in the form of a decision of the Committee of Ministers to be allowed to join an Enlarged or Enlarged Partial Agreement, following consultation of the non-member States already participating. International organizations may also be invited by the Committee of Ministers, following consultation of the non-member States already participating, to take part as an observer in the activities of a Partial, Enlarged Partial or Enlarged Agreement.

The European Union may be invited by the Committee of Ministers to participate in Partial, Enlarged Partial or Enlarged Agreements. The modalities of its participation are determined by the Committee of Ministers.

---

[69] CoE, ETS no. 148 (1992).

[70] CoE, ETS no. 157 (1995).

[71] CoE, ETS no.13 (1989).

[72] CoE, ETS no. 185 (2001).

[73] CoE, ETS no. 90 (1977).

[74] CoE, ETS no. 141 (1990).

[75] CoE, ETS no. 18 (1954).

[76] CoE, ETS no. 135 (1989).

[77] CoE, ETS no. 120 (1985).

[78] See in particular Statutory Resolution (93)28 by the Committee of Ministers on Partial and Enlarged Agreements (1993).

3.4.4.4 Relation with the European Union

Generally, over the years, the CoE has been increasingly dominated by the EU countries. This is also due to the increasing membership of the EU; nowadays EU member states constitute the majority of the CoE members. Therefore, for practical and legal reasons, there is a growing need for coordination between the EU and the CoE, e.g. to avoid incompatibilities between EU law and the draft conventions of the CoE. EU law also has an important impact on the drafting of CoE Conventions.

3.5 North Atlantic Treaty Organization (NATO)

3.5.1 Origin of the NATO

NATO is a political and military alliance whose primary goals are the collective defense of its members and the maintenance of democratic peace in the North Atlantic area as expressed in the preamble of the North Atlantic Treaty (sometimes also referred to as Washington Treaty), the formal agreement establishing NATO.[79] It was founded 1949 in Washington, when the Cold War broke out. It was also designed to create a powerful community based on Western democratic values to oppose the communist Soviet Union and the satellite states under its control, and to foster democratic peace in the North Atlantic Area. In addition, NATO also sought to prevent the revival of nationalist militarism in Europe by establishing a strong U.S. presence on the continent. To this end, it encouraged European political integration.[80]

The North Atlantic Treaty was signed by 12 states, including the USA and Canada,[81] on 4 April 1949 and came into force on 24 August 1949. Today, the organization comprises 31 members.[82] Following the Russian military aggression against Ukraine in February 2022, the former neutral countries Finland and Sweden decided to join NATO. All NATO member states have to respect the basic values of democracy, individual liberty and the rule of law.

---

[79] *"The Parties to this Treaty reaffirm their faith in the purposes and principles of the Charter of the United Nations and their desire to live in peace with all peoples and all governments. They are determined to safeguard the freedom, common heritage and civilisation of their peoples, founded on the principles of democracy, individual liberty and the rule of law. They seek to promote stability and well-being in the North Atlantic area. They are resolved to unite their efforts for collective defence and for the preservation of peace and security."* – NATO, *North Atlantic Treaty* (1949), Preamble.

[80] <https://www.nato.int/cps/ie/natohq/declassified_139339.htm> (accessed 9 March 2025).

3.5.2 *Main Goals and Purpose of NATO*

NATO has three core tasks: collective defence; crisis management; and cooperative security through partnerships. NATO has expressed a commitment to

> protecting its members through political and military means. It promotes democratic values and is dedicated to the peaceful resolution of disputes. If diplomatic efforts fail, it has the military power to undertake crisis-management operations. These are carried out under the collective defense clause of NATO's founding treaty - Article 5 of the Washington Treaty or under a United Nations mandate, alone or in cooperation with other countries and international organizations.[83]

Its main goal, however, is collective defense. Central to NATO as a military alliance is the so-called alliance clause as core obligation of the member states. In this regard, all NATO member states agree that

> *an armed attack against one or more of them in Europe or North America shall be considered an attack against them all and consequently they agree that, if such an armed attack occurs, each of them, in exercise of the right of individual or collective self-defence recognised by Article 51 of the Charter of the United Nations, will assist the Party or Parties so attacked by taking forthwith, individually and in concert with the other Parties, such action as it deems necessary, including the use of armed force, to restore and maintain the security of the North Atlantic area.*[84]

The clause thus lies at the heart of the alliance and creates a spirit of solidarity and cohesion among its members. Its functions are clear: it seeks to deter potential enemies from using armed force against a member state as it would amount to an attack against all member states. Thus, the alliance clause serves as a strong deterrence against potential attacks. Such clauses enable military alliances like NATO to contribute to international peace and security by preventing the use of military force. The clause further reveals strong interrelations between NATO's core purpose and the system of collective security of the UN Charter: as an alliance, an organization of collective defence, NATO's core purpose is based on Article 51 of the UN Charter stating the right of states to individual and collective self-defence.[85] Article 3 of the NATO Treaty commits in this context the member states "*by means*

---

[81] The signatories were Belgium, Denmark (with Greenland), France (with the French territories in Algeria), Great Britain (with Malta), Iceland, Italy, Canada, Luxembourg, the Netherlands, Norway, Portugal and the USA.

[82] They are: Albania, Belgium, Bulgaria, Canada, Croatia, Czech Republic, Denmark, Estonia, France, Finland, Germany, Greece, Hungary. Iceland, Italy, Latvia, Lithuania, Luxembourg, Montengro, Netherlands, North Macedonia, Norway, Poland, Portugal, Romania, Slovakia, Slovenia, Spain, Turkey, the United Kingdom and the United States.

[83] *What is NATO?*, available at <https://www.nato.int/nato-welcome/index.html> (accessed 9 March 2025).

[84] Art. 5 North Atlantic Treaty. For a concise commentary on Art. 5, see Tertrais (2016).

of continuous and effective self-help and mutual aid, [to] maintain and develop their individual and collective capacity to resist armed attack."

In addition, NATO and its member states are committed to the principle of the peaceful resolution of disputes and therefore settle

> *"any international dispute in which they may be involved by peaceful means in such a manner that international peace and security and justice are not endangered, and to refrain in their international relations from the threat or use of force in any manner inconsistent with the purposes of the United Nations."*[86]

The organization has the military power to undertake crisis management operations if diplomatic efforts to settle a dispute fail. These operations can be military or non-military and have to strictly observe the prerogatives of the UN Security Council with regard to the maintenance of international peace and security.

Contrary to the UN, NATO does not have an internal mechanism to settle disputes including institutionalized collective measures against member states. This is why the North Atlantic Treaty does not establish a system of collective security. However, the alliance promotes democratic values and enables its members to consult and cooperate on defence and security-related issues to solve problems, build trust and, in the long run, prevent conflicts among them. In this regard, Article 2 of the North Atlantic Treaty states that member states

> *"will seek to eliminate conflict in their international economic policies and will encourage economic collaboration between any or all of them."*

This is a remarkable provision for an organization focussing on security and collective defence. The drafters of the North Atlantic Treaty were apparently aware of the conflict potential of controversies regarding economic issues.

3.5.3 Organs of the NATO

3.5.3.1 North Atlantic Council

NATO's most important political organ is the North Atlantic Council, a plenary organ *"on which each of [the Member States] shall be represented to consider matters concerning the implementation of this Treaty"*.[87] The Council is made up of ambassadors of the member states and *is chaired by the Secretary General*; this is rather unusual in international organizations.[88] In addition, there are yearly or

---

[85] For a legal analysis of the interplay between NATO's collective self-defence and Art. 51 UNCh, see Simma (1999), p. 1 ss.

[86] Art. 1 North Atlantic Treaty.

biyearly formal summits with the Prime Ministers or the Head of States of the member states. The Council has no formal voting procedure, because NATO grants all allies an equal say. *Decisions are thus taken by consensus*, and a "NATO decision" is therefore the expression of the collective will of all 32 members countries.

According to Article 9, "*[t]he Council shall be so organized as to be able to meet promptly at any time.*" The Council has the power to make all the important decisions for the organization. The most far-reaching decision is the assessment that there is an armed attack against a member state, because this triggers the obligation of all the member states to assist the member under attack. The Council has further the power to establish subsidiary organs.[89]

3.5.3.2 Parliamentary Assembly

The NATO Parliamentary Assembly,[90] an inter-parliamentary organization, brings together legislators from NATO member states to consider security-related issues of common interest and concern. Although the Parliamentary Assembly is *independent of NATO and not regulated in the North Atlantic Treaty*, it acts as a *strong link between NATO and its member states' parliaments*, helping to build parliamentary and public consensus in support of Alliance policies. The main legal document regulating the Assembly's activities are the Assembly's rules of procedure, adopted in London 2019.[91]

The Parliamentary Assembly is composed of 281 delegates from NATO member countries who are nominated by their parliaments. The composition of each member state's delegation is based on the country's size and reflects the political composition of the parliament, therefore representing a broad spectrum of political opinions. The main executive organ of the Assembly is the Standing Committee, which is composed of the President, Vice-Presidents, Treasurer, Secretary General and the Head of each member delegation. Two sessions are held each year, in Spring and Autumn, in different countries. The Assembly has its own secretary general. Further, it has institutionalized ties with the OSCE Parliamentary Assembly, the Parliamentary Assembly of the Council of Europe (PACE) and the European Parliament which are also entitled to send delegations.

[87] Art. 9 North Atlantic Treaty.

[88] Usually, the chair rotates among member states.

[89] Art. 9 North Atlantic Treaty.

[90] <https://www.nato-pa.int> (accessed 9 March 2025).

[91] For the full text, see <https://www.nato-pa.int/view-file?filename=/sites/default/files/2020-01/187%20GEN%2019%20E%20Rules%20of%20Procedure%20London.pdf> (accessed 9 March 2025).

3.5.3.3 Euro-Atlantic Partnership Council (EAPC)

NATO also has established an informal body called the Euro-Atlantic Partnership Council (EAPC). Today, 50 nations, 32 NATO member states and 18 partner countries are part of this multilateral forum for dialogue and consultation on political and security-related issues among allies and partner countries. The EAPC provides the overall political framework for NATO's cooperation with partner countries in the Euro-Atlantic area and for the bilateral relationships developed between NATO and individual partner countries under the Partnership for Peace (PfP) program. Acting as a program of practical bilateral cooperation between individual Euro-Atlantic partner countries and NATO, the PfP allows partners to establish a unique relationship with NATO by choosing their own priorities for cooperation. An Individual Partnership and Cooperation Program is jointly developed and agreed between NATO and each partner country. All partners have access to the Partnership and Cooperation Menu, which consists of some 1400 activities for cooperation between NATO and the partners. EPAC and PfP are both schemes that regulate an association between an international organization and non-member states.[92]

3.5.3.4 Military and Civilian Administrative Structures

NATO has both military and civilian (political) administrative structures. The military structure includes the Military Committee, International Military Staff, Allied Command Operations, Supreme Headquarters Allied Power Europe (SHAPE) and Allied Command Transformation; it is based in Casteau, Belgium and composed of military of the member states. NATO itself has, however, very few military forces or equipment. Most of the forces remains under full national command and control until member states participate in NATO operations when the NATO command structure takes over.

The political department as well as the North Atlantic Council are based in the NATO headquarters in Brussels, which is also where member countries' national delegations and the liaison offices or diplomatic missions of partner countries are located. The work of these delegations and missions is supported by NATO's International Staff and International Military Staff, also based at the Headquarters. The international staff consists of representatives of the member states and is divided into various groups such as Private Office (PO), Political Affairs and Security Policy Division, Operation Division, Emerging Security Challenges Division, Defense Policy and Planning Division, Defense Investment Division, Public Diplomacy Division and Executive Management.

---

[92] See supra, Sect. 1.7.1.

3.5.4 *Crisis and Conflict Management by NATO Under Chapters VII and VIII of the UN Charter*

NATO is not only a military alliance designed to deter potential enemies with collective defense but also has been involved in crisis and conflict management activities, often under the umbrella of the UN Security Council as part of collective security.

Crisis management has thus become, at least until the Russian attack against Ukraine in 2022, another task of NATO. It employs a mix of political and military tools to manage crises. Crisis management takes place, of course, whenever there is a situation than can pose a threat to the security of a member state or the alliance at large or to the stability of a region of particular interest to the NATO countries. These crises can be political, military or humanitarian and can also arise from a natural disaster or as a consequence of technological disruptions. The member states decide on a case-by-case basis and by consensus whether to engage in a crisis management operation. So-called crisis response operations (CRO) cover all military operations conducted by NATO in a non-Article 5 situation. They support the peace process in a conflict area and are also called peace support operations.[93]

NATO crisis management operations and missions have included the former Yugoslavia, Afghanistan, Kosovo, the Mediterranean, the Gulf of Aden, Iraq, and support to African Union and Libya.[94] In some of the operations there was no authorization by the Security Council, such as in Kosovo and Iraq, but in most cases, NATO was involved as a main actor in UN-sponsored conflict managements.[95] It is clear that, under UN Charter, a UN Security authorization is necessary.

These conflict management activities include all the categories of pertinent activities under the UN Charter's Chapter VI or VII, i.e. peacekeeping, peace enforcement, conflict prevention, peacemaking, peace building and humanitarian missions. Humanitarian missions are conducted to alleviate human suffering. There are three main categories of humanitarian missions: disaster relief, refugee/displaced person assistance and humanitarian aid.[96] Humanitarian missions may precede or accompany humanitarian support provided by specialized non-governmental organizations.

---

[93] NATO's involvement in the Balkans and Afghanistan and its efforts in countering piracy off the Horn of Africa are examples of CROs.

[94] For an analysis of the cooperation between NATO and the UN in some of these operations (e.g. Bosnia and Afghanistan), see Harsch (2015).

[95] These are, in NATO's terminology, peace support operations, i.e. multi-functional operations conducted in support of an UN/OSCE mandate or at the invitation of a government involving military forces and diplomatic and humanitarian agencies and designed to achieve long-term political settlement or other conditions specified in the mandate. They include peacekeeping and peace enforcement as well as conflict prevention, peacemaking, peace building and humanitarian operations.

3.5.5 NATO's Development and Challenges

At the beginning of the 1960s, France was critical of the dominance of the US within NATO. In the course of his re-election in 1965, General Charles de Gaulle as French president demanded that the American and Canadian units acting on behalf of NATO stationed in France be commanded by the French. After the US refused, France withdrew from the NATO's integrated military command but rejoined it in 2009. France's participation in NATO operations has steadily increased since the 1990s, and it participated in all major alliance expeditionary operations, including Kosovo (KFOR) and Afghanistan (ISAF). One reason for this rapprochement to the NATO was the EU's failure to deal with the Yugoslavia crisis, which highlighted the fact that the NATO and the cooperation with the US were still necessary to safeguard Europe's collective security after the Cold War.[97] During the Yugoslav crisis in the 1990s, the US was reluctant to supply ground troops. This was viewed as a weakening of US commitment which placed more pressure on the European countries to take more responsibility to solve the Yugoslav crisis. This pressure intensified when the US began to address conflicts outside Europe and shifted its regional security focus. Essentially, as France was already supporting the NATO by supplying it with troops, it made sense to participate in NATO's military operations.

Europe has also pushed for the creation of its own European Security and Defense Policy which enables coordinated action by the European countries without US support. The EU has an interest in maintaining its own strength to deal with conflicts the US may not want to get involved in, such as in the Congo region or other areas which were colonies of some EU member states.[98] Therefore, the EU has created institutions devoted to defense such as the European Union Military Committee (EUMC) in 2001, which is the highest military body set up within the Council,[99] and the European Defense Agency, established in 2004.[100]

A particular challenge to NATO took place when the United States was attacked by terrorists on 11 September 2001. The Alliance's 1999 Strategic Concept already identified terrorism as one of the risks affecting NATO's security. On the evening of 12 September 2001, less than 24 hours after the attacks, and for the first time in NATO's history, the Allies invoked the principle of collective defense in Article 5 North Atlantic Treaty. The North Atlantic Council agreed that if it determined that the attack was directed from abroad against the United States, it would be regarded as an action covered by Article 5. On 2 October, once the Council had been briefed

---

[96] <https://www.nato.int/docu/logi-en/1997/lo-505.htm> (accessed 9 March 2025).

[97] For more information and analyses of NATO and the EU's responses to the Yugoslav crisis, see e.g. Kaufman (2002); Gazzini (2001), p. 391 ss.; and Anderson (2007), p. 328 ss.

[98] For an early analysis of European security in relation to the EU and NATO, see Cornish (1996), p. 751 ss.

on the results of investigations into the 9/11 attacks, it determined that they were regarded as an action covered by Article 5 of the NATO Treaty. NATO's response was unique, and, from a legal perspective, arguably an overly broad interpretation of Article 5. This is because Article 5 relates to military attacks by a state against a NATO member state and not a terrorist attack by non-state actors against a NATO member state. Nonetheless, Article 5 was invoked as an *"expression of transatlantic solidarity"*.[101]

The 2014 Ukraine crisis and Russia's annexation of Crimea in 2014 showed the need for a fast response task force.[102] These incidents generally revealed the necessity for NATO to maintain an efficient military force. As a result, NATO member states no longer decreased military budgets. In particular, the need for new and functioning equipment has been recognized by the European NATO members. The Russian attack against Ukraine on February 24, 2022, and the armed conflict that followed boosted NATO's role in Europe overnight and led member states to sharply increase their military spending. NATO's main purpose as defense alliance has become much more important because the aggressive conduct of Russia against some NATO countries such as the Baltic states. With the election of Donald Trump as US President in 2024 for a second term, increasingly profound tensions between the USA and the other NATO countries have come to light, with the President acting over the heads of NATO partners, particularly in the Ukraine conflict, and making demands on them that were in some cases excessive. It cannot be ruled out that the USA will leave NATO under Trump or that NATO, due to the unanimity rule, could become incapable to act.

References

Anderson S (2007) EU, NATO, and CSCE responses to the Yugoslav crisis: testing Europe's new security architecture. Eur Secur 4(2):328–353

Bailes AJK (2006) The politico-military dimension of OSCE. Helsinki Monitor 17(3):214–225

Borchardt KD (1987) European unification: the origins and growth of the European community, 2nd edn. Office for the Official Publications of the European Communities, Luxembourg

Bossong R, Hegemann H (eds) (2015) European civil security governance: diversity and cooperation in crisis and disaster management. Palgrave Macmillan, Vlandria/Hamburg

Cabranes JA (1978) Reflections on the Belgrade Meeting (1977–78) of the Conference on Security and Cooperation in Europe. Yale Stud World Public Order 4:274–290

Churchill W (1946) Speech to the Academic Youth. Speech at the Universität Zürich, 19. Sep 1946. https://www.legalanthology.ch/t/churchill_speech-to-the-academic-youth_1946.pdf

---

[99] <https://www.eeas.europa.eu/eeas/eumc_en> (accessed 9 March 2025).

[100] See <https://eda.europa.eu/> (accessed 9 March 2025).

[101] Rühle (2013), p. 54 ss.

[102] For an analysis of how the Ukraine conflict has affected the relationship between NATO and Russia, see Cross (2015), p. 151 ss. For an analysis of the conflict from the perspective of collective securitisation, see Sperling and Webber (2017), p. 19 ss.

Cornish P (1996) European security: the end of architecture and the new NATO. Int Aff 72(4): 751–769
Cross S (2015) NATO–Russia security challenges in the aftermath of Ukraine conflict: managing Black Sea security and beyond. Southeast Eur Black Sea Stud 15(2):151–177
CSS Analyses in Security Policy (2008) Kosovo's controversial independence. CSS Analyses in Security Policy 3(29). https://www.files.ethz.ch/isn/48155/css_analysen_nr29-0308_E.pdf
Deen-Racsmany Z (2000) A redistribution of authority between the UN and regional organizations in the field of the maintenance of peace and security? Leiden J Int Law 13(2):297–331
ECOWAS (1999) Protocol relating to the mechanism for conflict prevention, management, resolution, peacekeeping and security. ECOWAS Commission, Abuja. https://ecowas.int/wp-content/uploads/2024/08/Protocol-relating-to-the-Mechanism-for-conflict-prevention-Mgt-Resolution-etc.pdf
Freeman J (1991) Security and the CSCE process: the Stockholm Conference and beyond. Palgrave Macmillan, London
Galbreath DJ (2007) The organization for security and co-operation in Europe. Routledge, London
Gazzini T (2001) NATO coercive military activities in the Yugoslav crisis (1992–1999). EJIL 12: 391–435
Goldberg AJ (1979) The Belgrade Conference and international human rights. Natl Black Law J 6(2):179–182
Harsch MF (2015) The power of dependence: NATO-UN cooperation in crisis management. Oxford University Press, Oxford
Hollis S (2015) The role of regional organizations in disaster risk management. Palgrave Macmillan, London
Job BL (2004) The UN, regional organizations, and regional conflict: is there a viable role for the UN? In: Price RM, Zacher MW (eds) The United Nations and Global Security. Palgrave Macmillan, New York, pp 217–243
Kaufman JP (2002) NATO and the Former Yugoslavia: crisis, conflict, and the Atlantic alliance. Rowman & Littlefield Publishers, Lanham, MD
Killham EL (1984) The Madrid CSCE Conference. World Aff 146(4):340
Lachowski Z (2004) Confidence- and security-building measures in the New Europe. Oxford University Press, Oxford
Liskofsky S (1978) Human rights: from Helsinki to Belgrade. Am Jewish Year Book 78:121–145
Liskofsky S (1979) The Belgrade Conference. Am Jewish Year Book 79:152–159
Lodgaard (2007) The Stockholm CSBMs and the future of the CDE. Arms Control 8(2):155 ss
Olonisakin F (1996) UN co-operation with regional organizations in peacekeeping: the experience of ECOMOG and UNOMIL in Liberia. Int Peacekeep 3(3):33–51
Paliwal S (2010) The primacy of regional organizations in international peacekeeping: the African example. Va J Int Law 51(1):185–230
Perry V, Keil S (2013) The OSCE Mission in Bosnia and Herzegovina: testing the limits of ownership. Natl Pap 41(3):371–394
Reinalda B (2009) Routledge history of international organizations: from 1815 to the present day. Routledge, London
Ritsch FF (1970) Origins of the Council of Europe: Part One: The Post-War Unity Movements to the Hague Congress. Il Politico 35(1):69–94
Rühle M (2013) Reflections on 9/11: a view from NATO. In: Hallams E et al (eds) NATO Beyond 9/11: the transformation of the Atlantic alliance. Palgrave Macmillan, London, pp 54–66
Sica M (1996) The role of the OSCE in the former Yugoslavia after the Dayton Peace Agreement. Helsinki Monitor 7(2):5–12
Sidhu WPS (2020) Regional organizations. In: Weiss TG, Daws S (eds) The Oxford handbook on the United Nations, 2nd edn. Oxford University Press, Oxford, pp 345–362
Simma B (1999) NATO, the UN and the use of force: legal aspects. EJIL 10(1):1–40
Smok V (2015) Should Belarus join the Council of Europe? Belarus Digest, 5 March 2015. https://belarusdigest.com/story/should-belarus-join-the-council-of-europe/. Accessed 9 Mar 2025

Spandler K (2020) UNAMID and the legitimation of global-regional peacekeeping cooperation: partnership and friction in UN-AU relations. J Interv Statebuild 14(2):187–203
Sperling J, Webber M (2017) NATO and the Ukraine crisis: collective securitisation. Eur J Int Secur 2(1):19–46
Szasz P (1998) The law on economic sanctions. In: Schmitt MN, Green LC (eds) International law studies, vol 71. Naval War College, Newport, pp 455–481
Tertrais B (2016) Article 5 of the Washington Treaty: its origins, meaning and future. Research Paper No. 130, NATO Defense College, Rome
Thomas DC (2001) The Helsinki Effect: international norms, human rights, and the demise of communism. Princeton University Press, Princeton
Walter C (2009) Regional arrangements and the United Nations Charter. In: Wolfrum R (ed) Max Planck Encyclopedia of Public International Law. Oxford University Press, Oxford

Selected Bibliography

OSCE

Bortloff J (1996) Die Organisation für Sicherheit und Zusammenarbeit in Europa: eine völkerrechtliche Bestandesaufnahme. Drucker & Humblot, Berlin
Institute for Peace Research and Security Policy (ed) (2019) OSCE Yearbook 2018. Nomos, Baden-Baden
Sargsyan D, Zahorka H (2019) Organization for Security and Cooperation in Europe (OSCE): idea, history, challenges. Lambert Academic Publishing, Saarbrücken
Steinbrück M (2019) The legal framework of the OSCE. Nomos, Baden-Baden
Tavares R (2009) Regional security: the capacity of international organizations. Routledge, London

Council of Europe

Bond M (2012) Council of Europe: structure, history and issues in European politics. Routledge, London
Breuer M, Schmahl S (eds) (2017) The Council of Europe: its laws and policies. Oxford University Press, Oxford
Kleinsorge I (2010) Council of Europe. Nomos, Baden-Baden
Kolb R (2013) The European Union and the Council of Europe. Hart Publishing, Oxford

NATO

Fidler, Pregent, Vandurme A (2013) NATO, cyber defense, and international law. J Int Comp Law 4(1)
Gazzini T (2001) NATO coercive military activities in the Yugoslav crisis (1992–1999). EJIL 12: 391–435
Harsch MF (2015) The power of dependence: NATO-UN cooperation in crisis management. Oxford University Press, Oxford
Herd GP, Kriendler J (eds) (2013) Understanding NATO in the 21st century. Alliance Strategies, Security and Global. Routledge
Kaufman JP (2002) NATO and the former Yugoslavia: crisis, conflict, and the Atlantic alliance. Rowman & Littlefield Publishers, Lanham, MD

Kitchen V (2010) The globalization of NATO: intervention, security and identity. Routledge
Medcalf J (2005) NATO: a beginners guide. Oneworld Publications
Medcalf J (2008) Going global or going nowhere?: NATO's role in contemporary international security. Peter Lang
Nazemroaya MD (2012) The globalization of NATO. Clarity Press
Rees W (2011) The US-EU security relationship: the tensions between a European and a global agenda. Red Globe Press
Rühle M (2013) Reflections on 9/11: a view from NATO. In: Hallams E et al (eds) NATO Beyond 9/11: the transformation of the Atlantic alliance. Palgrave Macmillan, London, pp 54–66
Simma B (1999) NATO, the UN and the use of force: legal aspects. EJIL 10(1):1–40
Sloan SR (2010) Permanent alliance?: NATO and the transatlantic bargain from Truman to Obama. Continuum
Sperling J, Webber M (2017) NATO and the Ukraine crisis: collective securitisation. Eur J Int Secur 2(1):19–46
Tertrais B (2016) Article 5 of the Washington Treaty: its origins, meaning and future. Research Paper No. 130, NATO Defense College, Rome
Wheeler NJ (2000) Reflections on the legality and legitimacy of NATO's intervention in Kosovo. Int J Hum Rights 4(3–4):144–163

Chapter 4
Supranational Organizations: The European Union

4.1 Introduction

On 25 March 2017, the member states of the European Union (EU) celebrated the 60th anniversary of the 1957 Treaty of Rome that paved the way for the by far most developed supranational organization.[1] Based on the Treaty of Rome, the then six signatory states created the European Communities, the predecessor organization of the EU.

Even though the EU consisted in 2017 of 28 member states, only 27 member states celebrated the EU's anniversary by looking back to their collective achievements and discussing the organization's future. Given that the United Kingdom was about to leave the EU, it did not participate in any of the ceremonies. After submitting a total of three applications for EU membership (in 1961, 1967 and 1970) and finally becoming a member state in 1972, on 23 June 2016, the British voters decided in a consultative referendum to leave the EU, thereby putting an end to 45 years of membership. Subsequently, the two-year negotiation period between the UK and the EU began when the UK filed its application for withdrawal on 29 March 2017.[2] The UK finally left the EU, after extended negotiations, end of 2020.

The UK's reasons for leaving the EU were, among others, a historical aversion towards political influence from the European mainland and, more importantly, difficulties reaching political agreements on a European level. A significant portion

Special thanks to Ulrike Heinrich for her important contribution to the elaboration of this chapter.

[1]Treaty establishing the European Economic Community (EEC, EEC Treaty) and also the Treaty establishing the European Atomic Energy Community (EAEC, EAEC Treaty) both signed on 25 Mar 1957.

[2]For more details see <https://www.parliament.uk/business/publications/research/eu-referendum/negotiations/> (accessed 9 March 2025).

U. Saxer, *The Law of Global and European Organizations*, Springer Textbooks in Law, https://doi.org/10.1007/978-3-032-00067-5_4

of the British public considered the EU to be just an economic project. But the organization is much more than that. It is based on the *concept of functional integration*: by conferring some of their decision-making powers upon the EU institutions that the member states have created, the organization serves as the *main example of a supranational international organization.*

4.2 The Concept of Supranationalism

The EU is neither a nation state nor a traditional international organization nor a confederation of states. Accordingly, traditional categories of statehood or internationally recognized legal subjects are of little help to understand the EU's structure and nature which is coined by the concept of supranationalism.

4.2.1 Traditional Intergovernmental Organizations

Traditional, intergovernmental organizations are based on international treaties between its members (states or international organizations) that serve common purposes carried out by organs acting on behalf of the organization, not of the member states. The main purpose of traditional intergovernmental organizations is to develop common policies in the areas covered by the organizations' activities and to coordinate the implementation of these policies in the member states. The focus is thus on international cooperation and coordinating members' activities. Within traditional international organizations the member states' political and legal powers, i.e. their sovereignty, remain to a large extend unaffected.[3]

4.2.2 Supranational Organizations

4.2.2.1 Introduction

Contrary to traditional organizations, supranational institutions as the most recent category of law-based institutionalized interstate cooperation have the power to act partly independently of their member states, both politically and legally, because their member states have transferred some of their sovereign powers to the common superstructure.[4] Therefore, supranational organizations, like states, have the power

[3] As to the main features of traditional international organizations supra, Sect. 1.3.1.2.

[4] As to the concept of supranationally and the criteria to distinguish traditional intergovernmental from supranational organizations see also supra Sect. 1.3.2.1.

to develop specific policies in the policy areas transferred from the member states, to establish rules and to make decisions. Some of their legal acts are directly applicable in the member states without further domestic implementation and regulate also the conduct of individuals and companies.

Supranational organizations therefore do not only coordinate, as do traditional organizations, common policies developed under the umbrella of an organization; they above all *strive for legal and political integration in the framework of common institutions* and based on the organization's constitution and generally on common legal norms. Responsible for these differences from traditional intergovernmental organizations is the concept of functional integration, as the example of the EU's development shows.

4.2.2.2 The Concept of Functional Integration; Role of Interdependencies

States usually integrate in limited functional, technical and economic areas where they feel the need to cooperate more closely. As the development of the process of European integration shows, functional integration often starts in economy-related policy areas and expands then to other policy areas as interdependencies between the participating states grow, but also due to interrelations between different policy areas. The step, e.g., from regulating trade with certain goods to regulating common environmental standards applicable to these goods is not so far. This general process eventually results in an increased necessity to harmonize rules regulating further, functionally connected policy areas.

Interdependencies are the engine of European integration and the basis of the integration of states within a common superstructure. As the developments in Europe, but also of other international institutions such as the United Nations (UN) and the World Trade Organization (WTO) show, a consequence of interdependencies is a growing need to establish common rules and therefore an increase of the powers of these organizations and their organs. However, within the traditional structures of intergovernmental organizations, the focus remains generally on coordination rather than law-making and rule harmonization. This is different with supranational organizations where the *answer to increasing interdependencies are more common policies and laws*, and thus an expansion of political and legal integration.

4.2.2.3 Definition; Features

Even though various definitions have been developed in the literature, a generally agreed definition of the concept of supranationalism and the characteristics of a supranational organization is still missing. Most definitions are quite vague and do not capture fully what supranationalism means. Some definitions describe supranationalism as something between a federation and a confederation of states. Others define supranational organizations as something between a traditional organization and a federation. These explanations refer to the issue of sovereignty, which is certainly necessary but not conclusive to understanding supranationalism as it is not broad enough to encompass the concept.

Schermers and *Blokker*[5] in their seminal textbook list six characteristics of supranational organizations, namely:

- the power to make decisions binding on the member states;
- the power to make rules that directly bind the member states' inhabitants without the need to transform supranational rules and decisions into domestic law;
- the power to enforce its decisions without member state cooperation;
- the financial autonomy of the organization's organs; and
- the inability of a member state to unilaterally withdraw from the organization.[6]

As they are of the opinion that no organization meets all these criteria, *Schermer* and *Blokker* suggest using the term "supranational" in a relative rather than an absolute sense.

The basic, distinctive principle of a supranational organization is, however, that the *members partially transfer some national sovereignty rights to a common institution.*[7] This transfer of political and law-making powers in certain policy areas from states to a common institution is *by far the most important feature of supranational organizations* and has important structural, normative and institutional ramifications. *Structurally*, the transfer of rights and powers establishes the *authority of the organization and its institutions*. This transfer allows for a partial integration of policies and law-making in certain policy areas, which become the responsibility of the organization's organs. *Normatively, an independent legal system is established* that binds the organization's organs as well as member states and natural as well as legal persons. Its laws and decisions are partly directly applicable in the member states, including to individuals. This partly state-like functioning of a supranational organization and its law is the necessary consequence of the transfer of powers from member states to the organization. Due to this transfer, these powers prevail over the states' domestic powers. Consequently, the organization has *direct power over the member states' citizens* without the need to have the organization's acts implemented as domestic law. *Institutionally,* the organization's structure needs to secure adequate policy- and law-making and the rule of law. This implies, inter alia, the absence of expansive member states veto powers, at least partly independent organs exercising the organization's powers, and access by individuals and member states to a court for judicial review of the organization's

[5] Schermers and Blokker (2018), para. 61.

[6] This criterion has become moot because of an amendment to the Treaty establishing the European Union providing for a mechanism for Member States to leave the Union; see Art. 50 of the Treaty on European Union (TEU), introduced by the Treaty of Lisbon, 13 Dec 2007.

[7] See, e.g., definition in Wikipedia "Supranational Union": "Supranationalism is a method of decision-making in multi-national political communities, wherein power is transferred or delegated to an authority by governments of member states".

acts. Finally, the organization must *have an international legal personality* to be able to conclude international agreements in the areas of its competences.

4.3 Development, Nature and General Features of the European Union

4.3.1 Origin and Development: From the European Coal and Steel Community to the European Union

Although Tsar Alexander had already suggested the establishment of a permanent unification of the European countries in 1818,[8] it took another 130 years for the first step in this direction. The EU's institutional roots date back only to the 1950s when Belgium, France, Italy, Luxembourg, the Netherlands and Germany decided to enter into an economic cooperation based on the assumption that countries that trade with each other are less likely to go to war with each other. Accordingly, these six countries' first agreements dealt with coal and steel, the two most important materials to produce arms of any kind.

4.3.1.1 European Coal and Steel Community

In the aftermath of the Second World War, Europe was divided into two hostile blocks dominated by completely different political systems and ideologies. This conflict between the communist Eastern part of Europe and the capitalist Western part of Europe is also known as the *Cold War*. While Eastern Europe including Poland, Hungary, Romania, Bulgaria and the Eastern part of Germany was dominated by the Soviet Union, the United States of America protected Western Europe. Around 1950, to avoid an expansion of the Soviet Union's influence within Europe, Western European countries started to cooperate on the military and political level by, inter alia, building a common defense. Thus, the North Atlantic Treaty Organization (NATO)[9] and the Western European Union (WEU)[10] were founded. At around the same time, the Council of Europe was established; it aimed at achieving greater unity between the countries involved by upholding human rights and

[8] During a diplomatic meeting of France, Britain, Austria, Prussia and Russia which took place in Aachen 29 Sep—21 Nov 1818.

[9] Military alliance between several North American and European states based on the North Atlantic Treaty that was signed on 4 Apr 1949.

[10] Association of 10 countries (Belgium, France, Germany, Greece, Italy, Luxembourg, the Netherlands, Portugal, Spain, and the United Kingdom) built in 1955 that operated as a forum for the coordination of matters of European security and defense. Its powers were later transferred to the European Union. The organizations got dissolved in 2011.

democracy and promoting European culture.[11] To rebuild the economies of the Western European countries, a similar economic cooperation was needed.

Initially, in view of Germany's main role as an aggressor in two world wars, any form of cooperation involving this country turned out to be extremely difficult, especially given that relations between France and Germany had traditionally been very tense. Even though Germany was defeated, many countries still feared that Germany could regain its former economic strength and become an aggressive power again threatening peace and stability in Europe. Nevertheless, Germany's economic potential, its size and its strategically important geographical location in the heart of Europe made the country's speedy recovery very important for Europe. Many countries, including France, needed Germany's plentiful coal resources to develop their own steel industry.

Against this backdrop, on 9 May 1950, only 5 years after World War II ended with Germany's absolute surrender, the then French Minister of Foreign Affairs, Robert Schuman, presented a scheme for the permanent pacification of relations between France and Germany, which Jean Monnet, the Commissioner-General of the French National Planning Board, later elaborated on. This scheme was later called the Schuman Declaration,[12] and it mooted the idea of forming an economic community to integrate Europe's coal and steel industries. Believing that "*Europe will not be made at once, or according to a single plan*" and "*will be built through concrete achievements which first create a de facto solidarity*", Monnet and Schuman emphasized the importance of "*the elimination of the age-old opposition of France and Germany*".[13] To achieve these objectives, the scheme proposed to "*place Franco-German production of coal and steel as a whole under a common higher authority, within the framework of an organization open to the participation of the other countries of Europe*".[14] This was because "*by pooling basic production and by instituting a new higher authority, whose decisions will bind France, Germany, and other member countries, this proposal will lead to the realisation of the first concrete foundation of a European federation indispensable to the preservation of peace*".[15]

Schuman and Monnet wanted to create a supranational organization authorized by its Member States to make economic decisions on their behalf and to supervise the execution of the treaty on which the organization was based.[16] Compared to the

[11] See supra, Sect. 3.4.4.1.

[12] See <https://europa.eu/european-union/about-eu/symbols/europe-day/schuman-declaration_en> (accessed 9 March 2025).

[13] <http://www.robert-schuman.eu/en/declaration-of-9-may-1950> (accessed 9 March 2025).

[14] Ibid.

[15] Ibid.

[16] Structurally, the plan resembled the River Commissions of the nineteenth century; see supra, Sect. 1.2.2.2.

concept of intergovernmental organizations in which member states also work together but retain their full sovereignty, the assignation of sovereignty on certain matters to a third party promised a faster joint decision-making.

Due to the poor economic situation of many European countries as a consequence of WW2, the idea of promoting Europe's coal and steel industries attracted great interest. Apart from France and Germany, Italy and the Benelux countries (Belgium, Netherlands and Luxembourg) also joined the negotiations, with they thought that their own industry would benefit from being part of a common market for coal and steel. The negotiations took almost a year, because the states involved had to agree on the extent of power the new "higher authority" should be given. In addition, clarification on the higher authority's supervision was needed: How should and, more particularly, could the authority be controlled? Eventually, Germany and the Netherlands successfully insisted on the implementation of an additional body allowing the participating states to supervise the actions taken by the higher authority.

Subsequently, on 18 April 1951, France, Germany, Italy, Belgium, Netherlands and Luxembourg signed the Treaty establishing the European Coal and Steel Community stating that they *"institute among themselves a European Coal and Steel Community (ECSC), based on a common market, common objectives, and common institutions"*.[17] The Treaty, which came to be known as the *Treaty of Paris*, formed the ECSC with four main institutions, namely (i) a Council of Ministers representing the governments of all member states to jointly decide on non-contractual policies; (ii) a High Authority consisting of independent appointees authorized to make decisions based on the Treaty's provision; (iii) a Court of Justice composed of independent judges to interpret the Treaty and resolve conflicts between member states and the High Authority; and (iv) a Common Assembly consisting of members of national parliaments to monitor the High Authority's actions. Following the ECSC's mission *"to contribute to economic expansion, the development of employment and the improvement of the standard of living in the participating countries through the institution, in harmony with the general economy of the member states, of a common market"*, the Treaty requested all members of the High Authority to refrain from any action incompatible with the supranational character of their functions.[18] Following the ratification by the six founding member states, the ECSC came into force on 23 July 1952. The common market for coal, iron ore and scrap opened on 10 February 1953, closely followed by the market for steel that opened on 1 May 1953. Basically, the ECSC possessed already most of the structural features of supranationalism and provided the conceptual framework for the process of European integration.

[17] Art. 1 ECSC.

[18] Art. 2 ECSC.

4.3.1.2 European Economic Community

In the following years the call for cooperation between European countries grew louder. Due to fear of military attacks from the Soviet-dominated Eastern Europe, the French Prime Minister René Pleven proposed the establishment of a European Defence Community (EDC) to protect the borders of the western part of Germany. In addition, an entity to be named the European Political Community (EPC) was proposed in 1952 as a combination of the existing European Coal and Steel Community (ECSC) and the proposed European Defence Community (EDC). Both proposals did not receive a majority in the French Parliament and therewith failed. Other ideas gained more support: One was the establishment of a common market covering all types of economic activities that abandons internal tariffs and quotas etc. by establishing an external tariff (customs union) to boost Europe's economy. The other idea was the establishment of a European Atomic Energy Community to stimulate non-military cooperation in the nuclear energy sector.

On 25 March 1957, the six founding states of the ECSC signed the Treaty establishing the European Economic Community (EEC; EEC Treaty) and the Treaty establishing the European Atomic Energy Community (EAEC; EAEC Treaty) and thus agreed on the establishment of two new Communities. The EEC Treaty, which came to be known as the *Treaty of Rome*, has been concluded to enable people, goods, services and capital to move freely between the member states' borders, the EAEC Treaty to develop the non-military, peaceful use of nuclear energy (EAEC). *The EEC was created as a free trade area and a customs union according to Article XXIV Secs (4) to (9) of the General Agreement on Tariffs and Trade (GATT).*

The institutional structure of the EEC and the EAEC was like that of the ECSC. Both the EEC and the EAEC included four institutions, namely a Commission, a Council and, jointly with the ECSC, an Assembly and a Court. The new communities' supranational executive, the so-called Commission, had been less powerful than those in the ECSC. Even though both commissions were entitled to make legislative proposals, the implementation of the proposals was subject to the approval of the respective Council of Ministers. During the next years the EEC was very successful and, to set an example, eliminated custom duties 3 years earlier than planned.

4.3.1.3 European Communities

a) Establishment

To strengthen the relationship between the ECSC, the EAEC and the EEC, on 8 April 1965 the member states signed the Treaty establishing a Single Council and a Single Commission of the European Communities (Merger Treaty)[19] to merge the executive branches into a single institutional structure. Entered into force on 1 July 1967, the Merger Treaty replaced both the Council and Commission of the

[19] The Treaty is also referred to as Brussels Treaty.

EAEC as well as the Council and the High Authority of the ECSC with the Council of the EEC and its Commission. Accordingly, the three communities became jointly referred to as the European Communities. Although sharing common institutions such as the Court of Justice and the Parliamentary Assembly, the ECSC, the EEC and the EAEC still remained legally independent. Following the communities' merger, the Common Assembly of the ECSC was expanded to cover all three communities and quickly acquired the title European Parliament. Additionally, in 1974, the European Council consisting of the Heads of State and Government of the member states of the European Communities was established. Following its main task of providing political guidance, the European Council started to explore new possible areas of cooperation between member states and to develop appropriate policies.

b) Establishment of a Single Market and Further Developments

During the economic crisis of the early 1970s, the European Communities expanded from six to nine member states with the accession of the UK, Ireland and Denmark in 1973.[20] Due to the continuing existence of different kinds of non-tariff barriers to trade, the Commission developed common policies to reduce them and declared the completion of a single market as one of its key ambitions. Following a request by the European Council, the Commission established a proposal to remove all trade barriers by 1992. To meet this tight schedule, the decision-making in all policy areas relating to the single market needed to be simplified and complemented by a revision of the European Communities' foundational treaties.

During a summit held in Paris in October 1972, the Heads of State or Government, among others, reaffirmed 1980 to be the deadline for the achievement of an economic and monetary union. In 1978, at a European Council meeting held in Bremen, the member states reached an agreement to set up a European Monetary System (EMS).

Eight years later, on 27 and 28 February 1986, the member states signed the Single European Act (SEA). This first major revision of the Treaty of Rome aimed at adding a new impetus to the integration of the European countries and to complete the internal market by, among other things, amending the rules governing the operation of the existing institutions and expanding the powers of the European Communities, notably in the field of research and development, the environment and common foreign policy. A fully operational single market taking up the objectives of the common market was to be completed by 1 January 1993.

The SEA established several institutional changes by amending the Treaty of the EEC regarding the decision-making procedure within the Council, the Commission's powers, the European Parliament's powers and the Communities' responsibilities. In so doing, the SEA introduced, inter alia, a cooperation procedure and extended qualified majority voting at the place of unanimity to new areas. In

[20] In the end Norway did not became a member of the EU. The Norwegian citizens eligible to vote refused to join the European Community in 1972 and to join the EU in 1994 in referendums.

addition, it formalized the Economic and Monetary Union (EMU), a cooperation that was already discussed and developed outside of the treaties.

4.3.2 The Establishment of the European Union

4.3.2.1 Treaty of Maastricht

Having discussed the European Communities' expansion repeatedly, on 19 June 1983 the ten Heads of State or Government of the member states of the European Communities[21] adopted the *Solemn Declaration on European Union* expressing their desire to establish a European Union.[22] One decade later, on 7 February 1992, the member states signed the *Treaty of Maastricht on European Union (TEU, Maastricht Treaty, Treaty on European Union).* Commonly considered as the real genesis of the EU, the Maastricht Treaty contained several structural and content-related modifications.

The establishment of the European Union is a vivid example of the impact of functional integration on the powers of supranational organizations and the changing relations between the organization and its member states, resulting in a power shift from the states to their common superstructure. The continuing need to harmonize policy areas resulted in a spill-over to policy areas increasingly remote from economic issues. Therefore, the Maastricht Treaty expanded the powers of the Union considerably.

4.3.2.2 Three Pillars of the Union

Upon the entry into force of the Maastricht Treaty on 1 November 1993, the EEC became the European Community (EC) and the Treaty repositioned the EU by arranging all their duties on three pillars. Comprising the EC, the ECSC and the EAEC, the first pillar handled economic, social and environmental policies. The second pillar took care of all foreign policy and security matters, and the third pillar aimed at bringing together co-operation in the EU member states' fight against crime.[23]

[21] Greece joined the European Communities in 1981 marking the start for the "Mediterranean enlargement" (referring to the accession of Spain and Portugal that followed in 1986).

[22] See <http://aei.pitt.edu/1788/1/stuttgart_declaration_1983.pdf> (accessed 9 March 2025).

[23] The following chart is inspired by the homepage of the EU.

4.3.2.3 Institutional Changes

The Maastricht Treaty further created new institutions such as the European Central Bank, the European System of Central Banks, and the European Monetary Institute.

The Treaty also reinforced the powers of the European Parliament. The newly introduced instrument of co-decision enabled the European Parliament in certain policy areas to modify legislative proposals before approving them. Thus, next to the structural amendments, the Maastricht Treaty opened the way to political integration by introducing the concept of European citizenship, thereby representing a new stage in European integration.

When they signed the Maastricht Treaty, all EU member states committed themselves to joining the Euro zone once their economies met all the Treaty's requirements. Nevertheless, several EU member states managed to avoid this obligation. By negotiating opt-outs, the UK and Denmark could keep their own currency, and Sweden did not join the exchange rate mechanism necessary to adopt the Euro.

4.3.2.4 Expansion of Membership; Treaty of Amsterdam

In the following years several European countries decided to apply for membership. With Greece joining in 1981, Portugal and Spain joining in 1986 and Austria, Sweden and Finland joining in 1995 the EU had grown up to 15 member states. On 2 October 1997 all EU member states signed the *Treaty of Amsterdam amending the Treaty of the European Union, the Treaties establishing the European Communities and certain related acts* (Treaty of Amsterdam) that mainly focused on improving the democratic legitimacy of the European institutions. One of the Treaty's innovations was to devolve certain powers from national governments to the European Parliament, thereby increasing the institution's democratic powers and enhancing the Union's democratic legitimacy. By reforming the three pillars of the EU and the respective institutions, the Treaty of Amsterdam also aimed at helping the organization to better prepare for expansion. By signing the Treaty of Amsterdam, the EU member states also agreed on further coordination in Common Foreign and Security Policy (CFSP).

4.3.2.5 Monetary Union; Treaty of Nice

In the years following the Maastricht Treaty and the Treaty of Amsterdam, all EU member states but Denmark, Sweden and the UK worked towards implementing a monetary union. The European Central Bank started its operations in 1998, and from 1 January 2000 onwards, the exchange rates of all countries involved were fixed. Shortly before the implementation of the Euro, on 26 February 2001, the EU Member States signed the *Treaty of Nice amending the Treaty on European*

Union, the Treaties establishing the European Communities and certain related acts (Treaty of Nice). The changes made by the Treaty of Nice affected further reform of the institutions and the decision-making process. In addition, the composition of the European Parliament and the Commission were altered. On 1 January 2002, with the introduction of Euro banknotes and coins, the monetary union of the EU had been finalized.

4.3.2.6 Failed Constitutional Treaty

In 2004 ten more countries joined the EU.[24] Due to the increasing number of applicants, the member states agreed in giving the EU a consolidated constitution. Accordingly, on 29 October 2004 the *Treaty establishing a Constitution for Europe (Constitutional Treaty)* was signed to replace the existing EU treaties with a single text. Even though all EU member states signed the Constitutional Treaty, it was *never finally ratified.* The ratification process ended with the document's rejection by French and Dutch voters on 29 May and on 1 June 2005. In both countries, the supporters of the left-wing parties voted almost completely against the Constitutional Treaty. In addition, many supporters of social democratic parties and union members also joined this position. The opponents of the Constitutional Treaty emphasized the loss of national sovereignty.

4.3.2.7 Treaty of Lisbon

Given that the EU needed a revised legal basis, the next agreement, the *Treaty of Lisbon amending the Treaty on European Union and the Treaty establishing the European Community* (Treaty of Lisbon, Reform Treaty) got signed by the EU member states on 13 December 2007 and entered into force on 1 December 2009. This Treaty provided for several changes, many of which were already contained in the Constitutional Treaty of 2004. The EU member states agreed, among other things, on moving from unanimity to qualified majority voting in at least 45 policy areas in the Council of Ministers. In addition, the European Parliament obtained more powers. For example, the European Parliament was treated as a co-legislator to the Council of Ministers and, moreover, gained more weight in shaping the political agenda for Europe. Additionally, the EU received a consolidated legal personality. With the entry into force of the Lisbon Treaty, the EEC ceased to exist, and all of the organization's functions were transferred to the EU. Hence, the Treaty establishing the European Economic Community became the *Treaty on the Functioning of the European Union (TFEU).*

---

[24] Cyprus, the Czech Republic, Estonia, Hungary, Latvia, Lithuania, Malta, Poland, Slovakia and Slovenia.

A negative consequence of the monetary union was revealed during the financial crisis of 2008. Beginning in 2007, the crisis led to a destabilization of the entire world's financial system and plunged the global economy into recession. The consequences of the crisis also affected several EU member states. As a result of the EU's monetary union, the financial problems of individual countries impacted all Member States and weakened for a while the whole organization.

4.3.2.8 New Members; Brexit and Other Calls for Withdrawal

After Bulgaria, Romania (2007) and Croatia (2013) entered the EU, the organization reached the size of 28 member states. However, in the UK, on 23 June 2016, a slim majority of the voters chose in a consultative referendum UK's withdrawal from the EU (Brexit). Therefore, starting in 2016, the EU negotiated with the UK until the end of 2019 to regulate the consequences of Brexit. The withdrawal procedure, which was initiated by written communication of the UK to the EU Council on 29 March 2017, should have been completed by 29 March 2019. However, by this deadline, the Parliament in London rejected the draft withdrawal agreement between the UK and the EU for the third time. On 11 April 2019, the EU member states approved to postpone the Brexit until 31 October 2019. This was again extended to 31 January 2020 when the UK definitely left the EU.

With the refugee crisis starting in 2016, the calls for a withdrawal from the EU grew louder also in other EU member states. Events such as the civil war in Syria and the increased attacks of terrorist organizations in Afghanistan, Iraq and Syria led to mass migrations mainly towards the EU. The refugee crisis became the new battleground of competing interests within the EU. Questions such as how to deal with the increasing number of refugees and how to distribute them among the EU member states created further deep political rifts in the EU. Meanwhile, the economic problems that Brexit caused for the UK have largely silenced the desire to leave the EU. In addition, the EU was able to enact quickly sanctions against Russia as a collective reaction against the Russian war of aggression against Ukraine. The EU sanctions packages against Russia are unprecedented.

4.4 Member States of the European Union

4.4.1 Development of Membership

At present, the EU consists of 27 member states[25] and covers the majority of the more than 50 states located on the continent of Europe.[26] In addition, other states such as the Ukraine, Albania, Serbia, Georgia and Turkey[27] have expressed their interest in joining the EU. Initially, only six European states, namely Belgium, Germany, France, Italy, Luxembourg and the Netherlands, started to cooperate economically by founding the ECSC in 1951 and the EAEC as well as the EEC in 1957. With the establishment of the EEC, these six core states laid the cornerstone for a process that culminated in the creation of the EU in 1993.

The first enlargement of the EEC took place in 1973 with the accession of Denmark, Ireland and the United Kingdom, followed by Greece in 1981 and Spain and Portugal in 1986. With the formal establishment of the EU, the EEC's successor, more and more European states decided to join the supranational organization. In 1995, Austria, Finland and Sweden became part of the EU, increasing the number of Member States to 15. The largest growth of the EU took place in 2004 with the accession of Cyprus, Czech Republic, Estonia, Hungary, Latvia, Lithuania, Malta, Poland, Slovakia and Slovenia. In 2007 Bulgaria and Romania joined the alliance, followed by Croatia in 2013.[28]

4.4.1.1 Changes in Membership: Accession and Withdrawal

a) Legal Basis; Copenhagen Criteria

Dealing with the accession to the EU in more detail, Article 2 and 49 TEU read as follows:

> ***"Article 2***
> *The Union is founded on the values of respect for human dignity, freedom, democracy, equality, the rule of law and respect for human rights, including the rights of persons belonging to minorities. These values are common to the*

---

[25] For the complete list of EU member states see <https://europa.eu/european-union/about-eu/countries_en> (accessed 9 March 2025).

[26] The conceptions about how many European countries exist are diverging. Depending on the source, the European continent encompasses 47 till 53 independent states. See among others <https://www.worldatlas.com/geography/how-many-countries-are-in-europe.html> and <http://unstats.un.org/unsd/methods/m49/m49regin.htm#europe> (accessed 9 March 2025).

[27] For more information see below: Sect. 4.4.1.1.

[28] <https://ec.europa.eu/neighbourhood-enlargement/countries/detailed-country-information/croatia_en> (accessed 9 March 2025).

Member States in a society in which pluralism, non-discrimination, tolerance, justice, solidarity and equality between women and men prevail."

"Article 49

Any European State which respects the values referred to in Article 2 and is committed to promoting them may apply to become a member of the Union. The European Parliament and national Parliaments shall be notified of this application. The applicant State shall address its application to the Council, which shall act unanimously after consulting the Commission and after receiving the consent of the European Parliament, which shall act by a majority of its component members. The conditions of eligibility agreed upon by the European Council shall be taken into account.

The conditions of admission and the adjustments to the Treaties on which the Union is founded, which such admission entails, shall be the subject of an agreement between the Member States and the applicant State. This agreement shall be submitted for ratification by all the contracting States in accordance with their respective constitutional requirements."

As a general rule, any European country[29] may apply to join the EU, provided it satisfies the supranational organization's criteria for membership. The conditions for joining the EU, also known as the *Copenhagen criteria*,[30] have political, economic and legal aspects.[31] EU member states must respect and promote the organization's values such as democracy and human rights. In addition, EU member states must have a free-market economy and a stable democracy. Moreover, the country must agree to adopt or comply with all EU legislation.

b) Status of Candidate Country

European states that express their interest in becoming member of the supranational organization are divided into candidate countries and potential candidate countries. The classification depends on whether, and to what extent, these candidates fulfil the requirements for EU membership.

The current group of candidate countries consists of Albania, Montenegro, Serbia, the Former Yugoslav Republic of Macedonia, Turkey[32] and Ukraine. All candidate countries but Turkey are considered to be promising candidates.[33] To date,

---

[29] See supra, Sect. 4.4.2.

[30] Named after the European Council in Copenhagen in 1993 which defined them.

[31] For more details see <https://ec.europa.eu/neighbourhood-enlargement/policy/conditions-membership_en< (accessed 9 March 2025).

[32] <https://europa.eu/european-union/about-eu/countries_en> (accessed 9 March 2025).

[33] In 1987, Turkey applied to join what was then the EEC. It was declared eligible to join the EU in 1997 with accession negotiations starting in 2005. In recent years, the negotiations with Turkey have stalled. The 2023 Türkiye Report by the European Commission, dated 8 Nov 2023, concluded that Turkey continues to move further away from the EU, especially in the areas of the rule of law

the chances of Turkey becoming a Member State of the EU are regarded as small. The state's repeated human rights violations and its oft-criticized democratic deficits are considered as being not compatible with the values of the EU and its normative underpinnings. Currently, potential candidates that have been promised the prospect of joining the EU when they fulfil the requirements for EU membership are Bosnia and Herzegovina and Kosovo.[34]

c) Procedure; Negotiations

Becoming a member state of the EU is *a complex and long procedure*. The first step for every country wishing to join the EU is to submit a membership application to the Council. After receipt of all the application documents, the Council asks the Commission to assess the applicant's ability to meet the Copenhagen criteria. If the Commission affirms the applicant's ability, the Council must then agree on a framework for negotiations with the candidate country. The unanimous approval of all EU member governments is needed before membership negotiations can commence.

Formal membership negotiations between the candidate state and both the ministers and ambassadors of the EU member governments typically take the following form: Encompassing all the relevant policy areas, this intergovernmental conference covers all current EU legislation. Negotiation on all policy areas, also known as chapters, are formally opened on a subject-by-subject basis. Each applicant country must adopt a vast amount of EU rules and regulations as national law. As a result, the negotiation process lasts a very long time. To conclude membership negotiations, every single chapter needs to be closed. This requires every EU member government to be satisfied with the respective negotiation's results.

d) Accession Treaty

Upon the completion of all negotiations, the applicant country must sign an *Accession Treaty* containing details of the terms and conditions of membership, all transitional arrangements and deadlines, as well as details of financial arrangements. This treaty is *to be approved by the governments of all member states, the Commission and the Parliament*. Additionally, *every EU member state must ratify the Accession Treaty*. By joining the EU, new member states become party to the founding treaties and thus are subject to both the obligations and the privileges of the EU membership. The Union itself is not a party of the Accession Treaty.

---

and fundamental rights. The report highlighted ongoing concerns, noting that Turkey had made limited progress in addressing issues such as judicial independence, media freedom, and civil society. As a result, the prospects for Turkey's accession to the EU remain increasingly uncertain. See European Commission (2023).

[34] See <https://europa.eu/european-union/about-eu/countries_en> (accessed 9 March 2025).

4.4.2 *Leaving the European Union*

4.4.2.1 Instances; Brexit

The EEC saw two exits, namely Algeria in 1962 because of its independence from France, and Greenland in 1984.[35] In these two cases not a member state left the supranational organization, but only a part of the state's territory, either to create a new, independent state or to make use of a broad autonomy granted by the metropolitan state. These events therefore had no effect on membership either of France or Denmark. To date only the UK as a member state left the EU. Before the 2016 EU referendum Brexit result, a possible withdrawal from the EU had already been discussed several times in the UK. In a referendum held in 1975, about two thirds of the British voters chose to remain in the EEC. On 23 June 2016, the British people voted in a non-binding referendum to leave the EU[36] and on 29 March 2017, 9 months after the referendum and after 44 years of membership, the British government officially declared its intention to leave the EU. The execution of the Brexit made the UK the first former EU Member State.

4.4.2.2 Withdrawal from the EU

Originally, the withdrawal of a member state from the EC/EU was not expressly regulated; the EU treaties did not provide for such a procedure. It was therefore contested whether a member could, based on its sovereignty and right to self-determination, unilaterally withdraw from the Community or the Union respectively or whether the *pacta sunt servanda*-principle applied. It was only when the Treaty of Lisbon entered into force in 2009 that a member state's right to unilaterally withdraw from the supranational organization was explicitly recognized and regulated. Article 50 TEU reads as follows:

> ***"Article 50***
> 1. *Any Member State may decide to withdraw from the Union in accordance with its own constitutional requirements.*
> 2. *A Member State which decides to withdraw shall notify the European Council of its intention. In the light of the guidelines provided by the European Council, the Union shall negotiate and conclude an agreement with that State, setting out the arrangements for its withdrawal, taking account of the framework for its future relationship with the Union. That agreement shall be negotiated in accordance with Article 218(3) of the Treaty on the Functioning of the European Union. It shall be concluded on behalf of the Union by the*

[35] The Greenlanders are now Danish citizens but not EU citizens.

[36] For more details see <http://www.bbc.com/news/politics/eu_referendum/results> (accessed 9 March 2025).

Council, acting by a qualified majority, after obtaining the consent of the European Parliament.

3. *The Treaties shall cease to apply to the State in question from the date of entry into force of the withdrawal agreement or, failing that, two years after the notification referred to in paragraph 2, unless the European Council, in agreement with the Member State concerned, unanimously decides to extend this period.*
4. *For the purposes of paragraphs 2 and 3, the member of the European Council or of the Council representing the withdrawing Member State shall not participate in the discussions of the European Council or Council or in decisions concerning it. A qualified majority shall be defined in accordance with Article 238(3)(b) of the Treaty on the Functioning of the European Union.*
5. *If a State which has withdrawn from the Union asks to rejoin, its request shall be subject to the procedure referred to in Article 49."*

Article 50 TEU only provides a rough framework for the exit procedure. Since before the UK no member state had ever invoked Article 50 TEU, there are many uncertainties regarding the entire process. Simultaneously, the procedure's outcome is rather unpredictable. This was clearly evidenced by the way the UK left the Union.

Withdrawal from the EU is subject to each member state's constitutional requirements. Using the example of the UK, according to British law, the result of the referendum was not binding on Parliament.[37] Contrary to previous national referendums in the UK, where the respective law stipulated that the outcome should also be implemented, David Cameron's government did not pass a corresponding legislation for the EU referendum regulating a possible withdrawal from the EU. Despite all this, however, from a political point of view, disregarding the voters' decision was not considered as an option.[38]

First of all, to begin the exit procedure, the respective member state must notify the European Council of its intention to leave the EU. The notification is to be addressed to the leaders of the remaining member states together with the president of the European Council and the president of the European Commission. Following the notification, the European Council develops a set of guidelines for the negotiations. Based on these guidelines, the EU negotiates and concludes an agreement with the member state intending to leave. During these negotiations, also known as the "sunset period",[39] the European Commission establishes the arrangements for the

[37] <http://www.independent.co.uk/news/uk/politics/brexist-vote-eu-referendum-not-legally-binding-supreme-court-legal-challenge-art.-50-a7418706.html> (accessed 9 March 2025).

[38] According to a statement of the former UK Prime Minister, David Cameron, announced on 22 Feb 2016, "for a Prime Minister to ignore the express will of the British people to leave the EU would be not just wrong, but undemocratic", see <http://www.publications.parliament.uk/pa/cm201516/cmhansrd/cm160222/debtext/160222-0001.htm#16022210> (accessed 9 March 2025).

[39] Crossley et al. (2017).

member state's withdrawal by also considering the country's future relationship with the Union.[40]

All negotiations must be completed within 2 years from receipt of the notification. During these 2 years, the EU treaties continue to be applicable to the leaving member state, and all rights and obligations of the EU membership remain valid. Accordingly, the respective state is still obligated to pay its contributions to the EU budget and is still fully involved in the organization's decisions except for those dealing with its own withdrawal.[41]

To be valid, all agreements dealing with a member state's withdrawal need to be concluded by the European Council. In this regard, the *approval of both the respective member state and the qualified majority of the remaining EU member states is needed*, provided 65 percent of the remaining member states' population is represented.[42] In the case of the UK, at least 20 of the 27 remaining EU member states needed to approve the agreements. Last but not least, the *consent of the European Parliament* by simple majority is required.

If no agreement is reached within the stipulated time frame, the membership of the leaving state expires automatically, unless the parties involved decide to extend the deadline as in the case of Brexit. As to motivate all parties to conclude the agreement in time, an extension of the time limit has to be accepted by all EU member states unanimously. This requirement makes an extension rather unlikely. Nevertheless, in the case of the UK the EU member states approved to postponing the deadline for 6 months and then again for another 3 months.

4.4.2.3 Expulsion of an EU Member State

Apart from the autonomous decision of a member state to withdraw from the EU, do the treaties establishing the EU also provide for the expulsion of a member state by the supranational organization and/or by its members? The answer is no. However, the suspension of certain membership rights is an option regulated in the treaties. Dealing with the suspension of EU membership rights in more detail, Article 7 TEU, *the so-called "nuclear option"* reads as follows:

"Article 7

1. *On a reasoned proposal by one third of the Member States, by the European Parliament or by the European Commission, the Council, acting by a majority of four fifths of its members after obtaining the consent of the European Parliament, may determine that there is a clear risk of a serious breach by a*

---

[40] Indeed, two agreements are needed: one treaty on details of withdrawal, and one on the (then former) Member State's future relationship with the EU.

[41] Art. 50(3) TEU.

[42] For more details on the "qualified majority" according to EU law see <http://eur-lex.europa.eu/summary/glossary/qualified_majority.html?locale=en> (accessed 9 March 2025).

Member State of the values referred to in Article 2. Before making such a determination, the Council shall hear the Member State in question and may address recommendations to it, acting in accordance with the same procedure. The Council shall regularly verify that the grounds on which such a determination was made continue to apply.

2. *The European Council, acting by unanimity on a proposal by one third of the Member States or by the Commission and after obtaining the consent of the European Parliament, may determine the existence of a serious and persistent breach by a Member State of the values referred to in Article 2, after inviting the Member State in question to submit its observations.*
3. *Where a determination under paragraph 2 has been made, the Council, acting by a qualified majority, may decide to suspend certain of the rights deriving from the application of the Treaties to the Member State in question, including the voting rights of the representative of the government of that Member State in the Council. In doing so, the Council shall take into account the possible consequences of such a suspension on the rights and obligations of natural and legal persons. The obligations of the Member State in question under the Treaties shall in any case continue to be binding on that State.*
4. *The Council, acting by a qualified majority, may decide subsequently to vary or revoke measures taken under paragraph 3 in response to changes in the situation which led to their being imposed.*
5. *The voting arrangements applying to the European Parliament, the European Council and the Council for the purposes of this Article are laid down in Article 354 of the Treaty on the Functioning of the European Union."*

Having been designed to uphold the principles on which the EU is founded, namely liberty, democracy, respect for human rights and fundamental freedoms and the rule of law, Article 7 differentiates between the mere risk of a serious violation of the union's core values[43] and the final determination of the existence of a serious and persistent breach of these values. The suspension of a member state's rights, such as voting right in the Council, will be triggered if there is a serious and persistent breach of EU core values committed by the member state in question.

To initiate a review process, there must be a proposal by one third of the EU member states or the Commission criticizing a serious and persistent breach of EU core values committed by a member state. Following this, the affected member state is to be heard by the Council. Provided that the European Parliament gives its consent, the Council then decides based on all information available. In view of

[43] For identifying the mere risk of a serious violation of the EU's core values in a first step a reasoned proposal supported by either one third of the Member States, the European Parliament or the European Commission is needed. Upon receipt of the proposal the Member State concerned shall be heard by the Council. Provided that the European Parliament's consent is given, the Council shall than act by a majority of four fifths of its members. Once the mere risk of a serious violation of the values referred to in Art. 2 is determined, the Council makes recommendations to the respective Member States and constantly examines their implementation.

the potential serious consequences for the member state in question, the Council's decision must be unanimous.[44]

If the member state is found to have committed a serious and persistent breach of EU values, the Council may then *decide to suspend certain of the state's rights*. The Council's qualified majority must approve all sanctions. Nevertheless, only membership rights are sanctioned. The member state's obligations remain completely binding.

The EU has formally not used this procedure so far but has already requested some of its member states to change their laws to conform with the EU's basic values. In 2012 the EU had been concerned about a number of developments in Romania, especially regarding actions that appear to reduce the effective powers of independent institutions like the Constitutional Court. Accordingly, the Commission invited Romania to restore its rule of law in accordance with the respective EU standards.[45] In April 2017, the European Parliament strongly condemned policies of the Polish government. The list of allegations made by the EU Parliament was long and focused, among others, on the judicial reforms that from the point of view of the European Commission endangered the separation of powers in Poland and restricted the independence of courts, and on violations of the rule of law, freedom of expression and freedom of the media. Believing the actions of the Polish government and President have led to a "paralysis of the Constitutional Court", which is "a threat to democracy, human rights and the rule of law", the European Parliament since then launched several infringement procedures against Poland.[46] Also Hungary is in the focus. This country has long been accused of violations of fundamental rights and the separation of powers by the EU institutions, in particular by the Parliament. In February 2023, the European Commission referred a case against Hungary to the Court of Justice for its potential breach of several rights in the Charter of Fundamental Rights of the European Union (the Charter) and fundamental EU values laid

[44] Of course, the member state accused of serious violations of core values is excluded from the vote. The requirement of unanimity was the reason that neither Poland's nor Hungary's membership rights got suspended despite that these countries committed serious violations of important membership rights, because these two states protected each other and made an unanimous decision impossible.

[45] European Commission, *Report on Romania under the Cooperation and Verification Mechanism"*, 7 Jul 2012, available at: https://ec.europa.eu/commission/presscorner/api/files/document/print/en/memo_12_529/MEMO_12_529_EN.pdf (accessed 8 March 2025).

[46] The European Parliament urged Poland "not to proceed the new laws unless they fully guarantee the independence of the judiciary to implement all EU Commission and Venice Commission recommendations in full, to comply with the EU Court of Justice order to "immediately suspend large-scale logging" in the ancient Białowieża forest, to respect the right of freedom of assembly, to strongly condemn the "xenophobic and fascist march that took place in Warsaw" on Saturday, 11 Nov 2017, and to take a firm stand on women's rights, by providing free and accessible contraception without discrimination and making emergency contraception available without medical prescription", see European Parliament, *Resolution of 15 Nov 2017 on the Situation of the Rule of Law and Democracy in Poland* (2017/2931[RSP]).

down in Article 2 TEU.[47] This is the first time that a member state is referred to the Court of Justice for a potential breach of fundamental EU values laid down in Article 2 TEU. Background was a Hungarian law discriminating against LGBTIQ.

4.5 Main Aims of the European Union

The main aims of the EU are reflected in Article 3 TEU, which reads as follows:

> ***"Article 3***
> *(ex Article 2 TEU)*
>
> 1. *The Union's aim is to promote peace, its values and the well-being of its peoples.*
> 2. *The Union shall offer its citizens an area of freedom, security and justice without internal frontiers, in which the free movement of persons is ensured in conjunction with appropriate measures with respect to external border controls, asylum, immigration and the prevention and combating of crime.*
> 3. *The Union shall establish an internal market. It shall work for the sustainable development of Europe based on balanced economic growth and price stability, a highly competitive social market economy, aiming at full employment and social progress, and a high level of protection and improvement of the quality of the environment. It shall promote scientific and technological advance.*
> 4. *It shall combat social exclusion and discrimination, and shall promote social justice and protection, equality between women and men, solidarity between generations and protection of the rights of the child. It shall promote economic, social and territorial cohesion, and solidarity among Member States. It shall respect its rich cultural and linguistic diversity, and shall ensure that Europe's cultural heritage is safeguarded and enhanced.*
> 5. *The Union shall establish an economic and monetary union whose currency is the euro.*
> 6. *In its relations with the wider world, the Union shall uphold and promote its values and interests and contribute to the protection of its citizens. It shall contribute to peace, security, the sustainable development of the Earth, solidarity and mutual respect among peoples, free and fair trade, eradication of poverty and the protection of human rights, in particular the rights of the child, as well as to the strict observance and the development of international law, including respect for the principles of the United Nations Charter.*
> 7. *The Union shall pursue its objectives by appropriate means commensurate with the competences which are conferred upon it in the Treaties."*

[47] *European Commission v Hungary*, Case C-769/22.

These are broad and important purposes. At the time of the establishment of the EEC, the organization was by far not as ambitious. Its first and most important goal was *the creation of a common market*. The treaties that followed the EEC's establishment expanded this purpose with the creation of the Economic and Monetary Union (EMU), a Common Foreign and Security Policy and powers of the union in Justice and Domestic Affairs. The Maastricht Treaty in particular enhanced European political and economic integration by creating a single currency (the Euro), a unified foreign and security policy, and common citizenship rights and by advancing cooperation in the areas of immigration, asylum, and judicial affairs.[48]

Today, Union's goals are[49]:

- To promote peace, the Union's values and the well-being of its citizens;
- To offer freedom, security and justice without internal borders;
- To support sustainable development based on balanced economic growth and price stability, a highly competitive market economy with full employment and social progress, and environmental protection;
- To combat social exclusion and discrimination;
- To promote scientific and technological progress;
- To enhance economic, social and territorial cohesion and solidarity among member countries;
- To respect the Union's rich cultural and linguistic diversity.

These goals are s*upplemented by values that are common to all member states* and an integral part of the European way of life. These values are: the inviolability of human dignity; individual freedoms including the freedom of movement and all the individual freedoms and human rights protected by international human rights treaties as well as by the EU Charter of Fundamental Rights; equality as the same rights of all citizens before the law in all areas and as a principle directing European policies and legislation; democracy; and the rule of law. Given that these core obligations are laid out in the Lisbon Treaty and the EU Charter of fundamental rights and *form the foundation of the political systems of the member states*, they are the basis of the EU and its legal and political order.

The goals and purposes of the EU as defined in Article 3 TEU support the process of functional integration and reflect the EU's particularly legal nature as a supranational organization. Its goals are very broad and, regarding the policy areas, resemble, to a large extent, the goals of a state. However, it is very clear that the EU does not have all the powers a state usually has and that its purpose is still limited and based on treaties concluded between states, not on a constitution adopted by a democratic constituency.

---

[48] As to the historical developments see supra, Sect. 4.3.

[49] <https://europa.eu/european-union/about-eu/eu-in-brief_en> (accessed 9 March 2025).

The very broad delineation of the EU's purpose has important legal ramifications, particularly in the construction of the organization's and its institutions' powers. These powers must be interpreted in the context of the EU's broad purpose; therefore, the doctrines of *effet utile*[50] as well as of implied powers[51] find a rich area of application within the EU.

4.6 Legal Basis and Policy Areas

4.6.1 Legal Basis

The EU's legal basis is built on several founding, amending and accession treaties as well as additional protocols. The EU treaties are binding agreements between all the member states that set out the EU's objectives and rules. They regulate, e.g., the Union's decision-making procedures and its relationship with the member states. Even though the EU's institutions are involved in the drafting process, the *Union itself is not a party to these treaties.*

The treaties currently in force that form the legal basis of the EU are:

- Treaty on European Union[52];
- Treaty on the Functioning of the European Union[53];
- Treaty establishing the European Atomic Energy Community[54]
- Charter of Fundamental Rights of the European Union.[55]

To cover new areas of cooperation and increase the efficiency and transparency of the EU, the treaties are regularly amended, and often the European institutions get vested with new powers. Given that several countries have repeatedly expressed their interest in becoming part of the EU and have started negotiations with the organization, the number of accession treaties is likely to continue to increase in the future.

4.6.2 Policy Areas

Throughout the years, the EU has expanded its activities and engaged in a wide range of policy areas, though the degree of EU involvement differs according to the

---

[50] See supra, Sect. 1.11.3.

[51] See supra, Sect. 1.9.2.

[52] Consolidated Version, OJ C202/13 (2016).

[53] Consolidated Version, OJ C202/47 (2016).

[54] Consolidated Version, OJ C203/1 (2016).

[55] OJ C326/391 (2012).

policy area. The nature and extent of participation ranges from areas that are almost exclusively covered by the EU to others with a very weak participation of the EU due to a nearly exclusive decision-making authority of the member states.

Policy areas where *all major decisions are taken on the EU level* are:

- External Trade
- Competition policies
- Agriculture and Fisheries
- Currency (Euro)

Policy areas with a *strong involvement of the EU* are:

- Environmental issues
- Cross-border crimes
- Transport
- Research and Development
- Occupational health and safety
- Regional policies
- Internal market
- Development Aid

Policy areas with a *weak involvement of the EU* are:

- Defense
- Taxation
- Social policies
- Foreign policies
- Health care

Policy areas *almost exclusively determined by the Member States* are:

- Primary and secondary education
- Cultural policies
- Street crimes

4.7 Institutions and Organs of the European Union

4.7.1 Overview

The 1951 ECSC was based on five institutions representing the traditional separation of powers between the legislative, executive and judiciary branches of government. This included the High Authority (predecessor to the European Commission), the Common Assembly (predecessor to the European Parliament), the Special Council (equivalent to the current Council of the European Union) and the Court of Justice, supplemented by a Consultative Committee that was established alongside the High Authority to represent civil society.

The subsequent establishment of the EEC and the EU was accompanied by institutional changes. This shift of powers led to the creation of several new institutions. Today, the seven principal decision-making bodies of the EU listed in Article 13 TEU are:

- the European Parliament (Article 14 TEU);
- the European Council (Article 15 TEU);
- the Council of the European Union (Article 16 TEU);
- the European Commission (Article 17 TEU);
- the Court of Justice of the European Union (Article 19 TEU);
- the European Central Bank (Article 13(3) TEU); and
- the European Court of Auditors (Article 13(3) TEU).

Their establishment, powers and functions are described in the following section. Detailed provisions on these institutions are set out in the Treaty on the Functioning of the European Union (TFEU).

Other institutions, organs and interinstitutional bodies of the European Union are the European External Action Service (EEAS), the European Economic and Social Committee (EESC), the Committee of the Regions (CoR), the European Investment Bank (EIB), the European Ombudsman, the European Data Protection Supervisor (EDPS), the Computer Emergency Response Team (CERT), the European School of Administration, the European Personnel Selection Office and the Publications Office. Their functions are too specific for a general textbook and therefore will not be discussed.

4.7.2 European Parliament

4.7.2.1 Establishment of the European Parliament

The European Parliament's origin dates to the ECSC Common Assembly which first met on 10 September 1952. The Common Assembly was composed of 78 appointed representatives drawn from the Member States' national parliaments. Following the establishment of the EEC and the EAEC, the then enlarged Common Assembly (142 members) was shared by all three communities and renamed as European Parliamentary Assembly.

The European Parliamentary Assembly met for the first time in Strasbourg on 19 March 1958. Due to the subsequent change of the seating arrangements from sitting according to nationality to sitting according to political views (i.e. political parties), the European Parliamentary Assembly is considered the birth of modern European parliamentarism. On 20 March 1962 the organ changed its name to European Parliament.

The Common Assembly of the ECSC was a rather powerless body that monitored the activities of the High Authority, but without legislative powers. Over time, and simultaneously with the expansion of European supranationalism, the institution's competences have been considerably extended by shifting the power balance away from the Council and towards the European Parliament. The first direct elections of the European Parliament allowing EU citizens to elect the Members of Parliament took place in 1979. Subsequently, the European Parliament began to draft proposals addressing the functioning of the EU, such as the Draft Treaty establishing the European Union of 1984 (Draft Treaty). Even though this draft treaty was eventually not adopted, other treaties, such as the Treaty of Maastricht of 1992 and the Treaty of Lisbon of 2007, implemented many ideas contained in the Draft Treaty and allocated more powers to the European Parliament. Today, the *European Parliament shares the EU's legislative and the budgetary authority with the Council of the European Union*.

Unlike national parliaments, the European Parliament does not have a juxtaposition between the government on the one hand and opposition groups on the other. Depending on the respective topic to be discussed, the majorities continuously change. This political independence increases the influence of each individual Member of the European Parliament (MEPs) regarding legislative processes within the EU. During the meetings of the European Parliament, all MEPs are grouped by their political affiliation.

4.7.2.2 Powers and Functions of the European Parliament

The European Parliament *represents the democratic foundation of the EU*. Being directly elected by the people, the Union thus at least partly rests on popular sovereignty and has some democratic legitimacy. The Parliament serves as one of the law-making bodies of the EU together with the Commission and the Council. The *citizens of the EU directly elect the European Parliament* for a period of 5 years (Article 14(3) TEU) making the Parliament the only directly elected institution of the EU and the only directly elected supranational organ in the world. The number of MEPs is limited to 705 in total and the number of MEPs for each Member State is proportionate to the country's population. This is limited by the stipulation that each member state can delegate at least 6 but not more than 96 MEPs to the European Parliament.

The European Parliament's work takes place in three places. The general secretariat of the European Parliament is located in Luxembourg, the meetings of the whole Parliament's plenary sessions take place in Strasbourg and Brussels, and all committee meetings are held in Brussels. The President of the European Parliament represents the institution to other institutions and the outside world. Additionally, president's signature is required for enacting most EU laws and the EU budget.

The European Parliament has *wide-ranging legislative, supervisory and budgetary responsibilities*. In the field of legislation, the European Parliament, together with the Council of the European Union, passes EU laws that are based on the European Commission's proposals and decides on the EU budget. The Parliament also *supervises the work of the Commission and other EU bodies*. Its supervisory tasks include the democratic scrutiny of all other EU institutions, the observation of elections, the assessment of petitions of EU citizens, the supervision of the European Central Bank's monetary policies, the election of the President of the European Commission and the *approval of the European Commission as a body.* With regard to budgetary issues, the European Parliament, in cooperation with the European Council, determines the EU budget and approves the "Multiannual Financial Framework", the long-term budget of the EU.

The work of the European Parliament is divided into preparing legislation and adopting it at a later stage. To carrying out this work, the European Parliament has 20 committees and two subcommittees to examine proposals of the Commission for legislation in different policy areas. The MEPs and political groups within the EU body can put forward amendments to these proposals or even propose to reject a draft bill. *What they cannot do is to propose bills* because this is the *unique power of the Commission.* The subsequent adoption of the proposed legislation and amendments (if any) takes place in the European Parliament's plenary sessions, normally held in Strasbourg 4 days a month, during which all MEPs assemble in the chamber to cast final votes.

The Parliament can also be asked by the public to act on a certain issue if it is within the EU's remit. In this regard, any citizen of an EU member state, EU resident or company based in the EU is entitled to submit a petition to the European Parliament either by mail or online.

4.7.3 European Council

4.7.3.1 Establishment of the European Council

During the 1960s, the European leaders had assembled only for ceremonial events. Their first politically significant meeting took place at the Summit of the Heads of State or Government of the Member States of the European Communities held in The Hague from 1–2 December 1969. The Hague Conference tackled a number of important issues such as the creation of an economic and monetary union, the completion of the Common Agricultural Policy and the expansion of the then EEC to include the UK and other countries.

In the following years, similar meetings took place at irregular intervals. In 1974, these events finally led to the establishment of the European Council. Initially, the European Council was founded as an informal forum bringing together the Heads of State or Government of all member states. In 1992, the institution's status changed to "formal forum" and in 2009, the European Council became an official institution of the EU. Today, the meetings of the European Council include not only political leaders of the EU member states but also the President of the European Commission and the High Representative for Foreign Affairs and Security Policy.

4.7.3.2 Powers and Functions of the European Council

The European Council defines the EU's general political direction and priorities. By bringing together all leaders of the EU member states (Article 15(2) TEU), the European Council represents the *highest level of political cooperation between the member states.* The European Council is chaired by a President who is elected by the European Council for a once-renewable two-and-a-half-year term (Article 15(5) TEU). One of the President's tasks is to represent the EU to the outside world.

The European Council sets the political agenda of the EU by dealing foremost with complex and sensitive issues. It does this by, among other things, determining the EU's common foreign and security policy and nominating and appointing candidates to certain high-profile EU level roles in, for instance, the European Central Bank or the European Commission. The European Council is entitled to ask the European Commission to make a proposal on any issue it wants. In addition, it can order the Council of the European Union to deal with certain issues.

Basically, the European Council holds meetings 4 times a year in Brussels. In cases of urgency, the president of the European Council may convene additional meetings. Only the Heads of State and Government of the member states are allowed to participate in votes conducted during the meetings. The decisions of the European Council require consensus, i.e. unanimity where the EU Treaties provide, otherwise a qualified majority is sufficient (Article 15(4) TEU).

4.7.4 Council of the European Union

4.7.4.1 Establishment of the Council of the European Union

Like the European Parliament, the Council of the European Union was set up in the early 1950s. The forerunner of today's Council of the European Union was the Special Council provided for in the 1951 Treaty of Paris. Although it was established to exercise control over the High Authority's activities by issuing opinions, in the early years the Special Council's tasks were limited to informing the High Authority.

The structures of the EEC and EAEC also provided for a Council. Despite the same name, the new Councils were given more powers than the ECSC Special Council. The EEC Council's task was to *"ensure the co-ordination of the general economic policies of the Member States and to dispose a power of decisions"* (Article 145 EEC Treaty) while the EAEC Council was empowered to *"take all measures within its competence in order to co-ordinate the actions of member states and of the Community"* (Article 115 EAEC Treaty).

The subsequent signing of the Brussels Treaty to merge the communities' executives established a single Council, the Council of the European Communities, to replace the Special Council of the ECSC and the Councils of the EEC and the EAEC. Given that each community retained its legal independence, the new Council of the European Communities continued to act according to the powers given to it by the respective founding Treaties.

The final name change took place in 1993 when the Maastricht Treaty entered into force. The Maastricht Treaty, best known for establishing the EU, limited the powers of the European Commission, the European Parliament and the Court of Justice of the European Union, and authorized the Council of the European Union make decisions jointly with the European Parliament.

4.7.4.2 Powers and Functions of the Council of the European Union

The Council of the European Union, together with the European Parliament, *exercises legislative powers within the EU* (Article 16(1) TEU). *Composed of ministers from the EU member states*, the Council of the European Union is often referred to as the Council of Ministers. Its presidency changes between the EU member states on a six-month rotating basis.

The Council of the European Union has several tasks. Amongst its tasks are the adoption of EU law based on proposals from the European Commission, the coordination of policies of the EU member states and the development of the EU's foreign and security policy; the latter is based on guidelines developed by the European Council. Furthermore, the Council of the European Union concludes agreements between the EU and other states or international organizations and also drafts the EU's annual budget.

Unlike the European Parliament or the European Council, the Council of the European Union does not have fixed members. Depending on the policy area being discussed, the ministers responsible for a certain area meet in *ten different council configurations*, such as the Economic and Financial Council or the Agriculture and Fisheries Council. Council meetings take place in Brussels and Luxembourg, and most meetings are convened throughout the year, albeit irregularly. The General Affairs Council, the Foreign Affairs Council and the Council on Economic and Financial Affairs meet once a month.

In order to maintain consistency within the ten different council configurations, the General Affairs Council co-ordinates the work of the Council of the European Union, prepares for European Council meetings and deals with issues that cannot be assigned to only one special council formation.[56] In carrying out these tasks, the General Affairs Council is supported by the Permanent Representatives Committee which is composed of national ambassadors.

During the public meetings, the ministers, previously authorized by their government, discuss, amend and adopt laws, and coordinate policies. Their decisions require a qualified majority. 55% of member states, representing at least 65% of the EU population is needed, and actions can be blocked by at least four member states.

[56] Such as issues that for example can be assigned to both the Economic and Financial Council and the Agricultural Council.

There are, however, some exceptions with regard to sensitive topics like foreign policy and taxation, which would then need a unanimous vote. For procedural and administrative issues, however, only a simple majority is sufficient to reach a decision. The meetings are generally chaired by the minister of the country that currently holds the rotating presidency. The Foreign Affairs Council is permanently chaired by the EU High Representative for Foreign Affairs and Security Policy.

4.7.5 European Commission

4.7.5.1 Establishment of the European Commission

The European Commission's origin can be traced back to the High Authority of the European Coal and Steel Community consisting of nine members one from each of the ECAC's six member states, though Germany, France and Italy were given an extra member due to their relatively larger populations. Decisions were made with a simple majority of votes, and the High Authority appointed its own presidents. Jean Monnet, the first President and spiritual father of the Schuman Declaration, designed the High Authority as an independent supranational executive body equipped with significant independent powers to regulate the market for coal and steel. However, because the governments of the ECSC member states feared a great loss of their sovereignty, Monnet's plans were not fully implemented. The High Authority's tasks were mostly limited to the general oversight of the ECSC and the Community's functioning. Eventually, the institution became more bureaucratic than was originally planned.

The institutional structure of the EEC and the EAEC, established some years after the ECSC, was similar to that of the ECSC. In addition to the High Authority, two similar bodies were founded in 1958, namely the EEC Commission, which also had nine members, and the EAEC Commission consisting of only five members. The new commissions' tasks set out in the Treaty of Rome consisted of three basic functions: proposing new policies, overseeing the implementation of policies, and representing the EEC and EAEC community in external trade negotiations.

The 1960s were marked by conflicts over the amount of influence the EEC Commission would have on further European integration development. The French President, Charles de Gaulle, wanted the EEC Commission to be subordinated entirely to the EEC Council of Ministers. Walter Hallstein, president of the EEC Commission, sought to keep the Commission independent of the annual renewal of member states' contributions by introducing financial resources. Ultimately, both plans failed, and the EEC Commission's competencies were slightly reduced in the 1966 Luxembourg Compromise that settled the EEC's dispute in the agricultural policy and other policies.[57] In 1967, following the merger of the three communities, the High Authority, the EEC Commission and the EAEC Commission were replaced by the Commission of the European Communities. By taking up all functions and powers of the three institutions, the new Commission was now responsible for all policies of the European Communities.

In the following years, the Commission gradually lost its influence over the integration process and turned into an executive body. It was only when the SEA was adopted in 1986 that the Commission's areas of responsibility expanded slightly. Since the entry into force of the Maastricht Treaty on 1 November 1993, the Commission of the European Communities was renamed the European Commission, though the name change was not accompanied with more powers.

The EU Treaty reforms finalized in Amsterdam (1997) and Nice (2001) reorganized the Commission's composition and internal functioning. Subsequently, in order to maintain the Commission's effectiveness, a reduction in terms of the size of the Commission was discussed for the first time. Additionally, the powers of the president of the Commission were increased by among others authorizing him or her to decide as to the internal organization of the Commission, to allocate portfolios to the Commissioners and if necessary, reassign responsibilities during his term of office (Article 217 Treaty of Nice).

The Lisbon Treaty of 2009 brought about various changes for the European Commission. Among other things, the offices of the Committee on External Affairs and the High Representative for the Common Foreign and Security Policy (CFSP) were merged. This led to a better linkage between the Commission and the Council in the field of the CFSP, and the Commission was given more policy areas to act in.

4.7.5.2 Powers and Functions of the European Commission

The European Commission, also described as *the only body paid to think European*, exercises the powers conferred on it by Article 17 TEU. The institution is the *politically independent executive arm of the EU and promotes the general interest of the EU*. The European Commission is thus *like the government in a state system*. Its number of members corresponds to the number of member states.

The European Commission is the only institution tabling laws for adoption by both the European Parliament and the Council of the European Union. In this regard, the European Commission prepares proposals for new EU legislation on issues that cannot be dealt with effectively at the national level and also arbitrates in the legislative process. In addition, the European Commission, together with the Court of Justice of the European Union, ensures the enforcement of EU law, manages EU

---

[57] The Luxembourg Compromise gave a de facto veto power to every member state on topics that were a very important national interest. In such a case, the Council would seek to find a solution that all members could unanimously agree upon, regardless of whether the treaty required only a majority.

policies, and allocates as well as supervises the supranational organization's funding. The institution also represents the EU internationally by negotiating international agreements and participating in international bodies.

The Commission is currently composed of 27 Commissioners. This college of Commissioners includes the president of the Commission, his or her eight vice-presidents who act on the president's behalf and coordinate the work in their area of responsibility, and 18 further Commissioners. The latter are in charge of their specific portfolios that support the vice-presidents by submitting proposals to the College.

The Commissioners take charge of the institution's political direction for a period of 5 years, which corresponds to the five-year legislative period of the European Parliament. During their term of office, the Commissioners are not allowed to pursue any other professional activity. In addition, *governments must respect the Commissioner's independence* and must not attempt to influence them. The chair president is proposed by the European Council and elected by a majority of the MEPs. The president selects potential Commissioners based on suggestions from the EU countries, which later have to be approved by the European Council. The president also determines the distribution of the policy areas and selects potential vice-presidents. One of the vice presidents acts as the EU High Representative for Foreign Affairs and Security Policy and as Chairman of the Council on Foreign Affairs simultaneously, and thus assumes a dual function between the Commission and the Council of the European Union. In order to carry out its functions, *the whole European Commission needs to be approved by the European Parliament.*

Decisions within the European Commission are made based on collective responsibility, and all Commissioners have equal voting rights in the decision-making process. None of the Commissioners has any individual decision-making powers, except when authorized in certain situations. In general, *decisions within the European Commission are made by consensus.* In exceptional cases, decisions (votes) can also made by a simple majority.

4.7.6 Court of Justice of the European Union

4.7.6.1 Establishment of the European Court of Justice

The Court of Justice of the European Union (CJEU) was established in 1952 as part of the ECSC. Following the Treaty of Paris, the Court's mission was to ensure that *"in the interpretation and application of this treaty and of rules laid down for the interpretation thereof, the law is observed".*[58] Initially, the CJEU's jurisdiction was limited to disputes within ECSC treaties. Following the establishment of the EEC and the EAEC in 1958, the Court's area of competence expanded to all disputes

[58] Art. 31 of the Treaty establishing the European Coal and Steel Community (1951).

linked to the relevant treaties. Since 1989, the CJEU is considered to be one of the EU's main institutions.

4.7.6.2 Powers and Functions of the Court of Justice of the European Union

Apart from being an economic union, *the EU is also a legal union. The CJEU represents the rule of law*, one of the EU's paramount principles, and is responsible for the principle's utilization and enforcement. The Court is composed of one judge per member state and 11 advocates general (Article 19(2) TEU). All judges are appointed by the governments of the member states for a renewable term of 6 years by common accord after consultation with a panel responsible for giving an opinion on prospective candidates' suitability (Article 255 TFEU) and *enjoy full independence in their work.*

Serving as the highest authority in the European legal system,[59] the CJEU interprets EU law and settles legal disputes between national governments and EU institutions as well as between EU organs and between individuals and member states as to the proper application of EU law. It is functionally to a large extent *equivalent to a constitutional court.* As a general rule, however, only EU member states, the EU institutions and national courts can refer cases to the CJEU. In exceptional cases, however, individuals, companies or organizations are also allowed to take action against an EU institution for an alleged rights infringement. This is the case for appeals to the CJEU regarding decisions taken by the EU institutions in the field of competition, Community grants, contracts with EU institutions or the European public service.

The CJEU rules on cases brought before it. The institution's main activities include interpreting the law (*preliminary rulings*), enforcing the law (*infringement procedures*), annulling EU legal acts (*actions for annulment*), ensuring that the EU acts in appropriate cases (*actions for failure to act*) and sanctioning EU institutions (*actions for damages*).

The CJEU is divided into two courts, the *Court of Justice* and the *General Court* (Article 19(1) TEU). The Court of Justice, the highest court, deals with requests for preliminary rulings from national courts, certain actions for annulment, and appeals. The General Court rules on actions for annulment brought by individuals, companies and, in some cases, EU governments. Additionally, between 2005 and 2016 the European Union Civil Service Tribunal dealt with labour disputes between EU civil servants and the EU as their employer. The Civil Service Tribunal ceased to exist on 1 September 2016. All pending cases have been handed over to the General Court.

CJEU cases are assigned to one judge and one advocate general and are processed in two stages, one written and one oral. Proceedings begin with parties submitting written statements to the Court. The judge-rapporteur summarizes the statements that

[59] In matters of Union law, but not national law.

are later discussed at the Court's general meeting. The Court then decides on how many judges to assign to the case, whether a hearing needs to be held and whether an official opinion from the advocate general is required by law. The oral stage of proceedings consists of a public hearing, during which lawyers from both sides put their case to the judges and advocate general, who questions them. The advocate-general's duty is, *"with complete impartiality and independence, to make, in open court, reasoned submissions on cases"*.[60] With their submissions, the advocate-generals propose a solution and provide logical legal reasoning to reach the conclusion presented and help prepare the case for the Court of Justice. Their opinions contain research on the existing case law as well as on the legal points presented in Court.

4.7.7 European Central Bank

4.7.7.1 Establishment of the European Central Bank

The European Central Bank (ECB) was established in 1998, and it is the de facto successor of the European Monetary Institute (EMI). The EMI operated between 1994 and 1997 and served as the key monetary institution of the second phase of the Economic and Monetary Union of the EU by encouraging cooperation between the member states' national banks.

Although the scope of the ECB's work and expertise was already set out in the 1992 Treaty of Maastricht, the institution did not exercise its full powers until the euro was introduced on 1 January 1999. When the Treaty of Lisbon entered into force in 2007, the ECB formally received the status of one of the major EU institutions with independent powers.

4.7.7.2 Powers and Functions of the European Central Bank

The ECB's tasks as central bank are manifold and correspond largely to the *tasks of national central banks*. One of the main principles it rests on is its independence from the other EU institutions and from the member states.

The ECB sets the interest rates for lending money to commercial banks in the euro zone, controls money supply and inflation, manages the euro zone's foreign currency reserves, and the buying or selling of currencies to regulate exchange rates. It ensures that national authorities have adequate oversight over financial markets and institutions. It also ensures the proper functioning of payment systems and guarantees the safety and soundness of the European banking system. In addition, the ECB authorizes the production of Euro banknotes by euro zone countries,

[60] Art. 252(2) TFEU.

monitors price trends and assesses risks to price stability. The ECB plays a central role in times of economic turmoil such as in the Greek government debt crisis starting 2009 which became a European debt crisis, or during the Corona pandemic.

The *main operative organ of the ECB is the Executive Board* which monitors the institution's daily operations and is responsible for the implementation of monetary policies. The Executive Board consists of the President, the vice-president and four other members. They are all appointed by the European Council for non-renewable terms of 8 years. The president represents the ECB at high-level meetings in the EU, as well as internationally. The Governing Council is the main decision-making body of the Euro system. It encompasses the members of the executive board and the governors of the national central banks of the euro member countries. Its responsibilities include the definition of the monetary policies and key interest rates.

4.7.8 European Court of Auditors

4.7.8.1 Establishment of the European Court of Auditors

The creation of the European Court of Auditors (ECA) dates back to the 1975 Treaty of Brussels; it was formally established on 18 October 1977. In its early years, the ECA was not a formal institution but an external body designed to audit the finances and other financial matters of the European Communities. Subsequently, after it was formally established, the ECA replaced two separate institutions, namely the auditing bodies of the EEC and Euratom.

The 1992 Maastricht Treaty established the ECA's legal status. By becoming the fifth institution of the EU, the ECA gained new powers such as the ability to bring actions before the CJEU. With the entry into force of the Treaty of Amsterdam in 1997, the ECA gained the full power to audit the EU's entire finances.

4.7.8.2 Powers and Functions of the European Court of Auditors

The members of the ECA are appointed by the Council of the European Union upon consultation with the European Parliament. To date, the ECA consists of 27 members, one from each member state. All ECA members are chosen for a period of 6 years which can be extended. One of the ECA's members serves as president with a three-year term, which can also be extended. The ECA has independence from the institutions and bodies that it audits. It decides independently what to examine, how this examination is carried out and how or when to present the examination results. It is divided into several chambers, and these chambers submit reports and opinions to the members of the ECA for adoption before they become official.

Despite its name, the ECA has no judicial functions. The institution represents the interests of European taxpayers by monitoring the proper collection and use of EU funds and by improving the EU's financial management. *The ECA serves as an independent external auditor of the EU* but cannot initiate any legal action itself. Instead, it is committed to improving the management of the EU's budget and reports on the financial situation in general.

The ECA has several tasks and functions. It examines the EU's revenue and expenditure, reviews persons or organizations managing EU funds and produces test reports with results and recommendations for the European Commission and national governments. In this regard, there are three types of audits: accounting audits, conformity audits and performance audits. The ECA reports to the European Anti-Fraud Office on alleged fraud, corruption or other illegal activities committed by persons or organizations managing EU funds, prepares an annual report for the European Parliament and the Council of the European Union which the Parliament examines before approving the manner in which the budget is used by the Commission. The ECA also publishes preparatory acts on the financial management of the EU, position papers, surveys and other ad-hoc publications on financial issues.

4.8 Law-Making in the European Union

4.8.1 Sources of European Union Law

The EU has *its own legal order*. The EU is not only an economic and a political union, but also *a legal union*. Once a country becomes an EU member state, *EU law becomes part of its legal system*. The is a hierarchy of three sources of EU law: primary legislation, secondary legislation, and supplementary law. The distinction between primary and secondary legislation coincides with the general distinction between primary and secondary law in the law of international organizations.[61]

4.8.1.1 Primary Legislation

Primary legislation, also known as the primary source of law, is the most important source of EU law. It mainly comprises of the *founding treaties of the EU, namely the TEU, the TFEU, and the Charter of Fundamental Rights of the European Union (CFREU), but also includes the amending EU treaties*, the protocols annexed to founding Treaties amending Treaties, and the Treaties of Accession of new member states to the EU.

A special case are international agreements concluded by the EU. According to the case-law of the CJEU, international law takes precedence over (secondary) EU law: *'It should also be pointed out that, by virtue of Article 216(2) TFEU, where international agreements are concluded by the European Union they are binding upon its institutions and, consequently, they prevail over acts of the*

[61] See supra, Sect. 1.10.2.

European Union."[62] Thus, these agreements rank hierarchically between primary and secondary legislation.

4.8.1.2 Secondary Legislation

Law that stems from the principles, objectives and provisions of the founding treaties is labelled secondary law. The EU's secondary legislation consists of (quasi-) legislative acts and agreements. (Quasi-)Legislative acts can be divided into two groups: those listed in Article 288 TFEU and those not listed there. The acts listed in Article 288 TFEU are regulations, directives, decisions, recommendations and opinions, thus acts of legislation in the proper sense. These acts are adopted by the European institutions on the basis of the founding treaties, following a legislative procedure. The second group includes white and green papers and also "atypical" acts such as communications and recommendations.

4.8.1.3 Supplementary Law

As extensive as they are, the EU's primary and secondary law cannot comprehensively cover all possible situations that might arise; hence, supplementary law is needed to bridge the remaining gaps. Supplementary law includes *the case law of the CJEU*, *international law (written law, customs and usage)* that the CJEU is guided by when developing its case law, and *the general principles of law*. These principles are developed in the case law of the CJEU that have allowed the Court to implement rules in different domains not mentioned within the treaties.

4.9 Acts of the European Union

For achieving the aims of the EU, various legislation tools with different binding effects are available. Dealing with the legal acts of the EU Article 288 TFEU reads as follows:

> ***"Article 288 TFEU (ex Article 249 TEC)***
> *To exercise the Union's competences, the institutions shall adopt regulations, directives, decisions, recommendations and opinions.*
>
> *A regulation shall have general application. It shall be binding in its entirety and directly applicable in all Member States.*

---

[62] CJEU, *Air Transport Association of America and Others v Secretary of State for Energy and Climate Change* (Judgment) [2011] C-366/10, para. 50 (ECLI:EU:C:2011:864).

A directive shall be binding, as to the result to be achieved, upon each Member State to which it is addressed, but shall leave to the national authorities the choice of form and methods.

A decision shall be binding in its entirety. A decision which specifies those to whom it is addressed shall be binding only on them.

Recommendations and opinions shall have no binding force."

Accordingly, the European legislature distinguishes between regulations, directives, decisions, recommendations and opinions.

4.9.1 European Union Regulations

EU Regulations are, together with directives, the most important ways to enact EU law. They are *binding legislative acts that must be applied in its entirety across the whole EU by all the member state institutions* from the date of its entry into force.[63] EU Regulations *create rights and obligations for individuals* and can be based on by individuals in their relationship with other individuals, EU countries or EU authorities. Thus, their legal effect is *comparable to the legal effect of provisions of national law*. They are simultaneously, automatically and uniformly binding in the national legislation of all Member States. They *override all national laws dealing with the same subject matter*, and all subsequent national legislation must be consistent with and made in light of the respective EU Regulation. Accordingly, a great deal of care is required in drafting and formulating every EU Regulation.

4.9.2 European Union Directives

The EU Directive is a flexible *instrument used mainly to harmonize national laws*. EU Directives *set out a goal for EU member states to achieve by giving national authorities the choice of form and methods*. The measures that member states adopt must achieve the objectives set by the EU Directive. Unlike EU Regulations that are directly applicable to and within all EU member states like national law immediately after their entry into force, *EU Directives require domestic implementation* before individuals, businesses or governments can rely on them. In general, implementation must take place within 2 years; otherwise, the European Commission may initiate infringements proceedings, followed by proceedings against the defaulting member state before the CJEU.

[63] For more details see <http://eur-lex.europa.eu/legal-content/EN/TXT/?uri=URISERV%3Al14522> (accessed 9 March 2025).

Even though directives only take effect once they are implemented domestically, the *CJEU has developed a case law that a directive that is not implemented can have certain effects, too*. Provided that (i) the EU Directive's implementation into national law has not taken place or has been done incorrectly, (ii) the provisions of the respective EU Directive are unconditional and sufficiently clear and precise and (iii) the provisions of the directive give rights to individuals, individuals may rely on the EU Directive against an EU member state in court.[64]

4.9.3 European Union Decisions

EU Decisions are binding in its entirety and cannot be applied selectively or partially. They may be of general application but may also be specifically targeted at one or more addressees such as EU Member States, companies or even individuals. All EU decisions are binding on those to whom they are addressed.

4.9.4 Recommendations of the European Union

EU Recommendations are not binding on the recipients of the recommendations. Accordingly, there are no legal consequences for the recommendation's recipients if the recommendation goes ignored. By making a recommendation, EU institutions have the chance to make their views known and to suggest a line of action without imposing any legal obligations.

4.9.5 Opinions of the European Union

Opinions also allow EU institutions to make a statement without imposing any legal obligation on those to whom they are addressed. They can only be issued by certain organizations, namely the European Commission, the Council of the European Union, the European Parliament, the Committee of the Regions and the European Economic and Social Committee.

[64] CJEU, *Van Duyn v Home Office* (Judgment) (1974) C-41/74, para. 12 (ECLI:EU:C:1974:133).

4.9.6 Conflicts Between European and National Law: Primacy of EU Law

With the founding of the EU, member states have created an *independent, supranational legal system* in addition to their national legal systems. As a result of this parallelism, there may be cases of conflict between European law and national law. Hence, one fundamental principle of the supranational legal system of the EU is the *priority of application of EU law.* In cases where EU law and national law collide (including constitutional norms), *EU law regularly enjoys precedence over the member state's national law.* However, this is an application priority and not a priority with regard to validity: The national rule concerned still applies (e.g. for cases without a European connection) but cannot be relied on in cases where there is a governing EU law. EU law takes precedence over national law because EU law must be coherent, effective and autonomous in all EU member states in order to be effective, and so it has to be uniformly applied in all EU member states.

The primacy of EU law was already explained at an early stage by the CJEU and accepted in principle by the highest courts of the member states. In 1964, in the *Flaminio Costa v. E.N.E.L* decision,[65] the CJEU ruled that *"by contrast with ordinary international treaties, the EEC Treaty has created its own legal system which, on the entry into force of the treaty, became an integral part of the legal system of the member states and which their courts are bound to apply".*[66] By concluding the founding treaties, the EU member states have permanently limited their sovereign rights and created a new independent and self-sufficient legal body. If national law took precedence over EU law, the legal basis of the EU itself would be called into question. This was further confirmed by the Simmenthal II decision of the CJEU[67] where the Court stated the following:

> 21. It follows from the foregoing that every national court must, in a case within its jurisdiction, apply Community law in its entirety and protect rights which the latter confers on individuals and must accordingly set aside any provision of national law which may conflict with it, whether prior or subsequent to the Community rule.
>
> 22. Accordingly any provision of a national legal system and any legislative, administrative or judicial practice which might impair the effectiveness of Community law by withholding from the national court having jurisdiction to apply such law the power to do everything necessary at the moment of its application to set aside national legislative provisions which might prevent Community rules from having full force and effect are incompatible with those requirements which are the very essence of Community law.

The principle was further confirmed in an annex to the 2008 Treaty of Lisbon, the Declaration Concerning Primacy which restated a legal opinion of the Council Legal Service:

---

[65] CJEU, *Flaminio Costa v E.N.E.L* (Judgment) (1964) C-6/64, (ECLI:EU:C:1964:66O).

[66] Ibid., principle no. 3.

[67] CJEU, *Amministrazione delle Finanze dello Stato v Simmenthal SpA (Simmenthal II)* (Judgment) (1978) C-106/77 (ECLI:EU:C:1978:49), para. 21.

It results from the case-law of the Court of Justice that primacy of EC law is a cornerstone principle of Community law. According to the Court, this principle is inherent to the specific nature of the European Community. At the time of the first judgment of this established case law (Costa/ENEL, 15 July 1964, Case 6/641 [1] there was no mention of primacy in the treaty. It is still the case today. The fact that the principle of primacy will not be included in the future treaty shall not in any way change the existence of the principle and the existing case-law of the Court of Justice.

[1] It follows (…) that the law stemming from the treaty, an independent source of law, could not, because of its special and original nature, be overridden by domestic legal provisions, however framed, without being deprived of its character as Community law and without the legal basis of the Community itself being called into question.[68]

References

Crossley P et al (2017) Brexit: Time is of the essence. https://www.lexology.com/library/detail.aspx?g=49262904-2f23-425f-bb80-477b17f43466. Accessed 9 Mar 2025

European Commission (2023) Commission Staff Working Document: Türkiye 2023 Report. SWD (2023) 696 final, 8 Nov 2023. https://neighbourhood-enlargement.ec.europa.eu/system/files/2023-11/SWD_2023_696%20T%C3%BCrkiye%20report.pdf. Accessed 9 Mar 2025

Schermers HG, Blokker NM (2018) International institutional law, 6th edn. Brill Nijhoff, Boston/Leiden

[68] *Consolidated version of the Treaty on the Functioning of the European Union* - Declarations annexed to the Final Act of the Intergovernmental Conference which adopted the Treaty of Lisbon, signed on 13 Dec 2007 - A. Declarations Concerning Provisions of the Treaties, 17. Declaration concerning primacy (2008) OJ C115/344.

Chapter 5
Global Economic Organizations: WTO and the Institutions of Bretton Woods

5.1 Introduction; The Underpinnings of World Trade Rules

5.1.1 Background

5.1.1.1 Preliminary Remark

The World Trade Organization (WTO) deals with *world trade law and policies*. Together with the institutions of Bretton Woods, it plays a pivotal role in the steering of the world economy. As an institution, it was established in 1994 as the result of several years of multilateral negotiations. Before being brought to life, the General Agreement on Tariffs and Trade (GATT), a multilateral treaty adopted in 1949, was the main normative framework structuring trade negotiations and establishing basic trade law rules. *"The World Trade Organization (WTO) deals with the global rules of trade between nations. Its main function is to ensure that trade flows as smoothly, predictably, and freely as possible."*[1] As an organization, it provides the *common institutional framework* to discuss and develop global trade policies and to establish a common normative framework.[2] Its agreements form the legal basis and are a *quasi-constitution of international trade*.

Special thanks to Dominic Staiger and Steven Rüttimann for their important contribution to the elaboration of this chapter.

[1] <https://www.wto.org/english/thewto_e/thewto_e.htm> (accessed 9 March 2025).

[2] Cf. Art. II WTO Agreement: "(1) The WTO shall provide the common institutional framework for the conduct of trade relations among its Members in matters related to the agreements and associated legal instruments included in the Annexes to this Agreement."

U. Saxer, *The Law of Global and European Organizations*, Springer Textbooks in Law, https://doi.org/10.1007/978-3-032-00067-5_5

5.1.1.2 General Principles Regulating Economic Relations Between States: State Sovereignty Vs. Free Trade

The important role of the WTO is better understood against the background of general international law principles regulating economic relations between states. Historically, the economy of a country was an area in which state sovereignty played a pivotal role: Nation states valued their economies very highly and therefore would only rarely allow any incursion that would have weakened their freedom of action. Thus, for many centuries, *economy and trade were an area of nearly unhampered state sovereignty*. This was the main reason why almost no international trade rules developed. General international law did not, and still does not, require states to enter into economic relations, and there were only a very limited number of applicable rules and principles. States were free to introduce high tariffs or even import bans on certain goods as well as introduce other trade restrictions to protect their own economy. Clear international legal principles have been established only for cases of expropriation. According to these principles, a state must fully compensate the foreign subject who is forced to transfer assets, rights or titles to that state. Otherwise, countries were generally free to choose when and how to enter into economic relations with other states.

A concept opposed to this sovereignty-oriented approach is *the concept of free trade* which originated not as a legal concept, but as an *idea of political economy* developed at the end of the 18th and at the beginning of the nineteenth century. As a legal concept, it started to have an effect much later, after World War II, following the experience gained during the economic depression in the 1930s. Restrictive economic policies and currency devaluation caused by unilateral acts of many states had led to devastating deteriorating effects on the world economy and caused high unemployment in diverse countries. They were also responsible for social and political unrest in most parts of Europe, which fueled the rise of the Nazi and fascist movements. One of the main defects manifested itself in states overprotecting their economy against other economies by increasing import taxes and export restrictions. Such actions led not to an increase, but rather to a loss in wealth; in the very end, all states found themselves on the losing side because of a *spiral of unilateral trade restrictions designed to protect their domestic economies*.

5.1.1.3 After WW II: Establishment of GATT, IMF and World Bank; World Trade Liberalization

One response to this was the adoption of the GATT, which aimed at liberalizing world trade in goods as well as limiting trade barriers. The other response was the establishment of the Bretton Woods Institutions: The International Monetary Fund (IMF) and the World Bank. The IMF was created with the goal of establishing a stable worldwide currency system based on fixed exchange rates. Furthermore, the World Bank took on a very important role after WW II in supporting the economic reconstruction in countries affected by the war. Essentially, it was understood that a *liberalization of world trade and a stable currency exchange formed the two central pillars of a functioning world trade.* This was later supplemented by international arrangements protecting foreign investments.

However, the international political climate after World War II was not generally in favor of establishing binding international rules regulating the global economy as a free market economy. On the contrary, for decades there were strong divergences between national economic systems, and these divergences were an impediment to the establishment of common international trade rules, such as rules on free trade. Economic understandings pointed in two very different directions. On the one side stood the market-oriented Western world, and on the other the socialist and third world countries with a state-dominated economy and a very small private sector. This had an impact on the development of these organizations. Various states, especially communist ones, were not members or contracting parties for a long time,[3] and Third World states pressed for their particular concerns to be considered. With the end of communism, the membership base broadened greatly, and the idea of liberalizing the world economy became more prevalent.

Today, what have been tackled are not only the liberalization of world trade in goods but also of services and other aspects of international trade. It seems sometimes that the ideology and function behind the regulation of the international economy shares some traits with European (economic) integration; the process of liberalization shows a certain coerciveness in the sense that sectorial economic regulations tend to have an impact on neighboring economic sectors. From that there is often a call for further regulation of increasingly remote areas. For instance, internationally regulating pharmaceutical goods may have an impact on national public health policies because otherwise states could be tempted to erect trade barriers disguised as legal health requirements against the importation of pharmaceutical products. There is thus a need for internationally agreed principles on public health issues to secure importers' equal access to national markets. *Thus, attempts to regulate international trade are often accompanied by pressure to harmonize rules to secure the desired outcome of trade rules.* If the goal is to establish binding international rules for a global economy, it becomes unavoidable to regulate ever more sectors of the global economy, including investments, the free flow of capital and persons, and antitrust issues. The idea of functional integration thus also plays a role here, albeit less pronounced than in the process of European integration.

5.1.1.4 The Role of the IMF and of the World Bank

The WTO does not deal with issues outside of world trade regulation. However, it aims at creating a world trade order that functions according to established market principles. In doing so, *the WTO is supplemented by the Bretton Woods institutions.*

[3] In 1947, there were only 23 contracting states of GATT.

In 1944 the IMF and the International Bank for Reconstruction and Development (IBRD; also known as the World Bank) were launched at the *United Nations Monetary and Financial Conference* in Bretton Woods, New Hampshire, USA. The general idea of the conference was *to create an institutional basis for world trade* and, in this regard, to protect future generations from political and financial crises and to prevent further wars. The Bretton Woods Conference was attended by ministers of the 44 allied nations and had two major goals. The first and foremost goal was the fixing of exchange rates and stabilization of their conditions through the IMF to prevent currency fluctuations arising from balance of payments disparities. As the fixed currency exchange system was given up in the 70s, the IMF began focusing on finding solutions to the international deficit crises and supporting member states in dire financial need. The IMF therefore supports its member states in cases of payment balance deficits and thus secures international liquidity. The IMF's mission can be described as *the proactive coordination of balance of payments policies and the maintenance of a stabile monetary system* by creating a kind of insurance pool to which every member state is obligated to contribute funds. This insurance pool of funds is to be used as a backup if the system is about to fail. The idea was that no state should be able to gain advantages through its own regulations of foreign trade, and that free trade can only work smoothly if all states work together and play by the same rules. The states attending the Bretton Woods Conference also agreed on taking broad international action to promote foreign trade.[4] Additionally, nations should consult with each other and agree on international monetary changes which would affect them all.[5]

The second goal was to be accomplished with the help of the IBRD, which was tasked with *the objective of investing in development projects that foster reconstruction and development*. International investments were to be promoted, and special attention was to be given to states that suffered enemy occupation.[6] The World Bank Group nowadays plays a central role in the economic support (financial and knowhow) of developing countries. The Bretton Woods institutions are supplemented by the International Center for Settlement of Investment Disputes (ICSID) and the Multilateral Investment Guarantee Agency (MIGA) which both form safety mechanisms for international investments.

[4] *Final Act of the United Nations Monetary and Financial Conference*, Bretton Woods (1944), Annex C Sec. I.

[5] Ibid.

[6] *Final Act of the United Nations Monetary and Financial Conference*, Bretton Woods (1944), Annex C Sec. I., Sec. V.

5.2 The World Trade Organization (WTO)

5.2.1 Origin of the WTO: The Failed International Trade Organization (ITO); the GATT

As shortly explained, after both World Wars and the Great Depression the Western world felt the need for an institution governing the international economy to recover and regain economic health. Leading up to World War II, many states followed protectionist fiscal policies by setting up trade barriers to protect the domestic economy. Therefore, interstate trade got severely hampered. During the Second World War, national economies often served war-related purposes, and international trade was disrupted because of the many military conflicts worldwide.

During the Bretton Woods Conference, plans for the introduction of a third large institution, the International Trade Organization (ITO), were discussed, due to the need for an institution to address trade issues. Discussions about the ITO and its necessity were taken up again during the 1948 Conference on Trade and Employment in Havana, Cuba. The conference resulted in a draft agreement and the specification of the ITO's missions, which included the promotion of full employment and the development of international trade. However, due to the USA's refusal to ratify the agreement establishing the ITO,[7] the organization could not come into being. The USA did not approve the ITO charter because they objected to an international monitoring of national protectionist measures as provided for in the new institutional framework of the ITO. The US Congress did not even put the agreement to a vote as a rejection would have been certain.[8] Thus, while advocating the liberalization of international trade, the USA ironically strengthened their own protectionism and rejected the implementation of the ITO.

Founding an international trade organization without the USA—the globally dominating economic superpower—would not have made any sense at that time. Nonetheless, some efforts that were put into structuring the ITO were later utilized when the General Agreement on Tariffs and Trade (GATT) was adopted. At that time, there was a common understanding that, to decrease tariffs as quickly as possible, having a framework even before the Havana Charter came into force was pivotal. Therefore, Chapter IV of the ITO Charter *which regulated the trade of goods*, was adopted and introduced as a separate agreement, i.e. the GATT, in October 1947, coming into effect on 1 January 1948. The GATT was an international treaty and not an international organization and remained the only instrument regulating international commerce until the establishment of the WTO in 1995. It was for decades applied on the basis of a protocol on its provisional application, thus

[7] Zeiler (1999), p. 113.

[8] The US refusal is due to a constitutional specialty. On the one hand, the US congress—the legislative authority of the USA—holds the competency of promotion and regulation of commerce under US constitutional law. On the other hand, the executive authority—the president—holds the competency over foreign policy. This leads to a major trade-off regarding international trade law.

based on a temporary international agreement.[9] The GATT, as a simple agreement provisionally applied, became then an international forum for multilateral trade negotiations as the GATT's contracting parties discussed world trade regulation over various multilateral conferences (so called World Trade Rounds) until GATT was replaced by the WTO as an international organization. The original GATT text continues to be in force in a slightly adapted form as one of the main WTO agreements.

5.2.2 Protectionist State Measures and the Impact of Free Trade

5.2.2.1 Basic Principles of Free Trade Among States

GATT and WTO are based on *the concept of an internationally regulated free trade*. Free trade encompasses not only free exchange of goods as regulated by the GATT, but also trade in services, capital and other commodities. The—sometimes contested—general idea behind this is that *comprehensive free trade leads to so-called comparative advantages among the trade parties and thus create a win-win situation for all the states involved and their economies.*

The concept of comparative advantages was first developed by classical economist Adam Smith in 1776,[10] and later refined by economist David Ricardo in 1817.[11] The rule of comparative advantage says that two countries will both gain from trade if, in the absence of trade, they have different relative costs for producing the same goods. Accordingly, the theory postulates that goods and services should be produced where this can naturally happen in the most efficient way. Therefore, a trade party producing higher volumes of a certain good or a certain service usually has a comparative economic advantage over other countries. An *international division of labor* would eventually result, thus working towards the goal of gaining overall socio-economic wealth for all participating parties. In contrast, *protectionism isolates a country's economy against foreign competition and leads to efficiency losses* and thus to a reduction in socio-economic wealth. States which have a surplus production in certain goods should be able to export them to other states. Simultaneously, in areas where a state cannot fulfill the needs of its population through its own production of goods or services, imports should be made possible under suitably attractive conditions.

Based on this reasoning, free trade is not simply a zero-sum game as it results in advantages for all parties involved and regularly improves overall efficiency, thus

[9] As part of the Havana Charter, the GATT would have needed parliamentary approval, but not necessarily as a protocol regulating the GATT's provisional application.

[10] Smith (1904), p. 13.

[11] Ricardo (1821), chapter 7.

creating ideally economic win-win situations. However, in reality states have often preferred protectionist measures to promote short-term goals of domestic policies than to follow the principles of free trade.

5.2.2.2 Protectionist State Measures: An Overview

Over time, states have developed considerable imagination in developing a variety of protectionist measures, the most important being: tariffs; non-tariff barriers; subsidies; and dumping.

a) Import and Export Tariffs

Tariffs, i.e. a special duty levied at the border on imports of goods or services, have been the most popular protectionist measures. They are usually *designed to protect certain sectors of the domestic economy*. What are the effects of import tariffs on domestic consumers and producers? Because of a regulation-induced price increase, consumers and buyers will end up paying the import duty as they will not be able to buy the product at the non-tariffed price, or they will, if available, *switch to cheaper domestic alternatives*. This also affects the decision-making of the local producers. Behind these protective barriers, they have no incentive to innovate as they do not face serious competition.

However, such protectionist measures are very short-sighted. Tariffs can lead to *price increases and thus to higher costs, as well as fueling inflation*, which adversely affects disposable incomes. In a global economy characterized by the division of labor and global supply chains, e.g. the production and processing costs in the country levying the tariffs can also increase if they are levied on imported components. Moreover, once a state imposes tariffs on the import of goods or services, the exporting state will consider retaliating by also imposing tariffs on goods or services that the first country exports.[12] Absent any specific agreements between the states, such action is generally permissible under international law but will invariably result in goods from State A being hard or impossible to sell in State B. Ultimately, State A will experience a loss in wealth; and the same applies to State B in which the products can only be bought at a higher price. This was exactly what happened during the Great Depression before WW II. Under the umbrella of the WTO, the GATT aims exactly at avoiding such situations. The access to goods should be as easy and unencumbered as possible.

Export tariffs have different effects. They are basically imposed on rare goods and services of general importance to secure domestic availability and to avoid situation of domestic scarcity.

[12] This happened, e.g., when US President Trump decided in February/March 2025 to levy tariffs on products from Canada, Mexico and China. These countries immediately responded with tariffs on US products.

b) Non-tariff Barriers; State Monopolies

International trade can be encumbered not just by tariffs but also by non-tariff barriers. These *non-tariff barriers can be found in laws, judicial regulations or administrative practices of states*. They have, despite not imposing tariffs, a restrictive effect on international trade. *Import quotas* are one type of such non-tariff restrictions. Under import quotas only certain volumes of a good can be imported into a country. This regime is mostly ancillary to a requirement of approval for the import of the goods. States tend to utilize this mechanism when they are prohibited from imposing tariffs because of international agreements.

Another non-tariff restriction commonly used by governments is the *monopolization of the importation and distribution of a product*. For example, Sweden, before it became member of the European Union, monopolized the import and sale of alcoholic beverages.[13] A variety of reasons can justify a monopoly like the Swedish alcohol one, such as the protection of citizens' health, or fiscal reasons. Once such a monopoly exists, the state has full control over the determination of the amount to be imported.

There are many ways to implement non-tariff trade restrictions. An example is a regulation requiring state authority approval of foreign goods as well as laws relating to advertisement or packaging. For example, imports could be restricted by requiring a certain manufacturing process which essentially is only used by the country into which the goods are to be imported. A state could also require the production of a good or service to take place according to the country's domestic laws. The USA, for example, required that any tuna fish needs to be caught according to US law without endangering dolphins pursuant to a US law protecting marine life.[14]

Of course, there most certainly are *legitimate policy considerations behind regulations having a restrictive effect on international trade*, such as health, social, cultural or environmental policy considerations. The question is: how far may states go in restricting international trade when deciding on measures to implement certain policy goals? When are such goals a *simple pretext for illicit protectionist measures*? A seemingly non-trade political reason can be utilized to achieve an essentially trade-related goal, namely, to serve a protectionist purpose. This shows that the concept of free trade ultimately may limit the authority of a state to pass laws for the protection of, for instance, consumers or the environment to a far greater extent than it first appears. Generally, *under international free trade rules states must waive some of their sovereign rights* such as to impose tariffs, to impose a ban on the importation or on the exportation of certain goods, services and capital, to impose special taxes or to impose other, non-tariff barriers to trade to make free trade possible and to avoid any distortions in international trade.

---

[13] Nowadays there remains a distribution state monopoly whereas the importation monopoly had to be abolished due to Sweden's EU membership.

[14] See Marine Mammal Protection Act of 1972, 16 U.S.C. §§ 1361-1423h (2003); *United States — Restrictions on Imports of Tuna (Tuna-Dolphin I)*, GATT DS21/R (3 Sep 1991) [unadopted].

c) Subsidies

Distortion in international trade can also be caused by subsidies. A state can, for instance, subsidize a specific product, thus increasing its competitiveness in the national and international market by lowering its price so that it is cheaper than other similar products. Such action is often taken to protect or sustain jobs but can also be used to gain a long-term competitive advantage on the international market in hopes that competition will, in the long run, exit the market. Once this goal is reached, the subsidy can be removed and an even higher price than the original market price can be charged. Obviously, such measures are also a form of competitive distortion.

d) Dumping and Other Measures

'Price dumping' as an illicit trade conduct is regulated in Article VI GATT. It refers to the *export of goods on the international market at a lower price than in the country of origin*. In some instances, the export price can fall below the production costs. This quite aggressive tactic is *commonly used by private companies to expand their foreign market share*. Thus, even though dumping is not a state measure that distorts international trade because it origins from private companies, nevertheless, it potentially has the same distorting effect as state measures have. As a result, the GATT contains dumping-related rules.[15]

5.2.2.3 Impact of the Concept of Free Trade and International Trade Regulations on States

As the main argument for free trade, the comparative advantages theory requires states to accept limitations in sovereignty in matters relating to cross-border trade, such as the imposition of tariffs and non-tariff barriers and the decision to subsidize an industry and other measures, thus limiting their ability to protect their economy from foreign goods, services and capital. Moreover, free trade and international trade regulations may also affect non-trade-related policies of states, such as policies concerning health, environmental issues and others. There is often a tension between the requirements of free international trade on one hand, and often domestically driven political concerns in many areas on the other. Governments often prefer to follow domestic political needs rather than to observe international trade rules.

However, the GATT and the other basic WTO agreements do not strive for completely free global trade. They appreciate that complete international division of labor is impossible and that appropriate political trade measures are necessary. These measures may be national or international. Some preconditions for national protection measures are the fulfillment of certain material and procedural rules, under the supervision of the WTO organs. Nonetheless, the idea of comparative

[15] See infra, Sect. 5.2.5.5.

advantages had quite an important conceptual impact on the WTO and its main agreements.

5.2.3 *From the GATT to the WTO*

5.2.3.1 Structure and Framework of the GATT as an Agreement

The original GATT was introduced in 1947. Its articles were later amended several times and for a final time prior to its integration into the WTO (GATT 1994). Although the GATT 1947 framework was an international treaty rather than an international organization, it was structurally like an international organization despite lacking international legal personality. In 1994, the WTO, as a properly constituted international organization, supplanted the organizational structure of the GATT.

The GATT 1947 had four parts and the additional protocol of provisional application. The protocol forms an integral part of the GATT's legitimacy, since the agreement was not published as a separate document but as an attachment to the Final Act of the UN Conference on Trade and Employment.[16] The protocol therefore enforced the agreement among the initial contracting parties. Separate protocols of accession made the agreement applicable to the members that joined after 1947.

Part I of the GATT regulates the most important principle of the whole framework, the so-called *Most Favored Nation Principle (MFN, article 1).* This principle *requires a GATT state granting a trade concession to another GATT state to extend this advantage to all GATT states.* The MFN clause entails therefore *a principle of equal treatment of the GATT states as a method to generally reduce trade barriers.* This principle will be discussed in more details later.[17] Part I also consists of the Schedules of Concessions (Article II) which regulate the specific commitments that the contracting parties have made. Substantive matters are regulated in Part II which consists of arts. III–XXIII. They also will be discussed later.[18]

The focus of this chapter is on the procedural and structural provisions in Part III (Article XXIV–XXV). These provisions made it possible for the GATT 1947 to increasingly function like an international organization despite lacking a legal personality. Article XXV para. 1 states that the designated "Contracting Parties" shall meet up from time to time to give effect to the provisions involving joint action and to facilitate the operations and further the objectives of the agreement, thus

[16] The protocol is only found in the GATT 1947 providing for its application and legitimacy ever since the Havana Charter failed to spawn an institutionalized body governing international tariffs and trade as elaborated previously. As of the GATT 1994 the protocol was rendered unnecessary due to the introduction of the WTO body and therefore was not included in the updated text; cf. WTO Analytical Index, GATT 1994, Chapter I(A) no. 1(a)e.

[17] See infra, Sect. 5.2.5.2.

[18] See infra, Sect. 5.2.5.5.

implying a mandatory assembly of the contracting parties. Paras. 3 and 4 of the same article provide that each contracting party shall be entitled to have one vote at all meetings and joint decisions shall therefore be cast through the majority of votes. Furthermore, para. 5 states that exceptional circumstances shall allow for the possibility to waive an obligation imposed upon a contracting party, which requires that the decision is made by a two-third majority comprising more than half of the contracting parties. These far-reaching organizational regulations called for a structure capable of managing the workload.

5.2.3.2 Organs

The ITO and the GATT were very closely linked, since the GATT 1947 should have been the ITO's temporary provisions enforcement instrument. Nevertheless, the ITO failed as an institution, leaving the GATT as the only instrument regulating international trade. In an effort to save some of the structure the ITO would have provided, some structural parts were implemented into the GATT, *giving it an organizational-like appearance even though it was formally not an organization*. Organizational and structural questions, which otherwise would have been left for the ITO to decide, became an integral part of the GATT. Therefore, it increasingly acted as an international organization and integrated some structure into its operations by instituting the organs discussed in this chapter. Designed with the purpose of fulfilling the objectives of the GATT—including dispute resolution—the organs also had to oversee and control world trade. *The organs of the GATT 1947 were later integrated into the WTO structure in 1994.*

a) Contracting Parties Acting as a General Assembly

The main organ of the GATT was the totality of the contracting parties; thus, *the plenary organ acted as a General Assembly (GA)*. Each member state had one representative at the GA. Article XXV GATT provided that the delegates met once a year to hold the GA meeting, thereby giving effect to the provisions on joint action and furthering the objectives of the GATT. Moreover, the GA held a vast array of rights: e.g., information entitlements and consultation rights, approval and investigative rights, and the right to pass regulations. Voting powers were distributed equally among the contracting parties, with every state having one vote without considering the state's economic or political power as is done in the Bretton Woods institutions.[19] Despite that, the contracting parties would regularly bypass the voting process and *negotiate a current matter until a consensus among all parties was reached*. The fact that negotiations usually started off among the biggest trade partners and did not escalate even in the absence of an agreement gave the votes at least some form of weight distribution.

---

[19] Art. XXV(3) GATT 1947.

The decision-making process required unanimous votes on amendments to the Most-Favored-Nation treatment, the Schedules of Concessions (part I GATT) and on Article XXX GATT (regulating amendments). Other amendments to the GATT, including the granting of waivers, the inclusion of new contracting parties and the formation of a customs union or of a free trade area required a 2/3 majority. Any other decision would only have required a simple majority of delegate votes. However, the immediate effect of any decision would only have been binding for the parties voting in favor of it. *A contracting party could not be forced to accept a decision*; nor did the GATT provide any sanctioning mechanisms for when a contracting party did not accept a decision. For these parties, the decision would only be legally binding after they had accepted it, even if the majority had already embraced the decision.

The unanimity principle and the lack of a real weight distribution among voters had both advantages and disadvantages. On the one hand, unanimous decisions tend to be made slowly and are mostly reduced to the core questions, since any additional vote would naturally make finding complete acceptance by all contracting parties more difficult. On the other hand, equality among the contracting parties made it possible for a lot of them to participate in the first place. Smaller and less influential states would not have participated in the GATT if voting powers were distributed according to size and influence as their participation would have been deemed de facto impossible.

b) Council of Representatives

It was only in 1960 that the *GATT Council of Representatives* was established. A special GATT committee was asked to evaluate the organizational structure of the GATT a year earlier and proposed to the GA ways to improve it, which resulted in the founding of the council. Although primarily focused on the handling, application and reporting of factual issues arising between sessions of the GA, the council also supervised the activities of the committees, working groups and other organs acting on behalf of the contracting parties. Additionally, the council prepared the GA's sessions, conventions, conferences, trade negotiations (trade rounds) and carried out all other tasks delegated by the GA. The council was comprised of 66 representatives in total, which meant that not every contracting party had a permanent representative. Nevertheless, such parties were offered a seat when an issue involved or affected them.

c) Secretariat

Legally speaking, the GATT never actually had a Secretariat. Nonetheless, the term "GATT Secretariat" was used after the resources of the ITO Secretariat were merged into the GATT upon the ITO's failure. This was mainly due to practical reasons. Since then, the Secretariat has focused on administrative, organizational and legal matters (especially interpretation of the GATT treaty). These subject matters were further divided into three Departments: the Department of Trade and Development, the Department of Trade Policy and the Department of Conference Affairs and Administration. The majority of the workload was with the Department of Conference Affairs and Administration, since one of the Secretariat's main objectives was the planning, organization and moderation of trade negotiations and various other conferences, including post-conferential work such as issuing of reports and assistance in drafting rulings. Moreover, the Department of Trade and Development was focused on third world development as the WTO and World Bank are today, while analytics and statistics on world trade were assigned to the Department of Trade Policy.

d) Director-General
The Director-General overlooked the administrative work of the GATT and was therefore the head of the Secretariat. He was often referred to as the "manager" or "conciliator" of the treaty. The office of Director-General was created in 1965, succeeding the former office of Executive Secretary. His competencies were predominantly derived from the GATT treaty, in particular as regards his impact on trade negotiations. Apart from that, the Director-General also enjoyed informally acquired competencies—specifically, the Director-General stood as the so-called "*guardian of the GATT treaty*" as dubbed by former Director-General Olivier Long and therefore had the duty to make sure contracting parties were compliant with their GATT obligations.

e) Committees, Working Groups and Panels
The General Assembly and the Council could also create subsidiary, ad-hoc bodies which were entrusted with specific tasks, such as committees, panels or working groups. The committees mainly solved factual issues and answered specific problems of general significance to the contracting parties. They were put together from the contracting parties' delegates and did not have any time limits. Therefore, many of them became standing/permanent committees, such as the Committee on Trade and Development under Article XXXVIII para. 2(f) GATT, which monitored the application of part IV of the GATT. Working groups, on the other hand, were very much of a temporary nature. Like the committees, they were an assembly of delegates from the contracting parties. However, unlike the committees, their work was centered around specific trade issues and the submission of reports and conclusions thereof. The last category, the panels, used to be a group of external specialists, working independently from the contracting parties, that addressed individual issues which often involved settling disputes between two contracting parties.

5.2.3.3 The World Trade Rounds

a) General Remarks
To promote world trade, the GATT established the so-called World Trade Rounds. *Between 1947 and 1994, the GATT hosted a total of eight rounds.* The last, ninth round (Doha Round) was launched at the WTO's Fourth Ministerial Conference in Doha, Qatar, in November 2001. Each round is named either after the place it was held or the key initiator of the round such as the Dillon (1960–1961) and the Kennedy (1964–1967) rounds. The World Trade Rounds' initial primary purpose was to reduce tariffs in trade. Hereafter, negotiations on non-tariff barriers to trade,

contractual amendments, new agreements and treaties have steadily grown in importance. Tariff reductions can apply to either specific goods or to a general sector. This approach resulted in many bilateral negotiations being carried out based on reciprocity with the goal of reducing tariffs in a meaningful and efficient way, based on the MFN clause. Within the framework of these trade rounds, a vast number of trade policies, known as the GATT codes, were made. These agreements were *plurilateral agreements*: although made under the auspices of the GATT, these agreements were also made in parallel to the GATT, and therefore had their own GATT contracting states as parties. Such parallel agreements were welcomed: not only was the GATT hard to amend since a 2/3 majority of all contracting states was needed, but amendments were also only applicable to the members voting in favor of it (Article XXX para. 1 GATT).

b) Overview Over the Frist Seven Rounds
From 1947 to 1979 there were seven World Trade Rounds.

aa) First Round (Geneva Round) The first ever World Trade Round took place in the "Palais des Nation" in Geneva from April to October of 1947. Ever since the end of the Great Depression WW II, a significant portion of the international community embarked on a course of trade liberalization. Therefore, the Geneva trade negotiations were intended to be part of the ITO involvement, which was initially promoted by the USA after the US Congress authorized the President to generally reduce tariffs. Not yet knowing that the establishment of the ITO would fail, the parties were keen to achieve fast ratification of the GATT treaty since the US Congress limited the presidential tariff reduction authorization to 1947. The GATT was thus ratified a year prior to the Geneva round, and the contracting parties planned to later merge part II of the GATT into the ITO once it was established and keep parts I and III within the GATT.

Following the ratification, the Geneva round was used to negotiate tariffs and trade barriers in detail. After negotiating tariffs independently, product by product, the participating states eventually managed to reduce tariffs in trade significantly compared to the level in 1930. Nonetheless, no one suspected that the ITO would not be ratified by the very nation that promoted its creation. In 1948 the "Final Act of the United Nations Conference on Trade and Employment", commonly known as the Havana Charter, was successfully completed. It would have provided the basis for the ITO's establishment and was ratified by 53 states but, due to the US Congress' lack of approval, never by the USA. As explained earlier, the ITO without US participation would not have made sense, which is why the establishment of the ITO was abandoned in the end.

bb) Second Round (Annecy Round) During the second World Trade Round, which took place in Annecy, France, from April to August 1949, the GATT was expanded to include an additional 10 contracting states. As the GATT 1947 required unanimous voting on the inclusion of new contracting states, the GATT was amended during the 1948 Havana Conference to provide for a less onerous two-third majority. It also provided that a state which disapproved of a new contracting state being included could not be forced into trade concessions with it. Other than that, the Annecy Round was a rather inefficient round since the main goal of reducing tariffs in trade was only met by a 1–2% reduction. Compared to the Geneva Round, this was a rather low rate. Moreover, the Annecy Round was the least attended round; only 13 states participated.

cc) Third Round (Torquay Round) Already planned during the Annecy Round, the Torquay Round took place from September 1950 to April 1951 in Torquay, UK, under the topic of European trade market consolidation. The most significant result of the Torquay Round was the admission six new contracting states: West Germany (FRG), Austria, Peru, Philippines, South Korea and Turkey. The USA declared that the US Congress would fail to accept the Havana Charter, which turned out to be correct. However, the applicable US Trade act allowed the US President to decide on tariff reductions up to 50%. Moreover, the US Congress revoked the so-called "Peril Point Provisions", a set of minimal tariffs to protect local production, in favor of a less far-reaching "Escape Clause", which allowed tariff concessions to be revoked only if it was imminently necessary to protect local production. Thus, the USA were basically prepared to enter into serious trade negotiations. These negotiations were, however, overshadowed by a controversy between the USA and the Commonwealth of Nations as to preferential treatment schemes applicable within the Commonwealth that were qualified by the USA to be unfair. Despite this and the setback as to the creation of an international organization devoted to international trade, trade barriers were lowered but not in the extent the participating states expected. About 500 single negotiations were carried out in Torquay.

dd) Fourth Round (2nd Geneva Round) Dubbed the "Tariff Conference", the fourth round was held a second time in Geneva from January to May 1956. Despite the hopes of the contracting/attending states and the expansion of the scope of the GATT, the round was again rather unsuccessful; it resulted only in a general reduction in tariffs by 2–3%. A lot of the concessions that were obtained were not more than a kind of admission fee of the new contracting states. For the first time, the High Authority of the European Coal and Steel Community (ECSC) was present, representing its member states Belgium, West Germany (FRG, France, Italy, Luxemburg and the Netherlands. Moreover, the 2nd Geneva Round admitted a new member state, Japan.

ee) Fifth Round (Dillon Round) In September 1961, the fifth round began. It was named after Clarence Douglas Dillon, then-US Secretary of Treasury. The Dillon Round was the third round to be held in Geneva and lasted until July 1962 with a total of 26 states participating. The Dillon Round was the first to be named after its influencer, which in this case was due to Dillon's extensive efforts in promoting free trade under President John F. Kennedy. Other than that, the Dillon Round saw the introduction of three new signatory states, Cambodia, Israel and Portugal. However, the Dillon round was yet another unsuccessful round. The member states of the recently established European Economic Community (EEC) were considering merging their national trade zones into a single trade and customs union to match the USA's trade power.[20] Given that the customs union had an adverse effect on trade with third states the Dillon round was also devoted to the negotiations on trade concessions by the EEC member states to compensate these adverse effects. Moreover, the USA's anxiety over trade discrimination by the European Economic Community caused it to issue an offer of 20% reduction on US tariff to put some pressure on the EEC member states. Non-ECC members were generally interested in negotiations on general tariff reduction which resulted however in a mere 1% reduction.

ff) Sixth Round (Kennedy Round) After many rather unsuccessful tariff negotiations over the years, the sixth world trade round, which took place from May1964 to June 1967, resulted in substantial tariff reductions. By now, world trade rounds had become more complicated as more states participated in them than in earlier rounds. The opening meeting of the Kennedy Round was attended by 66 countries, thereby tripling the duration of the Kennedy Round compared to the Dillon Round, which already held the record of an 11-month duration. The Kennedy Round was the fourth round to be held in Geneva and the second round to be named after its influencer, US President John F. Kennedy despite Kennedy's assassination the year before. Kennedy had heavily influenced the establishment of the round when securing the US Trade Expansion Act of 1962 which entitled the US government again to tariff cuts of up to 50%. This was a reaction to the EEC's ever-growing influence in world trade, which was one of the major topics discussed during the round. Other negotiated topics were the removal of non-tariff barriers, preferential treatment for developing countries and the removal of agricultural trade restrictions. In addition, a few important documents were signed, namely: the 1967 GATT Anti-dumping Code, an additional agreement on chemical goods and a memorandum on the foundations for negotiations of a worldwide grain agreement. The results of the Kennedy Round were again noted in the national schedules of concession and, additionally, in the 1967 GATT Protocol. Worldwide tariff reductions involved $40 billion worth of goods, thus making it the most successful world trade round.

gg) Seventh Round (Tokyo Round) The seventh round lasted from September 1973 to October 1979, doubling the length of the Kennedy Round and cementing the trend of the increasing duration of world trade rounds. Now with 102 participating countries, the Tokyo Round led to further substantial tariff reductions and special agreements for the agricultural sector regarding crop, dairy and beef products. Moreover, the parties agreed on a framework for non-tariff trade restrictions and created the legal basis for the special position of developing countries within the GATT. The Tokyo Round was off to a slow start as the USA had domestic

[20] Nonetheless, the trade union was eventually delayed because France declined the project's first attempt.

problems—namely, the Watergate Affair[21] —to overcome and a rather protectionist trade policy on its agenda. Discussions over whether to grant MFN status to the USSR further slowed down the process of tackling the essential topics such as tariff reductions. Even after these issues were overcome, the difficulties in negotiations persisted when it came to the existing tariff differences between the USA and the EEC, the imbalances in agricultural trade and the difficulties in the registration and elimination of non-tariff trade barriers. Despite all these difficulties, the parties managed to achieve a significant reduction in tariffs of about 35%.

5.2.3.4 The Uruguay Round and the Establishment of the WTO

a) The Uruguay Round

The Uruguay Round in Punta del Este, Uruguay, was the eighth and last multilateral trade negotiation taking place under the auspices of the GATT 1947. Beginning in 1986 and ending over 80 months later in 1994, the Uruguay Round was the longest negotiation round under the old GATT and the first to be held in a developing country. What led to the Uruguay Round was the economic crisis that affected the world in the 1980s. This crisis caused many countries to raise tariffs and other trade barriers again to provide a minimal level of economic security for their national economies. The GATT was thus seen as ineffective and criticized as such. Therefore, the Uruguay Round, which ultimately produced the WTO, can be described as a restructuring process and a new beginning of international trade regulation, one that tried to fill gaps of the GATT.

The Uruguay round focused on institutional reforms in decision-making and arbitration mechanisms, the further reduction of trade barriers for industrial and agricultural production, the international regulation of transnational services (which resulted in the adoption of the GATS) and the setting of international legal standards for the protection of intellectual property rights (which resulted in the adoption of the TRIPS). As tariffs had already been significantly reduced, tariff negotiations only played a secondary role. In fact, the focus was on expanding free trade and strengthening the international economic order through an enhanced institutional framework. Consequentially, the resulting trade liberalization measures adopted during the Uruguay round were the most important of all previous world trade rounds. One special concern in the initial negotiations was the effect that the Tokyo Round had on world trade. Since the questions of how new agreements would be implemented into the GATT structure and to whom and how they would be applicable were still somewhat unsolved, the Tokyo Round had produced numerous side agreements solely

[21] The Watergate Affair refers to the political scandal in the United States during the early 1970s, following a break-in at the Democratic National Committee headquarters at the Watergate office complex in Washington, D.C., and the subsequent cover-up by members of the Nixon administration, leading to President Richard Nixon's resignation in 1974. For a detailed account, see Kutler (1990).

applicable to the GATT members that accepted them. To counter this development, negotiations on the functioning of the GATT were conducted to solve the issue.

b) The Marrakesh Agreement (Final Act) establishing the WTO

The negotiations of the Uruguay Round concluded with the signing of the Marrakesh Agreement (Final Act) on 15 April 1994 in Marrakesh, Morocco, which launched the WTO. The Marrakesh Agreement marked the beginning of a new dawn in the implementation of a comprehensive framework for world trade and is the most ambitious and far-reaching international trade agreement ever concluded.[22] Over 60 additional agreements, largely of an ancillary nature, were attached to the Final Act signed in Marrakesh. These agreements regulated the agricultural sector (on market entry, production-independent subsidies, and export subsidies), textiles and clothing, technical trade barriers, trade-relevant investments, anti-dumping, origin classification, import licensing, subsidies and safeguard clauses. However, it is important to note that all the annexed agreements, despite being negotiated in separate committees during the Uruguay Round as well as being separate agreements altogether, are associated with and subordinated to the Final Act of Marrakesh. This means that, *by agreeing to the Marrakesh Agreement, each state agreed to all the annexed agreements and endorsed the equally binding effect of each agreement for all emerging WTO members, with the exception of the so-called plurilateral agreements.*[23]

Leading trade reform into a new era, the *Marrakesh Agreement, which is the agreement establishing the WTO (WTO Agreement; WTO-A), acts as an umbrella agreement governing all its annexed agreements*. It has 16 Articles and regulates not only the WTO's scope of application, functions and structure but also its relations to other organizations, its secretariat structure, budget and contributions status as well as its decision-making process. As can be seen from the preamble, the contracting parties had the sincere desire to overcome the problems with the old trade system, in which a multilateral treaty—i.e. the GATT—had to act increasingly like an international organization without being one and thus reached its limits. Therefore, the *WTO was constructed as an organization with own legal personality and thus gave international trade the structure and guidelines it needed.* The structure came through the annexed agreements, especially the agreements in annex 1A through 1C. These agreements constitute the three main pillars of the WTO: *the GATT, the General Agreement on Trade in Service (GATS) and Trade-Related Aspects of Intellectual Property Rights (TRIPS).*

As part of the WTO's establishment, the GATT 1947 was formally dissolved and integrated as GATT 1994 into the WTO in 1994, following the Uruguay Round.[24]

---

[22] Van den Bossche and Zdouc (2017), p. 87.

[23] See infra, Sect. 5.2.3.2.

[24] See Art. II (4) WTO-A: 4. The General Agreement on Tariffs and Trade 1994 as specified in Annex 1A (hereinafter referred to as "GATT 1994") is legally distinct from the General Agreement on Tariffs and Trade, dated 30 Oct 1947, annexed to the Final Act Adopted at the Conclusion of the

Still, it is noteworthy that the GATT treaty and all the additional treaties under the GATT continue to make up the majority of the WTO's framework and is therefore the main pillar. The two other pillars, the GATS and TRIPS, were negotiated during the Uruguay round and were directly integrated into the WTO's new legal entity. Bearing in mind that the GATT makes up most of the WTO, it seems only logical that membership in the GATT was de facto converted into membership in the WTO. However, from a strictly legal point of view, the GATT contracting states were obliged to formally ratify the WTO agreements as original members.[25] Therefore, there was *no formal succession from GATT to WTO membership as there cannot be a formal succession from an agreement to an independent legal entity, i.e. an international organization.*

This is also true for the GATT organs and most of their structure which were informally taken over by and integrated into the WTO: no formal succession took place. Nonetheless, the office of the Director-General and his Secretariat have been kept completely intact, though the office was renamed General Director (GD). The Secretariat still has the same instructions and obligations. Additionally, the contracting parties' General Assembly has been adapted and merged into the Ministerial Conference, the highest-ranking plenary organ of the WTO that comprises representatives of all the member states. Consequently, the bodies of committees, working groups and panels were taken over as well and are subject to the Ministerial Conference. The General Council continues to exist in its same form and manages the daily business in between sessions of the Ministerial Conference. Additionally, the WTO involves three sub-councils which are thematically divided into the three pillars, GATT, GATS and TRIPS. These councils report to the Generl Council with the aim of assisting the General Council in his endeavour to better manage his workload, The GATT, GATS and TRIPS Councils which oversee the founctioning of the respective agreements (Article IV (5) WTO-A) have the power to create subordinate bodies such as committees, working groups and panels themselves.

Generally, the original members of the WTO were eager to establish not legal but de facto continuity between the GATT and the WTO, as far as this was possible. Therefore, Article XVI (1) of the WTO-A states that, except provided otherwise under the WTO-A *"or the Multilateral Trade Agreements, the WTO shall be guided by the decisions, procedures and customary practices followed by the CONTRACTING PARTIES to GATT 1947 and the bodies established in the framework of GATT 1947."*

Second Session of the Preparatory Committee of the United Nations Conference on Trade and Employment, as subsequently rectified, amended or modified (hereinafter referred to as "GATT 1947").

[25]Cf. Art. XI (1) WTO-A: "The contracting parties to GATT 1947 as of the date of entry into force of this Agreement, and the European Communities, which accept this Agreement and the Multilateral Trade Agreements and for which Schedules of Concessions and Commitments are annexed to GATT 1994 and for which Schedules of Specific Commitments are annexed to GATS shall become original Members of the WTO."

5.2.3.5 The Agreements Concluded in Marrakesh

The legal texts adopted in Marrakesh consist of about 60 agreements, annexes, decisions and understandings. The *umbrella agreement is the Agreement Establishing the WTO (WTO-A)*. This was followed by agreements for each of the three broad areas of trade that the WTO covers, i.e. *the GATT (for goods), the GATS (for services) and the TRIPS (for intellectual property); the Dispute Settlement Understanding (DSU); and the Trade Policy Review Mechanism (TRIM)*. Extra agreements and annexes deal with the special requirements of specific sectors or issues such as the Agreements regulating Subsidies and Countervailing Measures,[26] Anti-Dumping[27] or Rules of Origin,[28] or the plurilateral Agreements on Government Procurement.[29] Finally, detailed, and lengthy schedules (or lists) of commitments were made by individual countries allowing specific foreign products or service-providers access to their markets. For GATT, these are binding commitments on tariffs for goods in general, as well as combinations of tariffs and quotas for some agricultural goods. For GATS, the commitments specify how much access foreign service providers are allowed for specific sectors, and they include lists of types of services where individual countries decline to apply the MFN principle of non-discrimination.

5.2.4 The WTO as an International Organization: Institutional Aspects

5.2.4.1 The WTO as International Institution and Subject of International Law (Article I WTO-A)

The WTO is *the core institution to regulate and steer global trade*. Its legal basis is the *Marrakesh Agreement Establishing the World Trade Organization (WTO-A)*. Art I of the WTO-A clearly expresses the intention to create an international organization. In Article VIII WTO-A, the WTO is expressly characterized as a *subject of international law*. These clear statements must be understood against the background of the GATT: it was structurally like an international institution but lacked an international legal personality. Therefore, as an independent international legal entity, the WTO may enter into international agreements with states and other international organizations, be internationally liable for its conduct and is generally bound by international law.

---

[26] Agreement on Subsidies and Countervailing Measures, Annex 1A (1994), 1869 UNTS 14.

[27] Agreement on Implementation of Article VI of the General Agreement on Tariffs and Trade (1994), Annex 1A, 1868 UNTS 201 (Anti-Dumping Agreement).

[28] Agreement on Rules of Origin (1994), Annex 1A, 1868 UNTS 397.

[29] Revised Agreement on Government Procurement, adopted 30 Mar 2012, WTO Doc GPA/113.

5.2.4.2 Scope and Functions of the WTO (Articles II and III WTO-A)

Article II WTO-A sets out the scope of the organization. It provides that the WTO constitutes the institutional framework for trade relations between the WTO members and for the agreements reached during the Uruguay round (Art II (1) WTO Agreement). It is thus the international institution to discuss global trade issues and to make political and legal decisions regulating trade. *The WTO-A and the multilateral trade agreements such as the GATT 1994, the GATS and the TRIPS, the DSU and the TPRM agreement are all integral parts of the WTO agreement and bind all member states (Article II (2) WTO-A).* On the other hand, the plurilateral trade agreements on specific sectors such as the Agreement on Public Procurement only bind those member states that have signed them and, in accordance with the *pacta tertiis*-rule, *"do not create either obligations or rights for Members that have not accepted them"* (Article II (3) WTO-A).

Article III specifies the functions and duties of the WTO. The WTO must facilitate the implementation of the agreements reached in the Uruguay round and encourage the goals contained in the agreements (Article III (1) WTO-A). *One main function of the organization is thus to monitor the agreements and member states' compliance with their legal obligations under WTO law.* In this regard, and much more than other organizations, the WTO is explicitly *designed to enforce numerous complex international agreements and therefore acts as an international institutionalized facilitator and enforcer.* An institutional umpiring making institutionalized multilateral reactions in case of norm violations possible improves rule observance and compliance. Furthermore, the *WTO provides a negotiation forum* for all member states in which trade relations, including current trade issues and future policies, can be discussed. In this context, the WTO can also *assist in the implementation of the agreements* reached (Article III (2) WTO-A). The WTO also *settles disputes* in accordance with the Understanding on Rules and Procedures Governing the Settlement of Disputes (DSU) and the Trade Policy Review Mechanism (TPRM).

Article III (5) WTO-A provides for the organization's cooperation with the IMF and the World Bank and its affiliated agencies *"[w]ith a view to achieving greater coherence in global economic policy-making"*. Article V (1) WTO-A generally obliges the WTO General Council to *"make appropriate arrangements for effective cooperation with other intergovernmental organizations that have responsibilities related to the WTO"*. The IMF and the World Bank Group are particularly important for the WTO because their activities are very often trade-related or have an impact on trade. As such, the WTO, through consultation, must coordinate these activities. This is particularly the case for the IMF's currency and debt related tasks. Therefore, Article XV GATT specifically regulates cooperation between the GATT/WTO and the IMF regarding exchange arrangements.[30]

[30] According to Art. XV (1), WTO and IMF coordinate their policies regarding exchange questions within the jurisdiction of the IMF and questions of quantitative restrictions and other trade measures within the jurisdiction of the WTO. Whenever WTO organs consider or deal with problems

5.2.4.3 Organizational Structure (Article IV WTO-A)

The WTO's organizational structure is based on the GATT structure. The top organ is the *Ministerial Conference, the plenary organ that meets at least once every two years* (Art IV WTO-A). Between these conferences the General Council, consisting of member state representatives, functions as the main organ by carrying out the functions of the Ministerial Conference (Article IV (2) WTO-A). *The General Council is responsible for regularly inspecting the functioning of the agreements and ministerial decisions*. It can *act as a dispute resolution organ* or as a *trade policy review supervision mechanism*. Importantly, its powers expand to all WTO trade-related issues. Furthermore, it can create subsidiary organs such as councils responsible for certain areas under the WTO system. These councils are mentioned in Art IV (5) WTO-A and are responsible for trade of goods (GATT Council), trade in services (GATS Council) and any trade-related aspects of intellectual property rights (TRIPS Council). They supervise the functioning of the agreements in their area of responsibility.

Additionally, Article IV (7) WTO-A allows for the creation of committees. The supervision of plurilateral agreements naturally only applies to the member states which are party to it. As long as the organs conduct the supervision, these organs will act under the institutional framework of the WTO and are themselves supervised by the General Council.

Ongoing management is placed in the hands of the Secretariat with the General Director as head (Article VI WTO-A).

Structure of the WTO (Fig. 5.1)[31]:

5.2.4.4 Decision Making; Power of Authoritative Interpretation

The WTO has continued the practice under the 1947 GATT of passing resolutions *whenever possible by consensus*. This rule is incorporated in Article IX (1) WTO-A. A vote is held only if such a consensus cannot be reached. Every WTO member can cast one vote. The WTO agreement also contains an *explicit provision providing that the number of votes that the EU has is equal to the number of its member states who are also WTO members*. Decisions of the Ministerial Conference and the General

concerning monetary reserves, balances of payments or foreign exchange arrangements, they shall consult with the IMF (Art. XV (2)). The WTO organs further shall accept fact-related determinations of the IMF as to foreign exchange, monetary reserves and balances of payments, and as to whether action by a WTO member state in exchange matters is in accordance with the IMF Articles of Agreement. Art. XV (5) GATT further contains a reporting obligation of the WTO: If a WTO organ considers that exchange restrictions on payments and transfers in connection with imports are being applied by a WTO member states in a manner inconsistent with the exceptions according to the GATT for quantitative restrictions, it shall report thereon to the Fund.

[31] WTO (2022) WTO in brief. WTO, Geneva <https://www.wto.org/english/thewto_e/whatis_e/inbrief_e/inbr_e.htm> (accessed 9 March 2025).

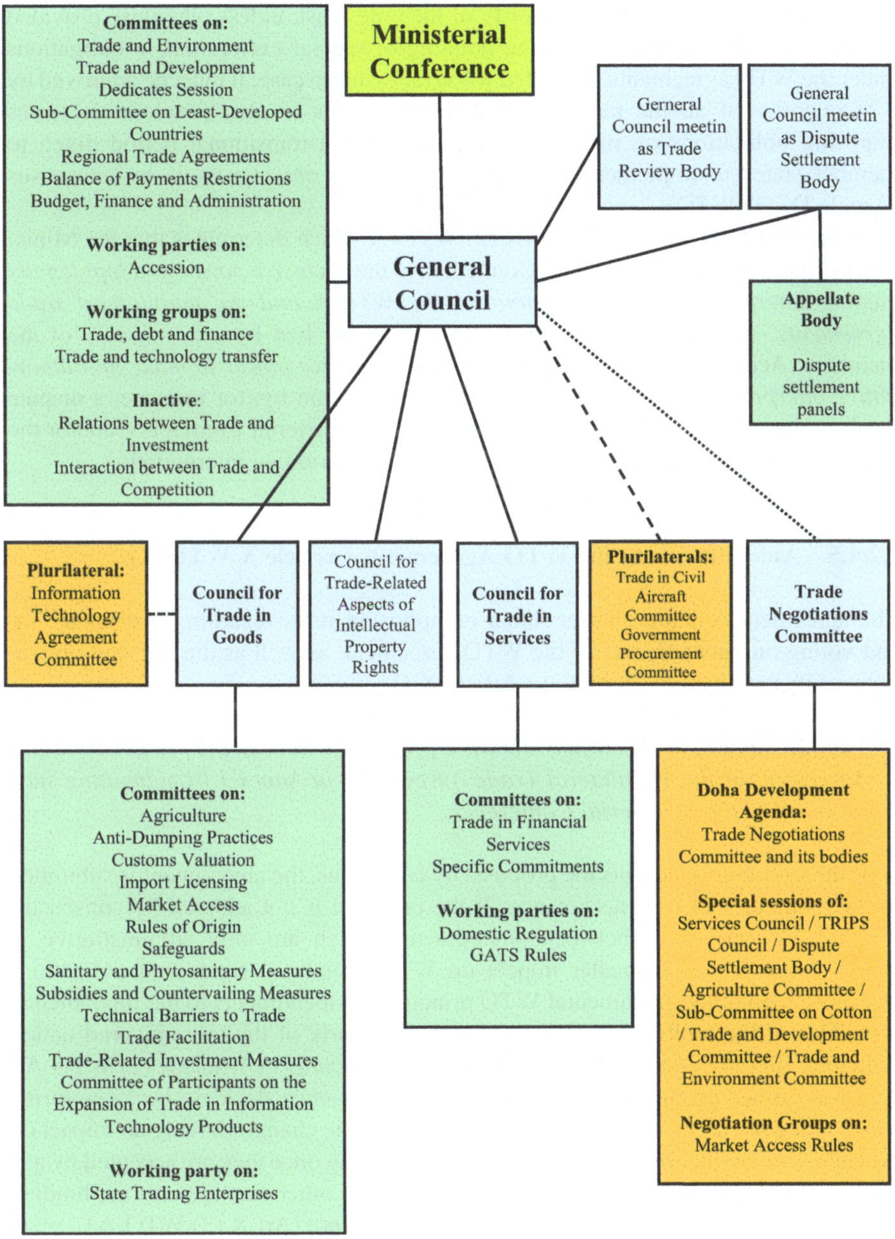

Fig. 5.1 WTO Structure. Own graphic inspired by WTO (2022) WTO in brief. WTO, Geneva <https://www.wto.org/english/thewto_e/whatis_e/inbrief_e/inbr_e.htm> (Accessed 8 March 2025)

Council are made by a simple majority of the votes cast, unless otherwise provided in one of the WTO agreements. The granting of special exemptions to obligations under the WTO agreements, so-called waivers, is such a case. It must be approved by a ¾ majority of all the members. Finally, decisions to alter previous decisions imposing obligations on member states, including a transitional period given to member states to implement these obligations, can only be made by consensus (Article IX (3) WTO).

A peculiar provision is Article IX (2) WTO-A which determines that the Ministerial Conference and the General Council have the *exclusive power to adopt legally binding interpretations of provisions in the WTO-A and the multilateral trade agreements*. A decision on interpretation can be reached by a ¾ majority of the members. Accordingly, these organs have the *exclusive power to make an authoritative interpretation*. This means that the interpretation by, for instance, a dispute resolution panel might not be authoritative, if the Ministerial Conference and/or the General Council requires panels to follow their authoritative interpretation.

5.2.4.5 Amendments to the WTO Agreements (Article X WTO-A)

The agreement contains further rather complicated rules regarding acceptance of, and voting on, amendments of the WTO agreement, as well as the relevant obligations of its members. According to Article X (1) WTO-A

> *"any Member of the WTO may initiate a proposal to amend the provisions of this Agreement or the Multilateral Trade Agreements in Annex 1 by submitting such proposal to the Ministerial Conference."*

If the Conference accepts the proposal by consensus, the amendment is submitted to the member states for acceptance. If the proposal is not adopted by consensus, Article X differentiates between amendments which are only administrative in nature, those having a greater impact on WTO members' rights and obligations and those regulating fundamental WTO principles. Amendments to the fundamental principles of the multilateral trade system, particularly of the most favored nation principle, are only effective once *approved by all members* (Article X (2) WTO-A). As to the other amendments, the ministerial conference decides, *by ¾ majority, which category such amendments should fall in*. Basic changes having an impact on the rights and obligations of member states are binding once they are accepted by a ¾ majority members' vote (Article X (3) WTO-A). All other amendments are binding for all members *when adopted with a 2/3 majority vote* (Art X (3) WTO-A).

5.2.4.6 Membership (Articles XI and XII WTO-A)

The WTO-A distinguishes between original members, i.e. contracting parties to GATT 1947, and new members that acceded to the WTO. As an organization, the

WTO is open to membership of states as well as of *"separate customs territories possessing full autonomy in the conduct of [their] external commercial relations and of the other matters provided for in this Agreement and the Multilateral Trade Agreements"*. The area of application of this provision is rather unclear. The only example is Taiwan which, because of its contested international status, acceded in 2002 not as a state but as a separate customs territory to the WTO. The provision could, however, also apply to associations of states that have established an institution of regional economic integration, thus a supranational organization, as full autonomy presupposes and implies independence from states.

Article XII (1) WTO-A provides for membership of new states as well as of these territories based *"on terms to be agreed between it and the WTO"*. Nonetheless, the regulation of membership of such associations remains rather obscure. What about voting rights? What about a simultaneous membership of states which are part of the custom territory? Is not an amendment to the WTO agreements necessary in most cases, as the example of the European Union shows whose membership is explicitly regulated in the WTO-A?

Thus, also the accession of a new member is usually based on an agreement on the terms of accession (Article XII (1) WTO-A) which must be approved by the Ministerial Conference by a two-thirds majority of the Members of the WTO (Article XII (2) WTO-A).

5.2.4.7 Categories of WTO Agreements

Article II WTO-A distinguishes between Multilateral Trade Agreements (Article II (2) WTO-A) and Plurilateral Trade Agreements (Article II (3) WTO-A). *Multilateral agreements are binding on all member states whereas plurilateral agreements are binding only on those members which have agreed to them.* New members therefore have to accept and ratify the package of multilateral agreements whereas accession to the plurilateral agreements is voluntary for them (Fig. 5.2).

5.2.5 The GATT

5.2.5.1 Scope of Application

The GATT 1994 replaced its predecessor, the GATT 1947. As stated in Annex 1A of the WTO Agreement, the GATT drafted during the Uruguay Round—hence the GATT 1994—is legally distinct form the GATT 1947 despite that the GATT 1994 had basically adopted the text of the GATT 1947. This drew criticism during the Uruguay Round. To reduce confusion, the GATT 1947 was consequentially disapplied, but remains an integral part of the GATT 1994 under the WTO. Therefore, according to Annex 1A of the WTO Agreement, the GATT consists of the GATT 1947, the provisions and legal instruments which entered into force under the

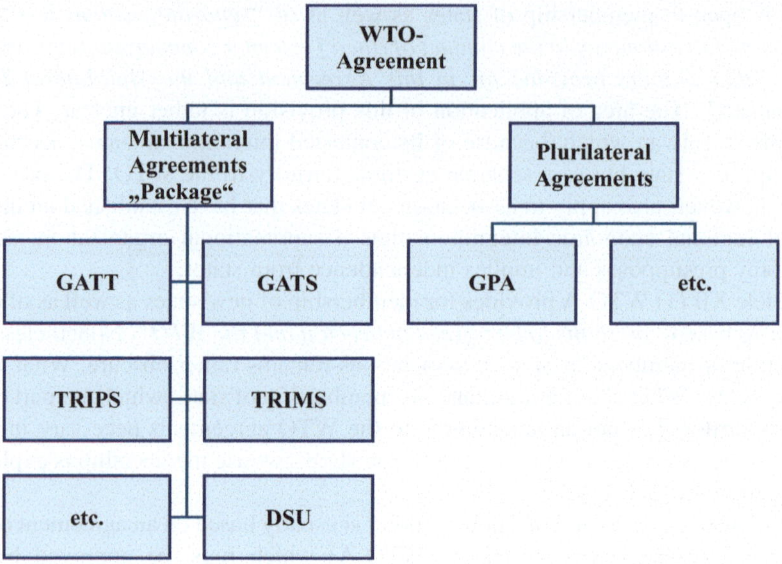

Fig. 5.2 WTO-Agreements. Own graphic

GATT 1947, the understanding in interpretation of GATT articles as well as the Marrakesh Protocol. The Protocol encompasses the combined national Schedules of Concession which contains over 25,000 pages.

The GATT deals with world trade in goods only because at that time global trade was foremost trade in goods. Thus, services were excluded from the GATT 1947. Also, international investments fall, for the most part, outside the GATT. The GATT aims at promoting world trade and free competition, encouraging investments, creating jobs, increasing economic development and wealth throughout the whole world. It also supports the best possible allocation of resources and a harmonious development of international trade relations. It is thus guided by the classic foundational principles of international free trade which were carried over in mostly the exact form to the WTO during the Uruguay World Trade Round.

5.2.5.2 General Principles, Including the Most Favored Nation (MFN) Clause

The GATT principles, most of which are also general WTO principles, are as follows:

a) The Principle of Non-Discrimination

Non-discrimination is mentioned in the preamble to the WTO Agreement as a key principle of global trade law. In the preamble, WTO members express their desire *to eliminate discriminatory treatment in international trade relations.*

Non-discrimination is represented in two WTO principles, the MFN treatment obligation and the national treatment obligation.

b) The Most Favored Nation Principle (MFN)

Articles I (1) and XIII GATT lay down the foundation of the MFN treatment principle. The *MFN obligation is a cornerstone of the GATT and one of the pillars of the WTO trading system*. The principle requires contracting parties to grant trade benefits of any kind not only to a single favored party, but equally to every other contracting party and their citizens.

The term is derived from the idea that the same benefits granted to a party's most favored trading partner are to be granted to the WTO community in the same form for equal or similar goods, thus *providing for a mechanism for a balanced abolishment of trade barriers*. As can be seen in Article I para. 1 GATT, the principle is applicable to the modalities surrounding not only goods originating in a specific trading partner state, but also goods bound for a trading partner state. Ever since the WTO was established (GATT 1994), the MFN treatment not only applies to goods but also to services (GATS)[32] and rights on intellectual property (TRIPS)[33] in an analogous way.

The MFN principle applies to *"same or similar goods."* However, neither the GATT 1947 nor the GATT 1994 managed to provide a general definition of what constitutes similar goods. Therefore, goods and services had to be and still are analyzed individually. There is a rich DSB panel practice on this.

Closely linked to the MFN principle is the *principle of reciprocity*. Reciprocity means that a state granting trade benefits of any kind to another state can expect the same—reciprocal—benefits from the receiving state. This can only be true for equally developed states, which is why the scope of application of reciprocity is limited. Exceptions involve generally any trade with less developed countries to give them comparative advantages.

c) The Principle of National Treatment

Contained in Article III GATT, this principle complements the MFN principle by setting an equilibrium not only regarding trade of goods between two countries (c.f. MFN), but also between the imported goods and the local goods of an importing country. This means that *foreign goods are not to be treated less favorably than comparable domestic goods once they have gone across the national frontiers* and have complied with all the import conditions. This principle has been implemented into the WTO's other pillars as well and therefore applies under the GATS to services and under TRIPS to intellectual property since 1994.

---

[32] Marrakesh Agreement Establishing the World Trade Organization, Annex 1B (1994) 1869 UNTS 183, Art. II.

[33] Marrakesh Agreement Establishing the World Trade Organization, Annex 1C (1994) 1869 UNTS 299, Art. 4.

d) Bindings and Enforceable Commitments
During multilateral negotiations, states regularly agree upon maximum levels of trade barriers to promote international trade. Although this issue appears to be mostly in the background, the agreement on such extremes is vital to international trade because it gives trade partners and companies stability and security regarding future changes in trade barriers. The resulting commitments are called "bindings" and are documented in the respective states' "schedules of concessions" (Article II GATT). These schedules then become an integral part of the states' obligations under the GATT.

e) Prohibition on Quantitative Trade Barriers
States abstain from imposing quantitative quotas on trade. Trade restrictions must be limited to tariffs because such measures are more transparent and affect trade a lot less than import quotas (*"tariffs-only-principle"*).

f) The Principle of Proportionality
The principle of proportionality means that the actions chosen by a state as part of domestic policies should be *the least damaging variant to international trade and trade relations*. This bans arbitrary actions by governments and prevents unnecessary trade restrictions and administrative burdens.

g) The Principle of Transparency
This principle secures a multilateral review process for the international trade community which *requires the publication of all trade-relevant laws, regulations and general applicable provisions*. This increases predictability of market conditions and discourages unfair treatment of foreign offers. Therefore, member states must specifically define the appropriate authorities from which other states can obtain information. The member states have the obligation to notify the WTO community about changes in national trade policies so they can be reviewed for compatibility with WTO law.

5.2.5.3 Exceptions to the Most Favoured Nation Principle

Although the MFN treatment provides a strong foundation for a balanced reduction in trade barriers, there are important exceptions to it. These primarily involve the ability to create free trade zones and preferential treatment of developing countries.

a) Preferential Treatment of Developing States
The preferential treatment of developing countries can be found in the waiver clause in Article XXV (5) GATT. According to this clause, contracting states are empowered to grant exemptions in the form of special permits, i.e. waivers, which form the basis for a preferential treatment of developing countries. With waivers, a country can grant benefits to developing countries without having to grant them to any other country as would be otherwise required by the MFN principle. This gives the *developing world competitive advantages over other states*. This specific treatment has been generally regulated in the so-called Enabling Clause, i.e. the

"Decision on Differential and More Favourable Treatment, Reciprocity and Fuller Participation of Developing Countries" which is an agreement of the GATT signatories concluded in 1979.[34] This allows for derogations from the MFN Treatment principle and therefore helps developing countries to get a competitive edge over other countries to balance out socio-economic inequalities.

b) Historical Exceptions
Furthermore, historically acquired preferences, also known as acquired rights or 'grandfather clause', constituted a huge part of exceptions. These are preferences which were settled before the GATT was established and which the contracting states were allowed to keep, giving those preferences priority over any future case to which the MFN would be applicable. Nevertheless, only import tariffs were affected by the grandfather clause, leaving quantitative restrictions (quotas) subjected to the MFN treatment.

c) Tariff Unions and Free Trade Zones
Tariff unions and free trade zones also constitute very important exceptions to the MFN treatment principle. The reason for this exemption is obvious: under the MFN clause, any preferential treatment must be accorded to all the WTO member states equally. Thus, w*ithout an exception to the MFN principle, it would not be possible to establish tariff unions or free trade zones between some WTO member states*; all the WTO members could profit from the free trade regime or preferential tariffs without an obligation to grant any concessions themselves to the members of the free trade zone or the tariff union. The prevailing view, however, when the GATT was negotiated was that *regional trade liberalization is a goal that serves the interest of all states*, and therefore, states should have incentives to enter into particular agreements regulating closer economic ties between them.

Tariff unions and free trade zones are regulated in Article XXIV (4)–(10) GATT. They are based on a bi- or multilateral treaty merging at least two trade areas into one new, bigger area which shares its benefits and duties as one body either as a free trade zone, a tariff union or even a supranational economic organization. Depending on the degree of integration, the members of such a special arrangement are considered by other world trade participants as one single actor. This allows for regions to merge their economies and shift their MFN obligations to a bigger body. Among the most notable examples of such arrangements are the North American Free Trade Agreement (NAFTA), consisting of Canada, USA and Mexico) and the European Union (EU). In the case of the EU, not only have its members agreed on the free trade of goods or services, but they have also agreed on free movement of people, making the EU's internal state borders open borders.

[34] *Decision on Differential and More Favourable Treatment, Reciprocity and Fuller Participation of Developing Countries (Enabling Clause)*, GATT Doc L/4903 (1979), BISD 26S/203.

5.2.5.4 General Exceptions; Policy Exceptions; Waivers

Further exceptions are contained in Article XIX (protection clause and countermeasures), Article XX (general exceptions), Article XXI (exceptions for ensuring security), Article XXII (protection of concessions and other advantages) and Article XXXV (non-application of the agreement between certain parties).

a) General Exceptions

The most important provision regulating exceptions is Article XX GATT on general exceptions. Almost all cases decided by the panels of the dispute settlement mechanism deal with this article of the GATT. According to this provision.

> *"... nothing in this Agreement shall be construed to prevent the adoption or enforcement by any contracting party of measures: (a) necessary to protect public morals; (b) necessary to protect human, animal or plant life or health; (c) ... (d) necessary to secure compliance with laws or regulations which are not inconsistent with the provisions of this Agreement, including those relating to customs enforcement, the enforcement of monopolies operated under paragraph 4 of Article II and Article XVII, the protection of patents, trade marks and copyrights, and the prevention of deceptive practices; (e) ... (f) imposed for the protection of national treasures of artistic, historic or archaeological value; (g) relating to the conservation of exhaustible natural resources if such measures are made effective in conjunction with restrictions on domestic production or consumption; ..."*

This is the legal basis according to which WTO member states may pursue *trade-relevant national policies and regulations for the protection of public interests* such as public morality, protection of life and health of humans and animals, the protection of natural resources etc. The provision shows that *WTO member states retain their political autonomy*, i.e. they do not transfer powers to an international organization, as would be the case for membership in a supranational organization. However, the exercise of this residual sovereign power is scrutinized by the WTO organs, in particular by the General Council responsible for the GATT, and by the dispute settlement panels if and when a member state brings a case to dispute settlement. The main issue, then, is whether national

> *"measures are not applied in a manner which would constitute a means of arbitrary or unjustifiable discrimination between countries where the same conditions prevail, or a disguised restriction on international trade"*

(Article XX (1) GATT). Thus, the GATT, like other international agreements, sets limits to the exercise of sovereign rights and therefore to the ways and means of pursuing national policy goals. For instance, restrictions on trade are not to be obscured by use of Article XX: Article XX is often deliberately misunderstood and misinterpreted by WTO member states to justify measures imposed to protect domestic economic sectors.

Conflicts surrounding the application of Article XX are resolved by panels as part of the GATT and WTO dispute settlement. In 1990, e.g., a panel had to decide on import restrictions and taxes on imported foreign cigarettes imposed by Thailand. To justify these restrictions, Thailand argued that foreign cigarettes contained substances which increased the harm to humans compared to local cigarettes. In its report the panel clearly stated that this was not the case and that the import restrictions had been unjustifiably imposed and thus the measure breached Article IX (2).[35] Although the panel clearly identified that cigarettes are harmful, nevertheless, the Thai legislature had other means of protecting its population than through discriminatory import restrictions.

b) National Security Exception (Article XXI)

Article XXI can be invoked to protect national security. This is especially the case in times of war or serious international tension (Article XXI (b) (iii)). Article XXI (c) can form the basis for a trade boycott against individual states. Article XXI (c) specifically refers to obligations under the UN Charter regarding the maintenance of international peace and security. This provision supplements Article 103 of the UN Charter which states that in the event of a conflict between the obligations of the UN Members under the Charter and their obligations under any other international agreement, their obligations under the Charter shall prevail.

c) Protection Clause (Article XIX)

The protection clause allows a country whose economy is endangered or seriously threatened by imports of a certain kind of products to annul temporarily part or all its obligations or concessions with regards to such products to protect its own economy. Once it invokes the protection clause, it *must still ensure that the MFN principle is complied with*; thus, differential treatment of its trade partners is not allowed. If a country wants to invoke the protection clause, it must begin negotiations with the affected countries (Article XIX (2)). The protection mechanisms have been specifically regulated in the *Agreement on Safeguards* (Safeguards Agreement) which concretizes Article XIX by allowing safeguard measures only once a special investigation has been carried out by the state, based on a previously agreed upon procedure, and the outcome of the investigation published according to Article X GATT 1994. The agreement also regulates the specific application of the safeguard measures. Therefore, an import volume restriction cannot reduce the quantity of imports to less than the average of the previous three representative years (Article 5 Safeguards Agreement). It can also only be applied for a period necessary to eliminate serious harm or to facilitate an adjustment period. It is further limited to a maximum period of 4 years (Article 4 Safeguards Agreement). Additionally, a commission is set up to monitor the protection measures (Article 13 Safeguards

---

[35] *Thailand – Restrictions on Importation of and Internal Taxes on Cigarettes* (1990) GATT Panel Report, DS10/R - 37S/200.

Agreement). A state wanting to impose protective measures must notify the commission immediately and begin consultations with it.

Sometimes, states have tried to agree on voluntary import or export limitations which were considered a way to get around Article XIX. Back in the 1980s, during the crisis faced by the American car industry, Japan and the USA agreed on the limitation of Japanese car imports into the USA. In recent times, US President Donald Trump during his first term tried to conclude analogous agreements. This voluntary limitation in the form of bilateral agreements undermined the GATT principles since more and more states started to regulate trade relations within this "grey area". This then led the GATT states to implement Article 11(1)(b) Safeguards Agreement during the Uruguay Round. According to this article, voluntary restrictions of exports or any other form of agreements on voluntary self-limitation or related measures are expressly prohibited.

d) Waivers

If none of the exceptions are applicable, the member states can still decide to exempt a member state from its obligations under unusual circumstances (Article XXV (5)). Under the WTO Agreement (Article IX (3)), a 3/4 majority of all member states is necessary. The decision is made by the Ministerial Conference. There are various groups of waivers in existence: Some states receive a waiver because they are undertaking a finance reform and thus need to adjust the tariffs. Others require the waiver to impose import restrictions to solve balance of payment problems. Commonly these waivers are granted to developing countries to protect certain industry sectors.

5.2.5.5 Non-Tariff Restrictions and Other Practices Impeding International Trade

a) Non-tariff Trade Restrictions in General

The GATT was always concerned with non-tariff trade restrictions which are sometimes more harmful to international trade than tariffs. Non-tariff trade restrictions include *quotas, subsidies, technical norms and restrictive custom procedures*. While reducing tariffs, some states have been increasingly looking to utilize these non-tariff measures as protective instruments even though they do not necessarily have an underlying trade-related rationale (i.e. technical standards for motor vehicles aiming at safety and the protection of the environment). The requirement to reduce non-tariff restriction is indirectly contained in Article III, VIII and XI GATT. However, there is no general prohibition. Only specific measures are explicitly prohibited or limited in their applicability, such as quotas and subsidies. On the other hand, *the prohibition on discrimination in Article III GATT requires equal treatment of imported and local goods as to, e.g., taxation, technical standards or other legal requirements*. Imported goods are not to be treated less favorably than goods produced within the country.

Apart from the creation of several other GATT complementing frameworks[36] on this topic, these technical trade restrictions have been addressed during the Uruguay Round which led to the establishment of the *Agreement on Technical Barriers to Trade*. It applies to technical rules and norms which have been implemented by a state due to e.g. the protection of consumers or the environment. The agreement prescribes that these technical rules and norms, as well as their certification and supervision, must not amount to an unnecessary trade restriction. Its aim is to improve the legal framework to give parties certainty in the area of technical norms and regulation.

b) Quotas

A basic GATT principle is *the prohibition of quotas. Only tariffs are allowed as restrictive trade practice* because they are more transparent and cause less disruption to trade. *Quotas are volume restrictions on export or import to or from a member country imposed by another member country.* Article XI expressly prohibits the use of such quotas by a member state; this is in line with the tariffs-only maxim. However, the GATT allows for a few exceptions. As far as a quota is permitted, Article XIII requires a nondiscriminatory application. Article XII allows for the required exception in cases where a country has serious balance of payment problems. Furthermore, export restrictions may be imposed if there is a shortage of a good. Import and export restrictions may also be utilized to reduce overproduction of, e.g., fishery or agricultural goods.

c) Subsidies (Article XVI GATT)

Distortion of competition can also be caused by subsidies, especially *export subsidies*. This area has grown since the 1970s through members such as the EU States which heavily subsidized steel and agricultural production. Other countries also grant public funding for ship production and the clothing and car industry. These subsidies are often the result of sectorial or regional employment politics to retain jobs. The subsidies can lead to tensions between member states, especially between the EU and the USA. As a counter measure, the USA has often imposed special tariffs (so-called countervailing duties) on subsidized goods.

The GATT contains an acknowledgement by the parties that subsidizing an export good can lead to adverse effects on other exporting or importing member states. The legal basis for subsidy regulations is set out in Article XVI GATT. Under the GATT 1947, if a state granted subsidies which led to market distortion, an aggrieved member state could counteract under Article VI GATT by imposing a tariff to offset the subsidy. This right could, however, only be exercised if the subsidy caused, or was likely to cause, substantial damage to an already existing branch of the aggrieved state's economy. Unlike in other instances where

[36] C.f. Agreement on the Application of Sanitary and Phytosanitary Measures (SPS Agreement) and the Agreement on Customs Valuation (Article VII of GATT 1994) as well as numerous rules on import licensing procedures.

countermeasures required GATT authorization, a party could impose such an offset tariff unilaterally if there were extraordinary circumstances.

However, this GATT regulation was ultimately seen as being unable to adequately solve subsidy issues, because the definition of a subsidy was unclear. Therefore, a subsidy codex was implemented in 1979. Because this codex was interpreted in various ways by different countries, international tensions arose once more. As a result, Article XVI GATT was supplemented by a new agreement, *the Agreement on Subsidies and Countervailing Measures*[37] as part of the results of the Uruguay Round. The Subsidies Agreement is the legal framework on subsidies and countermeasures and contains clear rules and procedures. It defines subsidies by addressing a wide range of government practices that affect international trade in like or similar manner if an undue advantage is conferred to domestic producers. This effect is described in Article XVI (1) GATT as *"any subsidy, including any form of income or price support, which operates directly or indirectly to increase exports of any product from, or to reduce imports of any product into, its territory"*. According to the Subsidy Agreement, a subsidy is a financial contribution by a government or any public body where, inter alia, a government practice involves a direct transfer of funds (e.g. grants, loans, and equity infusion) or potential direct transfers of funds or liabilities (e.g. loan guarantees); or government revenue that is otherwise due is foregone or not collected (e.g. fiscal incentives such as tax credits); or a government provides goods or services other than general infrastructure, or purchases goods; or there is any form of income or price support. Thus, a subsidy is usually financial assistance in form of a direct payment, the waiver of existing financial duties or a direct acquisition of goods by the state. A subsidy must specifically refer to a company or an industrial branch to fall under the terms of the GATT and the Subsidy Agreement. The countervailing measures provided for in the agreement can only be utilized where such specific subsidies are granted.

The Subsidy Agreement distinguishes in its part II between prohibited and actionable subsidies. Prohibited subsidies, which *are per se illegal, directly affect trade and have adverse effects on the specific state's interests*. They are tailored to bring out a specific export result and give preference to the domestic state's products. Prohibited subsidies are divided into two categories, export subsidies and local content subsidies.[38] Should any member state be affected by such prohibited subsidies, it can challenge them in the WTO dispute settlement procedure. *Most other subsidies, such as production subsidies, are considered actionable subsidies* by the Subsidy Agreement. Actionable subsidies can either be subject to WTO dispute settlement, or an affected state can implement countervailing measures against the subsidizing state. According to Article 5 Subsidy Agreement, these subsidies must

[37] Hereinafter: Subsidy Agreement.

[38] See Art. 3.1 Subsidy Agreement: "Except as provided in the Agreement on Agriculture, the following subsidies, within the meaning of Art. 1, shall be prohibited: (a) subsidies contingent, in law or in fact, whether solely or as one of several other conditions, upon export performance (..); (b) subsidies contingent, whether solely or as one of several other conditions, upon the use of domestic over imported goods."

damage an internal sector of another member state's economy, or otherwise substantially impede the interest of a member state, for sanctions to be imposed. Substantial damage is deemed to have occurred once a subsidy exceeds 5% of the value of a good. Furthermore, such damage can also be inflicted if subsidies are used to cover corporate losses in a specific sector of the economy. The subsidizing member must then prove that its actions do not cause damage of the mentioned kind to another aggrieved member state. The agreement permits all other subsidies. These can be non-specific subsidies as well as specific ones such as basic research, enhancement of underprivileged regions and the improvement of existing facilities to meet new environmental standards.[39] The agriculture sector is not covered by the agreement as it is regulated by a special agreement.[40]

Despite having an agreement regulating and thus legitimizing countermeasures, there is nevertheless a tendency to limit such unilateral rights. Therefore, there are extensive procedural requirements which the member state must follow if it wishes to impose a tariff as countermeasure. One such requirement is a detailed investigation into a prohibited subsidy. Such an investigation needs to be conducted independently by a public authority and within 18 months at the maximum. A causal connection also needs to be shown between the subsidy and damage caused to another member state's industrial sector. To prevent protectionism, the measures are only to be employed for a maximum of 5 years. Additionally, the investigating authority must stop the investigation if the subsidy amount is less than 1% of the price of the good.

d) Dumping (Article VI GATT)

Companies fix the prices of their products usually based on business considerations. In a market economy, companies have great freedom in setting product prices. Ultimately, these prices must be competitive and cover costs and generate a profit in the medium term. *Dumping prices are very low prices employed by companies to enter a market or to expand the market share.* Such prices may cause harm to competitors and potentially lead to market distortion and have an adverse impact on the affected sector of a country's economy. That is the reason why Article VI GATT contains general rules that define and prohibit dumping. It also provides for the option to impose anti-dumping tariffs, known as countervailing duties, to counter the effects of dumping. In urgent cases, these actions can be taken unilaterally (Art VI (6) GATT). These are regulated in more detail in the Agreement on Implementation of Article VI of the General Agreement on Tariffs and Trade 1994.[41]

According to Article VI (1) GATT, a good is classified as being dumped if it is brought into a market below its normal value, and its export price into another country is lower than the price of a similar good in the exporting country. In general,

---

[39] Art. 8 Subsidy Agreement.

[40] Agreement on Agriculture, Marrakesh Agreement Establishing the World Trade Organization, Annex 1A (1994), 1867 UNTS 410.

[41] Hereinafter: Implementation Agreement.

dumping occurs if a good is sold under its market value. As stated in Article VI (1): *"For the purposes of this Article, a product is to be considered as being introduced into the commerce of an importing country at less than its normal value, if the price of the product exported from one country to another (a) is less than the comparable price, in the ordinary course of trade, for the like product when destined for consumption in the exporting country."*[42] An example is the flooding of the oil market by the countries of the Organization of the Petroleum Exporting Countries (OPEC) in 2015 to financially undermine the process of oil fracking in Alaska by the US Government. The fracking process is technologically difficult and demanding and increases the cost of oil production. By flooding the market with cheap oil, OPEC hoped to stop the US' fracking activities since it would eventually be too expensive and have a low return on investment.

To ascertain whether a product is being dumped, the price of the product is compared to the price of a similar good. If the export price of a good is lower than the internal market price of a similar good, dumping has taken place. Anti-dumping tariffs can only be imposed if an internal industrial sector has been substantially damaged by the dumping practice.[43] In such a case, the aggrieved state must conduct an official investigation to ascertain if such damage has indeed occurred. Such an investigation is to be carried out in accordance with the Implementation Agreement which contains detailed rules to ascertain if dumping is used and the amount of damage caused.

Dumping is the undercutting of the market price by private companies. This is unlike the case of subsidies which are given by a state. What the two measures have in common is that, as is the case for subsidies, anti-dumping tariffs need to be reported to the WTO so that it can initiate a dispute resolution procedure. Market-distorting subsidies and dumping are usually counteracted by import tariffs of importing states to compensate for the distortion and deter such action.

5.2.5.6 TRIMs: Trade-Related Investment Measures

The TRIMs Agreement focuses on the relations between trade in goods and investments. The TRIMs Agreement was a reaction to national policies that impeded foreign investment; it was drafted and agreed upon during the Uruguay Round by all the WTO Members. As the preamble states, the TRIMs Agreement focuses on reducing the trade restrictive and distortive effects which domestic investment measures can have, as these measures would normally favor domestic industries rather than an open market for domestic and international market players alike.

[42] Cf. the definition in Art. 2(1) Implementation Agreement: For the purpose of this Agreement, a product is to be considered as being dumped, i.e. introduced into the commerce of another country at less than its normal value, if the export price of the product exported from one country to another is less than the comparable price, in the ordinary course of trade, for the like product when destined for consumption in the exporting country.

[43] Cf. Art 6(6) Implementation Agreement.

Therefore, the goal was to increase global economic growth by facilitating investments across international frontiers. Moreover, trade-related investment measures are stated as one of the four supply modes of services within the GATS.[44]

The compact agreement spreads over only nine articles. Article 1 regulates the coverage of the TRIMs, providing that the agreement applies to all investment measures related to trade in goods only; this refers to the regulations under the GATT. Article 2 then goes deeper into the relationship between the GATT and the TRIMs by referring to the principles of National Treatment (Article III GATT) and of General Elimination of Quantitative Restrictions (Article XI GATT). These GATT principles provide the legal basis of the TRIMS framework which predominantly consists of formal standards (e.g. notification, transparency and consultation requirements), leaving the exemplary and by far non-concluding list of inconsistent TRIMs to the Annex (Illustrative List). Article 7 of the TRIMs Agreement also establishes the Committee on Trade-Related Investment Measures which meets at least once a year to discuss current matters, or at the request of a member. The committee is self-organized and carries out the responsibilities assigned to it by the Council for Trade in Goods. The committee also annually reports to the Council.

5.2.6 GATS: General Agreement on Trade in Services

5.2.6.1 Introduction

The second large agreement under the WTO Agreement is the General Agreement on Trade in Services (GATS) which regulates trade in the tertiary sector. When the GATT was created, this sector was by far not as important and influential as it is today. Following the second industrial revolution, the secondary sector of most economies was usually the most significant and elaborated sector and responsible for domestic economic growth. However, because of the rapid growth of the tertiary sector, an international legal framework became necessary to extend global liberalization also to international trade in services. The GATS was adopted to fill this gap. It applies to all forms of international services and consists of a framework agreement, annexes and a list of mandatory and excluded services.[45] Hence, for the first time ever, services became part of the multilateral regulatory system of world trade, giving the WTO member states protection from discrimination and arbitrary conduct under international law. This symbolizes an important step away from the previous oft-criticized limitation on trade in goods *by expanding the basic principles regulating international trade to services as well.*

[44] See infra, Sect. 5.2.6.2.

[45] The excluded service sectors include the telecommunication, finance, audiovisual and ocean seafaring sectors.

However, the wholesale transfer of GATT principles to the GATS was, in practice, not possible due to the subject matters' fundamentally different nature; trade in services follows partly rules different from trade in goods. As a framework agreement, the GATS contains a few behavioral principles, some of them similar to the basic principles of the GATT, to facilitate progressive liberalization processes in the tertiary sector. In conjunction with its annexes, it addresses problems in relation to mobility of labor, financial services, air and sea transportation and telecommunications. Furthermore, *enforceable rights to market entry and to national treatment were created.*

The GATS is divided into two important parts. The first contains *general obligations and main principles* such as MFN treatment and the principle of transparency, but also exceptions. The second part regulates the *rules and principles regulating member states' specific commitments.*

5.2.6.2 Scope and Definitions (Article I GATS)

The very first provision, Article I GATS, regulates the scope and defines the most important terms. Article I (1) GATS stipulates that the agreement applies to measures taken by states which affect trade in services. As an international agreement, the GATS thus regulates measures regarding services with a cross-border component.

What is a service? Article I (3) (b) GATS defines the term "services" as *any service in any sector except services supplied in the exercise of governmental authority.* The latter refers to "*any service which is supplied neither on a commercial basis, nor in competition with one or more service suppliers*" (Article I (3) (c) GATS). Thus, according to Article I GATT, all of the main service areas and forms of international service fall under the GATS. To avoid a gap between the GATT and GATS, service sectors were included gradually; thus, all economic activities outside the production of industrial or agricultural goods are now covered.

Importantly, trade in most cases requires a movement of production factors abroad. This is especially the case with services that require personnel stationed in the foreign market, hence necessitating movements of persons or the establishment of a subsidiary in the foreign country. Therefore, trade in services is categorized into four supply modes according to Article I (2) GATS:

Cross-border

Consumption of services within the target country by a foreign supplier, enabling customers of the target country to consume the services through telecommunications or postal infrastructure.

Consumption abroad

Consumption of services rendered to consumers in other member states.

Commercial presence

The rendering of a service by an affiliated subsidiary or representative of a foreign service supplier within the target country, e.g. bank, hotel group, construction company.

Movement of natural persons

This involves the personal rendering of services through a foreign supplier (natural person) within the target country. It therefore does not matter whether the service is personally offered (such as a freelance worker) or offered by an employee on behalf of a service supplier such as, e.g., a consultancy firm, a hospital etc.

Thus, all services rendered under one of the headings are covered, except for services *"supplied in the exercise of governmental authority"*. What are measures by states? Instead of defining the measures per se, the GATS sets out the authorities whose measure would qualify as a measure by states. According to Article I (3) GATS, these authorities are *"central, regional or local governments and authorities", and non-governmental bodies in the exercise of delegated governmental powers*. Thus, "measures" refers to an exercise of governmental powers and are therefore authoritative, binding acts that regulate conduct.

5.2.6.3 General Obligations and Main Principles (Part II GATS)

a) Introduction

Part II of the GATS regulates general obligations that member states must comply with; these general obligations are independent of any concrete commitments by a member state. Some of these obligations and principles correspond to similar principles in the GATT; others are determined by the scope of the GATS and are therefore service-specific. The most significant articles are Article II which regulates the MFN principle, and Article III which sets out the principle of transparency. Furthermore, Article XII contains a similar rule regarding the protection of the payment balance in the GATT, with due regard to the general exceptions in Article XIV.

b) Most-Favored-Nation Treatment Obligation (Article II GATS)

The GATS regulates in Article II (1), as a basic obligation of the member states, the Most-Favored-Nation Treatment obligation. Hence, a member state is obliged to *"accord immediately and unconditionally to services and service suppliers of any other Member treatment no less favourable than that it accords to like services and service suppliers of any other country"* (Article II (1) GATS).

However, the MFN treatment does not apply absolutely. Excluded from the MFN treatment are free trade zones, and, mutatis mutandis, economic integration areas (Article V GATS) under the GATS. Moreover, Article VII GATS does not require a full application of the MFN to the assessment of foreign qualifications of service providers. A foreign qualification does not automatically need to be approved by another member state. However, the approval of a qualification is not to be used as a discriminatory tool nor as a hidden trade barrier. It must be based on objective criteria directly related to the quality of the service offered. In particular, since, e.g., doctors and attorneys are subject to national regulation, member states are not obliged to allow foreign doctors or attorneys to practice in a member state without any further requirements. The MFN treatment obligation entails, however, equal treatment of foreign service providers which allows all service providers as well as consumers to participate in the liberalization process.

c) Further Obligations and Principles
The principle of transparency contained in Article III GATS *obliges member states to publish promptly all relevant measures of general application which affect trade in services* and thus pertain to or affect the operation of the GATS. This obligation also applies to international agreements pertaining to or affecting trade in services to which a member state is a signatory. The principle of transparency is also *a fundamental rule of law standard.*

Such rule of law standards are further found in Article VI which deals with domestic regulations. This provision is applicable when a member state has entered specific commitments which grant foreign service providers market access. If this is the case, measures of general application affecting trade in services *must be administered in a reasonable, objective and impartial manner*. To ensure this, the member state must establish pertinent judicial proceedings and grant foreign service providers access to courts for review of decisions affecting trade in services under the commitments entered by the state. The procedures must provide for an objective and impartial review.

Another important principle is the *principle of recognition in Article VII GATS.* There is no general obligation of the member states to recognize the education or experience obtained, requirements met, or licenses or certifications granted in another member state. However, states may grant such recognition either unilaterally or based on agreements with other states. Although the MFN principle does not automatically apply, a state should nevertheless offer other interested states an "adequate opportunity" to negotiate recognition. Generally, the principle of non-discrimination applies, and recognition should not operate as a disguised restriction on trade in services.

d) Exceptions to the MFN and Other Principles
Like the GATT, the GATS regulates exceptions to MFN and other principles, mostly in a similar way to the GATT. An exception can be made by economic integration arrangements regulated in Article V GATS, and labor market integration agreements regulated in Article V *bis* GATS. As in the GATT, one important requirement is that such arrangements *shall not, in respect of other member states, raise the overall level of barriers to trade in services compared to the level prior to the arrangement.*

The GATS further provides in Article XIV for general exceptions, in Article XIV *bis* for security exceptions, and in Article X for emergency safeguard measures. Article XI und XII GATS make clear that a country may, under ordinary circumstances, not apply restrictions on international transfers and payments for current transactions relating to its specific commitments under the GATS, but only in the event of serious balance of payments and difficulties in external financial relations.

5.2.6.4 Rules on Specific Commitments (Part III)

Part II of the GATS contains all the general obligations of the member states, whereas the specific obligations are regulated in Part III. These *specific market entry obligations* are *separate commitments of each member state* and are *included in so-called country lists* which form an integral part of the GATS. Every member state's list *contains the service areas and obligations the member state has entered into to facilitate market entry for these services*. Some states have made reservations to certain service areas to which they restrict market entry. These reservations can take the form of quota restrictions or restrictions based on nationality. Ultimately, this means that market entry can only be restricted for service providers from member countries for which a country has made a reservation. These country-specific reservations have been negotiated bilaterally and are part of the entry price in participating in the GATS. The countries undertaking GATS obligations are evidenced by the lists, which specify the areas in which liberalization is to take place. The lists are negotiated bilaterally; however, based on the MFN principle, they apply to all member states. In addition, *states have generally to observe the principle of national treatments* according to Article XVII GATS.[46]

5.2.6.5 Parts IV to VI GATS

Part IV provides for the *continued liberalization of trade in services*, and therefore members shall enter into successive rounds of negotiation (Article XIX (1) GATS). This shows that, as with the GATT, the GATS has initiated *a process of liberalization* by increasingly reducing the impediments to global trade in services. Ultimately the goal is to further extend the country list and reduce the reservations on it. This will be achieved through further bilateral or multilateral negotiations, the results of which will extend to all states based on the MFN principle. Parts V and VI consist of some further provisions, in particular regarding the Dispute Settlement Process, which is common to all the contracts under the WTO Agreement.[47]

---

[46] The principle says that a state "shall accord to services and service suppliers of any other Member, in respect of all measures affecting the supply of services, treatment no less favorable than that it accords to its own like services and service suppliers."

[47] See infra, Sect. 5.2.9.

5.2.7 TRIPS: Trade-Related Aspects of Intellectual Property Rights

5.2.7.1 Subject Matter and Objectives

The third basic pillar of the WTO is the *Agreement on Trade-Related Aspects of Intellectual Property Rights (TRIPS)* which introduces basic trading rules for intellectual property. The agreement establishes minimum standards. Member states are free to go beyond them[48]; further, they have the autonomy to decide how to implement the TRIPS's provisions within their own legal system and practice.

That intellectual property (IP) was included in the discussions during the Uruguay Round reflects its growing overall importance and its extraordinary impact on the global economy; an ever-increasing part of the economy rests on patents, copyrights and IP rights. This is also reflected in Article 7 TRIPS which states the agreement's objectives: "*The protection and enforcement of intellectual property rights should contribute to the promotion of technological innovation and to the transfer and dissemination of technology, to the mutual advantage of producers and users of technological knowledge and in a manner conducive to social and economic welfare, and to a balance of rights and obligations.*" Extensive research and development costs of intellectual property such as, e.g., in the pharmaceutical industry, added to the need for protection, particularly because intellectual property piracy, imitations and counterfeiting pose a huge problem to international trade. In some states, intellectual property protection was virtually non-existent which caused imitated and pirated products to be distributed to the world market from these countries without payment of license fees. Therefore, these products are generally much cheaper than the original products. As a result, the manufacturers of the original products are insufficiently compensated for their development investments. This impairs innovation and disrupts international trade. In total the value of pirated and imitated goods exceeds 5% of total world trade.

Despite this, the TRIPS Agreement is repeatedly criticized. A central criticism is that the concept of intellectual property is determined by Western ideas of the legal protection of individual human creations by *establishing commercializable monopoly rights*. This is said to be primarily in the interest of large global companies based in the developed world, such as the US IT, entertainment and film industry, companies of the digital industry, or global pharmaceutical companies.[49] This would lead to an additional disadvantage for developing countries, e.g., in economic development, or in the field of health and in education, to name just a few. TRIPS is said *to be a form of neo-colonialism, overburdening developing countries*, which must adapt their legal system to very strict standards of Western origin that are foreign to them. This criticism must be taken seriously. However, it does not change the fact

---

[48] Art. I(1) TRIPS.

[49] See, e.g., Archibugi and Filippetti (2010), pp. 137–149.

that TRIPS is a central step forward in the global standardization of IP rights, not only in terms of their content, but also regarding the applicable procedures.

The TRIPS addresses copyright and related rights (i.e. the rights of performers, producers of sound recordings and broadcasting organizations), trademarks, geographical indications, industrial designs, patents including even the protection of new varieties of plants, the layout-designs of integrated circuits, and undisclosed information including trade secrets and test data. In so doing *it also concretizes the fundamental GATT principles for IP rights and stipulates rules stemming from the most notable international agreements in the area of intellectual property* (set out below). The TRIPS aims at increasing protection of intellectual property while simultaneously ensuring that no protective trade barriers are created through using excessive or overly complex intellectual property laws.

5.2.7.2 Basic Principles (Part I TRIPS)

The basic principles are listed in the first part of the TRIPS. One important obligation is the *national treatment obligation*.[50] According to this principle, a WTO member shall accord to the nationals of other Members treatment no less favorable than that it accords to its own nationals regarding the protection of intellectual property. The other basic principle is, like under GATT and GATS, the *MFN treatment obligation* which is to be found in Article 4(1) TRIPS. According to this obligation, any advantage, favor, privilege or immunity granted by a member to the nationals of any other country regarding the protection of intellectual property shall be accorded immediately and unconditionally to the nationals of all other members. In line with the general exceptions contained in the GATT and GATS, Article 8(1) allows states *"to adopt measures necessary to protect public health and nutrition, and to promote the public interest in sectors of vital importance to their socio-economic and technological development, provided that such measures are consistent with the provisions of this Agreement."*

The TRIPS defines the main elements of protection, i.e. the subject-matter to be protected, the concrete rights, exceptions to those rights, and the minimum duration of protection. In so doing, the TRIPS refers to the substantive provisions of the main conventions of the World Intellectual Property Organization (WIPO), the Paris Convention for the Protection of Industrial Property (Paris Convention), the Berne Convention for the Protection of Literary and Artistic Works (Berne Convention), the Rome Convention, and the Treaty on Intellectual Property in Respect of Integrated Circuits. The main substantive provisions of these conventions are explicitly referred to and thus become obligations under the TRIPS Agreement. The TRIPS thus contains provisions of public international law as well as international private law.

[50] Art. 3(1) TRIPS.

5.2.7.3 Protection of Private Rights (Part II TRIPS)

An important part of the TRIPS consists of rules which *grant enforceable rights to private individuals, and which impose concrete obligations on the states*. These rules form the core of the TRIPS, which means that private individuals can, at least to a certain extent, directly rely on the provisions vis-à-vis their state. However, it should be noted that the TRIPS *only applies to the trade-related aspects of intellectual property*. It is *not* an all-encompassing multilateral agreement on intellectual property.

As in the main pre-existing intellectual property conventions, the basic obligation of each member state is to accord the treatment regarding the protection of intellectual property provided for under the Agreement to the "persons" of other Members. "Persons" is defined in Article 1.3 as "nationals"; but it also includes persons, natural or legal, who are closely related to other Members without necessarily being nationals.

5.2.7.4 Enforcement (Part III TRIPS)

Part III of the TRIPS Agreement regulates member states' enforcement obligations. This requires them *to enact laws that permit effective action by national and foreign right holders against infringements* of intellectual property rights (IPR). The Agreement establishes certain general principles to be observed and implemented by the member states and applicable to all IPR enforcement procedures. Namely, they should be fair and equitable, not unnecessarily complicated or costly, and should not entail unreasonable time-limits or unwarranted delays.[51] They should also allow for judicial review of final administrative decisions.[52] In addition, it contains provisions on civil and administrative procedures and remedies, such as provisions regulating provisional measures, evidence, the right of information, injunctions, damages, indemnification, provisional measures, special requirements related to border measures and criminal procedures. Thus, the TRIPS specifies quite in detail the procedures and remedies that must be available under national law so that rights holders can effectively enforce their rights.

The TRIPS hence contains *international minimal judicial and administrative procedural standards which also reflect basic rule of law principles*. Article 41(5) TRIPS states that the agreement does not oblige states to create a specific judicial system for the enforcement of intellectual property rights. Indeed, it is most likely the case that no member state has done so. Therefore, the TRIPS principles are *de facto general requirements for the member states' judicial systems*.

---

[51] Art. 41(2) TRIPS.

[52] Art. 41(4) TRIPS.

5.2.8 Trade Policy Review Mechanism (TPRM)

Another important pillar of the WTO is the Trade Policy Review Mechanism (TPRM). The WTO Agreement establishes a review mechanism to enable the WTO bodies to evaluate, on a regular basis, *individual member state's trade policies and practices and their impact on the functioning of the multilateral trading system.* The mechanism is *not designed to serve as an enforcement mechanism* of specific obligations under the Agreements; neither is it designed for dispute settlement, or to impose new policy commitments on member states. However. an integral part of the WTO's work is the monitoring of national trade policies and the ways in which they are applied. This is in line with the *monitoring role that organs of international organizations often have*, i.e. to monitor their member states' conduct as to their compliance and their execution of an organization's purpose, rules and policies. As far as the WTO is concerned, a credible trade policy review process is a necessity: mishandled or even unlawful trade policies can have a huge adverse impact on the global economy and may severely undermine the whole WTO structure. Thus, a review mechanism allows for better control of member states' trade policy activities and their adherence to existing rules, disciplines and commitments under the multilateral trade agreements.

Introduced early during the Uruguay Round and later finalized and confirmed as an integral part of the WTO Agreement in 1995, this review mechanism was not really new; the GATT 1947 had already established a similar mechanism. However, this mechanism only affected trade in goods because the other agreements did not exist yet. The newly designed TPRM was therefore implemented as an annex to the WTO Agreement, making it applicable to all other agreements thereunder. Still, one might ask how exactly the TPRM seeks to ensure transparency and promote socio-economic growth. To be involved in international trade, market players require as much market information as possible. The first way that the TPRM ensures transparency is by *requiring the market players, i.e. the WTO member states, to report specific measures, policies or laws affecting international trade to the WTO* and its members immediately. This allows for a collective appreciation and evaluation of the full range of the states' trade policies and practices and thus, the impact on the functioning of the multilateral trading system as demanded in the objectives of the TPRM.

The second way that the TPRM seeks to ensure transparency is through the *WTO's regular review of its members' trade policies*. The review process is set out in subsection C of the TPRM; this subsection also establishes the *Trade Policy Review Body (TPRB)* . Even though the actual organ of the TPRB is none other than the WTO General Council, it still conducts its work under the name of the TPRB. The procedure is focused not only on the greater goals of international trade, but also on the socio-economic and developmental needs of each country under review. By ensuring that trade policy reviews are held on a regular basis, states are encouraged to follow the WTO's specific country recommendations more closely. Generally, all the members are reviewed regularly, though the frequency of the review varies according to the size and economic influence of the country in question. Therefore, the four biggest market players, which are the USA, the European Union, Japan and China, are reviewed more frequently than others, i.e. they are scrutinized every other year. The following 16 states, also measured by economic power, are scrutinized every 4 years. Finally, the remaining countries are scrutinized every 6 years, leaving developing countries the possibility of extending the scrutiny period to beyond 6 years.

5.2.9 Regulation of Dispute Settlement: The Dispute Settlement Understanding (DSU)

5.2.9.1 General Remarks

The rules on dispute settlement form one of the backbones of the WTO system. Disputes in the WTO are essentially broken promises; they usually arise when one country adopts a trade policy measure or takes some action that one or more fellow WTO members considers to be a breach of the WTO agreements, or to be a failure to live up to obligations. WTO members have agreed that if they believe fellow members are violating trade rules, they will settle the dispute through the multilateral system instead of acting unilaterally against the offending member. Thus, one of the major achievements of the Uruguay Round and the Marrakesh Agreements is the *eradication of unilateralism* by providing official procedures to formally decide and settle trade disputes. For states, this means abiding by the agreed procedures and respecting judgments.[53]

The general idea of such a dispute settlement body is not new to the international community. It had already been introduced to the GATT 1947, but it was mostly ineffective. The GATT envisaged only a very rudimentary system of dispute settlement incorporating primary consultations as well as arbitration procedures. Under this procedure, panels were created to investigate disputes. Although the procedure was arbitrational in character, its primary aim was to find an amicable solution between the parties. The ultimate settlement of the dispute rested with the GATT Council. However, its decision only carried the weight of a recommendation and had no legal consequences or force. It only became a form of secondary GATT law if the signatory states to the GATT accepted the decision. To determine whether or not to accept the decision, the parties to the dispute had a right to vote on it, though in practice, these decisions were reached by consensus. According to this system, a panel decision also required the consent of the losing party.

[53] Unfortunately, unilateralism in trade policy has increased significantly in recent years. In particular, the US, under re-elected President Trump, has taken measures that violate WTO law. At the same time, the US is preventing the election of new judges to the Appellate Body, so that the dispute settlement is currently not really functioning.

The GATT 1947 dispute settlement system was also ineffective for another reason. Many technical requirements which have been incorporated into the dispute settlement body under the WTO, such as fixed timelines in which a dispute was to be decided, did not exist under the GATT 1947. Therefore, cases were dragged out inconclusively over long periods of time, and if a ruling was eventually produced, a single member state could easily block its approval. Hence, during the Uruguay Round, the dispute settlement system was reworked completely. The result was the thoroughly structured and organized framework in the *"Understanding on Rules and Procedures Governing the Settlement of Disputes"* (DSU), annexed to the WTO Agreement (annex 2). The core concept was to create one single mechanism that would apply to all WTO Agreements and treaties alike. The system was thus reformed towards achieving a real Dispute Settlement Body (DSB). Among its competencies are the creation of a panel, the acceptance of recommendations for settlement, supervision of decisions and recommendations as well as the power to grant a member state the right to suspend its obligations under the GATT and/or the other agreements.[54] The DSU system provides the WTO with clearly defined rules on how to settle disputes. According to these rules, a single party can no longer unilaterally block the approval of a recommendation to resolve the dispute. The system also includes an appeal procedure against recommendations made by the panels.

All this has been *a major breakthrough in trade history*, since this procedure paves the way for the application of the principles of fairness, open dealing and mutual benefit. Moreover, it secures peace and promotes socio-economic growth internationally. Hence, the DSU introduced a *unique, very elaborate and highly efficient system of court-like adjudication of interstate trade disputes* which is also the WTO's last resort of enforcement when states do not comply with WTO rules. The rules on dispute settlement are thus the *very central pillar of the multilateral trading system* and the WTO's major contribution to the stability of the global economic system.[55]

Unfortunately, since 2019 the United States have been blocking the DSU-system by vetoing new appointments to the appellate body, which severely jeopardizes the functioning of the entire dispute settlement and generally the idea of a rules-based multilateral trading system. One consequence thereof is that there is no functioning legal remedy against first-instance panel reports to that appeals remain without a final decision but remain in a legal void. At the same time are appealed panel reports not enforceable.

---

[54] Art. 2 para. 1 DSU.

[55] <http://www.wto.org/english/thewto_e/whatis_e/tif_e/disp1_e.htm> (accessed 9 March 2025). Unfortunately the WTO dispute settlement is in a serious crisis. Its appeals mechanism is not functioning because the United States has been blocking appointments to the Appellate Body, which has led to most panel reports being appealed "into the void" and leaving the dispute unresolved. As a result, it has become difficult right for members states to enforce WTO obligations through complaints against measures they believe are in violation.

5.2.9.2 Overview of the DSU-System

The system is based on clearly defined rules, including timeframes in which a case is to be completed. It introduced greater discipline to settle a case in a timely manner, but with flexible deadlines at various stages of the process. The agreement emphasizes that *prompt dispute settlement is essential if the WTO is to function effectively.* It further sets out, in considerable detail, the procedures and the timetable to be followed in resolving disputes.

According to Article 1 DSU, the *dispute settlement procedure applies to nearly all treaties and agreements* signed during the Uruguay Round, especially the WTO Agreement, the GATT, the GATS and TRIPS. Additionally, it is also applicable to some plurilateral trade agreements.[56] It is therefore a universal mechanism for the settlement of disputes arising from the WTO agreements. This is of central importance because, apart from the EU, *there is no international organization which has a similar quasi-judiciary dispute settlement mechanism.* This shows importance with which the parties viewed their obligations when they signed the agreements that resulted from the Uruguay round.

Article 2 DSU addresses the status of the DSB. It has the power to set up panels, supervise decisions and recommendations and grant a waiver of obligations under the WTO commitments. It is the *central organ of the WTO dispute settlement system.*

If a member state believes that another member state has violated its obligations and thus interfered with its rights, it can enter into consultation with that member state. The member state allegedly in breach is obligated to reply within 10 days and to start consultations within 30 days. The start and progress of the consultation must be communicated to the DSB.

If no consultations are possible within 60 days or if the member state in breach rejects consultation, the aggrieved member state has the right to convene a dispute settlement panel. In important cases, these timeframes can be shortened. A panel is composed of three trade (law) experts from countries other than the two in dispute. If a party rejects a panel member, the General Director of the WTO must establish a new panel within 60 days. Once established, the panel must present a report within 6 months or, in urgent cases, within 3 months. However, because it is a mere recommendation to the DSB, the report is neither final nor binding. Notwithstanding that, the panel report is accepted as long as the DSB does not reject it unanimously within 60 days, or a party to the dispute does not object to it within the same timeframe by appealing to the Appellate Body. Thus, the Uruguay Round agreement made it impossible for the country that lost a case to block the ruling from being adopted. *Rulings are thus automatically adopted unless they are rejected by*

[56] The applicability of the DSU to plurilateral agreements is subject to the adoption of a decision by the parties to each of these agreements setting out the terms for the application of the DSU to the individual agreement, including any special and additional rules or procedures (Appendix 1 of the DSU). The Committee on Government Procurement has taken such a decision, but not the Committee on Trade in Civil Aircraft for the Agreement on Trade in Civil Aircraft; cf. <https://www.wto.org/english/tratop_e/dispu_e/disp_settlement_cbt_e/c1s5p1_e.htm> (accessed 9 March 2025).

consensus. Any country wanting to block a ruling must persuade all other WTO members (including the counterparty in the case) to share its view. That is almost impossible.

The standing appellate body has the power to review the panel report if a party to the dispute objects to the panel report within 60 days of the report being issued. An appeal is *limited to legal arguments*, which means that political and economic considerations cannot be directly argued. 3 of the 7 members of the appellate body decide on the appeal. They have the power to uphold the report, modify it or reject certain conclusions drawn from it. This procedure should not take more than 90 days and generally takes only 60 days. The appellate body also decides by way of a report, which will be accepted if the DSB does not object by consensus within 30 days. The DSB has to decide on the matter within 30 days of publication of the appellate body's report. Accepted appellate decisions must be complied with by the parties to the dispute. *In total, the duration of the procedure, starting with the setting up of the panel up to the decision on the report, should not take more than 9 months; and if there is an appeal, not more than 12 months.* The agreed time limits are flexible, and if the case is considered urgent (e.g. if perishable goods are involved), it is accelerated as much as possible.

After the report is accepted, the party in breach must inform the DSB the steps it will take to rectify its breach. The DSB then supervises the implementation of the report. If the results of the report are not implemented, the aggrieved party can *demand from the DSB the right to utilize countermeasures against the party in breach*. Article 22 stipulates the options a party has. In general, the countermeasure must refer to the economic area where the original breach occurred. Should this be impossible, concessions can be suspended in other economic areas.

Although much of the procedure does resemble a court or tribunal, the preferred solution is for the countries concerned to discuss their problems and settle the dispute by themselves. The first stage is therefore consultations between the governments concerned, and even when the case has progressed to other stages, consultation and mediation are still always possible.[57] The point very often is not to pass judgment, and the priority is to settle disputes through consultations if possible. Moreover, the DSU even provides for this method in Article 5.1, allowing for assistance through good offices, conciliation or mediation.

An overview on the dispute settlement provides the following flow charts (Fig. 5.3)[58]:

[57] <http://www.wto.org/english/thewto_e/whatis_e/tif_e/disp1_e.htm> (accessed 9 March 2025).

[58] <https://www.wto.org/english/tratop_e/dispu_e/disp_settlement_cbt_e/c6s1p1_e.htm> (accessed 9 March 2025).

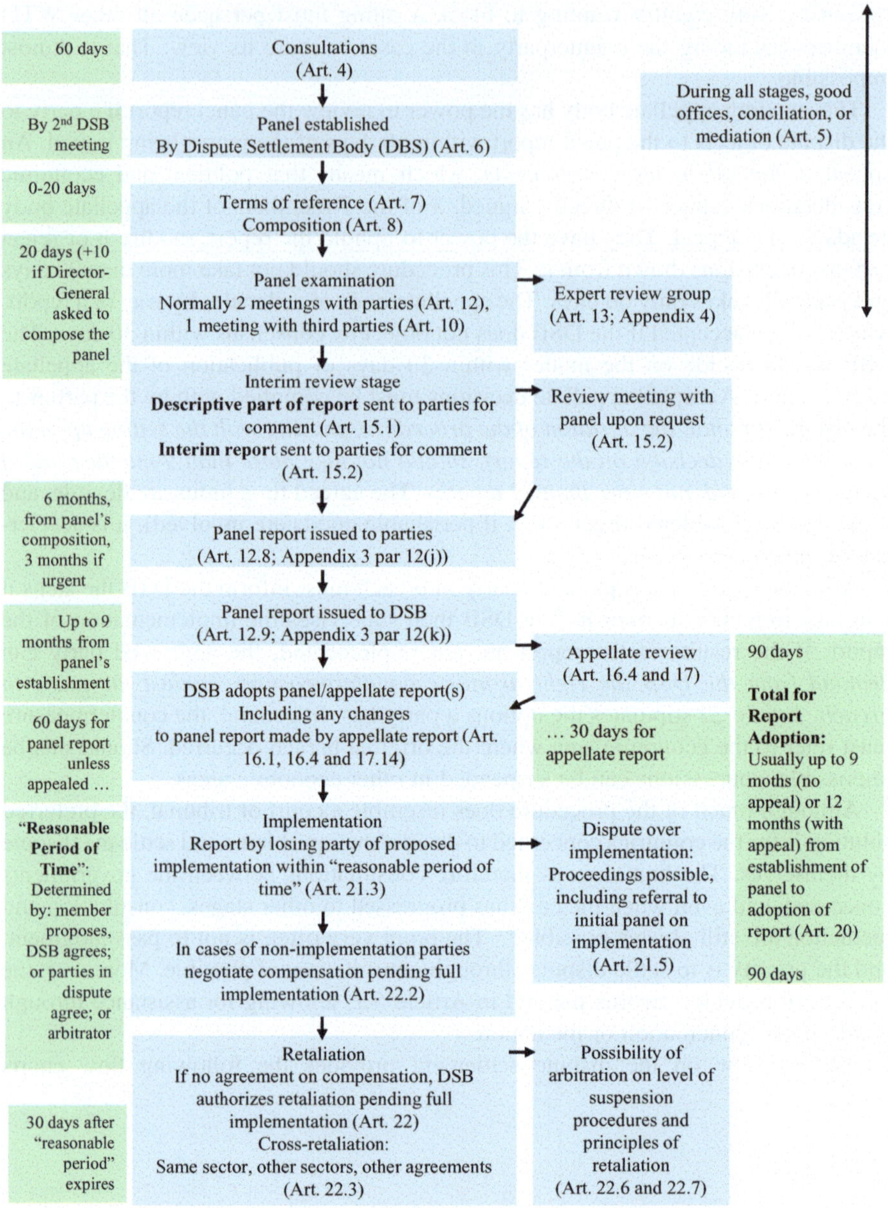

Fig. 5.3 Dispute Settlement. Own graphic inspired by WTO (2024) Dispute settlement: Introduction to dispute settlement in the WTO. WTO, Geneva https://www.wto.org/english/tratop_e/dispu_e/disp_settlement_cbt_e/c6s1p1_e.htm (accessed 8 March 2025)

5.2.10 Regional Economic Integration

Regional economic integration plays a central role in worldwide trade relations. Although the WTO aims to create the political and legal framework for global trade, already when the GATT came into force in 1947, the contracting states considered closer economic ties between states in a region based on treaties as an option or even a necessity because economic intercourse normally takes place primarily between neighboring countries and with countries in the same region. *In view of close mutual interdependencies in regions, there is therefore often a need for more detailed regional regulations.* However, due to the principle of most-favored-nation treatment that applies to all WTO basic agreements (GATT, GATS, TRIPS) this would only possible to a very limited extent: When a WTO member enters into a regional integration arrangement, or—in the terminology of the WTO—regional trade agreements (RTA) through which it grants more favorable conditions to its trade with other parties to that arrangement than to other WTO members' trade, it departs from the guiding principle of the MFN clause and of non-discrimination defined in Article I of GATT, Article II of GATS, and elsewhere. As a basic rule, genuine trade advantages that individual states grant each other must be passed on to all WTO states as a consequence of the most-favored-nation obligation. This would make it impossible, e.g., to create free trade areas and customs unions.

However, such obstacles to regional economic cooperation would have contradicted a fundamental idea of the GATT and now the WTO, namely, to promote and liberalize interstate trade generally with a view to overall prosperity gains. Therefore, it makes sense to provide an exception to the MFN principle for regional economic integration and to allow preferential trade agreements. As of March 2025, 373 RTAs were in force.[59] This shows how important regional economic integration is. RTAs are also particularly popular when liberalization steps fail to materialize or progress sluggishly at the global level. However, care must be taken to ensure that regional economic integration does not occur at the expense of states not participating in it, as this would contradict the general goal of promoting global trade in the interest of all states involved.[60]

Article XXIV (4) GATT therefore recognizes

> *"the desirability of increasing freedom of trade by the development, through voluntary agreements, of closer integration between the economies of the countries parties to such agreements"*

and that customs unions or free-trade areas facilitate trade between the states involved and not to raise barriers to the trade with other states. As a consequence, the

---

[59] See https://rtais.wto.org/UI/PublicMaintainRTAHome.aspx (visited March 7, 2025).

[60] This was stressed in the Nairobi Ministerial Declaration, adopted on 19 Dec 2015 (WT/MIN(15)/DEC), para. 28: "We reaffirm the need to ensure that Regional Trade Agreements (RTAs) remain complementary to, not a substitute for, the multilateral trading system."

GATT does not prevent, e.g., the formation of customs unions or of free-trade areas and even of economic supranational organizations (Article XXIV (5) GATT). However, states entering RTAs must observe rules which are to be found in Article XXIV GATT as to trade in goods and Article V GATS as to services. The basic principle is quite simple: *RTAs must cover more or less all trade between the participating states and may overall not raise additional trade barriers with non-participating, third states.* RTAs have to be notified to the WTO. The *Committee on Regional Trade Agreements (CRTA)* monitors individual regional agreements as to their conformity with WTO law and policies, this based on a transparency mechanism which provides for early announcement of any RTA and notification to the WTO.[61]

5.3 International Monetary Fund (IMF)[62]

5.3.1 Introduction: The Institutions of Bretton Woods

The first half of the twentieth century was characterized by two world wars causing enormous physical and economic destruction in Europe. In addition, the "Great Depression" of the 1930s following a hyperinflation in Germany and the breakdown of the New York stock market in 1929 led to economic devastation in both Europe and the United States. In the 1930s, as part of and a reaction to the Great Depression, many countries tried to insulate their failing economies against foreign influence by raising foreign trade barriers, devaluing their currencies to compete successfully on the international export markets and limiting their citizens' rights to hold foreign currency. These restrictive measures led to a sharp decline in world trade followed by rising unemployment rates and a general decline in living standards.

These events evidenced the necessity of an institutionalized international monetary system based on clear, enforceable rules that among others would stabilize currency exchange rates. Already in the early 1940s, even though the end of the Second World War (WW 2) was not yet foreseeable, the later victorious powers, the United States of America (US) and the United Kingdom (UK), were already thinking about how the world economy should continue after the end of the war. At this particular time, the idea of an international organization emerged. To prevent a further economic disaster, this organization should ensure exchange rate stability, monitor the member states' monetary policies and help to eliminate trade restrictions.

[61] See *Transparency Mechanism for Regional Trade Agreements*, Decision of 14 Dec 2006, WT/L/671, Decision of the General Council to establish on a provisional basis a new transparency mechanism for all RTAs.

[62] *Special thanks to Ulrike Heinrich und Dominic Staiger for their important contribution to the elaboration of this chapter.

Having that in mind, on August 14, 1941, US President Franklin D. Roosevelt and UK Prime Minister Winston S. Churchill signed a joint statement, the *"Atlantic Charter"*, containing the common principles of their international policy: no territorial aggrandizement; no territorial changes made against the wishes of the people (self-determination); restoration of self-government to those deprived to it; reduction of trade restriction; global cooperation to secure better economic and social conditions for all; freedom from fear and want; freedom of the seas; abandonment of the use of force; and disarmament of aggressor nations.[63] Thus, also the reduction of trade restrictions as well as international economic cooperation was already then put on the international agenda.

In the subsequent years, early plans for the post-war world economic order emerged. The "White-Plan" developed by Harry Dexter White, senior U.S. Treasury department official, and presented by the US in 1943 suggested the creation of an International Stabilization Fund to grant loans to member states. The Fund's main objective was the maintenance of fixed exchange rates by giving its approval to major devaluations and influencing the economic policies of debtor countries. A plan presented by the UK, the so-called Keynes Plan developed by John Maynard Keynes, one of the most influential economists of the twentieth century, included the creation of a supranational Central Bank to support countries with current account deficits.

On July 1, 1944, thus only some weeks after beginning of the Allied invasion of Normandy which was decisive in defeating Germany and ending World War II in April 1945, 730 delegates from all allied nations including the Soviet Union met for the United Nations Monetary and Financial Conference in the US mountain village of Bretton Woods, New Hampshire. The participants of the conference held at the Mount Washington Hotel sought to make financial arrangements for the postwar world after the expected defeat of Germany and Japan. In so doing, they planned to build *a framework for economic co-operation to avoid a repetition of the competitive devaluations that had contributed to the 1930s Great Depression*. The conference faced two factions: the Americans, led by Harry Dexter White, and the British, headed by John Maynard Keynes. The Americans favored free trade, fewer controls and restrictions, and fixed exchange rates. The British pursued a plan to allow controlling intervention and to keep exchange rates free. Regardless of the different objectives, both parties aimed at avoiding a repetition of the destructive policies that could spark another conflict.

The participating states were aware that *the stability of the international monetary system is an essential prerequisite for functioning global trade*. This requires stable, predictable exchange rates and the convertibility of currencies. Consequently, in the course of the conference, the participating 44 states negotiated a new international monetary system. The so-called Bretton Woods system of monetary management established the rules for commercial and financial relations among the world's major

---

[63] See Wikipedia, Atlantic Charter,< https://en.wikipedia.org/wiki/Atlantic_Charter> (accessed 9 March 2025).

industrial states. Being the *first example of a fully negotiated monetary order*, the Bretton Woods system intended to ensure stability of the monetary system by governing monetary relations among independent nation-states.

Two important organizations with different responsibilities were established. The *International Monetary Fund (IMF) whose primary purpose was and is to ensure the stability of the international monetary system*, and the *World Bank mainly focusing on economic development and investments*. With the foundation of these two organizations, a cornerstone was set for the stability of the international monetary system. Later, other organizations were established in the framework of the World Bank, namely the International Finance Corporation (IFC, established 1956),[64] the International Development Association (IDA, established 1960),[65]the Multilateral Investment Guarantee Agency (MIGA),[66] and the International Center for the Settlement of Investment Disputes.[67] All these organizations together form the *World Bank Group which, together with the IMF, constitute the Bretton Woods system*.

The institutions of Bretton Woods have structural similarities that distinguish them from most other international organizations. They are *partly modeled on corporations*. Members are obliged to make a *capital contribution*, the amount of which depends on each member's economic strength, and which also determines voting rights. The decision-making of the institutions is thus not determined by the principle of one state, one vote, but by the different capital contributions of the states, which means that the economically strongest states can exert essential influence. The Bretton Woods institutions as financial institutions are thus *largely capitalist in structure*. In addition to this, the provisions of the agreements establishing these institutions are often highly technical and reflect the language of the world of finance.

5.3.2 Development of the IMF; Purposes

Following the United Nations Monetary and Financial Conference of Bretton Woods, the IMF, also known as the Fund, formally came into existence on 27 December 1945, when the first countries ratified its Articles of Agreement (*Articles of Agreement of the International Monetary Fund*, IMF Agreement). After the first IMF projects started in May 1946, the organization's operational activities began on 1 March 1947. At this time, the international organization already had 40 Member States. The first big expansion of the IMF's membership took place

[64] For details see infra, Sect. 5.4.5.

[65] For details see infra, Sect. 5.4.4.

[66] For details see infra, Sect. 5.4.6.

[67] For details see infra, Sect. 5.4.7.

in the late 1950s and the 1960s. During that time, many African countries became independent and applied for membership.

The purposes of the International Monetary Fund are regulated in Article I of the IMF Agreement. Its general goal is *"to promote international monetary cooperation through a permanent institution which provides the machinery for consultation and collaboration on international monetary problems"* (Article I (i) IMF Agreement). This should contribute to the expansion and balanced growth of international trade (Article I (ii) IMF Agreement). Therefore, the IMF is responsible for and promotes *"exchange stability, to maintain orderly exchange arrangements among members, and to avoid competitive exchange depreciation"* which were rampant in the interwar period. This requires a multilateral system of payment and the elimination of foreign exchange restrictions because such measures hamper business transactions and therefore international trade (Article I (iv) IMF Agreement). However, individual trade may cause a negative trade balance which usually also has a negative impact on a country's balance of payments, particularly on its debt and currency. An important purpose of the IMF is to help states with balance of payments difficulties (Article I (v) IMF Agreement), by providing them access to funds necessary to restore the equilibrium of the balance of payment. The reason for this is that such situations have an adverse impact on the currencies of the countries affected by such problems and sometimes force these countries to impose foreign exchange restrictions. In this regard the IMF functions more like a bank for states in economic trouble than as a fund.

5.3.3 "Gold Standard", Fixed Exchange Rate and Breakdown of the Old System

5.3.3.1 Establishment of the Gold Standard

These goals were implemented by establishing the so-called Gold Standard, a system of pegged, or stable, currency exchange rates. This system, also known as Bretton Woods system, required that each unit of a country's currency represents a fixed weight of gold. As to that, each IMF member declared a value for its currency relative to the US dollar, and in turn the US Treasury tied the dollar to gold by agreeing to buy and sell gold to other governments at then $35 per ounce. Maintaining this parity required the member countries' central banks to keep adequate stocks of gold. In case a member country failed to maintain sound economic policies, gold would move from one country to another, which tended to cause deflation in the country losing gold or inflation in the country receiving the gold. For example, if a country was importing more than it was exporting thus creating a current account deficit but was not receiving sufficient loans from abroad to pay for all the imports, the central bank would start losing gold reserves. This was supposed to set off a chain of events that would cause prices to decrease and ultimately result in a reduction in imports and an increase in exports, which would reduce the current account deficit. The country experiencing the corresponding current account surplus (for every country with a current account deficit there is a country with a matching current account surplus) would experience the opposite effect.

5.3.3.2 System of Fixed Exchange Rates

Between 1945 and 1971, all countries joining the IMF agreed to this fundamental principle of the IMF to keep their exchange rates fixed. Adjustments of these fixed rates required the correction of a fundamental disequilibrium in the balance of payments. Initially, each correction required the IMF's approval. However, the UK was not willing to give up total sovereignty of the value of its pound sterling. Thereupon, the IMF agreed to allow adjustments up to 10% without its approval.

Member states with a balance of payment deficit could borrow money from the IMF. The Fund itself supplied the money needed to fill the gap created by the trade imbalance. Thus, the exposure of a single country was limited to the amount in the fund. This consideration was important given that at the time the IMF was established the US did not want to supply all the funds needed for balancing the disequilibrium created by the reconstruction of Europe after the WW2 and given that at that time Europe had to import a large part of the necessary goods as domestic production was destroyed.

5.3.3.3 The Collapse of the Old System in 1971

The established "par value"—system prevailed until 1971. At this time, US President Richard Nixon suspended the convertibility of the dollar (and dollar reserves held by other governments) into gold. There were several reasons for this. Already by the early 1960s, the U.S. dollar's fixed value against gold, under the Bretton Woods system of fixed exchange rates, was considered as overvalued. A sizable increase in domestic spending on President Lyndon Johnson's Great Society programs and a rise in military spending caused by the Vietnam War gradually worsened the economic situation in the US because of, as it was perceived at that time, the overvaluation of the dollar which had an adverse impact on US exports because it made US products and services expensive abroad and at the same time the import of foreign products and services to the US cheap which also adversely affected domestic production.

This crisis marked the breakdown of the system. After an attempt to revive the fixed exchange rates failed, by March 1973 the major currencies began to float against each other. Floating exchange rates means that a currency's value is determined in the foreign exchange (FOREX) market, thus by the market forces depending on the permanently changing demand for a country's labor, capital, and currency. Central banks sometimes intervene for political and/or macroeconomic reason by buying and selling significant amounts of the domestic currency to influence the exchange rate and, e.g., to fight speculative manipulations against their currencies on the Forex markets.

Following the collapse of the Bretton Woods system, IMF member states have been free to choose any form of exchange arrangement except pegging their currency to gold. They are allowed to peg their currency to another currency or a basket of currencies, to adopt the currency of another country, to participate in a currency bloc, or to form part of a monetary union.[68] This was made possible based on an amendment to the IMF Articles of Agreement adopted in 1978.[69]

5.3.3.4 Developments After the Breakdown of the System of Fixed Exchange Rates

With the collapse of the fixed currency system, the IMF had to redefine its role. Before the end of the Gold Standard, its main tasks were to monitor the system of fixed exchange rate and the respective arrangements between states and to provide funds to states to enable them to overcome balance of payments problems which could also adversely affect world economy. Beginning in the mid-1970s, the IMF started to see its role as an *institution generally monitoring global economy and surveilling the economic performance of its member countries* instead of simply overseeing the exchange rates. An important focus was to help states in economic troubles to avoid the spreading of these troubles which could possibly result in a regional or even global financial and economic crisis. An important role played and continue to play the so-called conditionalities. *Conditionalities are the contractually agreed conditions and policies of the IMF to be observed by states requesting financial resources from the IMF.* They have their legal basis in Article V(3) of the IMF Agreement. The conditionalities should incentivize states to address the roots of their economic difficulties by making structural adjustments in their policies.[70]

From the mid-1970s, the IMF sought to respond in particular to the balance of payments difficulties of the world's poorest countries and generally of the developing countries. For that purpose, the IMF deepened in the 1990s cooperation with the World Bank to commonly address the economic problems of the world's poorest countries.[71] But also more developed countries were forced to seek the IMF's financial assistance and advice. The crises which required interventions by the IMF included Mexico (1982), Brazil (1987), the so-called Asian crisis (Thailand,

[68] For further reference see <https://www.imf.org/external/about/histend.htm> (accessed 9 March 2025).

[69] Art. IV IMF Agreement - *Obligations Regarding Exchange Arrangements*, Amendment effective 1 Apr 1978, as per Board of Governors' Resolution No. 31-4, adopted 30 Apr 1976.

[70] See also infra, Sect. 5.3.8.1.

[71] These activities included the Initiative for Heavily Indebted Poor Countries (HIPC, 1996) and the Multilateral Debt Relief (MDR) supplementing the HIPC Initiative.

Indonesia, Korea and other Asian countries, 1997–98) and Russia (1998). The IMF's main goal was to prevent the spreading of these crises which would have threatened the global financial and currency system and thus the world economy at large. Other countries in need of IMF financial support included Argentina (during the 1998–2002; Argentine great depression), Uruguay (2002 Uruguay banking crisis) and Greece (2010 and 2011, to avoid Greece's bankruptcy). A very important challenge to the IMF was the COVID-19 pandemic, during which the IMF mobilizes more than USD 1 trillion to fight the consequences of the pandemic for particularly affected or vulnerable states. 25 member countries received immediate debt relief to under the IMF's Catastrophe Containment and Relief Trust (CCRT) program.

5.3.4 *International Status*

The IMF Agreement provides that the Fund shall possess full juridical personality, and in particular, the capacity to contract, to acquire and dispose of immovable and movable property, and to institute legal proceedings (Article IX (2) IMF Agreement).

To enable the IMF to fulfill all its functions, each IMF Member State grants the Fund's status, immunities, and privileges within its territory (Article IX IMF Agreement). This includes immunity from judicial process and other actions, immunity of archives, freedom of assets from restrictions, privilege for communications, immunities and privileges of officers and employees and immunities from taxation (Article IX (3–9) IMF Agreement). The legal complexities surrounding these immunities were notably highlighted in the 2011 case involving then managing director Dominique Strauss-Kahn, where questions arose regarding the extent of immunity provided to high-ranking officials under international law for non-official conduct.[72]

5.3.5 *Membership*

5.3.5.1 Original and Other Members

As all international organizations is the IMF governed by its Member States. The IMF Agreement distinguishes between original members (Article II (1) IMF Agreement) and other members (Article II (2) IMF Agreement).

Original members of the IMF are those of the countries whose governments accepted membership before December 31, 1945 (Article II (1) IMF Agreement).[73]

[72] United States v Dominique Strauss-Kahn, *People of the State of New York v Dominique Strauss-Kahn*, 2011 NY Slip Op 21,114 (NY Sup Ct 2011).

[73] This includes Belgium, Bolivia, Canada, Chile, China, Colombia, Czechoslovakia, Dominican Republic, Ecuador, Egypt, Ethiopia, France, Greece, Guatemala, Honduras, Iceland, India, Iran,

Member States that joined the IMF later are considered as "other members". Despite these different categories, all the members have basically the same legal status. There are no privileges of the original members.

5.3.5.2 Accession to the IMF

Any state may apply for membership of the IMF. Membership is open at such times and in accordance with such terms as may be prescribed by the IMF Board of Governors (Article II (2) IMF Agreement) which also decides on the admission of new members. A pre-existing UN membership is not required.[74] IMF membership is almost universal.[75] An accession requires the new member inter alia to pay a quota subscription and to refrain from restrictions on exchange of foreign currencies. Members are generally required to share information on economic data with other countries and with the IMF. In return they get inter alia access to information on economic policies for all member countries, access to technical assistance in banking, fiscal affairs, and exchange rate policies and financial support if they suffer financial difficulties.

5.3.5.3 Withdrawal of Membership

a) Voluntarily withdrawal

Each Member State may withdraw from the IMF at any time. A member's withdrawal becomes effective on the day the IMF receives a written notice to that effect (Article XXVL (1) IMF Agreement). The voluntary withdrawal does not affect the Member State's obligations to repay existing IMF loans. The subsequent settlement of the leaving state's IMF accounts shall be made with reasonable dispatch (Article XXVI (3) IMF Agreement). Countries that voluntarily withdrew from the membership were Poland (1950; readmitted in 1986), Cuba (1964) and Indonesia (1965, readmitted in 1967).

b) Compulsory withdrawal

In addition to voluntary withdrawal, the IMF Agreement also regulates the compulsory withdrawal of a Member State. This procedure is the last step in a series of

---

Iraq, Luxembourg, Mexico, Netherlands, Norway, Paraguay, Peru, Philippines, South Africa, United Kingdom, United States, and Yugoslavia. Costa Rica, Poland, Brazil, Uruguay, and Cuba signed the Articles by that date, too, but their membership became effective a little later upon deposit of their respective instruments of acceptance.

[74] Switzerland, e.g., joined the IMF before it became UN member. Kosovo is currently not a UN but nonetheless an IMF member.

[75] The IMF has 190 member countries as of 2023, with the latest member being the Principality of Andorra, which joined in Oct 2020. Only Cuba, East Timor, North Korea, Liechtenstein, Monaco, Taiwan, and Vatican City are not members.

escalating measures that the IMF applies to members that fail to meet their obligations under the IMF Agreement. The exclusion of IMF membership runs in stages. Hence, before any action against a Member State is taken, the respective country will be informed in reasonable time of the complaint and will be given the opportunity for stating its case, both orally and in writing (Article XXVI (2) (d) IMF Agreement).

In case a Member State fails to fulfil any of its obligations under the IMF Agreement, the IMF may first declare the respective Member State ineligible to use the general resources of the Fund (Article XXVI (2) (a) IMF Agreement). If the IMF member—even after a reasonable period of time—persists in its failure to fulfil any of its obligations, the Fund may suspend its voting rights. This decision requires 70 percent of the Fund's total voting power. The same applies to the suspension's termination (Article XXVI (2) (b) IMF Agreement). Provided, the Member State continues on failing to fulfill its obligations, the IMF Board of Governors decides about its compulsory withdrawal from the IMF. This decision requires 85 percent of the total voting power (Article XXVI (2) (c) IMF Agreement). So far, no Member State has been expelled from the IMF.

5.3.6 *Organs*

To perform its duties, the IMF has the following organs: the Board of Governors (Article XII (2) IMF Agreement), the Executive Board (Article XII (3) IMF Agreement), the Managing Director (Article XII (4) IMF Agreement), the International Monetary and Financial Committee (IMFC), the Development Committee, and the Administrative Tribunal (Fig. 5.4).

5.3.6.1 Board of Governors

The IMF Board of Governors serves as the Fund's *highest decision-making body and plenary organ*. The Board consists of *one Governor per member country*. Each member country appoints its Governor and one alternate Governor, usually the minister of finance or (rather rare) the head of the national central bank. In support of its work, the Board of Governors gets advice from two committees, the *International Monetary and Financial Committee (IMFC)* and the *Development Committee*.

Even though the Board of Governors has delegated most of its powers to the IMF Executive Board, it retains several functions. These include, among others, the right to approve quota increases, special drawing right (SDR) allocations, the admittance of new members, compulsory withdrawal of members, and amendments to the Articles of Agreement and By-Laws. Moreover, the Board of Governors elects or

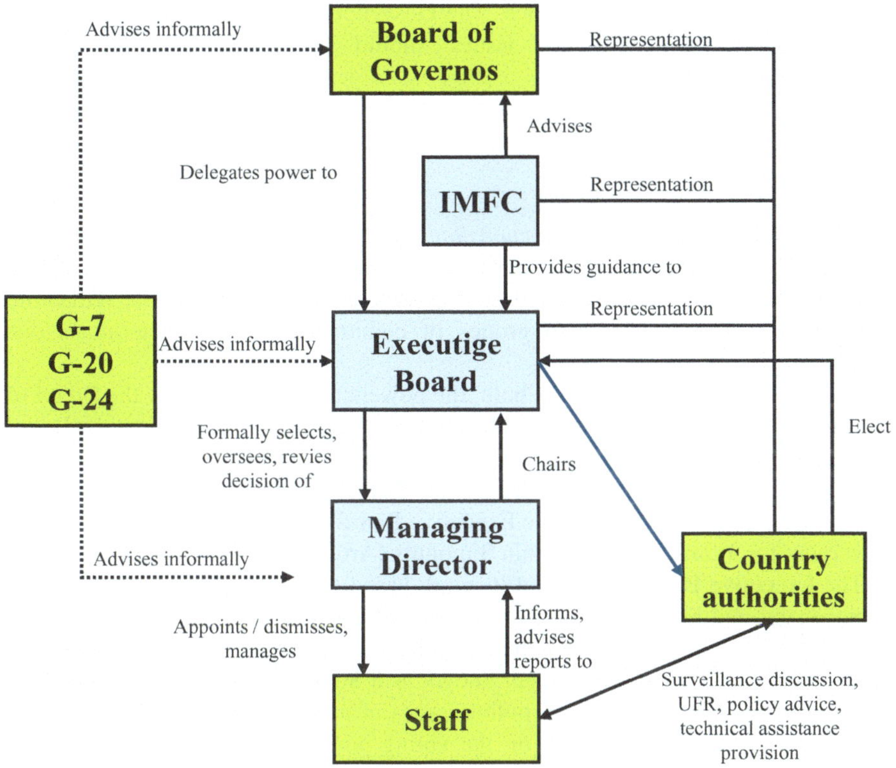

Fig. 5.4 IMF stylized view. Own graphic

appoints directors of the Executive Board and is the ultimate arbiter on issues related to the interpretation of the IMF Agreement. The Board of Governors thus has *the power of authentic interpretation of the IMF Articles of Agreement.*[76] Usually, votes at the Board of Governors are taken by mail-in ballot. The quota of a Governor's country determines its voting power in the Board.

Once a year, in September or October, the Board of Governors meets with the World Bank at the IMF–World Bank Annual Meetings. In recent years, these meetings have customarily been held in Washington for two consecutive years and in another member country in the third year. One Governor of the Board together with a Governor of the World Bank chairs the Annual Meeting, with the chairmanship rotating among the membership each year. The Annual Meetings include plenary sessions, during which the IMF and World Bank Governors consult with one another and present their respective countries' views on current issues in

[76] Art. XXIX(b) IMF Agreement.

international economics and finance. The Governors also make decisions on how current international monetary issues should be addressed and approve corresponding resolutions.

5.3.6.2 Executive Board

The IMF Executive Board is *responsible for the organization's daily work.* It consists of 24 Directors and is *chaired by the Managing Director.* The Member States holding the five largest quotas appoint one Director each. The remaining member countries have formed groups of countries; each one determines one Director.

The Executive Board exercises both, the powers transferred to it by the Board of Governors, and the powers conferred by the IMF Agreement. In so doing, the Board is also responsible for making a first decision in case Member States cannot agree on the interpretation of certain Articles of the IMF Agreement (power of authentic interpretation). This decision of the Executive Board can be referred to the Board of Governors for a final decision within 3 months (Article XXIX IMF Agreement).

The Executive Board carries out its work based on papers prepared by the IMF Management and Staff. The Board holds formal and informal meetings and meets several times each week. Following most formal meetings, the Executive Board summarizes its views in a document known as a Summing Up. Informal meetings may be held to discuss complex policy issues at a preliminary stage. The voting power of each Director depends on the voting power of the countries he or she represents. However, decisions of the Executive Board are normally taken based on consensus.

5.3.6.3 Managing Director

The IMF Managing Director is basically a powerful Secretary-General and combines two functions. He or she controls the Executive Board, what is quite unusual in international organizations,[77] and further is head of the IMF staff. The Managing Director is therefore responsible for the staff's organization, appointment, and dismissal. He or she is supported by a First Deputy Managing Director and three Deputy Managing Directors. According to an informal agreement between the US and some western European countries, the IMF Managing Director is always a European, and an American always occupies the position of the First Deputy Managing Director.

[77] Another example is NATO's Secretary-General heading the Council; see supra, Sect. 3.5.3.1.

5.3.6.4 Further Organs

a) International Monetary and Financial Committee (IMFC)
The IMFC acts as an advisory body for the Board of Governors. The Committee consists of 24 members, drawn from the pool of the Board of Governors, which represent all of the Fund's Member States. The IMFC meets twice a year during the IMF Spring and Annual Meetings to discuss matters of common concern affecting the global economy and for advising the IMF on the direction of its work. As to that, at the end of each Meeting, the Committee issues a joint communiqué summarizing its views and providing guidance for the IMF's work program during the 6 months leading up to the next Meeting. The IMFC voting operates by consensus.

b) Development Committee
The Development Committee is a joint committee representing the full membership of the IMF and the World Bank. It mainly serves as a forum for building intergovernmental consensus on critical development issues. In addition, the Development Committee advises the Boards of Governors of the IMF and the World Bank on issues related to economic development in emerging and developing countries. Just like the IMFC, the committee consists of 24 members (usually ministers of finance or development).

c) Administrative Tribunal
The IMF Administrative Tribunal serves as an independent judicial forum for the *resolution of disputes arising between the IMF and its staff members*. The Tribunal is composed of five members, including the President, and takes its decisions by a panel consisting of the President and two other members designated by the President.

The members of the Tribunal are completely independent in the exercise of their duties. They may not have any prior or present employment relationship with the IMF. Moreover, they are not eligible for staff employment with the Fund following the end of their service with the Tribunal.

5.3.7 Decision-Making; Voting

Unlike the General Assembly of the United Nations, where each country has one vote, decision-making at the IMF has always been designed to reflect the relative position of an IMF Member State in the global economy.

Within the IMF, *voting power is based on a quota system*. Each Member State has a number of basic votes plus one additional vote for each special drawing right (SDR) of 100,000 of a member's quota (Article XII (5) (a) (ii) IMF Agreement). The total votes of each Member State equal the sum of its basic votes and its quota-based votes. Since 2008, each state's number of basic votes equals 5.502% of the Fund's total votes (Article XII (5) (a) (i) IMF Agreement). In the recent past, the IMF started reforms to ensure that its governance structures adequately reflect fundamental changes taking place in the world economy. This current number of basic votes represents close to a tripling of the number prior to the effectiveness of the IMF reform of 2008.

Except as otherwise specifically provided, all IMF decisions shall be made by a majority of the votes cast (Article XII (5) (c) IMF Agreement). Most essential governance decisions, such as quota adjustments, *require a 85 percent supermajority*. To date, the US is (and has always been) the only country able to block a supermajority on its own by having 831.407 votes (16,52 percent of the total). Other states with large voting shares are Japan (309.670 votes: 6,15 percent of the total), China (306.294 votes: 6,09 of the total), Germany (267.809 votes: 5,38 percent of the total), the UK (203.016 votes: 4,03 percent of the total), France (203.016 votes: 4,03 percent of the total) and Italy (152.165 votes: 3,02 percent of the total). The EU Member States plus the UK combine 25,6 percent of the total vote, which, assuming an effective coordination of the Member States' views and actions, gives the EU a de facto veto power as well.

Quotas are an essential component of the governance structure of the IMF. They not only define the influence Member States exert in the decision-making processes but also their financial commitments and access to financing in case of need.[78]

The important decisions within the framework of the IMF are regularly pre-discussed and de facto pre-decided by the G 7 or the G 20 countries. The weighting of votes based on economic strength makes this possible.

5.3.8 Activities of the IMF

The Fund's core responsibilities towards its Member States include surveillance at the global, regional, and country levels, technical assistance and training, and financial support. The IMF's economic and financial research and statistics is supporting these activities.

5.3.8.1 Surveillance

The IMF promotes economic stability and global growth of its Member States and, to that end, encourages its members to adopt sound economic and financial policies. By regularly *monitoring global, regional, and national economic developments* the Fund seeks to assess the impact of its members' policies on other economies. This surveillance helps the Fund to identify potential risks to stability for recommending appropriate policy adjustments needed to sustain economic growth as well as

[78] See infra, Sect. 5.3.9.1.

financial and economic stability. The IMF periodically reviews its surveillance and monitoring activities.

The IMF surveillance involves annual in-depth appraisals of each IMF Member State's economic situation. During visits, IMF staff together with government and central bank officials discuss risks to domestic and global stability, focusing on exchange rates and monetary, fiscal, and regulatory policies. Given that comprehensive discussions with a broad array of groups lead to better evaluations, IMF staff also meet with other stakeholders, including members of the legislature and representatives from the business community, labor unions, and civil society. Upon completion of their evaluation the IMF staff report their findings to the IMF Executive Board for discussion. The Board, in turn, delivers its view on the report to the country's authorities.

In recent years, surveillance has become more transparent. Accordingly, IMF Member States have started to publish a press release summarizing the staff report and accompanying analysis, as well as the views of the Board.

5.3.8.2 Technical Assistance and Training

The IMF offers technical assistance and training to help its Member States strengthen their capacity to design and implement effective policies. This technical assistance refers to mainly four areas, namely monetary and financial policies; fiscal policy and management; compilation, management, dissemination, and improvement of statistical data; and economic and financial legislation.

5.3.8.3 Lending

The IMF provides loans to Member States that experience actual or potential balance of payments problems. It assists Member States hit by crises but also provides precautionary financing to help Member States prevent and insure against crises. The Fund's financial support enables the respective country to rebuild its international reserves, stabilize its currency, continue paying for imports, and to restore conditions for strong economic growth, while undertaking policies to correct underlying problems. Unlike development banks, the *IMF does not lend money to specific projects*. On that regard, the terms "loans" and "lending" are not entirely accurate. The needy Member State purchases SDRs (see Sect. 2.9.5 below) or currency from the IMF by paying in its own currency and under the condition that the member will repurchase its own currency again from the IMF at a later date.

The IMF gets its financial resources primarily through its members' payment of quotas. Other major sources are multilateral and bilateral loans. Currently, the IMF's total resources amount to about SDR 982 billion. Setting aside a liquidity buffer and considering that only resources of Member States with strong external position are used for lending, this results into a capacity for lending of about SDR 715 billion (around US$ 1 trillion).

The causes of crises are varied and complex, and can be domestic, external, or both. Depending on the needs of the respective Member State, the IMF offers different types of financial support. A country facing a sudden drop in the prices of key exports may need speedy financial assistance while a country suffering from severe capital outflows may need to address the problems that led to the loss of investor confidence. To meet the changing needs of its Member States, the IMF continuously refines its lending arrangements. The level of access to the IMF's lending facilities depends on the quota of the Member State.

The IMF provides financial support upon request by its Member States. The IMF Agreement states in Article V (1) that a member *"shall deal with the Fund only through its Treasury, central bank, stabilization fund, or other similar fiscal agency, and the Fund shall deal only with or through the same agencies."* This provision refers to operations and transactions of the Fund and therefore also applies to arrangements giving a state access to the Fund's financial resources and limits the member states' organizational autonomy.

If a member facing financial problems requests the Fund for support, the IMF staff team holds discussions with the country's government to assess both its economic and financial situation and its financing needs. The legal basis is Article V Section 3 of the Articles of Agreement regulating the conditions governing the use of the IMF's general resources which reads as follows: "*(a) The Fund shall adopt policies on the use of its general resources, including policies on stand-by or similar arrangements, and may adopt special policies for special balance of payments problems, that will assist members to solve their balance of payments problems in a manner consistent with the provisions of this Agreement and that will establish adequate safeguards for the temporary use of the general resources of the Fund*".

Usually, financial support of the IMF depends on the *effective implementation of economic policies and measures agreed on with the IMF (policy conditionality)*. The Fund can provide this temporary financing under 'adequate safeguards' to countries experiencing balance of payments problems. In exchange for this support, countries must agree to implement IMF-designed policy reform packages—or 'conditionality'—administered through a lending program. This may include the reduction of fiscal deficit, the privatization of state-owned enterprises, and the implementation of certain laws such as banking regulations (i.e. anti-money laundering), spending or taxation. The conditions vary depending on the Member State's needs and the goals the member has agreed to implement for resolving balance of payment problems. As structural measures are hard to measure in a quantitative sense, the IMF generally sets goals to pass a law by a predetermined date. In the course of time, conditions are often renegotiated and adjusted depending on the situation in the Member State.[79] These conditionalities are sometimes highly controversial and criticized for political and economic reasons. A part of the critique opines that the conditions often unduly infringe state sovereignty and democratic decision-making as states are forced by an international institution to accept deep intrusions in matters of domestic policies even if the majority of the people is against the conditions imposed by the IMF. Another criticism is that the conditions reflect a neoliberal economic concept leading to an impoverishment of parts of the population as these countries are not fit for neoliberal prescriptions.[80]

The disbursement of the loans requires the approval by the Fund's Executive Board. For this, the Member State submits a Letter of Intent (LoI) and a further detailed Memorandum of Understanding (MoU) to the Board. Once the Executive Board approves the arrangement with the Member State, IMF resources will be released. Usually, the payment is made in installments depending on the implementation of the policy actions.

5.3.8.4 Facilities

Over the years, the IMF has developed various types of loan arrangements. These so-called facilities are tailored to address the specific circumstances of the Fund's diverse membership by differing in their aims and repayment schedule as well as in the interest rates charged.

Special consideration is given to low-income countries. These countries may receive *financial support on concessional terms*, which means there is a period with no interest rates. This support is available through the Poverty Reduction and Growth Trust (PRGT). Since the start of the Covid-19-pandemic, lending from the PRGT has risen very sharply in response to the unprecedented and urgent needs of low-income countries. Other facilities available to these countries include the Extended Credit Facility (ECF), the Standby Credit Facility (SCF) and the Rapid Credit Facility (RCF).[81]

Non-concessional loans are subject to the IMF's market-related interest rate. This includes, among others:

---

[79] See Dreher (2009), pp. 233–267.

[80] See for a quantitative analysis of the impact of conditionality and the methodological issues connected to that Stubbs et al. (2020), pp. 29–73.

[81] IML Lending consists of the following programs and facilities: Resilience and Sustainability Facility (RSF), Rapid Financing Instrument, Rapid Credit Facility (RCF), Policy Coordination Instrument (PCI), Policy Support Instrument (PSI), Protecting IMF Resources - Safeguards Assessments of Central Banks, Short-term Liquidity Line (SLL), Standby Credit Facility (SCF), Extended Credit Facility (ECF), Stand-By Arrangement (SBA), Post Financing Assessment (PFA), Precautionary and Liquidity Line (PLL), Extended Fund Facility (EFF), Trade Integration Mechanism (TIM), Flexible Credit Line (FCL), IMF Conditionality, Exogenous Shocks Facility- High Access Component (ESF-HAC), see also <https://www.imf.org/en/About/Factsheets/IMF-Lending> (accessed 9 March 2025).

- Stand-By Arrangements (SBA) to address short-term or potential balance of payments problems;
- Flexible Credit Lines (FCL) built to help members with already strong policies to prevent or mitigate crises and boost market confidence during periods of heightened risks;
- Extended Fund Facilities (EFF) serving as the IMF's main tool for medium-term support to countries facing protracted balance of payments problems; and
- Rapid Financing Instruments (RFI) to provide rapid assistance to countries with urgent balance of payments need, including from commodity price shocks, natural disasters, and domestic fragilities.

The maximum amount that a country can borrow from the IMF varies depending on the type of loan. Typically, the access limit is a multiple of the country's IMF quota. This limit may be exceeded in exceptional circumstances. The SBS, the FCL and the EFF have no pre-set cap on access.

5.3.8.5 Special Drawing Rights (SDR)

In 1969, the IMF created *the Special Drawing Rights as an international reserve asset* to supplement its members' official reserves. Being neither a currency nor a claim on the IMF, SDRs serve as a potential claim on the freely usable currencies of IMF members and can be exchanged for these currencies. With the collapse of the Bretton Woods system in 1973 and the shift of major currencies to floating exchange rate regimes, the reliance on the SDR as a global reserve asset decreased. Nonetheless, SDR allocations can play an important role in providing liquidity and supplementing member countries' official reserves.

The value of an SDR is based on *a basket of the world's five leading currencies*. Initially, the SDR was defined as equivalent to 0.888671 grams of fine gold. This was also equivalent to one U.S. dollar. Since the collapse of the Bretton Woods system, the currency value of the SDR is determined daily by the IMF by summing these values in U.S. dollars, based on market exchange rates, of five major currencies: the euro, Japanese yen, yuan, pound sterling, and the U.S. dollar. The SDR valuation is normally reviewed every 5 years.

SDR is an accounting unit for IMF transactions with member countries and a stable asset in countries' international reserves. It provides the basis for calculating the interest rate charged to members on their non-concessional borrowing from the IMF and paid to members for their remunerated creditor positions in the IMF. It is also the interest paid to members on their SDR holdings and charged on their SDR allocation. The SDR also serves as the unit of some other international organizations.

5.3.9 Obligations of IMF Member States

5.3.9.1 Subscribe to Quotas

When joining the IMF, each Member State is assigned an *initial quota denominated in Special Drawing Rights (SDR)*. The IMF quotas *reflect the IMF members' economic size and characteristics*. They are calculated according to a defined formula.[82] To reflect economic changes, the IMF Board of Governors reviews the quotas at least every 5 years (Article III (2) IMF Agreement).

The Member States' quotas play several key roles in the IMF. Not only do they *determine each Member State's voting power*. They also decide on each country's subscription by establishing the extent of resources each Member State needs to provide to the IMF at the appropriate depository (Article III (1) IMF Agreement).

The Member State with the largest quota hosts the principal office of the Fund (currently Washington, D.C., United States). The five member countries with the largest quota decide on the location of depositaries for the Fund's gold holdings.

5.3.9.2 Obligations Regarding Exchange Agreements

To achieve the goals of the IMF, its Member States are obliged to collaborate with both, the Fund and other member countries. In so doing, the IMF Agreement among others obliges all Member States:

- to direct its economic and financial policies toward the objective of fostering orderly economic growth with reasonable price stability;
- to promote stability by fostering orderly underlying economic and financial conditions and a monetary system that does not tend to produce erratic disruptions; and
- to avoid manipulating exchange rates or the international monetary system *to prevent effective balance of payments adjustment or to gain an unfair competitive advantage over other members* (Article IV section 1 IMF Agreement).

In addition, Member States need to inform the Fund of the exchange arrangements they intend to apply to fulfil these obligations (Article IV section 2(a) IMF Agreement).

[82] Each quota is a weighted average of a Member State's gross domestic product (GDP) (weight of 50 percent), openness (30 percent), economic variability (15 percent), and international reserves (5 percent). For this purpose, the GDP is measured through a blend of GDP—based on market exchange rates (weight of 60 percent)—and on purchasing power parities (PPP) exchange rates (40 percent). The calculation also includes a "compression factor" that reduces the dispersion in calculated quota shares across members.

The IMF is given vast surveillance powers to oversee the international monetary system and the compliance of its Member States with their obligations mentioned above (Article IV (3) IMF Agreement). The Fund exercises firm surveillance over its members' exchange rate policies and may adopt specific principles for the guidance of its Member States. Vice versa, each member of the IMF needs to provide the Fund with the information necessary for such surveillance and, if requested, shall consult with the Fund its exchange rate policies.

5.3.9.3 Further General Obligations

With membership, the states commit to a number of other obligations. These include the avoidance of restrictions on current payments and of discriminatory currency practices, the convertibility of foreign-held balances, furnishing of information, consultation between members regarding existing international agreements, and the collaboration regarding policies on reserve assets (Article VIII IMF Agreement).

5.3.9.4 Relations with Other International Organizations and Non-member Countries

The IMF Agreement provides that the Fund shall cooperate within the terms of this Agreement with any general international organization with a general purpose or with specialized responsibilities in related fields (Article X IMF Agreement).[83] *The closest cooperation is with the World Bank (IBDR).* Both organizations belong to the family of Bretton Woods institutions and have as a common goal to raise living standards of the populations of their member states. Their *activities are to a certain extent complementary*: the IMF's approach is a macroeconomic one and implies assistance to states to reach financial stability as a precondition of economic well-being and growth while the World Bank's focus is usually on concrete projects contributing to long-term economic development and poverty reduction.

Regarding non-member states Article XI defines as a general obligation of the member states to avoid and to prevent transactions and practices in relation to these states that would be contrary to the IMF Agreement and the purposes of the IMF.

[83] However, any arrangements for such cooperation, which would involve a modification of any provision of the IMF Agreement, may be effected only after amendment to the IMF Agreement under its Art. XXVIII.

5.4 The World Bank Group[84]

As one of the world's largest international organizations for funding development aid, the World Bank Group is focusing on the improvement of sustainable growth and socioeconomic wealth in developing countries all over the world. *Its main goal is to reduce poverty* through financial, administrative as well as social services provided to its member countries while its mission is to fight said poverty by "*helping people help themselves.*"[85]

5.4.1 History

Conceived during World War II at Bretton Woods, New Hampshire, the World Bank initially helped rebuild Europe after the war. Its first loan of $250 million was to France in 1947 for post-war reconstruction. Reconstruction has remained an important focus of the Bank's work, given the natural disasters, humanitarian emergencies, and post-conflict rehabilitation needs that affect developing and transition economies. The Bank itself is set up as a Group, encompassing its two lead funding institutions and further three institutions which were later established: the *International Bank for Reconstruction and Development (IBRD)*, the *International Development Association (IDA)*, the *International Finance Corporation (IFC)*, the *Multilateral Investment Guarantee Agency (MIGA)*, and the *International Centre for Settlement of Investment Disputes (ICSID)*. The purposes of these organizations are complementary: the IBRD is an organization financing development projects and policies, IDA provides very low-interest loans to particularly poor countries, IFC contributes to private sector investment and provides advice, MIGA is an insurance for investments against political risk, and ICSID is an institution to settle investment disputes between investors and host countries.

During the initial consultations leading up to the establishment of the World Bank, the topic on whether the World Bank should be solely responsible for development or for reconstruction was hotly debated. The European countries were naturally interested in reconstruction of their war-torn countries, whereas the developing countries such as Mexico wanted the focus to be on development aid. Essentially a compromise was reached by initially setting the focus on reconstruction (of post-war Europe) but including development as a key factor as well as requiring

[84]*Special thanks to Ulrike Heinrich und Dominic Staiger for their important contribution to the elaboration of this chapter.

[85]World Bank (2011), p. 1.

an equitable balance between reconstruction and development projects.[86] Following this historical compromise, the first loans in favor of development purpose, totaling 16 billion USD, were granted to Chile in 1948.

In the 1980s, the Bank was pushed in many directions: early in the decade, the Bank was brought face to face with macroeconomic and debt rescheduling issues. Later in the decade, social and environmental issues assumed center stage, and an increasingly vocal civil society accused the Bank of not observing its own policies in some high-profile projects. The Bank has effectively engaged with partners and clients in complex emergencies from post-conflict work in Bosnia to post-crisis assistance in East Asia to post-hurricane clean-up in Central America to post-earthquake support in Turkey, in Kosovo, East Timor and during the Covid-19 pandemic—to list only a few instances of World Bank Group involvement.

Following criticism, the Group established the *Millennium Development Goals* (MDGs)[87] in the year 2000 in accordance with the United Nations' Millennium Declaration.[88] The MDGs are the World Banks eight formulated development goals which should have been reached within a 15-year time window. The goals committed the international community to a global and sustainable socioeconomic progress and include:

- Eradication of extreme poverty and hunger
- Achievement of universal primary education
- Promotion of gender equality and empowerment of women
- Reduction of child mortality
- Improvement of maternal health
- Combat against HIV/AIDS, malaria and other diseases
- Ensuring environmental sustainability
- Development of a global partnership for development

The goals were only partly reached. The MDGs were succeeded in 2016 by the *Sustainable Development Goals* (SDGs), adopted by the UN General Assembly[89] and consisting of 17 sustainable development goals.

5.4.2 Common Structure

Although the five members of the World Bank Group are *independent from each other* and have their *own legal personality as well as their very own founding documents*, they do share strong ties. The institutions largely have common

---

[86] Art. III, sec. 1(a) IBRD Agreement.

[87] *Millennium Development Goals* (2000), <https://www.un.org/millenniumgoals/;> (accessed 9 March 2025); furthermore, see also Fukuda-Parr (2004), 389 ss.

[88] A/RES/55/2 (2000).

[89] *Transforming our world: the 2030 Agenda for Sustainable Development*, A/RES/70/1 (2015).

headquarters and personnel which are considered the group's most strategic asset. The World Bank institutions together employ approximately 15'000 professionals and administrative personnel on a full-time basis. Roughly 60% of them operate from Washington DC, USA, where the headquarters are based. The other 40% are based in offices reaching over 110 developing countries. This percentage pursues the early initiated trend of moving more personnel out from the headquarters into the countries the group works with to achieve deepen relations and integration into the markets, governments and businesses the Group finances.

The main institutions of the World Bank Group are structurally similar to the IMF: They are *based on a capital to be subscribed to by the member states which also determines the voting power of each member*. The *Boards of Governors (BoG)* are politically the most important organs. They oversee the work of the IBRD as well as the IDA and IFC (both ex officio) and consist of two representatives of each member state which either are officials at ministerial level or head of their central bank. The positions these representatives hold are Governor and the Alternate Governor of the BoG. As the IDA's and IFC's governor offices are assigned ex officio, they are held by the same individuals as the IBRD's. The remaining MIGA and ICSID officials are appointed either separately or differently. The Boards meet annually and are concerned with the central business of the World Bank such as: membership admission or suspension, financial statement reviewing and budgeting, formal cooperation agreements with other international institutions as well as handling of further powers, the Boards have not delegated.

Because of its annual meeting schedule, the IBRD delegates general operations and daily business such as policy decisions and approval of lending proposals to the *Boards of Executive Directors (BoED)*. Again, as with the BoG, the BoED's officials are represented by the same individuals throughout the IBRD, IDA and IFC. The latter two are assigned ex officio as well. The Board of the IBRD meets at least twice a week to discuss business and *consists of 25 Executive Directors*, which are elected by the IBRD's member states of which the 6 largest shareholders (USA, JAP, PRC, GER, FRA and UK) appoint one each. The remaining Executive Directors are appointed by so-called constituencies, which are groups of member countries mostly representing geographic regions.

Head representative of the World Bank Group is its *president*, who is elected by the BoED for a term of 5 years, leaving open the possibility for a renewal. The president is in charge of overall management and business administration according to the decisions of the BoED. Moreover, he serves as a chair for the BoED (including the MIGA's Board) as well as the ICSID's Administrative Council. The president holds no voting power and has to report to the BoED while the IBRD's and IDA's organizational units report to him.

5.4.3 International Bank for Reconstruction and Development (IBRD)

5.4.3.1 Main Functions, Membership, Voting

The IBRD was established in 1944 as the first of the five international financial institutions under the roof of the Word Bank, providing financial services, strategic and coordination services as well as knowledge services to its borrowing member counties.[90] The Bank itself describes its role as the *primary financier of development projects in the Third World*. The World Bank has become the *Third World's largest creditor*[91] and is the largest multi-national lending and technical agency dealing with Third World development.

The IBRD counts a total of 189 member states for which it provides the above-mentioned functions and by which it is owned. As stated in the Articles of Agreement, membership is only open to members of the IMF.[92] Membership to the IBRD is mandatory to become a member to the other four institutions of the World Bank Group. Structurally is the IBRD modelled after the example of the IMF. To become member, as under the IMF Agreement, the subscription of capital is required. Also voting follows the rules of the IMF: Thus, the voting powers of the member states depend on their economic strength. This refers to the Board of Governors as well as to the Board of Executive Directors. In the Board of Governors, each Governor representing its state has 250 votes plus the Member state's variable share of votes. As under the IMF Agreement, there are qualified majority requirements depending on the concrete issue which might include a super majority of 85% which gives, like in the IMF, the U.S.A. de facto a veto power. The Board of Executive Directors usually decides, however, based on consensus.

5.4.3.2 Purposes

According to Article I IBRD Agreement, the World Bank has the following purposes:

i. *To assist in the reconstruction and development of territories of members by facilitating the investment of capital for productive purposes, including the restoration of economies destroyed or disrupted by war, the reconversion of productive facilities to peacetime needs and the encouragement of the development of productive facilities and resources in less developed countries.*

---

[90] <https://www.worldbank.org/en/who-we-are/ibrd> (accessed 9 March 2025).

[91] Together the countries of the Third World owe the World Bank Group more than 160 billion U.S. dollars; cf. <https://data.worldbank.org/indicator/DT.DOD.DLXF.CD?year=2022> (accessed 9 March 2025).

[92] Art. II(1) Articles of Agreement.

ii. *To promote private foreign investment by means of guarantees or participations in loans and other investments made by private investors; and when private capital is not available on reasonable terms, to supplement private investment by providing, on suitable conditions, finance for productive purposes out of its own capital, funds raised by it and its other resources.*
iii. *To promote the long-range balanced growth of international trade and the maintenance of equilibrium in balances of payments by encouraging International investment for the development of the productive resources of members, thereby assisting in raising productivity, the standard of living and conditions of labor in their territories.*
iv. *To arrange the loans made or guaranteed by it in relation to international loans through other channels so that the more useful and urgent projects, large and small alike, will be dealt with first.*
v. *To conduct its operations with due regard to the effect of international investment on business conditions in the territories of members and, in the immediate postwar years, to assist in bringing about a smooth transition from a wartime to a peacetime economy.*

As it is reflected in these provisions, the *promotion of investments* is one of the main purposes of the World Bank. The Bank assists by granting loans and providing other forms of financial assistance for concrete projects to support development and for investments in areas such as education, health, public administration, infrastructure, financial and private sector development, agriculture, and environmental and natural resource management. Some projects are co-financed with governments, other multilateral institutions, commercial banks, export credit agencies, and/or private investors.

Historically, the IBRD was established to *reconstruct post-war Europe* followed by the development of the *member states struggling which finding hold in the global economy*.[93] Over decades the IBRD's task list has been continuously extended, giving it the power to assist reconstruction and development in middle-income and poorer, less creditworthy countries. This is achieved through the IBRD's ability to borrow money at favorable conditions from capital markets, thus making as well as facilitating capital investment *"by means of guarantees or participations in loans and other investments made by private investors"*.[94] The bank strives for a well-balanced and sustainable growth of international trade and for improving productivity, living standards and labor conditions in its member states. This *long-term loan business is the IBRD's main instrument* in providing its aid in reconstruction and development. Furthermore, IBRD offers risk management products as well as analytical and advisory services. This enables members to access social (human development), political (governance) and financial aid. The informational

[93] World Bank (2011), 14 ss.

[94] Art. I(2) Articles of Agreement.

foundation of these loans lays in the so called "Country Assistance Strategy", a strategy worked out mutually with each country concerning the scope and bias.

5.4.3.3 Capital Basis

All this puts the bank in need of large amounts of capital, most of which is raised on the global capital market (nowadays $50 to 60 billion a year). However, the bank cross-finances its capital needs through loan repayments, returns and member subscriptions of base capital shares which are correlative to the specific country's economic size, according to the Articles of Agreement. Therefore, countries with larger stakes have more power in the IBRD's decision-making process. The bank holds a total of USD 10,000,000,000 in stock capital. Largest stakeholder are the United States of America holding approximately 15.98% of subscribed capital. Further strengthening the bank and allowing for favorable conditions, the IBRD has an AAA rating since 1959 which is based upon four pillars as they follow:

- *Prudent financial policies and substantial liquidity*
  Legally limited lending and a maximum gearing ratio (ratio of long-term debt compared to equity capital) of 1:1 render the bank's business prudential and conservative.
- *Quality Loan portfolio*
  High quality and reputation are achieved through AAA ratings, restriction to state or state-guaranteed investments, limitation of loan concentration and restrictive policies of capital freezing in case of debtor's delay.
- *Consistent profitability*
  Over the past decade, the IBRD has consistently reported positive net income, averaging approximately $1.4 billion in annual profit.
- *Diversified shareholder base*
  Backup through massive shareholder support of its 189 member states with a current capital of USD 276 billion (as of 30 June 2023)[95]

5.4.4 International Development Association (IDA)

5.4.4.1 Purpose

Another institution under the roof of the World Bank Group is the IDA, which was founded in 1960 placing *special focus on less developed member countries and complementing the IBRD's measures.*[96] IBRD and IDA are together regarded as the World Bank as understood in the media. Nonetheless it must be said that the IDA

[95] For all see <https://financesapp.worldbank.org/summaryinfo/ibrd/> (accessed 9 March 2025).

[96] Art. I IDA Articles of Agreement.

stands completely independent, has its own legal personality and is not subject to regulations and decisions made by the IBRD (see also Article VI (6) IDA Articles of Agreement). As mentioned earlier on, membership is only open to members of the IBRD and therefore members of the IMF.

According to Article I of the IDA Articles of Agreement, the organization has as purposes

> *"to promote economic development, increase productivity and thus raise standards of living in the less-developed areas of the world included within the Association's member-ship, in particular by providing finance to meet their important develop-mental requirements on terms which are more flexible and bear less heavily on the balance of payments than those of conventional loans, thereby furthering the developmental objectives of the International Bank for Reconstruction and Development (hereinafter called "the Bank") and supplementing its activities."*

Concentrating on those member countries with almost no financial resources, i.e. the poorest countries, the association can provide better borrowing conditions than the IBRD—in fact it offers loans with very low or even free of interests and provides them with longer running times (25–40 years). Furthermore, the IDA is strongly involved in the sector of debt relief, helping poor and indebted countries settle their finance through its two major initiatives, the Heavily Indebted Poor Countries (HIPC) Initiative and the Multilateral Debt Relief Initiative (MDRI). Having supported over 100 countries since its foundation, the IDA has become the *number one institution within the World Bank Group to fight poverty.*[97] IDA's support ranges over a variety of different development investments from education and health care to environmental and economic activities, ultimately serving for equality, economic growth, job creation, higher incomes and improved living conditions.

5.4.4.2 Capital Basis

Comparable to the IBRD, IDA finances its funds through raising capital on the global financial markets. Despite this, most of its funds come from donations and contributions of its member countries as well as borrower repayments and contributions from the IBRD and the International Finance Corporation (IFC). The IDA's financial strategy is discussed tri-annually in so called replenishment meetings held by donors and borrower country representatives.

[97] <https://www.worldbank.org/en/news/feature/2024/01/31/record-ida-replenishment-essential-as-debt-crisis-looms> (accessed 9 March 2025).

5.4.4.3 Allocation of Funds

Since the financial needs of the member countries exceed the IDA's funds, the association must systematically allocate its funds to eligible recipients. To differentiate its business from the IBRD's, an eligible recipient is defined as *a country not creditworthy enough to qualify for IBRD support and with a Gross National Income (GNI) per capita below an annually updated threshold.* There are exceptions if the country fails to meet the IBRD's requirements but has a higher-than-threshold GNI. Contrary, there are also countries who have a lower-than-threshold GNI but still are considered creditworthy by means of the IBRD. Such countries are considered "blend" countries and are mutually eligible to IDA support. Following the eligibility qualification, IDA then reviews a country's size, portfolio performance according to their economy management and its implementation of policies to promote growth and reduce poverty which all together form the IDA Country Performance Rating (IDA rating). Above all that stand IDA internal policies demanding a sub-Saharan African focus and an allocation of 50% of the total resources to that area. The fact whether an interest rate is applied to a loan is dependent on the specific country's IDA rating.

5.4.4.4 Structure and Decision-Making

The structure and decision-making follow the model of the IBRD: The president as well as the members of the Board of Governors and of the Board of the Executive Directors of the IBRD are ex officio president or members of the respective boards of the IDA (Article VI (2, 4 and 5) IDA Articles of Agreement). As to decision-making the votes are weighted as in the IBRD and depend on a country's subscription (Article VI (3) IDA Articles of Agreement).

5.4.4.5 Power of Authentic Interpretation

Article X (a) provides that any dispute between the organization and a member state or between member states as to the interpretation of controversial provisions of the IDA Articles of Agreement shall be decided by the Executive Directors. According to Article X (b), any member, so not only members parties to a dispute, may refer the Executive Directors' decision to the Board of Governors for final decision. These organs thus have *the power of authentic interpretation.*[98]

[98] As to authentic interpretation cf. Gold (1996), 34 ss.

5.4.4.6 Termination of Membership—Settlement of Accounts

Another provision, Article VII (4), regulates in detail the financial consequences of the termination of a state's membership, including the settlement of accounts against the background of a country's subscriptions. Article VII (4) (b) requires that this be addressed in an agreement between IDA and the withdrawing country, which specifies the amounts to be paid by the country as a result of its contributions and the timing and currencies of their payment. This is also in the interest of the IDA. Since the capital contributions are used to finance loans, a country's withdrawal could result in a need for refinancing for outstanding loans. The IDA needs sufficient time for this refinancing.

This Article also contains rules which apply if the country leaving IDA and the organization do not come to an agreement within 6 months. These rules also have an important impact on the negotiations between IDA and the country's government. The government is relieved from any further liability except for *"amounts due and unpaid on the date when the government ceased to be a member and which in the opinion of the Association are needed by it to meet its commitments as of that date under its financing operations"*.[99] The same rule applies to the country's subscription. A leaving member receives a pro rata share of all principal repayments received by IDA after the date on which the country ceases to be a member on loans contracted prior thereto. IDA always has the option to withhold any amount due to the country as long as this country has a liability as borrower or grantor and may upon maturity set off these amounts.

5.4.5 International Finance Corporation (IFC)

A further institution under the roof of the World Bank is the International Finance Corporation IFC, established in 1956. According to Article 1 of the IFC Articles of Agreement, the IFC has as purpose *"to further economic development by encouraging the growth of productive private enterprise in member countries, particularly in the less developed areas, thus supplementing the activities of the International Bank for Reconstruction and Development"*. This is done in cooperation with private investors, by inter alia assisting in financing the establishment, improvement, and expansion of productive private enterprises when there is no governmental guarantee of repayment and if sufficient private capital is not available on reasonable terms. IFC further seeks to bring together investment opportunities, domestic and foreign private capital, and experienced management, and finally seeks to stimulate, and to help create conditions conducive to, the flow of private capital, domestic and foreign, into productive investment in member countries.

[99] Art. VII(4c) IDA Articles of Agreement.

Complementary to the activities of the IBRD, the IFC is designed *to improve private sector development through investment services, advisory services and asset management.* To achieve its purpose, IFC offers development impact solutions through firm-level interventions (direct investments and advisory services), standard-setting, and business enabling environment work. Being the World Bank's private sector arm, IFC promotes socioeconomic growth through the creation of jobs, the generation of tax revenue, improvement of corporate governance as well as the improvement of environmental performance and contributions to local communities thus pushing commercial businesses and private financial institutions within member states.

Again, membership is open only to IBRD members. Structurally, also this organization follows the model of IBRD, including decision-making based on the weighted votes depending on a member's capital subscription.

Looking closer at the services the IFC provides, the corporation considerably differs from the IBRD and IDA. Investment services clearly being its central products in offer, the IFC provides equity finance, long-term loans, syndicated loans, loan guarantees, trade finance, structured and securitized finance, local currency financing, private equity, and investment funds as well as risk management products to regions that would otherwise be deemed too risky by investors. Altogether the IFC holds an investment portfolio summing up to USD 70.7 billion spread over nearly 2868 companies in 109 countries (as of June 2024). Participation in IFC in a company's activities is by investors usually regarded as a quality label.

Although it still is a new business branch, the *IFC's asset management* can—from a fiscal viewpoint—be considered its second most influential business branch, totaling in assets of USD 10.1 billion (as of 2023) managed by the IFC and spread over 13 different funds. The funds are controlled by the IFC's Asset Management Company (AMC) which established the first fund, the *IFC Global Capitalization Fund*, in 2009. It was mainly called into life to help systematically important banks in emerging markets. The fund was followed by the *IFC African, Latin American, and Caribbean Fund* (2010) for equity and equity related investments, the *Africa Capitalization Fund* (2010) for investments in systematically important commercial banks, the *IFC Russian Bank Capitalization Fund* (2012) for investments in mid-sized commercial banks, the *IFC Catalyst Fund* (2012) as fund for funds and the *IFC Global Infrastructure Fund* (2013) for investments in the infrastructure sector. Other funds established since 2013 include the *IFC Financial Institutions Growth Fund* (2015), which focuses on equity investments in financial institutions in developing countries; the *IFC Emerging Asia Fund* (2016), which provides equity investments to foster economic growth and poverty reduction in Asia; the *IFC MCPP Infrastructure Fund* (2016), which mobilizes private investment into infrastructure projects in emerging markets; the *IFC Middle East and North Africa Fund* (2017), focusing on investments in private enterprises across the Middle East and North Africa; and the *Women Entrepreneurs Debt Fund* (2018), providing financing to women entrepreneurs through local banks.

Thirdly, IFC provides *advisory services.* With an investment volume of over USD 1.4 billion, the corporation provides advice, problem solving and training to companies, industries and governments in five business areas, managing over 800 projects across more than 100 countries. In particular it helps in getting access to finance through increasing availability and affordability of financial services. Also, the corporation handles business climate issues, environmental and social sustainability concerns, helps to develop viable markets and finally, advises governments in public-private partnerships and their structural aspects so basic infrastructure can be strengthened.

5.4.6 Multilateral Investment Guarantee Agency (MIGA)

5.4.6.1 Structure, Organs

The Multilateral Investment Guarantee Agency (MIGA) as an international organization also part of the World Bank Group was established in 1988. Structurally, the MIGA is similarly built as the IBDR, although differences remain. Founding document is the Convention establishing MIGA. Most prominent difference is the setting of Governors. At the BoG's place there is the MIGAs Council of Governors (CoG) which vests the agency's corporate powers within the council, except such powers that are conferred to another organ. The council is otherwise governed identically, and its representatives are open to being the same individuals as on the BoG. The same applies for the BoD which is also an organ of the MIGA.

The MIGA Convention regulates the powers of the Board as well as of the Council to render binding interpretations of the Convention's provisions the same way as the IDA Articles of Agreement.[100]

5.4.6.2 Purpose: Insurance for Private Investors Against Political Risks

MIGA provides *insurance against political risks and offers credit enhancement guarantees to protect foreign direct investments (only) in developing countries* (Article 14 MIGA Convention). As stated in Article 2 MIGA Convention, the objective of MIGA is

> *"to encourage the flow of investments for productive purposes among member countries, and in particular to developing member countries, thus supplementing the activities of the International Bank for Reconstruction and Development (hereinafter referred to as the Bank), the International Finance Corporation and other international development finance institutions. To serve its objective, the Agency shall: (a) issue guarantees, including coinsurance and reinsurance,*

---

[100] Art. 56 MIGA Convention; as to the analogous provision under the IDA Articles of Agreement see supra, Sect. 5.4.4.4.

against non-commercial risks in respect of investments in a member country which flow from other member countries; (b) carry out appropriate complementary activities to promote the flow of investments to and among developing member countries; and (c) exercise such other incidental powers as shall be necessary or desirable in the furtherance of its objectives."

Such insurances should encourage private investors to invest in developing countries where risks without the insurance would be too high to be attractive for investments and for which it is *difficult to find a private insurance prepared to cover these risks at reasonable terms*. Thus, the agency's main product—it's insurance guarantees—protect investors from a variety of aspects which are not subject to basic insurance models. The risks covered by MIGA are foremost *political risks* and include restrictions on currency transfer, expropriation and similar measures, breach of contract by the host government, and war and civil disturbances (Article 11 MIGA Convention).

The contracts are concluded between MIGA and the investors at terms generally defined by the Board. They need the *approval of the host state* (Article 15 MIGA Convention). These contracts give *private investors an international standing* in their relations with MIGA as well as with the host country. The sole fact that an investment is insured by an international institution like MIGA against risks for which the host state is responsible reduces that probability that these risks will materialize because this would not only create a controversy between the host state and the investor, but also between the host state and MIGA as insurer under the obligation to indemnify the investors.

5.4.6.3 Development Fields

The MIGA has four prioritized development fields in which it sees the greatest change potential. These are:

- First, *investments in IDA-eligible countries,* which are often underserved by private sector insurers due to heightened risks, benefit significantly from MIGA's political risk insurance. This allows for foreign investments that can substantially enhance development outcomes.
- Second, *investments in conflict-affected countries* play a crucial role in sustainable development post-crisis. MIGA facilitates these investments by offering insurance products that provide security to investors even after donor aid diminishes, thus fostering long-term growth.
- Third, MIGA supports *complex projects in infrastructure and extractive industries*, addressing essential needs such as power and water supply. These projects are executed in line with international standards, including environmental and social governance, ensuring that they contribute effectively to a country's development.

– Finally, MIGA is committed to supporting *South-South investments*, South-South meaning the investment between developing states which are growing in prominence as a key component of global foreign direct investment (FDI). By providing political risk insurance, particularly to local financial institutions that face challenges in mitigating political risks, MIGA ensures that these investments can proceed, contributing to broader regional development.

5.4.6.4 The Liquidation of MIGA

MIGA is one of the very few organizations whose liquidation is explicitly regulated in the treaty establishing the organization. Article 55 of the MIGA Convention gives the Council the power, by special majority, to decide to liquidate the organizations. This implies the cessation of the activities and the settlement of MIGA's assets and obligations, in particular the outstanding guarantees to investors. As explicitly stated in Article 55(b),

> *"[n]o distribution of assets shall be made to members until all liabilities to holders of guarantees and other creditors shall have been discharged or provided for and until the Council shall have decided to make such distribution. (c) Subject to the foregoing, the Agency shall distribute its remaining assets to members in proportion to each member's share in the subscribed capital."*

Distributions to members are, however, only made when members have settled all outstanding claims by MIGA against them.

5.4.7 International Centre for the Settlement of Investment Disputes (ICSID)

5.4.7.1 Purpose

MIGA's purpose is to encourage and protect foreign investments. This is also true for the International Center for the Settlement of Invest Disputes (ICSID), the fifth of the World Bank Group institutions. The ICSID is the *Bank's instrument for arbitration and conciliation in case of controversies between investors and host states*. Based on the *Convention on the Settlement of Investment Disputes between States and Nationals of Other States (Washington Convention)*, the ICSID supports the Bank's efforts in foreign investments. The convention establishes the institution and regulates jurisdiction and the main available methods to settle controversies between investors and the host state, i.e. conciliation and arbitration. The convention is supplemented by a set of three rules, i.e. the Rules of Procedure for the Institution of Conciliation and Arbitration Proceedings (Institution Rules), the Rules of

Procedure for Conciliation Proceedings (Conciliation Rules), and the Rules of Procedure for Arbitration Proceedings (Arbitration Rules).

The main purpose of the ICSID as an independent institution is basically to make available to host states and investors *the infrastructure for arbitration or conciliation proceeding in case of controversies between them and to administer these dispute resolution proceedings*. This is very similar to the arbitration and conciliation facilities provided for by private institutions such as the International Chamber of Commerce (ICC). The difference is that ICSID is not a private but an international, intergovernmental institution and that its jurisdiction *ratione materiae* is confined to investments and *ratione personae* to litigations between states and private investors. Otherwise, the concrete functioning is very similar to private arbitration and conciliation institutions.

Ever since the ICSID has seen an ongoing increase in importance as it is the main dispute resolution organ for the settlement of investment disputes between private corporations and public entities or countries. This is due to its considerably large size, number of adjudicated cases and countless investment treaties referring to its arbitration facilities, which has made it the leading institution in this field. The ICSID currently holds 154 so-called contracting states as members. In addition to arbitration and conciliation, which is ICSID's main business, it is also active in research and publishing in arbitrational law and investment law.

5.4.7.2 Structure

The ICSIDs structure is clearly different from the other World Bank institutions and consists of two main organs, the Administrative Council and the Secretariat. Each member state assigns one representative to the Council which in most cases is the ex officio assigned IBRD Governor if not appointed differently by the member state. Chairman of the Administrative Council is the World Bank President (assigned ex officio), although he or she does not have any voting powers. Being the governing organ of the ICSID, the Council elects the Secretary-General and Deputy Secretary-General, adopts regulations and rules, adopts the ICSID budget and approves the annual report on ICSID operations. The Secretariat then serves all the administrative tasks like the support for initiation and conduction of ICSID proceedings, assistance in the constitution of conciliation commissions, support of arbitral tribunals as well as ad hoc committees and case administration. Mostly financed through the World Bank, ICSID holds annual meetings together with the rest of the Bank Group and the IMF. The ICSID mainly operates as a secretariat whose Secretary-General is its legal representative and is selected by the Administrative Council every 6 years.

5.4.7.3 Activities

The ICSID offers three different types of services. It provides facilities for arbitration and conciliation, deals with certain proceedings outside the scope of the ICSID's convention (e.g. one party is not an ICSID member) and appoints arbitrators for ad hoc arbitration proceedings. As one easily could assume, the ICSID does not arbitrate or conciliate disputes by itself. Therefore, only the institutional and procedural framework are initialized through the ICSID. Once the parties agree on and file for an ICSID settlement, they cannot recall their request. Disputes are then settled through either of the two sets of procedural rules which the center provides:

a) ICSID Convention, Rules and Regulations
These are gathered documents consisting of the Convention on the Settlement of Investment Disputes between States and Nationals of Other States, the Report of Executive Directors of the IBRD on the Convention, the Administrative and Financial Regulations, the Institution Rules, the Conciliation Rules and the Arbitration Rules. The Convention, Rules and Regulations are the main framework used to govern proceedings.

b) ICSID Additional Facility Rules
In addition, the ICSID has established the Additional Facility Rules to govern proceedings between states and nationals of other states which normally would not fall under the scope of application of the ICSID. These are proceedings such as fact-finding proceedings, proceedings in which one of the parties is neither a contracting state or a national of a contracting state as well as proceedings in which at least one of the parties is a contracting country or national of such and a dispute subject which does not arise from an investment but at least is not just a commercial transaction.

The far most important activity of the ICSID is the administration of arbitration proceedings. Since the center's inception, the arbitral tribunals have heard and decided hundreds of cases. The center's jurisdiction is established in a treaty between the investor and the host state or, with the central government's consent, a subdivision of the host state (Article 25 ICSID Convention). The exhaustion of local remedies rule only applies if the host states insist on this rule's application (Article 26 ICSID Convention). One of the reasons that investors seek ICSID arbitration is often exactly that they consider the host state's court not independent enough to decide in an unbiased, fair way controversies under investment treaties concluded by their own government.

Arbitration starts with the filling of a request of arbitration with the Secretary General. The secretariat is then administering the arbitration. The Arbitral Tribunal is usually composed of three judges. One is nominated by each of the parties, the president is nominated by both parties. If the parties are not able to agree on the president, then nomination is up to the Chairman of the ICSID Administrative Council which is ex officio the World Bank president. The award is basically final. There is no appeal available against the award available.

References

Archibugi D, Filippetti A (2010) The globalisation of intellectual property rights: four learned lessons and four theses. Global Pol 1:137–149

Dreher A (2009) IMF conditionality: theory and evidence. Public Choice 141:233–267. https://doi.org/10.1007/s11127-009-9486-z

Fukuda-Parr S (2004) Millennium development goals: why they matter. Glob Gov 10(4):395–402

Gold J (1996) Interpretation: the IMF and international law. Kluwer Law International, Boston

Kutler SI (1990) The wars of Watergate: the last crisis of Richard Nixon. Alfred A. Knopf, New York

Ricardo D (1821) On the principles of political economy and taxation, 3rd edn. John Murray, London

Smith A (1904) In: Cannan E (ed) An inquiry into the nature and causes of the wealth of nations. Methuen & Co Ltd, London

Stubbs T et al (2020) How to evaluate the effects of IMF conditionality: an extension of quantitative approaches and an empirical application to public education spending. Rev Int Org 15:29–73. https://doi.org/10.1007/s11558-018-9332-5

Van Den Bossche P, Zdouc W (2017) The law and policy of the World Trade Organization, 4th edn. Cambridge University Press, Cambridge

World Bank (2011) A guide to the World Bank, 3rd edn. World Bank Publications, Washington, DC. https://doi.org/10.1596/978-0-8213-8545-6

Zeiler TW (1999) Free trade, free world: the advent of GATT. University of North Carolina Press, Chapel Hill

Chapter 6
Non-Governmental Organizations (NGOs)

6.1 Definition and Objectives

6.1.1 Introduction: The Concept of Non-Governmental Organizations (NGO)

The previous chapters have discussed traditional, governmental international organizations, focusing on their normative and governance structures, processes and goals. Other important actors on the international stage are non-governmental organizations (NGOs). NGOs, like intergovernmental organizations, play a decisive role and have an important impact in the international system. Today, over 7500 international NGOs and tens of thousands of local NGOs are active around the globe.[1] In their fields of activity, they contribute to the policies of states and international organizations. In practice, NGOs often belong to the influential players in the decision-making process of international organizations. Some NGOs have a significant impact based on their knowledge, membership and funding.

Before the UN was established in 1945, a variety of names were used for what is known as an NGO today as the term NGO did not gain currency before the end of World War II when it was created as a neologism. Before that, terms such as "association", "special interest group", "social movement", "voluntary organization", and "civil society organization" were the more prominently used terminology. For example, the Union of International Associations (UIA) was created in 1910 by an agreement between representatives of 132 civil society bodies and 13 governments. What was known as an international association at the time is now known as an NGO; indeed, the UIA is classified as an international non-governmental

Special thanks to Dominic Staiger for his important contribution to the elaboration of this chapter.

[1] Willetts (2011), p. xvi.

U. Saxer, *The Law of Global and European Organizations*, Springer Textbooks in Law, https://doi.org/10.1007/978-3-032-00067-5_6

organization today. Initially, the League of Nations had formal contacts only with traditional intergovernmental treaty-based bodies, but informal contacts with private organizations also developed over time.

The breakthrough at the international level for the term "non-governmental organization" came by way of the Article 71 UN Charter which recognizes an official role for NGOs in the UN system. However, it was then unclear what the term means and what associations should be recognized as NGOs. Contrary to US Secretary of State Edward R. Stettinius, the chairman of the US delegation to the conference that drafted the Charter, who announced that *"this paragraph stands on its own and needs no interpretation"*, some grievance about *"the rather condescending terminology"* and *"humble wording"* of Article 71 has been expressed by NGO leaders and others with the benefit of hindsight.[2] Nowadays there is a special procedure for recognizing an NGO according to Article 71 UN Charter.[3]

As the term NGOs was first mentioned in Article 71, the specifics of NGO involvement in and influence on the UN still had to be determined. Also this is now comprehensively regulated in ECOSOC Resolution 1996/31 of 25 July 1996 on the *Consultative Relationship Between the United Nations and Non-governmental Organizations*.

6.1.2 Definition)

At the international level, legal standards to define and regulate NGOs have not yet been established,[4] so that there is no internationally recognized, official definition. In general, however, NGOs are considered as

- independent, voluntary self-governing associations or organizations;
- with private, non-governmental membership;
- which have a general or public non-sovereign purpose and pursue essentially non-profit objectives;[5]
- display transnational activities;
- -have a structure as an institution with a headquarter;
- and governed by the law of a state and not by international law.[6]

There are therefore important structural differences between an NGO and a traditional International Organization (IO). One obvious distinction is that IOs are established by intergovernmental agreements while NGOs are established via the cooperation of private individuals or associations based on the law of the state in

[2] Fenaux (1978), p. 194; Shestack (1978), p. 97.

[3] See infra, Sect. 6.2.2.1.

[4] Martens (2003).

[5] This does not include political parties; cf. Council of Europe Publishing, *Legal status of non-governmental organisations in Europe*, CM/Rec(2007)14 and explanatory memorandum, 7.

[6] See also supra, Sect. 1.3.1.4.

which they are based.[7] Thus, NGOs are governed by national law, IOs by international law. Members of IOs are sovereign entities such as states and other IOs, whereas members of NGOs are individuals, private associations and/or companies. As a general rule, all NGOs must be independent of governments to be recognized as such. However, this rule which stems from the very nature and the denomination of NGOs and also applies to UN-recognized NGOs has been relaxed today as governments are often involved in the activities of NGOs in some form, e.g. through the funding they provide, but they should not have an impact on an NGO's basic decisions.[8]

A list of official criteria for an NGO can be found in rules of the ECOSOC regulating consultative status of NGOs in the UN system.[9] According to these rules of the UN system, an NGO

- must been in existence (officially recognized by a government) for at least two years,
- must have established headquarters, a democratically adopted constitution, authority to speak for its members, a representative structure, appropriate mechanisms of accountability and democratic and transparent decision-making processes;
- has as its main financial resources the contributions of the national affiliates or other components or of individual members.

Organizations established by governments or intergovernmental agreements are not considered NGOs.[10] There are, however, hybrid international institutions in which states are actively involved and trans-national corporations.

6.1.3 Objectives

One effect of the globalization of communication is to make it logistically and financially easier for small groups of people separated by thousands of miles to establish and maintain cooperation. This has led to the creation of improved, simple, and cheap communication facilities, which makes it for NGOs much easier to operate transnationally. *Many NGOs operate globally*, though not all NGOs choose to do so. The scope of the different NGOs' operations varies from local organizations solely operating in one small town to large global bureaucracies with a

[7] That distinction holds even when IOs provide formal institutional roles for NGOs; cf. Charnovitz (2006), p. 352.

[8] For a discussion of some of the negative effects reliance of government funding can have, see Hirsch (2013).

[9] ECOSOC, *Consultative relationship between the United Nations and non-governmental organizations*, E/1996/31 (1996).

[10] UN DESA, *Introduction to ECOSOC Consultative Status*, <https://ecosoc.un.org/en/ngo/consultative-status> (accessed 9 March 2025).

presence in many countries. The crucial factor that determines whether an NGO operates transnationally is the NGO's goals and funding. Discrete NGOs may first become well established in several countries before they decide to form an international NGO, as a loose federation, to exchange information and learn from each other's experience. This has been the case with trade unions and women's organizations. Other national NGOs may first have the goal of influencing their own government's policies but then decide to seek support from foreign governments and foreign or international NGOs. For instance, environmental NGOs in developing countries have found support from transnational networks to be crucial to their ability to carry out their functions. Other NGOs decided from the start that they would be more effective as a transnational organization and thus set up branches simultaneously in several countries. Examples of such NGOs are Amnesty International and Friends of the Earth which started in the United Kingdom and the United States respectively but eventually established branches in many countries. Finally, NGOs can be based in one country but have transnational goals. For many years, the UK-based Oxfam and US-based CARE raised funds for international disaster relief and development before joining international federations, and then later establishing branches in other countries.

NGOs mainly *use public communication to advance their goals.*[11] Indeed, NGOs are, to a large extent, information and communication networks that seek t*o raise awareness of and gain support for their causes*, so as to ultimately shape government action. Their main objective is public advocacy for wide-ranging interests such as humanitarian concerns and activities, environmental protection, the promotion of health, human rights (including minority rights and rights of particularly vulnerable persons and groups), scientific, cultural, charitable, philanthropic, and education issues. Some NGOs also promote sports, the protection of specific plants and rare animals. Hence, *NGOs represent civil society and its interests on the international level.*

The issues that form the subject of NGO advocacy are usually cross-border ones, as they affect a large part of the world's populations. For example, environmental issues such as the destruction of the rain forest is a climate change issue with global repercussions. The ever-increasing regional and global interdependencies regarding important political, social, environmental, economic, cultural and other issues, has led to a proliferation of NGOs to represent non-governmental interests. Over the last few decades, NGOs have significantly increased in numbers and influence. Today, most NGOs advocate for specific issues. In the course of their work, *they internationalize matters that were previously purely domestic* such as human rights issues not regulated by global agreements (e.g. protection of minorities, rights of women, children, migrants, indigenous peoples, human rights aspects of sexual orientation etc.), review and report on a state's compliance with their international obligations

[11]However, humanitarian NGOs of course display other, concrete activities such as medical assistance, food deliveries, shelters etc.

either as parties to international agreements or as members of international organizations, and provide their expertise to the work of international organizations.

In addition, NGOs with *humanitarian objectives* are pivotal: There are few international and national conflicts in which they are not or cannot be active. Without their involvement, the civilian population would suffer even more from the conflicts. Finally, some NGOs play a very important role in the further development of international law, particularly in the area of human rights and humanitarian international law. This will be demonstrated with the example of the International Committee of the Red Cross.[12]

Finally, NGOs play a central role in global development cooperation. Already in 1998, a report by the UN Secretary General highlighted that NGOs provide the second largest source of development assistance, thus underlining their importance to the global society.[13]

6.2 International Legal Status of NGOs

6.2.1 General Rule: No International Legal Personality

Although NGOs have considerable political influence, the traditional view of international law as a domain in which states and inter-governmental international organizations are the central actors means that NGOs do not have international legal personality. The general rule is that they are vested with domestic legal personality only.

Nonetheless, there are exceptional cases where NGOs possess a limited international legal personality as they are recognized as limited subjects of international law based on specific provisions in international agreements. An example is the International Committee of the Red Cross (ICRC) which has been given the mandate from state parties to the 1949 Geneva Conventions and their Additional Protocols of 1977 to protect victims of armed conflicts, both international and internal. Thus, its limited international legal personality is derived from the Geneva Conventions and their Additional Protocols. Second, the consultative status given by the ECOSOC to NGOs grants some international legal personality to these NGOs.

There is an ongoing debate as to whether NGOs should possess international legal personality. This requires a nuanced approach that considers the immensely different nature of various NGOs. Broadly speaking, three categories of actors can be distinguished: first, NGOs recognized under customary international law as possessing legal personality such as the Maltese Order as a special case,[14] second,

---

[12] See infra, Sect. 6.2.2.2.

[13] *Arrangements and Practices for the Interaction of Non-Governmental Organizations in All Activities of the United Nations System,* Report of the SG, A/53/170 (1998), para. 2.

[14] Crawford (2019), p. 114 ss.

NGOs whose legal capacity is recognized in an international treaty such as the ICRC, and/or dependent upon an agreement or acquiescence of states,[15] and finally the vast majority of all other NGOs without any international legal personality. The second category of NGOs has international legal personality functionally limited to the powers necessary to carry out the tasks which lie at the core of their raison d'être.

Arguments raised against NGOs more concrete international standing are their lack of representation: unlike democratically elected state actors, NGOs generally only represent an interest group and not the citizenry. Furthermore, their vast number would pose significant logistical issues if they all are subjects of international law and therefore to be accepted by international organizations and state as partners. The current practice of granting status to selected NGOs under the UN seems more accurate and efficient.[16] Greater access to the international decision-making process is also problematic because some NGOs receive private funds, which has the potential to affect their independence.

Generally, however, there is a slow shift towards recognizing not only states and governmental international organizations, i.e. traditional subjects of international law, but also other entities as relevant international actors which are fundamental to the functioning of the international legal order and which participate, often based on soft law or agreements, in activities alongside state agencies and international organizations. *Global public policy networks, e.g., often are rather networks than legal entities and are comprised by governments, global companies, actors from civil society such as NGOs and international organizations and institutions.* They develop specific policies and rules and coordinate the implementation. Their expertise is important also with regard to the creation of new international norms. This is also the case with NGOs. Their expertise on a particular subject qualifies them to be recognized as legitimate authority. Thus, there are important reasons to give NGOs a more concrete international standing or a formal position.

6.2.2 Special Status Regulations

6.2.2.1 Article 71 UN Charter and Article V (2) WTO-A

As mentioned previously, one exception to the NGOs' lack of international legal status is Article 71 of the UN Charter which provides that NGOs have a consultation status: "*The Economic and Social Council may make suitable arrangements for consultation with non-governmental organizations which are concerned with matters within its competence. Such arrangements may be made with international organizations and, where appropriate, with national organizations after consultation with the Member of the United Nations concerned.*"

[15] Brownlie (1998), p. 35.

[16] Wedgwood (1999), p. 29.

This status is specifically regulated in the ECOSOC Resolution 1996/31. Consultative status is granted by the ECOSOC upon recommendation of the UN Committee on NGOs. The Committee is responsible for accrediting NGOs with consultative status at the UN. While not all transnational NGOs will be eligible for ECOSOC consultative status as some NGOs are concerned with matters beyond the ECOSOC's competence, nevertheless, Article 71 arguably provides an authoritative statement that NGOs have a legitimate place in international diplomacy. Consultative relationships may be established with international, regional, sub-regional and even national non-governmental organizations.

The World Trade Organization (WTO) officially recognizes NGOs pursuant to Article V (2) WTO Agreement[17] which contains a specific reference to NGOs and provides that the *"General Council may make appropriate arrangements for consultation and cooperation with non-governmental organizations concerned with matter related to those of the WTO"*. In 1996, the General Council adopted guidelines for NGOs[18] which recognize the role that NGOs can play to increase awareness of the WTO's activities.[19] Pursuant to these guidelines, NGOs could attend the Plenary Sessions of the First WTO Ministerial Conference in Singapore in 1996. Further, NGO applications to register would be accepted by the WTO Secretariat on the basis of Article V (2).[20]

Similarly, international organizations such as the United Nations Conference on Trade and Development (UNCTAD) and the International Labour Organization (ILO) allow for NGO participation. In contrast, the International Bank for Reconstruction and Development ('World Bank') and the International Monetary Fund (IMF), do not provide an explicit legal basis for NGO involvement.

6.2.2.2 The Geneva Conventions and the ICRC

According to common Article 9 and Article 10 of the 1949 Geneva Conventions, the provisions of the Conventions *"constitute no obstacle to the humanitarian activities which the International Committee of the Red Cross or any other impartial humanitarian organization may, subject to the consent of the Parties to the conflict concerned, undertake for the protection of wounded and sick, medical personnel and chaplains, and for their relief."*[21] Thus, this provision grants impartial

[17] For a similar NGO approval procedure and the available status at the UN, see <https://ecosoc.un.org/en/ngo/> (accessed 9 March 2025).

[18] WTO General Council, *Guidelines for Arrangements on Relations with Non-Governmental Organizations*, adopted on 18 Jul 1996, WT/L/162.

[19] Art. II *Guidelines for Arrangements*.

[20] For more details see WTO, Relations with Non-Governmental Organisations, <https://www.wto.org/english/forums_e/ngo_e/intro_e.htm> (accessed 9 March 2025).

[21] This is the wording of Art. 9 of the Convention (I) for the Amelioration of the Condition of the Wounded and Sick in Armed Forces in the Field, Geneva, 12 Aug 1949. The wording of the other 1949 Geneva Conventions in analogous.

humanitarian organizations, i.e. humanitarian NGOs, the right to offer to the parties to an international armed conflict, to undertake humanitarian activities. The International Committee of the Red Cross (ICRC) is explicitly mentioned. This is why the ICRC is a partial subject of international law, due to its particular role under the 1949 Geneva Conventions. Such an offer is to be assessed by a state party to a conflict in good faith and in accordance with international obligations of humanitarian law. Depending on the circumstances, a refusal may violate these obligations.[22] However, the consent of the states parties to the armed conflict is required before humanitarian NGOs can operate in the country. NGOs thus do not have a right per se to provide aid in a country. In any case, the party offering the aid must be both impartial and established for humanitarian purposes to fall under the 1949 Geneva Agreements. The gravity of a certain situation might therefore justify the NGO's intervention when the requirements under the Agreement and Protocol are met.

6.2.2.3 A Hybrid Case: The European Convention on the Recognition of the Legal Personality of International Non-Governmental Organizations

The *European Convention on the Recognition of the Legal Personality of International Non-Governmental Organizations*, adopted by the Council of Europe in 1984, is a central step forward in the development of an NGO international legal framework.[23] The Convention recognizes that NGOs carry out valuable work for the international community in accordance with the UN Charter and the Statute of the Council of Europe, and so the Convention was adopted to facilitate the activities of NGOs on the European level. Article 1 of the Convention sets out the four conditions that the NGO must meet to fall under the Convention's ambit. First, the activity of the NGO must not be for profit and be of international utility, i.e. it must benefit not just a local community. Second, the NGO must be established by an instrument governed by the national laws of a party to the Convention. Third, the NGO must conduct its activities with effect in at least two states. Fourth, the NGO must have its statutory office in one of the Convention's member states, and its central management and control office in the territory of that member state, or another member state. As NGOs are private entities, they are not allowed to exercise the prerogative rights of a public authority.[24] The NGO's legal status, and rights and responsibilities, are governed by the law of the member state where the NGO's statutory office is located.

[22] See, e.g. a refusal that would violate Art. 54(1) of the 1977 Additional Protocol I to the 1949 Geneva Conventions which provides: "Starvation of civilians as a method of warfare is prohibited."

[23] The full version of the Convention can be downloaded at <https://rm.coe.int/168007a67c> (accessed 9 March 2025).

[24] For more details see the Explanatory Report on the Convention, para. 7; available on the website of the Council of Europe, <http://conventions.coe.int/treaty/EN/Reports/Html/124.htm> (accessed 9 March 2025).

In contrast to the UN's consultative status requirements, the Convention only imposes minimal requirements. Particularly, it does not demand a democratic constitution or democratic membership requirements. Further, it is only a regional solution to the questions relating to the NGOs' standing. The Convention's rules are hybrid insofar as they set out, on the European level, the obligation of the contracting states to recognize in their jurisdiction the legal personality of NGOs even if they were established under the laws of another contracting state. However, the Convention does not establish or recognize an international legal personality of national or international NGOs.

6.2.3 Revocation of Status in the UN

To maintain their status, NGOs must comply with the rules set by the international organization by which they have been accredited. The UN's ECOSOC rules, e.g., require NGOs to undertake to *"conform at all times to the principles governing the establishment and nature of their consultative relations with the Council"*.[25] In this regard, the UN can generally suspend or revoke the NGO's consultative status in three situations. First, the NGO behaves in a manner contrary to the UN Charter, which includes unsubstantiated or politically motivated acts against a UN member state incompatible with the UN's purpose. In such a situation, the NGO's consultative status can be suspended for up to 3 years. Second, if there is evidence that the NGO is funded by proceeds of criminal activities, suspension or withdrawal of the NGO's consultative status will be warranted. Third, given that consultative status is granted to aid the UN and its subsidiary organs in carrying out the relevant activities, this status can also be suspended or withdrawn if the NGO fails to make a positive or effective contribution to the UN within three years.

Nonetheless, NGOs' status in the UN is unique in that the UN officially recognizes NGOs' right to participate in the relevant processes. Other inter-governmental organizations do not have the procedure to grant this explicit right.

6.3 Roles and Activities

Before the 1990s, NGOs were seen as a rather remote phenomenon on the international political level. Generally, the NGOs that were already present internationally voiced their opinion strongly, but no tangible effect on the international community was observed. As exceptions, well-known NGOs such as Amnesty International, Human Rights Watch and Médecins Sans Frontières had already made an impact on policy making internationally.

[25] E/RES/1996/31, para. 57(b-c).

6.3.1 *Participation in Institutionalized International Conflict and Crisis Management*

All of this changed in the 1990s when NGOs started to assist and participate in collective conflict and crisis management under the auspices of the UN Security Council or other regional organizations. An early example is the 1992 UN Security Council Resolution on the conflict in former Yugoslavia, which called on states *"and, as appropriate, international humanitarian organizations to collate substantiated information"* relating to violations of humanitarian law.[26] In a 2003 resolution on Sierra Leone, the Security Council called on *"States, international organizations and non-governmental organizations to continue to support the National Recovery Strategy of the Government of Sierra Leone"*.[27] This practice of the UN Security Council, confirmed in many other conflicts, recognizes the important role of NGOs as indispensable partners in institutionalized international crisis and conflict management.

6.3.2 *Raising International Awareness of International Issues*

The main purpose and role of NGOs is *to promote their specific cause by raising awareness of problems and issues connected to the cause* and to press internationally for political, practical and/or legal solutions. In this context, NGOs are helpful *in bringing the views of civil society in different countries to the international level.* It is in this way that they can be viewed as an integral part of the international political framework. Today, NGOs insist on being heard on the issues that they advocate. This success can be attributed to their high level of expertise and professionalism. To fall into the realm of international law and politics, the NGO's cause must be international, including regional.

A further important factor is the NGOs' utilization of global communication which allows them to voice their opinion and concerns internationally even when states try to exclude them from discussions. Any such state action would result in the spotlight being placed on precisely the issues that the state attempted to shield from public discussion.

At the national level, NGOs often advance their causes by trying to persuade legislators to enact new laws or amend existing ones. Their power becomes apparent when national law-makers refuse to engage with them. In such instances, NGOs turn to their international networks to place pressure on other governments through local NGOs so as to influence the government in question to listen to them. Thus, if a state

[26] S/RES/ 771 (1992), para. 5.

[27] S/RES/1470 (2003), para. 8.

does not wish to discuss certain matters with an NGO, it might face pressure from other states which have been lobbied to advance the issue. Refusing to engage with NGOs is often no longer an effective way to avoid controversial issues. This is particularly the case with issues which originally belonged to the states' domaine réservé as, e.g., human rights issues.

NGO often endorse or participate in transnational advocacy networks, which have been defined as *"networks of activists, distinguishable largely by the centrality of principled ideas or values in motivating their formation"*.[28] Very often, more than one NGO is involved in such a network together with individuals with special expertise or interest in the field.

Trans-national corporations also sometimes form interest groups in form of NGOs which then consult with the UN in their area of expertise. Thus, their interests are introduced to the international decision-making level through NGOs. Domestically, they use more direct methods such as funding electoral campaign to influence election outcomes; consequently, this can sometimes affect who gets appointed to represent the country in international organizations, which could, in turn, affect their interest.

Very often, the issues that NGOs advance are part of a wide array of policy issues to be decided at a particular meeting. For example, the WTO rounds frequently discuss a wide variety of issues around the core trade topics, such as health and environmental concerns. Thus, NGOs must maintain a certain degree of flexibility on some issues to advance their core goals and not to become stuck on issues that may well be decided later. It is a simple trade off in bridging the gap between the varying interests of the parties involved in international policy-making.

6.3.3 Contribution to International Law-Making

NGOs, with their expertise in particular areas, participate directly and indirectly in the process of international law-making by influencing national governments, be it within the framework of international or regional organizations, or at international conferences where important multilateral agreements are drafted and signed. One can even say that NGOs play a vital role in the international legal environment as they possess vast resources and have in-depth knowledge on highly specific topics. This means that NGOs can react to crises much faster than most international organizations, whose complex political structures significantly slow down the decision-making process. Based on these capabilities, many NGOs today have advisory status in many IOs so that the NGO can contribute its expert knowledge of a particular situation and to assist in the IO's decision- and law-making process.

NGOs have been successful, e.g., in pressing for the 1997 Convention on the Prohibition of the Use, Stockpiling, Production and Transfer of Anti-Personnel

[28] Keck and Sikkink (1998), p. 1.

Mines and on their Destruction, also known as the Ottawa Treaty. After many decades of lobbying, NGOs were instrumental in bringing the process to a successful conclusion. Importantly, the US and Russia, as well as many other big powers, did not sign the Convention. Despite this, the NGOs still managed to conclude the Convention without any support from the superpowers, thus demonstrating their strength. Generally, NGOs may, based on their expertise, contribute to the further development of international law and politics in their areas of concern.

This contribution might seem puzzling because international law is traditionally understood as a product of state positivism, and international politics belongs to the sphere of state sovereignty. The key to this puzzle is the nature of NGOs. Like the state, the NGO is composed of individuals, but in contrast to the state, the NGO enjoys a voluntary relationship with the individual. Individuals support and join an NGO when they are committed to its purpose. This purpose and the organization confer an authority to NGOs—that is, a moral authority rather than a legal one. What thus distinguishes NGOs from IOs are their voluntary and self-motivated nature. While IOs' mandates are agreed to and limited by states, NGOs gain influence through their values and the attractiveness of their ideas. However, an NGO's influence is not guaranteed, including even the ICRC. Influence must be constantly cultivated engaging with members and civil society.[29]

6.3.4 Monitoring Compliance with International Obligations

NGOs also monitor international actors' compliance with their international obligations. Therefore, NGOs can be essential when it comes to treaty enforcement. For example, the activities of the ICRC have their basis in Geneva Conventions; thus, without appropriate international recognition of the ICRC and its role the treaty would not be enforceable in its current form. The ICRC tends to use discreet methods; going public when parties violate international humanitarian law is rather the exception. The reason for this is probably the ICRC's quasi-official status under international humanitarian law. For other NGOs, going public is one of the methods used to ensure compliance with international legal obligations. In "The New Sovereignty", Abram Chayes and Antonia Chayes devote a chapter to the impact that NGOs have on treaty compliance, and state that *"[i]n a real sense, [NGOs] supply the personnel and resources for managing compliance that states have become increasingly reluctant to provide."*[30] *Naming and shaming non-compliant states and public authorities*, multinational corporations, combatant groups and insurgents is one of the main soft powers that NGOs possess. That said, some recent developments have reduced NGOs' role in naming and shaming. In 2015, the UN appointed

[29] Charnovitz (2006), p. 348.

[30] Chayes and Chayes (1995), p. 250 s.

a Special Rapporteur on the right to privacy,[31] and part of the Special Rapporteur's mandate is to report on alleged violations of the right to privacy, which was previously carried out by NGOs. It has now been recognized as an important part of the UN's privacy protection goals and has thus been formally implemented.

Over the last decades, NGOs' role has continued to expand beyond naming and shaming. For example, the parties to the *UNECE Convention on Access to Information, Public Participation in Decision-making and Access to Justice in Environmental Matters*, usually known as the Aarhus Convention, agreed to give NGOs observer status when candidates are nominated to the Convention's Compliance Committee[32] and thus actively shape policy. There have also been various instances where NGOs played an important role within a domestic political system in pressing the government to meet its treaty obligations.

6.3.5 Communication

Generally, NGOs have found ways to attach themselves to IOs and to be present at negotiations of multilateral agreements. This allows them to lobby for many causes.[33] Lobbying always implies communication. In this regard, NGOs' communication can be public or nonpublic. Public communication refers to rallying support for causes on the streets and in the media; nonpublic communication refers to the NGOs' lobbying of politicians and other activities within the decision-making body's institutional framework. Most NGOs' main power is their impact on public communication and perception of issues, made possible by their active use of the internet to communicate across the globe. Subsequently, these NGOs also pushed for the implementation of electronic communication which was first used at the Earth Summit[34] to facilitate the exchange of information between members of the Summit and keep them updated on events unfolding in parallel discussions. The use and efficiency gain of such new technology would not have been possible without the NGOs' commitment. They assisted governments and universities around the world

[31] <https://www.ohchr.org/en/issues/privacy/sr/pages/srprivacyindex.aspx> (accessed 9 March 2025).

[32] First Meeting of the Parties to the Aarhus Convention, Decision 1/7, UECE/MP.PP/2/Add.8 (2004), Annex, para. 4 (2004). NGOs can also submit communications alleging noncompliance by a party to the Convention. See Report of the Compliance Committee, ECE/MP.PP/2005/13, paras. 24 ss. The Aarhus Convention is the Convention on Access to Information, Public Participation in Decision-Making and Access to Justice in Environmental Matters, Jun 25, 1998, 38 ILM 517 (1999).

[33] Charnovitz (2006), p. 349.

[34] The Earth Summit was The United Nations Conference on Environment and Development (UNCED), also known as the Rio Conference, a major United Nations conference held in Rio de Janeiro from June 3 to June 14, 1992.

in designing and setting up the appropriate structures for this new technology.[35] Thus, although not clearly visible to the general population, NGOs drive important developments that benefit humanity and at large and reshape global society.[36]

6.3.6 Critical Perspectives on NGOs

NGOs influence international politics and the political landscape in various ways, including lobbying, demonstrations, civil movements or technical expertise. Inevitably, many NGOs infringe on states' interests in some way, especially when it comes to causes such as human rights or environmental protection which are seen as controversial in some countries. Since the fact that some countries regard these causes as controversial is exactly why the NGOs were and are established, they invariably attract criticism from the relevant states. Some states, such as Russia, Turkey, Poland and Hungary, have established laws that limit and hinder NGOs' activities to suppress unwanted views and prevent the dissemination of incriminating information of governmental abuses.

One such very early incident occurred in 1985 when the executive branch of the French foreign intelligence service sunk Greenpeace's flagship, the Rainbow Warrior, at the Port of Auckland, New Zealand, killing a Dutch-Portuguese photographer. The ship was on its way to Muroroa to protest against France's plans of conducting atomic testing in the French Polynesian atoll. As this was a clear violation of New Zealand's sovereignty, which in turn violated international law, a diplomatic conflict between France and New Zealand ensued. The dispute was also referred to the UN.[37] Thus, an indirect consequence of NGOs' actions is unwanted conflicts between states when their actions are directed against a state's interest.

There have also been political objections to NGOs because of the influence that NGOs can have. Generally, many arguments against NGOs' involvement on the international level are politically motivated and thus must be approached with caution. This is especially the case when individual states criticize the activities of particular NGOs, claiming that they interfere in internal affairs or commit illegal acts. Other forms of criticism relate to efficiency, the selection of recipients of humanitarian or other assistance, etc.

[35] Srinivas (2015).

[36] For example in the area of economic development NGOs raise a massive amount of money and have a significant impact on local society. See Hénon et al. (2014), p. 109 ss.

[37] Ultimately the dispute between the two states was resolved through a special proceeding which was chaired by the UN Secretary General. See *Rainbow Warrior Arbitration (New Zealand v. France)*, Award, Jul 6, 1986, 82 ILR 499 (1989).

6.4 Relationship between IOs and NGOs

6.4.1 General Remarks

Non-governmental organizations have played an important role since the founding of the United Nations. They are an excellent source of information about violations of international law, as they have first-hand knowledge of potential misconduct by members states through their international operations. NGOs can also place considerable pressure on states to comply with international treaties or agreements without risking the diplomatic skirmishes that might occur between states. In addition to their participation in global organizations like the UN and the WTO, NGOs participate in the activities of regional organizations such as the Council of Europe and the EU. *NGOs generally support the activities of international organizations.*

NGOs often seek to influence the policymaking, standard-setting and law-making proceedings of regional and international intergovernmental organizations. There are several ways in which NGOs are connected to intergovernmental organizations. One way, and as discussed earlier, is an official accreditation to an intergovernmental organization such as the UN or the WTO. The other ways are more indirect: They try to access the organizations' secretariats and the decision-making organs to influence their policies as well as the policies of individual member state governments. Therefore, the cities in which important I(G)Os are headquartered are also the headquarters of many related international NGOs.

Furthermore, involvement in projects on the ground enables NGOs to gain a better understanding of the practical issues and allows them to assist IOs in establishing an appropriate framework. In most cases, local populations have difficulties relating to an IO because it is a remote body with which these populations ordinarily do not and cannot interact. Thus, NGOs are helpful in carrying these people's voices back to the IO and the international arena.

6.4.2 NGOs and the UN

Article 71 UN Charter provides the general legal framework regulating the relationship between the UN and NGOs. As stated by the former Secretary-General Kofi Anan in his 2000 Millennium Report: "*We also need to adapt our deliberate work so it can benefit fully from the contributions of civil society. Already, civil society organizations have made an important contribution to articulating and defending global norms. It is clear that the United Nations and the world's people have much to gain from opening the Organization further to this vital source of energy and expertise – just as we have gained from closer institutional links and practical cooperation with national parliaments.*"[38]

The 2003 Cardoso Report sought to enhance participation and relations between the UN and NGOs.[39] The report highlighted, however, the divide in representation between the rich global North and the poorer regions in the South. The framework has its flaws. The accreditation process costs on average 26000 USD for an NGO and requires a long list of supporting documents to be submitted.[40] For many smaller NGOs in the South, these costs, the lengthiness of the process and their inability to get all the required documents pose significant hurdles to becoming accredited to the UN.

NGOs are civil society organizations. In working with the UN, NGOs often form *an issue caucus* to determine the strategy for the advancement of a policy making process. These caucuses are temporary and are dissolved once the UN sessions on the issue are concluded. Furthermore, there are *NGO-based governance networks* which aim at increasing NGO participation in various policy making forums within the UN system. They are open to all NGOs and do not advance any specific policy. In the UN system, these networks are called *Facilitating Committees* or *NGO Steering Committee* when they relate to an organ or a permanent institution belonging to the UN. They support NGO members' full participation in meetings by informing them about events and, if necessary, by raising funds for their travel. The overall goal is to enhance the quality of the policy making process by ensuring all relevant actors can voice their opinion.

There are not only NGOs purposing idealistic, humanitarian and other non-commercial goals, but also organizations with more economical, business-related purposes. The largest NGOs by capital include BRAC,[41] the Wikimedia Foundation which aims at improving education and facilitating access to knowledge, and the New York based Acumen Fund supplying seed capital in developing countries to enable the growth of startups. To participate in UN consultations, these organizations with economic goals must comply with 10 principles. These principles are respect for human rights in their own work; not being complicit in human rights abuses by others; upholding the rights of trades unions; eliminating forced labor; abolishing child labor; eliminating discrimination in employment; supporting a precautionary approach to environmental questions; promoting environmental responsibility; encouraging the use of environmentally friendly technology and fighting all forms of corruption. Despite these requirements, many NGOs

[38] *'We the Peoples': The Role of the United Nations, 21st century*, UN SG Report, A/54/2000 (2000), 69.

[39] *Report of the Panel of Eminent Persons on United Nations—Civil Society Relations* (2004). Former president of Brazil Fernando Henrique Cardoso was the chair of the panel.

[40] *We the Peoples: Civil society, the United Nations and global governance*, UN SG Report, A/58/817 (2004), 54.

[41] A rural development group enabling microfinancing.

refuse to work with these organizations under a special framework as they view the organizations' commercial interests as irreconcilable with NGO objectives.

The main point of controversy over an NGO's conduct is the extent of its advocacy and some questionable activities. Some examples include aggressive publications or links to separatist organizations that reflect negatively on certain NGOs.[42] By bringing to the table controversial opinions derived from questionable sources, NGOs' advisory status is placed in jeopardy. To maintain a high level of independence in the UN's decision making, reports which are prepared and heavily influenced by NGO participation in the various sub-committees must reflect an independent and fully informed decision-making process. Otherwise, interested parties will gain the upper hand and advance one-sided views on the international level. This is because much of the groundwork is done by committees and sub-organs within the UN from which the General Assembly only receives the final reports.

6.4.3 NGOs and the ECOSOC: Resolution 1996/31

6.4.3.1 First Institutional Arrangements

In 1945, when the UN first consciously used the term "non-governmental organization" in Article 71 UN Charter, it was envisioned that NGOs would only have consultative status within the ECOSOC. Therefore, the ECOSOC appointed an NGO Committee to manage NGO applications for consultative status, supervise the agreed terms made with the NGOs, and manage relations between the NGOs and the ECOSOC. The NGO Committee was also tasked with evaluating applications from NGOs who wished to be reclassified to a higher status category. From 1968, the Committee was also to study NGO reports on their work and to determine the appropriate action to take on controversial NGOs such as revoking their consultative status. The decisions of the Committee on the revocation of status could be overruled by ECOSOC itself, which happened in a few instances.

The ECOSOC also adopted secondary law regulating the relations between the UN and the NGOs. In 1950, the ECOSOC passed the Arrangements for Consultation with Non-Governmental Organizations resolution; it was subsequently amended in 1968 and 1996.[43] The currently applied legal basis is ECOSOC Res 1996/31.

[42] *Report of the Committee on Non-Governmental Organizations*, E/2000/88 (2000), paras. 70 ss.

[43] *Consultative relationship between the United Nations and non-governmental organizations*, E/RES/1996/31 (1996).

6.4.3.2 ECOSOC Resolution 1996/31

a) General Remarks

Part 1 of the resolution sets out the *"Principles to be applied in the establishment of consultative relations"* and declares that the *"organization shall be concerned with matters falling in the competence of the Economic and Social Council and its subsidiary bodies. Consultative relationships may be established with international, regional, subregional and national organizations, in conformity with the Charter and the principles and criteria established under the present resolution."*

The ECOSOC Committee on NGOs reviews applications for consultative status twice a year, in January (regular session) and in May (resumed session). The Committee does not decide but recommends. These recommendations, contained in a report for the January session and one report for the May session, are reviewed by ECOSOC in April and July respectively. In most cases, ECOSOC decides to approve the recommendations. In very rare cases, it does not. Even controversial organizations such as the US National Rifle Association (NRA) have been accredited by the UN, thus highlighting that the UN applies a broad definition of NGO. There are no rules as to what is a "bad" or "good" NGO because social values and opinions in the areas in which NGOs operate differ widely around the globe. *Most transnational actors can thus expect to gain recognition as NGOs by the UN, provided they are not individual companies, criminals, or violent groups and they do not exist solely to oppose an individual government.* However, their influence may vary significantly based on their nature and representation.

National NGOs may be admitted after the Member State to which the NGO belongs has been consulted. Further provisions are made as to competence, established headquarters, democratic processes, authority, accountability to its members, funding etc. Although the resolution recognizes *"the evolving relationship between the United Nations and non-governmental organizations"*,[44] it is made explicitly clear that *"the granting, suspension and withdrawal of consultative status, as well as the interpretation of norms and decisions relating to this matter, are the prerogative of Member States exercised through the Economic and Social Council and its Committee on Non-Governmental Organizations."*[45]

b) Categories of Consultative Status

Part 2 of the resolution sets out the principles governing the nature of the consultative arrangements. Importantly, it highlights the clear distinction between the UN Charter participation without vote in the deliberations of the Council according to 69 and 70 UN Charter, and the arrangements for consultation with NGOs according to Article 71 UN Charter. According to Articles 69 and 70 UN Charter, the ECOSOC may invite States not members of the ECOSOC, and specialized UN agencies to participate in the deliberation, but without vote. The rights of NGOs

[44] Ibid., para. 17.

[45] Ibid., para. 15.

according to Article 71 go less far. The Charter makes a *clear distinction between the rights of states and specialized agencies on one side, and the consultative status of NGOs*. This distinction is fundamental; the arrangements for consultation should not accord non-governmental organizations the same participation rights that are granted to States and specialized agencies.[46] Generally, although today NGOs are usually viewed in a positive light, e.g. the IMF, the UN Security Council but also most of other organizations and their organs object formally integrating them into their decision-making process in whatever form.

Consultative status provides NGOs with access to ECOSOC and its many subsidiary bodies, the UN's various human rights mechanisms, ad-hoc processes, as well as special events organized by the President of the General Assembly. Currently there are according to the ECOSOC rules three tiers of participation: general consultative status, special consultative status and roster status:

- *General consultative status* is reserved for *large international NGOs whose area of work cover most of the issues on the agenda of ECOSOC* and its subsidiary bodies. These tend to be large, established international NGOs with a broad geographical reach. Over the last decade this number has remained constant at around 140 NGOs. NGOs on this list include International Alliance of Woman (since 1947), Institute of International Law (since 2017), and International Council on Social Welfare (since 1972).[47]
- *Special consultative status* is granted to NGOs that *have a special competence* in, and are concerned specifically with, only a few of the fields of activity covered by the ECOSOC. These NGOs tend to be smaller and more recently established. The number of these NGOs has increased significantly and is currently close to 2000. NGOs on this list include Aboriginal Legal Services of West Australia, Africa Unite and LGBT Denmark.
- Organizations that apply for consultative status but do not fit in the two categories are usually included in the *so-called roster*. These NGOs tend to have a rather narrow and/or technical focus. NGOs that have formal status with other UN bodies or specialized agencies (e.g. FAO, ILO, UNCTAD, UNESCO, UNIDO, WHO), can be included on the ECOSOC Roster. The roster lists NGOs that ECOSOC or the UN Secretary-General considers can make *"occasional and useful contributions to the work of the Council or its subsidiary bodies."*[48] The general roster contains much more than 1000 NGOs.

As of 31 December 2022, 6343 NGOs enjoyed active consultative status with ECOSOC.[49] Being placed in the highest category, i.e. general consultative status,

---

[46] Ibid., para. 18.

[47] For a complete list and a search option see <https://ecosoc.un.org/en/ngo/consultative-status> (accessed 9 March 2025).

[48] Ibid, para. 24.

[49] See ECOSOC, Introduction to ECOSOC Consultative Status, https://ecosoc.un.org/en/ngo/consultative-status#:~:text=As%20of%2031%20December%202022,active%20consultative%20status%20with%20ECOSOC.

grants substantial rights such as the right to request a discussion point to be set on the agenda in the same manner as member states or secretary-generals and other important figures in an IO. Such a right is substantial considering that in national parliaments, only members of parliament can table discussion points. Thus, such a classification is only given to the most important and reliable organizations such as Amnesty International or the ICRC.

6.4.4 NGOs and the WTO

The WTO is explicitly empowered to engage with NGOs by the Marrakesh Agreement (WTO Agreement). Specifically, Article V (2) of the WTO Agreement states that the General Council may make appropriate arrangements for consultation and cooperation with non-governmental organizations concerned with matters related to those of the WTO.

In 1996, the General Council of the WTO adopted the *"Guidelines for Arrangements on Relations with Non-Governmental Organizations"*.[50] The Guidelines state that Members recognize that NGOs can play a role *"to increase the awareness of the public in respect of WTO activities"* and that NGOs are a 'valuable resource" that can *"contribute to the accuracy and richness of the public debate"*.

These Guidelines also establish the limits of NGO participation by referring to the special status of the WTO, which is both an intergovernmental organization based on a binding treaty of rights and obligations among its members and a forum for negotiations. The General Council instructed only the WTO Secretariat to engage with NGOs which effectively barred NGOs from participation in the activities of WTO bodies.

In practice, the main forms of engagement between WTO and NGOs are: attendance of the formal plenary meetings of the Ministerial Conference; public symposia and forums on WTO-related issues; access to WTO information; regular informal briefings; opportunities for information exchange; informal meetings; the Informal NGO Advisory Body; and involvement in dispute settlement.

There are a few arguments in favor of strong NGO involvement in WTO activities. These arguments are not necessarily WTO specific but apply also to many other international organizations. First, NGO participation will enhance the WTO's decision-making process because *NGOs will provide information, arguments, and perspectives that governments may not possess* or may not want to bring forward. Additionally, NGOs have *a wealth of specialized knowledge, resources, and analytical capacity*. In fact, governments often lack the resources and the

[50] WT/L/162 (1996).

necessary expertise to investigate certain issues. Second, *NGO participation is civil society participation* and will therefore increase the WTO's legitimacy as it is still viewed as a body without attachment to national parliament that carries out most of its work in a non-public setting without democratic participation. Indeed, the WTO's decision-making has been described as undemocratic and lacking in transparency because it does not involve, either directly or through representation, those who will be affected by the decisions. Furthermore, decisions must be reached as a result of an open and transparent exchange of rational arguments. The WTO's legitimacy, and public confidence in it, are likely to increase if NGOs have the opportunity to be heard and to observe the decision-making process. Furthermore, NGOs can play an important role in disseminating information at the national level, thus ensuring broader public support and understanding. Third, *transnational interests and concerns may not be adequately represented by a national government.* By allowing NGO involvement in WTO discussions, NGOs can raise important international issues to the WTO. Finally, civil society participation in debates at the national level is only an option in those WTO Members which are open and democratic. This is not the case for all WTO Members. Allowing NGOs to be heard at the WTO can thus compensate for the fact that NGOs are not always heard at the national level in every country.

6.4.5 NGOs Before International Courts

6.4.5.1 Amicus Curiae Briefs

There are national court systems like, e.g., in the U.S.A where NGOs can file amici curiae briefs in court proceedings. Such practice is particularly common in national courts when the legal issues in question fall within the NGO's expertise and will affect their operation, or the group on whose behalf they advocate. These submissions outline the effects of a particular decision from the NGO's perspective. The submissions also enable the court to gain a better understanding of the facts of the case as NGOs often have vast resources and materials on the subject matter in questions and are particularly able to foresee the effects of a decision on those who will be affected by it.

NGO submissions could also be a vital part of the decision-making process of international courts, and indeed, there are increasingly international courts and tribunals accepting some kind of NGO involvement. However, the International Court of Justice (ICJ), e.g., has remained skeptical of third-party submissions for two reasons. First, there might the the risk of opening the floodgates if NGO submissions are allowed. Second, since NGOs have a vested interest in the relevant issues, there is a risk that NGO submissions might introduce an element of bias to the ICJ's decisions. Despite this skepticism, *amicus curiae briefs from NGOs are increasingly playing a role in international courts.*

6.4.5.2 NGOs, the International Court of Justice, and the International Criminal Court

It is well-established that only states have standing before the ICJ. Nonetheless, the ICJ has the option of *calling an NGO as an expert witness* and introducing the NGO's view on a subject through such means.[51] Although NGO submissions are generally not allowed, the ICJ has the procedural power to request them according to the specific circumstances of every case. In addition, NGOs sometimes manage to introduce their opinions through a backdoor, as was the case with the ICJ Nuclear Weapons Advisory Opinion.[52] A project was launched in 1992 by three UN organizations to get the UN to pass, or threaten to pass, a resolution on the legality of using nuclear weapons. This project saw various NGOs lobbying and drawing public support for such an advisory opinion collecting a total of over 3.5 million signatures opposing the use of nuclear weapons.[53] The efforts initially resulted in the World Health Organization (WHO) requesting an opinion from the ICJ.[54] The ICJ declined to issue such an opinion because it was of the view that the legal question put before it lacked the necessary connection to the WHO's scope of activities so that the request was an act *ultra vires*.[55] This led to the UN General Assembly submitting a request for the opinion[56] which the ICJ accepted.[57] The heavy NGO involvement in the request for the opinion arguably suggests that the request came about because of the NGOs' demand. This raised the issue of NGO's influence on states in the UN General Assembly. In essence, some judges thought that the NGOs' influence went so far as to raise doubts about whether the request for an opinion was made by the free will of the states in the General Assembly. Others disagreed, stating that the representatives of the states carry out their essential function by bringing the opinion of their constituents, which include the NGOs, to the GA.[58] In any event, this example shows that although NGOs do not have legal standing, they may influence states' opinion through their lobbying activities.

Similarly, the Rome Statute of the International Criminal Court (ICC) does not allow NGOs to bring cases before the court. This right is only granted to state parties, the UN and the ICC Prosecutor. The ICC, however, often seeks additional information from NGOs when hearing cases as NGOs will invariably have firsthand

---

[51] Art. 50 ICJ Statute.

[52] *Request for an Advisory Opinion from the international Court of Justice in the Legality of the Threat or Use of Nuclear Weapons*, A/49/75 (1994).

[53] Reference in the Written Statement of the Government of the United Kingdom in the case of the' Legality of the Threat or Use of Nuclear Weapons' (ICJ, Jun 1995), paras. 1.2, 2.2 s.

[54] *Legality of the Threat or Use of Nuclear Weapons*, Advisory Opinion, ICJ Rep. 226 (1996), para. 84.

[55] Boisson de Chazournes and Sands (1999), p. 4.

[56] A/Res 49/75K (1994).

[57] *Legality of the Threat or Use of Nuclear Weapons*, Advisory Opinion, ICJ Rep. 226 (1996), 226.

[58] See e.g. Higgins (1997), p. 215.

information on the specific circumstances in country based on their humanitarian presence during war times or other support measures.

6.4.5.3 Amicus Curiae Submissions in WTO Dispute Settlement Proceedings

Only states have standing in WTO dispute settlement proceedings. The DSU does not regulate whether NGOs may submit amicus curiae briefs in such proceedings. It is, however, recognized that the panels' authority to seek information from any relevant source according to Article 13 DSU *allows panels also to take into consideration unsolicited submissions as relevant information.*[59] Amicus curiae submissions play not a role in panel proceedings but also and even more in Appellate Body proceedings. If NGO briefs are part of the submission of a party, they are treated as party statements and not as an independent source. An unsolicited independent NGO amicus curiae submission is considered if the submission contains in the eyes of the Appellate Body valuable information or statements.

6.4.5.4 NGOs and the European Court of Justice

Under the statute of the ECJ, Member States and the European Commission may submit their written observations on a case pending before the Court; they have general standing. This is different with NGOs; for them it is difficult to obtain standing as is evidenced by decisions referring to Greenpace. In the case *Stichting Greenpeace Council (Greenpeace International) and others v. Commission*[60] the question was whether Greenpeace had standing to challenge a decision of the European Commission to grant financial assistance from the European Regional Development Fund for the construction of 2 power plants in the Canary Islands. Greenpeace alleged a violation of EU law. The ECJ held that Greenpeace did not have standing. As an association formed for the protection of the collective interests of a category of persons, Greenpeace could not be considered to be directly and individually concerned by a measure affecting the general interests of that category. Essentially, a sufficiently strong interest by the NGO is necessary before it will be

[59] Art. 13, Right to Seek Information, states: "1. Each panel shall have the right to seek information and technical advice from any individual or body which it deems appropriate.... 2. Panels may seek information from any relevant source and may consult experts to obtain their opinion on certain aspects of the matter. With respect to a factual issue concerning a scientific or other technical matter raised by a party to a dispute, a panel may request an advisory report in writing from an expert review group..."

[60] *Stichting Greenpeace Council (Greenpeace International) and Others v. Commission of the European Communities*, Case T-585/93, Judgment of the Court of First Instance (5th Chamber), 1995 (ECR II-02205).

granted standing. In another case[61] the ECJ confirmed this jurisprudence. Greenpeace Energy requested the annulment of a Commission's decision approving State aid for a nuclear power plant. It is clear that the nuclear power station will have a significant impact on the environment. According to the ECJ, Greenpeace Energy as a potential competitor on the energy market failed to show that its competitive position would be substantially affected by the State aid.

In contrast, the CJEU confirmed standing of the Front Polisario, the internationally recognized organization representing the interests of the people of Western Sahara, to challenge agreements concluded between the EU and Morocco which were also applicable to the territory of Western Sahara. Polisario, inter alia, claimed a violation of the right of self-determination of the people of Western Sahara by these agreements. The Court recalled that *"according to settled case-law, the condition that a natural or legal person must be directly concerned by the decision which that person is contesting requires that two cumulative conditions be satisfied, namely that the measure being contested, first, directly affects the legal situation of that person and, second, leaves no discretion to the addressees who are entrusted with the task of implementing it, such implementation being purely automatic and resulting solely from EU provisions without the application of other intermediate rules..».*[62] It then assessed that Front Polisario, by its action for annulment, *«was seeking to protect the people of Western Sahara's right to self-determination, as already recognized by the Court of Justice in paragraphs 88, 91 and 105 of the judgment of 21 December 2016, Council v Front Polisario (C104/16 P, EU:C:2016: 973). »*[63] It further stated that *"[a]lthough it has not been officially recognised as being the exclusive representative of the people of Western Sahara, Front Polisario is, according to the resolutions of the highest bodies of the United Nations, including those of the United Nations Security Council referred to in paragraph 31 of the present judgment, a privileged interlocutor in the process conducted under the auspices of the United Nations with a view to determining the future status of Western Sahara. It also participates in other international fora in order to defend that people's right to self-determination.*[64] *(90) Those particular circumstances allow the finding that Front Polisario is entitled to contest, before the EU judicature, the legality of an act of the Union which directly affects the legal situation of the people of Western Sahara in its capacity as holder of the right to self-determination where that act individually concerns that people or, if the act is a regulatory act, where it does not entail implementing measures."* Of course, this is to some extent a special case as a result of the international recognition of the Polisario Front as an advocate for the people of Western Sahara. However, this case shows that in the EU,

---

[61] *Greenpeace Energy eG v European Commission*, Case C-640/16 P, Judgment of the Court of First Instance (8th Chamber), 2017 (ECLI:EU:C:2017:752).

[62] Joint Cases C-779/21 P. Commission v Front Polisario and C-779/21 P, Council v. Front Polisario, Judgment (Gand Chamber) of Oct 4, 2024 (ECLI:EU:C:2024:835) para. 87.

[63] Ibid. para. 88.

[64] Ibid. para. 89.

the procedural rights of NGOs and other non-state actors can, depending on the circumstances, go quite far.

References

Boisson De Chazournes L, Sands P (eds) (1999) International law, the international court of justice and nuclear weapons. Cambridge University Press, Cambridge

Brownlie I (1998) The rule of law in international affairs – international law at the fiftieth anniversary of the United Nations. Springer, Netherlands, The Hague

Charnovitz S (2006) Nongovernmental organisations and international law. Am J Int Law 100(2): 348–372

Chayes A, Chayes AH (1995) The new sovereignty: compliance with international regulatory agreements. Harvard University Press, Cambridge

Council of Europe (2007) Legal status of non-governmental organisations in Europe. CM/Rec (2007)14 and explanatory memorandum. Council of Europe Publishing, Strasbourg. https://rm.coe.int/16807096b7. Accessed 9 Mar 2025

Crawford J (2019) Brownlie's principles of public international law, 9th edn. Oxford University Press, Oxford

Fenaux R (1978) The transnational family of associations (INGOs) and the new world order. Transnatl Assoc 30(4):192–199

Hénon S et al (2014) The changing role of NGOs and civil society in financing sustainable development. OECD Development Co-operation Report:109–119

Higgins JR (1997) The reformation in international law. In: Rawlings R (ed) Law, society and economy: centenary essays for the London school of economics and political science 1895–1995. Yale University Press, Oxford, pp 125–145

Hirsch A (2013) NGOs, government censorship and you. Right Now. https://rightnow.org.au/opinion/ngos-government-censorship-and-philanthropy/. Accessed 9 Mar 2025

Keck ME, Sikkink K (1998) Activists beyond borders: advocacy networks in international politics. Cornell University Press, Ithaca, NY

Martens K (2003) Examining the (Non-)Status of NGOs. Indiana J Glob Legal Stud 10(2):1–24

Shestack A (1978) The economics of nonprofit institutions: studies in structure and policy. Oxford University Press, Oxford

Srinivas H (2015) Internet use: NGOs in action. GDRC Research Output E-103. https://www.gdrc.org/ngo/internet-ngos.html. Accessed 9 Mar 2025

Wedgwood R (1999) Legal personality and the role of non-governmental organizations and non-state political entities in the United Nations system. In: Hofmann R (ed) Non-state actors as new subjects of international law: international law – from the traditional state order towards the law of the global community, Proceedings of an international symposium of the Kiel Walther-Schücking-Institute of International Law, March 25 to 28, 1998. Duncker & Humblot, Berlin, pp 21–36

Willetts P (2011) Non-governmental organizations in world politics. Routledge, Abingdon

Index

U. Saxer, *The Law of Global and European Organizations*, Springer Textbooks in Law, https://doi.org/10.1007/978-3-032-00067-5

The manufacturer's authorised representative in the EU is Springer
Nature Customer Service Centre GmbH, Europaplatz 3, 69115 Heidelberg,
Germany. If you have any concerns regarding our products, please
contact ProductSafety@springernature.com

Printed and bound by CPI Group (UK) Ltd, Croydon, CR0 4YY
01/10/2026
02225971-0014